# Freedom Taking Place

## War, Women, and Culture at the Intersection of Ukraine, Poland, and Belarus

Edited with an Introduction by

**Jessica Zychowicz**

Series in Sociology

VERNON PRESS

*In the Americas:*
Vernon Press
1000 N West Street, Suite 1200,
Wilmington, Delaware 19801
United States

*In the rest of the world:*
Vernon Press
C/Sancti Espiritu 17,
Malaga, 29006
Spain

Series in Sociology

Library of Congress Control Number: 2022921586

ISBN: 978-1-64889-878-5

Also available: 978-1-64889-590-6 [Hardback]; 978-1-64889-690-3 [PDF, E-Book]

Product and company names mentioned in this work are the trademarks of their respective owners. While every care has been taken in preparing this work, neither the authors nor Vernon Art and Science Inc. may be held responsible for any loss or damage caused or alleged to be caused directly or indirectly by the information contained in it.

Every effort has been made to trace all copyright holders, but if any have been inadvertently overlooked the publisher will be pleased to include any necessary credits in any subsequent reprint or edition.

Cover design by Vernon Press.

Cover image: Lesia Khomenko, *Drawing on Maidan,* Carbon paper, gel pen, A4, 2013-2014. In collection of Revolution of Dignity Museum, Kyiv.

This book is dedicated to
forging peace in Ukraine
the 2020-2021 demonstrations in Belarus and Poland
and all who defend democracy

# Table of Contents

# List of Figures

# Author Biographies

**Dr. Svitlana Biedarieva** is an art historian, artist, and curator with an interest in Eastern European and Latin American art. She has taught art history and global history at the Universidad de las Américas Puebla, the Universidad Iberoamericana, the Universidad de Anáhuac Norte, and the Courtauld Institute of Art. Biedarieva is a member of the Association for Slavic, East European, and Eurasian Studies and the Society of Historians of Eastern European, Eurasian, and Russian Art. In 2019-2020, she has curated the exhibition *At the Front Line: Ukrainian Art, 2013-2019* in Mexico City and Winnipeg, Canada. Her edited books include *Contemporary Ukrainian and Baltic Art: Political and Social Perspectives, 1991-2021* (Stuttgart: ibidem Press, 2021) and *At the Front Line: Ukrainian Art, 2013-2019* (Mexico City: Editorial 17, 2020, co-edited with Hanna Deikun). Biedarieva's papers have been published by, among other outlets, October (MIT Press), *Art Margins Online* (MIT Press), *Space and Culture* (SAGE), *post at MoMA*, and *Revue Critique d'Art* (University of Rennes 2). In 2022, Biedarieva was selected as the CEC ArtsLink International Fellow" to "In 2022/23, Biedarieva was selected as the George F. Kennan Fellow at the Kennan Institute, Wilson Center, and the Non-Resident Visiting Fellow at the George Washington University for her research, the CEC ArtsLink International Fellow for her curatorial work, and the Prince Claus Seed Award Laureate for her artistic work.

**Oksana Briukhovetska** – born, lived and has worked predominantly in Kyiv, Ukraine. She graduated from National Academy of Visual Arts and Architecture in Kyiv in 2003. She worked as an artist, curator, graphic designer, participated in exhibitions in Ukraine and abroad, and published articles about art as well as short prose. From 2009 to 2019, she worked as a curator at the Visual Culture Research Center (VCRC), Kyiv, where she curated exhibitions, public events and publishing projects. Some of the early exhibitions that she co-curated – *Ukrainian Body* (2012) and *Lockout* (2014) had a significant public resonance. From 2011 she became involved in feminism and from 2015-2017 has organized three international feminist exhibitions in VCRC: *Motherhood; What in me is Feminine?* and *TEXTUS: Embroidery, Textile, Feminism*, which aimed at strengthening the voices of women artists within the Ukrainian art scene and in international collaboration. In 2017-2019 she participated in research on feminist art in East Europe and France within the Tandem-Ukraine project and co-edited and published a collection of interviews, *The Right to Truth: Conversations on Art and Feminism*. (VCRC, 2019). In 2018 she was a co-curator of the *Warsaw Under Construction X* festival (collaboration of VCRC and Museum of Modern Art in Warsaw) where she curated the "I am Ukrainka" poster campaign about Ukrainian women migrant workers in Poland that was widely discussed in the media and in Ukrainian television. In 2020 she came to the United States, where she started to work on the book on race and racism interviewing people in the U.S. about Black Lives Matter protests. In 2021 she was a co-curator of the Ukrainian chapter of the Secondary Archive project, which represents women artists of East Europe. In 2021 she entered the MFA program at Stamps School of Art and Design at the University of Michigan.

**Dr. Joanna Dobkowska-Kubacka** holds a Ph.D. from the Faculty of Philosophy and History at the University of Łódź. From 2018-2019 she conducted research at the Facultad de Geografía e Historia, the University of Santiago de Compostela in Spain. The final thesis she wrote in Spanish was a comparative analysis of the situation of Spanish and Polish female artists in the second half of the nineteenth century. In 2019-2021 she held the position of Polish Doctoral Fellow at the Wirth Institute for Austrian and Central European Studies at the University of Alberta. She also holds an MA in art history from Warsaw University along with postgraduate studies in history. In her thesis, she analyzed the iconography of heretics in Latin Europe's art from the 9-16th centuries. Her research interests include women's studies, critical art studies, and the phenomenon of rebellion in the context of art and religion. Joanna works also as a journalist and editor, collaborating with many Polish magazines (including *Polityka. Salon*). She is also an author. She has published three books: two novels and one in popular science; the most recent (co-authored with Joanna Wasilewska) is entitled, *W cieniu koronkowej parasolki: O modzie i obyczajach w XIX wieku* (*In the shade of a lace umbrella. About fashion and customs in the nineteenth century*) and received an award at the Popular Science Book Fair 2017. organized by Adam Mickiewicz University in Poznań (Poland).

**Dr. hab. Agnieszka Graff** is a feminist scholar as well as activist and media commentator living in Poland. An associate professor at the American Studies Center, University of Warsaw, she teaches courses in US culture, literature and film, African American studies, feminism and gender studies. Her articles on gender in Polish and US culture have appeared in collected volumes and academic journals, including *Public Culture, Feminist Studies, Signs,* and *East European Politics and Societies.* She has authored several books of feminist essays in Polish: *Świat bez kobiet* (*World without Women,* 2001, new edition 2021); *Rykoszetem* (*Stray Bullets – Gender, Sexuality and Nation,* 2008), *Magma* (*The Quagmire Effect,* 2010), *Matka Feministka* (*Mother and Feminist,* 2014). She writes for major journals and newspapers, including Oko.press and *Gazeta Wyborcza.* She has also authored introductions to Polish editions of feminist classics: Betty Friedan's *Feminine Mystique* (2012), Susan Faludi's *Backlash* (2013), and Audre Lorde's *Sister Outsider* (2015). Her most recent book is *Anti-gender Politics in the Populist Moment,* co-authored by Elżbieta Korolczuk (Routledge, 2021, open access).

**Kateryna Iakovlenko** is a Ukrainian visual culture researcher, writer, and curator focusing on art and culture during sociopolitical transformation and war. Among her publications is the book *Why There Are Great Women Artists in Ukrainian Art* (2019) and *Euphoria and Fatigue: Ukrainian Art and Society after 2014* (special issue of *Obieg* magazine, coedited with Tatiana Kochubinska, 2019). Currently, she is Cultural Editor-in-Chief of Suspilne.media (Kyiv) and a visiting scholar at the UCL School of Slavonic and East European Studies (2022–23).

**Dr. Małgorzata Jankowska** – art historian, lecturer and curator. Associate Professor at the Academy of Fine Arts Gdańsk (Department of History and Theory of Art). Associated with the Nicolaus Copernicus University (2002-2019). Her early research was based on the film experiments of Polish female and male artists (Artists' film. Sketches from the history of the visual film and photo-media movement in Poland 1957 – 1981). Main research interests focus on the issues of contemporary art in a broadly defined cultural context, with particular emphasis on new media art (bio art) and relationships between art, science and technology, especially the position of female artists in the field of new media art. She is a member of the Polish section of the International Association of Art Critics (AICA). From 2001-2016 she cooperated with Wozownia Art Gallery in Toruń, creating exhibitions and programs dedicated to, among others, performance and new media art. Organizer of interdisciplinary conferences: Twilight of the Anthropocene (2020, Academy of Fine Arts Gda sk), and the conference Bio-presence. Art in the Biotechnological World (2021, Academy of Fine Arts Gdańsk). She has published numerous articles and essays in journals, such as: "Algorithmic revolution. Art, gender and machine" or "Bacteria in the service of art and art for the love of bacteria. About Anna Dumitru's oeuvre."

**Dr. Magdalena Furmanik-Kowalska** – art critic and historian. Since 2021 she has been the research manager of Art & Modern Foundation (Fundacja Art & Modern). In 2014 she completed her PhD in the field of Art Studies at Nicolaus Copernicus University in Torun. The postgraduate course Gender Studies graduated at the University of Warsaw in 2009. From 2016 to 2020, the Associate Director of the Study Centre of the Polish Institute of World Art Studies. Member of the Polish section of International Association of Art Critics (AICA). Co-organizer of several international conferences on Asian art. Curator of many exhibitions of Polish contemporary art. Author of the book *Uwikłane w kulturę. O twórczości współczesnych artystek japońskich i chińskich* [Culture trouble: The Contemporary Art of Japanese and Chinese Women] and many articles on contemporary art. Co-editor of the publications *Costume – mirror of culture, The art of dress, dress in art,* and *What does (not) suit a man? Male clothes in art and culture.*

**Veranika Laputska** was most recently a research fellow at the United States Holocaust Memorial Museum. She is a Ph.D. Candidate at the Graduate School for Social Research, Institute of Philosophy and Sociology at the Polish Academy of Sciences and is a Co-Founder of the EAST Center. Her dissertation examines visual propaganda at national commemorations in modern Belarus. Laputska holds a Specialist Diploma in International Relations from Belarusian State University, an MA in European Studies from European Humanities University, an MA in East European Studies from Warsaw University, and an MA in Economy and Society from Lancaster University. Laputska was a recipient of the Rothschild Scholarship for the Naomi Prawer Kadar International Yiddish Summer Program at Tel Aviv University in 2019 and YIVO Full Scholarship for Uriel Weinreich Program in Yiddish Language, Literature and Culture in 2018. She holds a diploma in Gender Studies from Lund University (2009), and also completed an American Institute on Political and Economic Systems program at Georgetown / Charles Universities (2011). Laputska consults international and regional organizations and funds on media and democratization. In addition, she is working on two book projects about Belarus with Distinguished Professor David R. Marples at the University of Alberta, Canada; one on the politics of memory around sites of mass extermination in Belarus and another on the 2020 Belarusian protests. In 2022 she was a Mandel Center for Advanced Holocaust Studies Fellow at the Jack, Joseph and Morton Mandel Center for Advanced Holocaust Studies at the United States Holocaust Memorial Museum, working on the project "Maly Traścianiec and Other Forgotten Holocaust Sites in Belarus." Her research interests include the study of nationalism and the politics of memory as well as media, visual, and Jewish studies.

**Dr. Maria Mayerchyk** has a double affiliation with the University of Greifswald (Alexander von Humboldt Fellow) and the Ethnology Institute of the National Academy of Sciences of Ukraine (Senior Research Fellow). In the past, she was visiting professor at the University of Alberta (Canada) and visiting researcher at Harvard University (USA), Lund University (Sweden), and the University of South Florida (USA). Dr. Mayerchyk holds a Candidate of Sciences degree in History specializing in Ethnology. She teaches courses on queer, gender, feminism, diaspora, folklore and Ukrainian culture in Germany, Canada, and Ukraine. Maria authored/edited seven books in English and Ukrainian. Her current monograph, "Coloniality of the Indecent: Erotic Folklore in the Modern Design of Sexuality," is being translated into English. Her research interests include decolonial option, queer and feminist epistemologies, Eastern European studies, diaspora studies, and critical folklore studies.

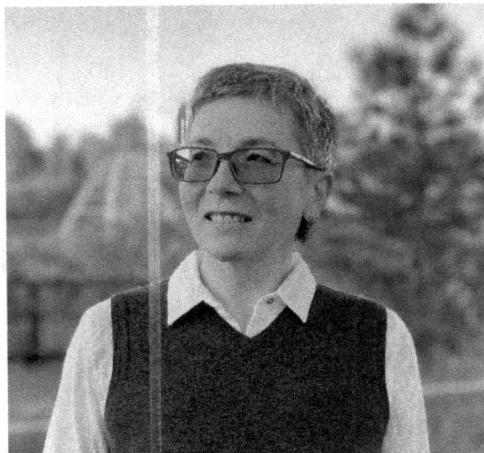

**Dr. Olga Plakhotnik** is a researcher and Chair of Ukrainian Cultural Studies at the University of Greifswald. She is also a PI of the BMBF-funded project "(Un)Disciplined: Pluralizing Ukrainian Studies—Understanding the War in Ukraine"— a research network comprising scholars from the universities of Greifswald, Regensburg, and Giessen. Olga's area of expertise includes feminist epistemologies and methodologies, feminist and queer pedagogies, contemporary feminist, LGBT+ and queer activisms in Ukraine. She holds a Ph.D. in sociology from the Open University (UK) and a Candidate of Sciences degree in philosophy from the National Aerospace University in Kharkiv (Ukraine). **Drs. Plakhotnik and Mayerchyk** are editors-in-chief of the refereed journal *Feminist Critique: East European Journal of Feminist and Queer Studies* (http://feminist.krytyka.com/en ). They co-authored a number of publications in feminist and queer studies. Their recent joint publications include chapters " 'Uneventful' Feminist Protest in Post-Maidan Ukraine: Nation and Coloniality Revisited" (in *Postcolonial and Postsocialist Dialogues,* Routledge 2021) and "Pride Contested: Geopolitics of Liberation at the Buffer Periphery of Europe" (forthcoming in *lambda nordica*).

**Dr. Natallia Paulovich** holds a doctorate in Sociology from the Graduate School for Social Research of the Institute of Philosophy and Sociology of the Polish Academy of Sciences, as well as an MA from the Belarusian State University in Minsk (Faculty of History). Her doctoral dissertation focused on the socio-cultural changes in Georgia after the collapse of the Soviet Union, and their connection to the transformation of female position in society under the new, neo(liberal) regime. Her current research interests focus on the gendered aspects of the Belarusian protests in 2020 and their aftermath. She is also researching feminist critiques of sports culture. Natallia's articles have appeared in: Anthropology of the Contemporary Middle East and Central Eurasia; Journal of Caucasian Studies, Special Issue: Gender in the Caucasus and Diaspora and Slavic Review. Dr. Paulovich is currently pursuing postdoctoral research and is also teaching yoga.

**Dr. Iryna Shuvalova** is a Postdoctoral Fellow at University of Oslo, Norway. She holds a PhD in Slavonic Studies from the University of Cambridge, where she was a Gates Cambridge scholar, and an MA in Comparative Literature from Dartmouth College, where she was a Fulbright scholar. Her most recent publications in *REGION: Regional Studies of Russia, Eastern Europe and Central Asia* (2021) and in *East/West: Journal of Ukrainian Studies* (2022) explore the construction of identity narratives during the Russo-Ukrainian war through the prism of popular songs, while her 2021 essay "The Mova I Live In" featured in the *Los Angeles Review of Books* examined multilingualism in Ukrainian society. Her forthcoming book is entitled *"Donbas Is My Sparta": Identity and Belonging in the Songs of the Russo-Ukrainian War*. Shuvalova is also an award-winning poet and translator. Her most recent and fifth book of poetry *Stoneorchardwoods* (*"Kamin'sadlis"*) has been named book of the year by Ukraine's Litakcent Prize for Literature and received the Special Prize of the Lviv UNESCO City of Literature Book Award. In 2009, she co-edited *120 Pages of "Sodom,"* the first anthology of queer writing in Ukraine. Her research interests lie at the intersection of politics and culture in Eastern Europe and Eurasia, particularly as viewed through the prism of conflict and dissent.

**Antonina Stebur** is a curator, art historian, art critic. She holds an MA in Visual and Cultural Studies from the European Humanities University and graduated from the School of Engaged Art "Chto Delat" (What is to be done?). She lectures on activist practices in contemporary arts at the Universität der Künste Berlin and the European College of Liberal Art (Minsk, Belarus). Antonina is a co-founder of the #damaudobnayavbytu (convenient woman in everyday life) project on gender discrimination in Belarus and other ex-Soviet countries, a co-founder Spaika.media, a research platform about activist political art and performance, co-initiator of The International Coalition of Cultural Workers Against the War in Ukraine (www.antiwarcoalition.art). The authors of *The History of Belarusian Photography* book, co-author Hanna Samarskaya. She is a co-curator of the exhibitions *Every Day. Art. Solidarity. Resistance*, which is currently on view in Mistetsky Arsenal, (Kyiv, Ukraine), exhibitions on inclusion in art— *Names* (Brest, Minsk, Vitebsk, Belarus), I *was approaching the city that I hadn't known yet*, Dnipro (Ukraine), and others. Her research interests include feminism, post-Soviet studies, political art, performance studies, grassroots activism, access to public space, tactics of resistance and solidarity, creating social infrastructures.

**Dr. Nataliya Tchermalykh** is a visual and legal anthropologist. She is currently a postdoctoral teaching and research fellow at the Interdisciplinary Center for Children's Rights Studies at the University of Geneva. In 2019, she completed her doctoral degree in Anthropology and Sociology at the Graduate Institute of International and Development Studies in Geneva (Switzerland). Her research interests encompass socio-legal studies, legal anthropology, visual anthropology and art. In 2014 she published *Paysages Instables. Des Artistes Ukrainiens entre Révolution et Guerre* [*Shifting Landscapes. Ukrainian Artists between Revolution and War*], published jointly by Editions de la Galerie Pangée (Montreal) and Rodovid (Kyiv).

**Dr. Jessica Zychowicz** is the Director of Fulbright Ukraine & IIE: Institute of International Education, Kyiv Office. She recently published her monograph, *Superfluous Women: Art, Feminism, and Revolution in Twenty-First Century Ukraine* (University of Toronto Press 2020). The book has been reviewed in multiple languages and countries; it won the American Association for Ukrainian Studies Book Prize; the Honorable Mention for the Omelijan Pritsak Prize for Ukrainian Studies from Harvard University; and the Honorable Mention for the Scaglione Prize in Slavic Studies at the Modern Languages Association (MLA)—the first ever to win this award for any book on Ukraine since the prize was established in 1992. The book will soon be published in Poland by the Museum of Modern Art in Warsaw with Karakter Press; and in Ukraine on Krytyka Press. In 2017-2018 Dr. Zychowicz was a U.S. Fulbright Scholar to Kyiv-Mohyla Academy, where she taught courses in sociology and conducted archival research toward another monograph. She has authored numerous articles on revolution and women/gender studies. She has also been a Research Fellow at the University of Toronto Munk School of Global Affairs (2015-2016), a Visiting Scholar at Uppsala University's Institute for Russian and East European Studies in Sweden (Fall 2019), and a Visiting Scholar as the 2018-2021 Stasiuk Fellow of the University of Alberta in the Contemporary Ukraine Studies Program (CUSP). Dr. Zychowicz is a Board Member of the Association for Women in Slavic Studies (AWSS), an Advisory Board member of H-Net H-Ukraine, and is a founding co-editor of the Forum for Race and Postcolonialism at *Krytyka*.com. Over the past five years, she has been an invited keynote speaker at the Ireland Museum of Modern Art, and invited speaker at Cultural Foundation Schloss Wiepersdorf in Germany, University of St. Andrew's in

Edinburgh, Scotland, NYU's Center for European and Mediterranean Studies, University of Arkansas, and many others. She earned her doctorate at the University of Michigan and holds a degree in English literature from U.C. Berkeley. For more information: https://www.jes-zychowicz.com/.

# I.
# Introduction

Jessica Zychowicz

At the intersection of Poland, Ukraine, and Belarus, there is an imaginary of political and cultural coordinates. The escalation of an all-out war on Ukraine in 2022 shifted the idea of "democracy" in the region into a critical defense of global proportions. The regional links between opposition movements in Poland, Ukraine, and Belarus that were led by women were already moving into view long before the war but came into sharp focus in 2021. After February 24, 2022, when Putin expanded the war he had been waging for eight years in Ukraine's Donbas, it seemed to experts that the world had been asleep until that moment. The global awakening to Russia's war on Ukraine is ongoing and continues to reveal the importance of the civic language(s) that feminists in these three countries had been developing in order to confront the steadily rising threat of authoritarianism. Much of the vocabulary of this new language stems from street actions and protests across the region since the early 2000s, facilitated by the growth of social media, as well as past experiences in the Orange Revolution in the case of Ukraine, and in joining the E.U. in the case of Poland. Key legislative changes have also been introduced permitting visa-free travel to/from Ukraine, and some protections for gender minorities were entered into law in Poland and Ukraine, albeit often unenforced and weakened by opponents. The civic vocabulary of feminist discourse is not limited by linguistic differences between spoken languages but recognized for its immediacy and transferability; it is "a new poetics," as Agnieszka Graff writes in her chapter about, in her words, the appearance of "angry women" in response to Poland's ultra-conservative PiS government. This book is about these women and more: it speaks with and through the anger of women everywhere who share their ideas and experiences in the interest of articulating a freer future.

This book brings together fifteen established scholars/authors with expertise in the immediate contexts of Ukraine, Poland, and Belarus in which all live and work, but also formal research methodologies, and firsthand observation developed in dialogue in international residencies, fellowships, exchanges, exhibitions, etc. The topics addressed in each chapter have evolved from individual sustained research concerning the past two decades, a timeframe that has involved ongoing occupation and cease-fire violations by Russia-backed separatists in Ukraine's Donbas, a situation that has now engulfed all of Ukraine and has also permanently changed Belarus and Poland. Each of these authors supplies valuable frameworks that they have developed in their scholarly work and artistic practices, which concern the relationship between power and language. Language is understood here as an extension of the body, producing knowledge that informs the interpretive lenses for the readings of case studies, which results in a kind of annotation of this language. Nearly all of these chapters were written during the past two years, as feminist protests were unfolding, but before the war escalated, all shed light on how we understand the recent events of mass protest, revolution, and war today. This is true not only in the more proximate impact on societies within and between shared borders (broadly defined) but also in shaping a language capable of shifting how individuals and institutions relate to one another amid the war, which is now at the center of global concern. This capacity is sought through a shared ethics that emerges in these texts most clearly in reference to inclusive, more nuanced, accurate understandings of transitions through and out of social, legal, military, and other forms of conflict. Such transitions must be inclusive of a more equitable future that guarantees security and democracy for the most diverse, widest possible range of cultures and peoples.

What can scholars do? What is our role in wartime? We can begin, as these chapters suggest, by opening ourselves to comparative approaches to our own "areas" – disciplines, national contexts, and topics. This anthology starts with the premise that "post-Soviet" is a global condition, situated at the intersections of power, body, social communication. We are only at the beginning of determining models for understanding how information and data are changing borders and who can cross them safely. Borders are also formed and reprogrammed, and this can be weaponized as data modeled on the flow of people, and of bodies, along with capital and goods. In 2021 Poland and Belarus witnessed how Lukashenko and Putin coordinated the weaponization of refugees from the MENA region on the Polish-Belarusian border. This unleashed an effective propaganda campaign of xenophobia within the E.U. Undoing or interrogating traditional ways of organizing knowledge can also help to break apart divisive narratives in disinformation campaigns and historical revisionism (not only Putin's but also in the closed media spaces of China, Iran, Turkey, etc.). By utilizing visual language analyses and combining different viewpoints on war from Poland, Ukraine, and Belarus, we are able to construct a contemporary history that evidences women's activism over time as a key component of civil society in recent decades, including revolutions in these countries of which the processes are ongoing and intertwined with the conditions of war.

A challenge to this contemporary historiography are the conditions of war itself. International evidence collections and investigations, now led by the International Criminal Court at The Hague, are underway to document the crimes and atrocities that are occurring daily at the time of the writing of this book. Further to these massive and much-needed documentation efforts, there were efforts by women activists prior to the escalation of Russia's war on Ukraine, amid complex challenges to the data collection. The necessity of simultaneous description of a historical trajectory of women's activism with human rights infractions, and now war crimes, also unfolds on the civic-legislative plane of Ukraine, which continues to shift oftentimes in relations with Poland and Belarus. Depicting human rights infringements includes gender analyses, yet should not be taken for granted as automatically considered. Early civilian efforts at documenting the war beginning in 2014 show only the nascent legal and social contexts of gender analysis within infractions in/near lines of military conflict that have intensified with the full-scale escalation of the war. An overwhelming amount of work is needed.

The renowned think tank ICTJ: International Center for Transitional Justice published a recent policy paper with guidelines for documenting the war in Ukraine.[1] In this paper, ICTJ offers a constructive critique of the Nobel Peace Prize given to the Ukrainian NGO Center for Civil Society for their civilian documentation of war crimes. ICTJ points out a need for more state support, official training, and the unreliability of reports due to factors such as bias and trauma, including the introduction of exaggeration for "fears of appearing disloyal" during wartime. The report also points to investigators needing more localized trainers. While it is not feasible to expect trainers to emerge from among traumatized populations, there can be lessons gained by leaders from studying the landscape of activism prior to the escalation, and by drawing out challenges and insights faced by women activists who early on started developing strategies for understanding the war, inclusive of revolution. An overwhelming amount of support will be needed for future investigations of rape, abduction of children, and gendered violence being committed now.

To help students and researchers working on gender in transitional justice out of conflict to peacetime, we can protect freedom of thought, speech, and action. We can inoculate from the information war: we can create a

---

[1] Anna Myriam Roccatello, "In Ukraine, Justice for Victims Is More Than Criminal Accountability," *ICTJ: International Center for Transitional Justice,* July 1, 2022, at https:// www.ictj.org/latest-news/ukraine-justice-victims-more-criminal-accountability. Accessed December 20, 2022.

more nuanced descriptive language that can have a legal impact, and that can increase our vigilance to mechanisms which seek to undermine clear lenses for analysis of gender or human rights issues– valid areas of legislation and concern–with weaponized discursive tools that are clearly authoritarian and manipulative. We can analyze these mechanisms through language in order to understand them vis-à-vis the Soviet context as a litmus for democracy, and a dual source of either confusion or greater cross-cultural solidarity around, for example, feminism today. As the chapters in this book make clear, feminist protest in Poland, Ukraine, and Belarus has become the avant-garde for a broader twenty-first-century civic vocabulary for democracy. But to interpret this language involves some de-coding, which is facilitated by scholarly/critical reflection through visual and written texts, and oftentimes this also involves understanding the ways in which political and administrative state power rely on gendered subjectivity to maintain authority, often to oppressive, and even violent ends. In these chapters by fifteen scholars from Poland, Belarus, and Ukraine the comparative historical knowledge between these three countries illuminates not "just" state sovereignty but an advanced language for civic and human rights more broadly.

## Structure of the Book

The timing of this volume responds to war that has been raging for a decade, but also the role of women as revolutionaries in Poland and Belarus in 2020-2021, and in 2013-2014 in Ukraine, as well as to security analyses that frame Ukraine's sovereignty strategically; as having regional and increasingly global implications. The critical approaches of each of these authors to their subjects is enriched by their diversity as scholars, critics, activists, curators and artists—each representing decades of research on their subject area. Their comparative approaches, in combination with firsthand experience in these countries, is also an invaluable and shared methodological quality that makes these authors' approaches to the study of gender—and the role of thinking women in a democracy—particularly critical and invaluable." For example, many texts include the early historical roots for contemporary debates about the body by looking at how gender was constructed in the twentieth century and was represented in official propaganda, as well as in underground, nonconformist, and other intellectual and creative experiments. Writers, intellectuals, artists, and others, on unofficial levels, were paving the way for changing gender roles on the one hand, spreading knowledge about the body and the self, but on the other hand, as citizens, were also expected to "become Soviet or communist" by adhering to strict state-mandated protocols on their messages, behaviors, activities, associates, and any number of other parameters. Those individuals who did not conform, or did so in unorthodox ways, subscribed to ideas that challenged broader tendencies toward the state's cooptation and regulation of the very idea of female emancipation in the twentieth century; such oppressive tendencies toward control and censorship have, we recognize now in the context of war, violently resurfaced around the globe.

The thirteen chapters are organized into three thematic sections. The first section, *On Unity and Autonomy: Unmaking Vulnerable Subjectivity* explores representations of gender in documentary expository, performance, film, and music. All five chapters involve questioning how individual identity comes into conflict with mass identity and mass identifications with historical change and political upheaval. Ukraine's two revolutions in the 2000s feature in two of the chapters, but the opening chapter of this section concerns the 1990s as an origin point for a theory of "dispossession" with the aim of reversing how the war today engenders further modes of dehumanization and absence. The war features prominently in the chapter about popular music in the Donbas since the outset of the war in 2014 in particular where notions of female/femininity are activated with strength, androgyny, autonomy by performers who challenge binary divides that would ascribe vulnerability to women in times of war.

The second section, *On Crossing Borders: Past as a Litmus of Freedom of Expression,* begins with the women of Poland during the mid-late nineteenth century who challenged gender norms by navigating and inventing, out of necessity, new professional roles for themselves within the arts. The following chapter, also set in Poland, continues this emancipatory thread in tracing a continuous narrative thread encompassing women artists from the post-WWII era through present-day Poland. These chapters weave between the past and the present in a commentary on the present paradigm in their focus on women's demands for freedom of expression and legal rights—the two inextricably bound with both leaving a past behind (failed uprisings against the Tsar in the case of the 19th century, and Nazi occupation in the case of postwar). The final two chapters each focus on perceptions of gender in the 1990s, and post-Soviet Ukraine. The shaping of racial narratives intersecting with class and women's rights informs both chapters, though geographically different from the other two, on Poland, there can be found many similarities criss-crossing and intersecting these four chapters, especially as concerns women's fight to claim and own their professional lives as artists, writers, intellectuals in their own right—in this concept of freedom these chapters also address how motherhood and notions of familial obligation or duty can be reinvented to work for, rather than against, the female intellectual or female artist. If any escape from the past could be possible the escape from the double-burden of domestic and factory work in the PRL and Soviet context is underlined.

The third and final section, *On Social Transformation: Text, Body, Protest Ballot*, takes a close look at the leading role of women in the street protests in Belarus and Poland in 2020 and 2021. Three of the chapters are by Belarusian scholars, one also being a curator who left Minsk for Kyiv and was part of the team that installed one of the largest exhibitions of contemporary Belarusian art to date, which was dedicated to the women's marches. The role of aesthetics in social transformation is central to the analyses in this chapter and the final one, which focuses on the feminist protests in Poland. All of the chapters provide useful in-depth overviews of the electoral situations in these countries at this time, yet with the added understanding and critical points of analysis on how legislation shapes gender and vice-versa.

Woven through all sections are questions within trajectories of exploration that share many areas of focus and, hopefully, will provoke even further research: biopolitics in the production of citizenship; reproductive rights, including ethics and debates around abortion; the labor of parenting; access to fairly paid intellectual and creative work; equities in hiring and the workplace; class formation in the mediatized era; the development of the far-right and anti-gender movements; sexual/bodily shame; imaginaries of non-normativity; religion and the church; legislation on anti-discrimination; decolonization; the production of private/public divides; activism and mass discourse against domestic violence; counterintuitive lines of solidarity that span sociolinguistic and national borders; the (non)feminization of poverty; etc.

## Contexts: War and Democracy, or, Feminism and its Opponents

The connections between people and ideas within women's struggles across these countries have continually increased over the past decade. A visa-free travel regime within the E.U. for Ukrainian citizens was introduced in late 2017; this was a key outcome of the 2013-2014 Maidan Revolution. Women-led demonstrations increased steadily from the mid-2000s with Manifa marches in Poland inspiring the reinvigoration of the Women's March in Ukraine in 2008. Participants from Poland and Ukraine and also Belarus collaborated closely on projects, exhibitions, conferences, and publications with women throughout Central and Eastern Europe. Sweden, Germany, the Czech Republic, Latvia, and Lithuania became key partners due to favorable policies for women and gender equality and funding for projects with "eastern neighborhood" countries on the backdrop of discussions about E.U. association agreements. Feminist discourse grew in proportion to state and NGO funding, but there also existed grassroots and underground or radical experimental and highly sophisticated philosophical discussion about the future of the idea in its wider emancipative potential.

On college campuses, younger millennial generations with the rise of the #MeToo movement, known in Ukraine as #ЯнеБоюсяСказати began to contest feminism as too divided into academic versus populist versions. A focus on domestic violence, abortion, and the church became part of wider efforts to reinsert feminism into the populist mainstream. Widespread feminist protests named "Black Protests" in Poland emerged at this time, as did more overt demands for Anti-Discrimination policies after the Maidan Revolution of Dignity 2013-14 in Ukraine; and in 2020 in Belarus. The first section of this book includes a chapter about Ukraine's post-Maidan revolutionary context by anthropologist Nataliya Tchermalykh in which she explores intergenerational affective communities concerning political upheaval, and desire for social change in Ukraine. She presents compelling conclusions about the impact of the revolution on the view of history and the course of the nation's future by observing her students' visual engagement in the recent aftermath of the violence on the Maidan: " 'We felt that the country was in the stage of a rough cut . . .': Vernacular documentation, Political Affects and the Ideological Functions of Catharsis, *A case-study of a screening at Dom Kino, Ukraine.*"

The focus on post-Maidan visual communication as generative of new affective senses of belonging also informs the closing chapter of this section by the present author, in which I take a comparative approach to one Canadian and one Ukrainian artist's depictions of generational, national, and gendered discourse around the body and social belonging.

Attuned readers may notice that the authors in this volume are not concerned with parsing the "waves" of feminism; indeed, such analysis in the new feminist turn is abandoned for more anthropological descriptions of action, and close readings of experimental speech, visual material, and performance. The categorical thinking and grouping of "waves" is not considered as useful as a tool for documenting freedom of expression that spans waves; rather, comparative approaches to contexts past and present reveal regressive vectors of legislation on discrimination and censorship, which are the baseline from which struggles for emancipation begin. Common figures of speech are also discernible in the aesthetic patterns of the protests and artistic expression across these chapters. These patterns emerge in what Graff describes in the final chapter of this volume: "it is a community of the imagination . . . a revolution of image, text and song . . . a certain language of expression." She proposes a question about the phenomena around feminism that she observes in Poland, asking: "Who is this newly emergent female subject that speaks to the female 'people'?." Collectively, the authors of this book might be said to be asking the same question. Each closely examines how culture-makers are engaged with bringing about a public that can be addressed in unison.

The opposite of the community presupposed by feminist civic language shapes its lexicon as well; these are its opponents, whose antidemocracy attacks can be traced over the past decade in the countries to Russia's nearest neighbors: again, in a triangulation of cultural relations with Poland, Ukraine, and Belarus. The mainstream reception of terms like "feminism" and "gender" as so-called alien imports from the West by far-right groups within these countries is significant. The latter two cases share some additional features: Belarus and Ukraine are post-Soviet, non-E.U. countries that Putin views as satellites of the Russian Federation in his vision of *Russkii Mir* (Russian World) ideology. The *Russkii Mir* is propagated at the expense of all who contest it; it is a combination of imperial and neo-Soviet erasure of modern borders, modern institutions, journalistic freedom, and now one could also argue, in terms of the West's economic sanctions on Russia, has also created an ethical litmus test for global commerce and enterprise.

In the weaponization of "gender" and "feminism" by anti-democracy campaigns waged by far-right groups, Putin's primary targets have also been the E.U. and U.S. A general backlash to women's rights demonstrations ensued in the West, not always stemming from Russia. However, in the regional context under examination, readers from Europe and the U.S. will find useful analyses throughout this book that can serve as further evidence in staking points of comparison for universal human rights protections. The refugee crisis at the Belarusian-Polish border throughout 2021 should be mentioned in this context as well, as it unfolded in parallel on the same global media landscapes controlled by opponents to the women's rights and LGBTQ movements. The convergences between anti-immigrant and xenophobic sentiments with anti-feminism and homophobia are as significant as they are consequential. The global aspects of these sentiments demand a critical examination of how the debates and appropriations of "gender" and "feminism" have evolved not only locally, but also in international relations with/in/between Poland, Ukraine, and Belarus before and since Russia's war started in Donbas in 2014. The war is being waged on global scale beyond material tanks and gas shutoffs; it is about more than territorial capture. The war unfolds on cultural fronts and dis/information campaigns aimed at weakening cohesion around democratic ideals and institutions.

Not only in the context of war, but also in peacetime, feminism in these countries, as elsewhere, does not appear as a single idea nor can it or should it be united into one "front." Feminism in protests often travels with LGBTQ discourse, but is not identical to it, and has internal differences, especially in some cases regarding gay male hegemony over the communities advocating for social change. Feminism is named and debated widely within these countries and these debates have their own trajectories.[2] It appears differently in each of these texts, sometimes in relation to the individual author's views, or in critiques of wider society. For example, as is pointed out by all three of the contributors from Belarus, Veranika Laputska, Natallia Paulovich, and Antonina Stebur: the frontwomen leaders of the opposition movement to Lukashenko in 2021 actively distanced themselves from the term feminism. Here these critical voices provide context, and also show where Belarusian women have chosen to reclaim feminism and "women's rights" as fundamental to society and worth fighting for: Laputska gives a close analysis of how women conforming to the state are implicated in rigged elections; Paulovich asks whether feminism is worth including into the agenda; and Laputska shows how artists have utilized the lack of attention to obvious connections between police brutality against the mainstream women's marches with domestic violence as a symptom of deeper sociopolitical authoritarian patriarchal issues. All mention the three opposition leaders, Sviatlana Tsikhanouskaya, Veranika Tsepkalo, and Maria Kolesnikova, and their public statements as an opportunity to point out the wider gains and losses of such distance in fighting for both broader social change and for women's rights, as women.

To further the above point that feminism is never a united "front," feminists can, and certainly now do, ally with a seemingly more and more united front against authoritarianism in Belarus, Ukraine, and Poland. Yet even this alliance is not a given, but emerges through its ongoing articulation by actions and voices on the ground and in discourse, many featured in this book. Since the military actions by Russia-backed separatists in 2014, the focus on women's rights in sovereign Ukraine has continued to converge with securing veterans' rights and women's representation in the military, while responding to the social needs of Ukraine's internally displaced populations. This dynamic in many ways mirrors the women's organizations on the territories of modern Ukraine, Belarus, and Poland in WWI and WWII.[3]

---

[2] For a concise overview regarding Ukraine see: Olesya Khromeychuk, Tamara Martsenyuk, Emily Channell-Justice, Jessica Zychowicz, "Ukraine (finally) Treats Women's Activism Seriously," *The Ukrainian Quarterly*, no. 2 (Summer 2021): 47–54.

[3] For a history of women's civic organizing, especially Ukrainian women, in this region in WWI and pre-WWII twentieth century see: Martha Bohachevsky-Chomiak, *Feminists Despite Themselves: Women in Ukrainian Community Life, 1884-1939* (Edmonton: University of Alberta Press, 1988). Sociologist Tamara Martsenyuk has conducted extensive research and authored numerous reports on human rights in the context of women veterans and IDPs since 2014. She is one of the founding researchers on the wider project initiated in 2014 entitled "Invisible Battalion 3.0: Sexual Harassment in the

The wide variety of feminisms is as numerous within these chapters as it is within these countries, in Western Europe, in North America, and indeed anywhere women have developed and documented their own epistemology and activism. In this context, it is important to recognize and trace unique histories of origin narratives and imports/borrowings that move East-West, in both directions. For example, feminism as a term largely entered Ukraine's cultural landscape in the 1990s with writers like Oksana Zabuzhko and new translations of Virginia Woolf. This origin point appears in several chapters in this volume, especially in the two by Ukrainian authors/curators Oksana Briukhovetska and Kateryna Iakovlenko that look specifically at this period.[4] This origin is important, but it is not the only one, as both of these authors point out, as the Soviets introduced ideological dogma and indoctrination concerning race and sexuality that persist today. A grappling with this past appears throughout all of the texts in this volume and complicates especially the abortion policy debates between these countries, which distinguish the discussion in the post-Soviet context (where abortion bans have not been introduced) from the Polish one in its primary association with anti-clericalism and the Catholic Church. Communist discourse on "The Woman Question" in all three of these countries has, historically, come into conflict with "feminism" as a perceived importation from the West. The idea of women fighting for emancipation was in communist doctrine inseparable from the proletarian struggle. Today feminism is demonized by its opponents as either a Soviet-era Marxist point of dogma, or an alien import from the West. Feminism is perceived by these opponents as a dangerous "immoral" force they equate with the E.U., as documented in slogans such as "Keep Gay-Europa out of Ukraine" or the "No LGBT Zone" signage in Poland.

---

Military Sphere" in collaboration with the Institute for Gender Programs: https://invisible battalion.org/en/invisbat-2/ Accessed September 10, 2022.

[4] Kateryna Iakovlenko co-authored a companion essay collection by artists from the exhibition dedicated to contemporary art by women in Ukraine, entitled *A Space of One's Own*, Kyiv: PinchukArtCenter, November 2018. Kateryna Iakovlenko, ed., *Чому в українському мистецтві є великі художниці* [*Why There are Such Great Artists in Ukrainian Art*] (Ukraine: PinchukArtCentre, 2019). The exhibition converged with the centennial of suffragism. For a historical account in a transatlantic context see: Jessica Zychowicz "A New Dawn at the Centennial of Suffragism: Artistic Representation in Transeuropean and Transatlantic Kyiv," *Contemporary Ukrainian and Baltic Art: Political and Social Perspectives, 1991-2021*, ed. Svitlana Biedarieva (New York: Columbia University Press and Ibidem-Verlag, 2021). For a review of the exhibit in the context of the history of suffragism see: Jessica Zychowicz "Ми, Аутсайдерки: Вірджинія Вулф і фемінізм у глобалній перспективі [We Outsiders: Virginia Woolf and Feminism in Global Perspective]," KORYDOR (February 5, 2019) online.

Conflicts around feminism and gender in reference to the church and the communist past have produced tensions at sites that demand further research. Embodied creative expression by artists and activists written about here, or in some cases artists that contributors to this volume work with as curators, or when they speak as artists themselves working at these sites, for example, are important forms of communication for circumventing biopolitical control and censorship. For example, Iryna Shuvalova explores this in case studies of performances by a female war veteran who built a successful career as a popular singer pushing against traditional representations of "femininity" in Ukrainian society. She presents compelling evidence of how non-conforming representations of gender identity challenge limitations in the politics of citizenship and access to civil rights in wartime. Music and media performances with wide followings that complicate "femininity" in military contexts become powerful sources of agency against systemic violence. The idea of women fighting for their rights has its opponents in all three countries, and these opponents continually exploit the idea. Artistic experiments, then, in the context of regimes that exploit the human body as a political tool, when studied critically, become "more than art."

### Geographical Scope

Beginning in 2014, Russia's war on Ukraine's Donbas triggered an ever-aggressive regional invasion of divisive propaganda and provocation, with the aim of splitting off democratic solidarities and social pluralism in the countries closest culturally, linguistically, and territorially to Ukraine. While Poland, unlike Belarus and Ukraine, was never Soviet, the Polish case is relevant for understanding modern nationhood in these countries. Poland, now a member of NATO and having recently transitioned to full E.U. membership, had centuries served as the nearest "European Other" in the imagination of the Tsar (and in its post-partition/occupation successive Sejm parliament, which comprised Europe's first democratic senate). It is also true that Polish nobles represented in the Sejm were never in alignment with the national project of Ukraine under construction by intellectuals. Polish landlords who held votes in the Sejm often maintained colonial agendas to acquire serfs in developing power relations with Orthodox populations between Warsaw and Moscow. People living in these territories self-defined with a wide variety of ethnic identities at different points in history, the most predominant being Ruthenian, Cossack, and Jewish, with the latter population not permitted to live further east in Russia than the Pale of Settlement. There were many German nobles in the city of Kyiv as well. Yet at different points, all of these populations were ruled by successive occupiers in these territories, with the Russian Imperial Tsardom being the most consistent across the Kyiv and Warsaw regions. Autonomous modern Ukrainian statehood found expression only briefly in 1918, then again in a contested sense in 1941, but it was not until 1991, with the fall of the USSR, that Ukraine finally became a full sovereign state with its post-WWII borders intact—up until 2015 with Russia's annexation of Crimea and occupation of Luhansk and Donetsk.

Over the longer term, pacts, compromises, and alliances between Poland and Ukraine have arisen, usually in pragmatic arrangements aimed to buffer Moscow, often between individual dissenters against Soviet power, or in earlier periods, wherever those identifying with the respective national projects allied themselves with "modernity" or against the Tsar and serfdom in the case of the 1864 "Springtime of Nations" across Europe. Numerous examples over the 19th c. include Polish uprisings within the country's Russian partition and Polish members of the Decembrists in their resistance to Tsardom. For populations working to forge independent Ukrainian and Belarusian states, 19th c. ethnic folk expressions held significance, as did 20th c. Stalinist Soviet national policy outlawing such expressions, punishable by death. How could such a banal form as folk art earn someone a one-way trip to a remote Siberian work prison (GULAG), or execution? Because art carries with it the power markers of historic paradigms. Folk expressions were also symbolic of the emancipation of serfdom in the 19th c., which had openly challenged the seat of power in Moscow. The iron fist of Stalinism in the twentieth century then demanded absolute conformity and loyalty to the regime—Ukraine and Belarus, in any slight expression of nationhood, were categorically disallowed. Folk embroidery would not belie an emancipative rebellion, uprising, or challenge to Stalin.

Today, Putin often quotes from Stalin. In a striking contemporary visual response to these speeches, chapter twelve features cross stitch folk embroidery by Belarusian artist Rufina Bazlova, created in the image of protests in Minsk in 2021, led by women who were beaten in the streets by riot police. Images and art play an increasingly central role in building communities with shared political identifications, as is explored by the Belarusian author/curator Antonina Stebur in her chapter, " 'People have nothing to oppose to state violence except their fragile bodies': Configurations of Feminism in Belarusian Protest Art," on the aesthetics of the resistance to Lukashenko's dictatorship. Stebur was one of two women in a team of five curators of the first major contemporary exhibition of Belarusian art; it was named after the protests' rallying cry, "*Kazhdie den!*": *Everyday. Art. Solidarity. Resistance,* and consisted of over 100 works in all media formats. Many works were created during the protests, largely about violence inflicted during them; many works were by women, some created inside prisons or detention centers. The exhibition was installed in Kyiv's largest state-supported museum, Mystetskyi Arsenal (Art Arsenal) in Spring/ Summer 2021.[5]

Global responses to the war in Ukraine will determine the future survival of democratic societies well beyond the nation's borders. This war is also being waged in information spheres: culture, texts, images. The deeper sociopolitical ramifications of this war when it was initially being fought in Donbas were first and most vehemently felt as anti-democracy and anti-gender/anti-feminist propaganda in the region of Ukraine, Belarus, and Poland, then made themselves visible globally. Years before Trump took office, his campaign manager, Paul Manafort, was already employed as campaign manager for Viktor Yanukovych, the Kremlin-backed president of Ukraine. The Maidan Revolution of Dignity of 2013–2014 resulted in Yanukovych's ouster, but an uneven media war continued, with Kremlin-backed vectors of information like "Stop Gender!" finding fertile ground in Ukraine and Eastern Europe, aimed more generally at weakening not only growing LGBTQ and Women's Rights marches, but peaceful civic demonstrations throughout the West. In their chapter, "Between the Time of Nation and Feminist Time: Genealogies of Feminist Protest in Ukraine," the sociologists Olga Plakhotnik and Maria Mayerchyk provide an in-depth analysis of this period and of dynamics within Ukrainian feminist activism. Written from the position of two critical scholars at the center of organizing women's marches in Kyiv since their resurgence in 2008, the chapter also represents Plakhotnik and Mayerchyk's wider ongoing critiques of the marches.

## Conceptualizing Freedom: Civic Language

The idea of *freedom* in the twenty-first century does not stand apart as a purely physical location marked by national borders. This is not to argue that location does not matter; quite the opposite, as in the Internet Age, information is increasingly co-determinate of physical freedom. Protest in the physical and virtual landscapes is less tethered to place and national borders. A demonstration is locally rooted while being globally accessible on the Internet. Today, information moves at the speed of light and electricity; it is more diffuse and acquires meaning through anonymous editing, comments, posts, producing visual content layered with political meaning through viral videos and memes. For example, the Belarus marches and the Polish feminist demonstrations circulated on media surfaces through icons and hashtags: in the former instance,

---

[5] A virtual version of the exhibition, held partly during a lockdown, could be viewed on the museum website: "Kazhdie den!" Exhibition. Kyiv March 25–June 6, 2022. Mystetskyi Arsenal Museum website: https://artarsenal.in.ua/en/vystavka/evere-day-art-solidarity-resistance/. Accessed November 18, 2022.

with a heart, a fist, and a peace sign standing in for the three women opposition leaders, and with a pink lightning bolt on #Strajk Kobiet in the second instance.

Feminist 1970s critical theories of media and the public sphere have become relevant again. The information-dense space of protests across Poland and Belarus in 2020 and 2021, and of war in Ukraine, provide ground for imagining what a "new" or differently defined and repositioned avatar of the conscientious objector or human-rights defender can mean in vocalizing a specific position or acting on a public stance. In their chapter, Furmanik-Kowalska and Jankowska, writing from Poland, mine the vibrant history of women artists after 1945, providing extensive examples in a trajectory of resilience in the face of trauma, autonomy from dependence on male professional gatekeepers, and the innovative integration of new media into creative work. The chapter traces how women became visible and possibilities in art expanded, not least because of rebuilding Poland after the German occupation, and because of women's deft maneuvers in dealing with PRL-era censorship, overcoming patriarchy in the art system while securing the right to own their name and their individual genius.

Across and within the three countries studied here, diverse representations of feminism in the media's linguistic landscape have emerged through artworks in resonant ways, creating affective communities of activists. Feminism is also being appropriated, weaponized, and demonized by opponents. The feminist and gender protests in Eastern Europe have maintained a growing resistance against authoritarianism. Agnieszka Graff points out that in Poland by 2018, feminists were being recognized as frontline defenders of democracy, no longer "marginal to politics." Graff traces how, since 2015, feminism here has *gained a public*. She describes this in terms of war: "This war – involving the rise of radical nationalism and described by sociologists in terms of 'symbolic thickening'– has what may be termed a spiritual dimension. It is experienced by many as a struggle between good and evil. Against the rise of fascism, against the dissolution of democratic dreams, there is an equally radical rebellion. Witches, madwomen, and rebels are emerging from the darkness in defense of the good – democracy, freedom and pluralism. On the other side, they see evil – nationalism, misogyny, ossified tradition, unspeakable cruelty."[6] Her observations reveal a war that is even deeper than and precedes the bombs now falling on Ukraine—and that in this sense is not limited to any one nation's territory, but is global. Feminist protest is a medium with which new civic languages have emerged, directly confronting attacks on democracy. Again, not as a united

---

[6] Marta Kotwas and Jan Kubik, "Symbolic Thickening of Public Culture and the Rise of Right-Wing Populism in Poland," *East European Politics and Societies* 33, no. 2 (2019): 435–471.

front, but as a deliberately fractured and nuanced range of relations, terms, interactions, networks, and sociopolitical exchanges that repeat and solidify various enactments of selfhood, autonomy, and resilience in demanding one's rights. Women are at the forefront of this communication, which is inextricably tied to how one positions their body vis-à-vis institutions, including the state and police that represent civic power structures.

A central observation to be drawn from this book is that today's war in Ukraine is not "just" about Russia versus Ukraine—it is the next stage of the Maidan Revolution, not limited this time to Kyiv's Maidan but taking place in information warfare globally. How western nations choose to respond militarily or economically involves many thorny issues, yet another, possibly more lasting issue—this volume's concern is how to deal with new forms of attacks on democracy in the overt degradation of culture, civic freedoms, and pluralism. As some have pointed out, in 2013 the term appearing most often in the Polish press was not "Maidan Revolution," but "Stop Gender!" What this shows us is that Putin was already engaged in full information warfare against the E.U. at the time of the Maidan Revolution in Kyiv. The moment Kyiv's central square was clear and the barricades removed, Russia annexed Crimea on a false referendum and occupied Donbas on the pretext of "separatists" claiming territory based on false essentialist claims, including ethnolinguistic territorial arguments. Since the Revolution of 2013-2014 (and earlier), feminists and women activists have remained at the center of the struggle for democracy, in the belly of the beast as authoritarians observing that moment have risen in Poland, Ukraine, and Belarus—and not only. China has recently proclaimed any "Color Revolutions" to be a threat, referring to the 2004 Orange Revolution, when Ukraine responded to the rigging of its presidential election. Scholars possess rhetorical competence and unique approaches to questions of injustice, tyranny, violence, and social exclusion that can help to shed light on problems outlined here. What verbal and visual civic languages are activists working with at the intersection of Ukraine, Poland, Belarus? How can these languages facilitate even broader communication about human rights and democracy?

Freedom of expression on all sides of the political spectrum has become tantamount to an attack on identity, and thus on the body as an ideological tool of state, society, institutions. The global conservative turn underway since 2016, to include the rise of far-right groups, fits this pattern, and it has not spared these three countries. In an important sense, this feature of their respective sociopolitical landscapes makes them thoroughly "normal" examples of the same retrograde tendencies afflicting all post-industrial democracies in the twenty-first century. Some have drawn this justifiable conclusion from extensive case studies on the post-Soviet context and include Ukraine as key evidence of a "competitive authoritarianism" or of autocratic structures that persist regionally as a stable frame.[7] At the same time, unique challenges underpin the region, such as oligarchy and economic interdependencies on fossil-fuel infrastructures.[8] Each of the three national contexts are distinct in their particular challenges, yet they also share historical features that differ from the West, such as the experience of the communist experiment, occupation by the Nazi German regime and/or Soviet state, and loss of life during WWII. In all three countries, these features shape lived experience and memories of the past, especially regarding intergenerational communication and how individuals understand themselves vis-à-vis systems of state authority, including participation in elections and motivation to join demonstrations. The shared feminist civic languages examined in this book are an outgrowth of links between scholars and with demonstrators on the ground, forced by historical circumstances to fight a war defined in terms of culture, language, and information—of stolen ballots, social discrimination, and degraded rights.

While this volume's driving questions are grounded in local historical contexts, new frameworks are applied to uncover unconventional, interdisciplinary, and comparative approaches to gender and culture and examine how societies replicate power systems. In Ukraine today, for example, urban space is marked by memorials being contested in the context of Decommunization Laws introduced after the Maidan Revolution, which address the removal of Lenin statues. These debates indicate similar tensions, as the residual Soviet past comes into conflict with present negotiations on ideological meanings attached to the physical landscape. The Decommunization Laws, applied in 2015 in blanket unilateral decisions in ways that can bring to mind the reflex to reject "feminism" by wielding local associations with Bolshevist propaganda about imports of Western decadence, have been criticized by artists after state institutions shut down exhibitions that presented Soviet-era symbols (even when the "point" was to critique and discuss those symbols). The Decommunization Laws provide interesting comparisons with populist stances taken in the U.S. in 2018–2020 to resist removal of statues commemorating Civil War figures,

---

[7] The term "competitive authoritarianism" is derived from a situation of "pluralism by default," capturing the situation entered by Ukraine and other post-Soviet states in the shoring up of public resources by elites after the fall of the USSR. See: Lucan A. Way and Steven Levitsky, *Competitive Authoritarianism: Hybrid Regimes After the Cold War* (Cambridge: Cambridge University Press, 2010).

[8] The politics and extensive infrastructure involvement of Eastern and Central Europe in fossil fuels and other energy interdependencies stemming from the Russian Federation is well documented. See: Margarita M. Balmaceda, *Russian Energy Chains: The Remaking of Technopolitics from Siberia to Ukraine to the European Union* (New York: Columbia University Press, 2021).

including the Confederate General Robert E. Lee. Oksana Briukhovetska's chapter, "Beyond Three Colors, Exploring Soviet Memory of Race as an Artist," is written from her perspective as a feminist artist from Kyiv participating in the Black Lives Matter protests in New Orleans. Briukhovetska delves into significant differences and misunderstandings between nations in Cold War era understandings of race, and delves under the surface into social mechanisms underlying ideological content of Soviet socialist realism, which she argues is still residual today.

In post-Soviet Ukraine, the attempt to veil or erase the past by demolishing and outlawing Soviet-era symbols replicates the same overreach the Soviet state had used in seeking to censor and preemptively manipulate the subjects of its regime. This contradiction is pointed out today in Kyiv by civic cultural activist movements such as #SaveKyivModernism, who argue not in support of Soviet monuments but for opening the *process* of debate in the legislation of public space. They, like gender activists, prefer putting the terrors of communism on display to repeating Soviet-style gestures of unilateral erasure. It is worth noting that in Kyiv, Warsaw, and Minsk, many in the urban- and gender-activism communities overlap due to LGBT+ and Women's Marches, which is partly owed to to the shared space of the street march in providing ideas with visibility. The chapter by Svitlana Biedarieva, "Women's History as the History of Dispossession in Ukrainian Documentary Art," explores how artists working with critical historical themes navigate the constant sense of history being erased in the post-Soviet space, concurrent with and set within the contemporary context of Russia's war on Ukraine, which seeks to erase or weaponize cultural activity.

One historical point of reference for our overall project is an anthology published in Canada just after the fall of the USSR. *Two Lands, New Visions* differed from this book in its focus on literature and geographical scope: organized into Canadian-Ukrainian and Ukrainian writers, it did not explicitly name feminism as a mode of inquiry and did not work across contexts within Europe.[9] Yet it was important for marking Ukraine's transformation out of communism, and one of its two editors remains among the most highly regarded and interesting observers of communism's end in Ukraine. Solomea Pavlychko, who was from Kyiv, became a major voice for feminism in Ukraine when *Two Lands, New Visions* was published. Pavlychko had spent a year on a Canadian fellowship at the University of Alberta in Edmonton. She met the authors and feminists Janice Kulyk Keefer and Myrna Kostash, the latter a towering figure in the canon of Canadian literature who then, with the

---

[9] Kulyk Keefer, Janice and Solomea Pavlychko, eds. *Two Lands, New Visions: Stories from Canada and Ukraine* (Saskatchewan: Coteau Books, 1998).

Canadian historian Bohdan Krawchenko, took on the project of translating into English the letters Pavlychko wrote upon returning to Kyiv in the tumultuous year 1991, addressed to Dr. Krawchenko in Edmonton. In them, Pavlychko sets down her eyewitness accounts from inside the Writers' Union, the National Literature University, and the Verkhovna Rada (Presidential Parliament) as she participates in the fall of the USSR. Her seminal description of this key turning point in Ukraine's history was published as *Letters from Kyiv*.[10] In the letters, Pavlychko remarks in several places on her intellectual projects and mentions her aim to publish a feminist anthology. Tragically, these plans were cut short by her untimely death.

The present anthology and its title stand not in place of the one Solomea Pavlychko projected, but alongside it and other ideas yet to materialize, as a challenge to revisit the earlier aims that she and others of her generation set out to achieve. Some of those others, including Oksana Briukhovetska's father, were among the circles Pavlychko knew and mentioned in her letters from Kyiv. Today, given the war underway on all levels, we are witnessing a new phase in the end of the Soviet Union, in which Putin's revanchism threatens to return to that authoritarian past, at the expense of global post-WWII security architecture. The chapters here contain missives in the form of artworks, and chart blueprints that can be useful resource guides for the new feminist language growing out of protest cultures of the 2000s.

*Freedom Taking Place: Power, War, Women, and Culture at the Intersection of Ukraine, Poland, and Belarus* is dedicated to scholars, writers, and artists who have faced persecution, but especially to women writers and intellectuals and those who have fought to secure a place for themselves within the professionalization of scholarly and creative discourse. Women throughout time have successfully found ways to overcome or circumvent barriers to access in aligning their ideological aims with their work. They have managed to find professional resources, oftentimes with one another's mutual assistance, in order to achieve historical representation in both writing and the visual arts. This is largely the subject of the chapter by Joanna Dobkowska, "No Need for Genius—Good Taste Is Enough: Conditional Permission on Women's Professional Art Practices in the Kingdom of Poland in the Nineteenth and Early Twentieth Centuries." In it, Dobkowska provides a descriptive account of this problem in a historical time period that is the earliest within this book. Like those pioneers in art and writing, countless women writers in every country of the world have, throughout history, been pushed out of the creative and intellectual professions, or remained

---

[10] Solomea Pavlychko *Letters from Kyiv*, ed. Bohdan Krawchenko, transl. Myrna Kostash (Edmonton: CIUS Press, 1992).

unnamed or unseen or forced to bear the brunt of "women's work" in supporting men's careers ahead of their own. In response to this injustice, women are now translating, compiling, archiving, and preserving accounts of contemporaneous events as seen and experienced by women, people of color, the working classes, the undocumented. The texts in this volume are part of this wider effort and capture many intersections, many differences—race, class, gender, national, social—as sources of creativity and empowerment. These differences are motivating the new feminist language that is part of this broad turn, a paradigmatic shift that continues amid the brutal war, with its impacts and repercussions being felt first and strongest in the countries from which these authors are writing. Their texts will undoubtedly be banned by some countries, where the clock has been set back to a time when "freedom of thought" existed, nonsensically, as a legal category, when *thought itself*, whether in words, images, or actions, was historically barred to those who chose to identify as female or any other marker that failed to conform to accepted tradition. This book breaks with systems of rhetorical expression that, in remaining antithetical to this new language of feminism, can lead to imagination kill.

The rich soil of protest provides case studies both for material acts of solidarity and mutual assistance and for new definitions and sign systems for marking out the future *ways of knowing, and thus ways of inhabiting and legislating* rights: empowering citizens' voices even in times of revolution and war. Women's rights have played a central role in Belarus within the larger opposition movement, and in the democracy movement in Poland under the PiS government, and in post-Maidan Ukraine, where the nine-year struggle to convince the West of Russia's aggression in what was known for too long in global mass media as "the Donbas conflict" appears to have culminated in what is now painfully referred to everywhere as simply "the war." The women at the forefront of civic struggles for democracy in Ukraine, Poland, and Belarus, especially when the recent years of mass women's demonstrations within these nations are closely studied alongside one another, can help to nuance the politicization and conceptualization of what opposition movements are, and can become. Our shared objective here is to inoculate freedom of expression against further entrenching authoritarianism. This book is a stab— but not in the dark or alone—by women who are both at war and against war: feminists who think, write, fight, protest, vote. At different points in history, these acts have been forbidden not only to women but others as well, due to invasions, forced occupations, and repressions of various kinds, some in name only and others cemented into regimes.

The alternative to freedom taking place? Nowhere.

—Jessica Zychowicz, Kyiv/Warszawa, 2022

# II.
# On Unity and Autonomy:
# Unmaking Vulnerable Subjectivity

Chapter 1

# Women's History as the History of Dispossession in Ukrainian Documentary Art

Svitlana Biedarieva

**Abstract**

This chapter focuses on the artistic work that portrays the lives of women during wartime in Ukraine, providing evidence of resilience amidst war-caused displacement, dispossession, and trauma. The author analyzes the works of three artists, namely Maria Kulikovska, Alevtina Kakhidze, and Lia Dostlieva, to explore how art transforms society during periods of great uncertainty, such as the one preceding Russia's attempt at a full-scale invasion in February 2022. The artists' works reflect war-related changes in public and private spheres, drawing from personal stories and family histories. The chapter examines how the central notion of dispossession pervades Ukrainian art, conveying the sense of loss experienced by everyone in Ukrainian society since the beginning of the war in 2014.

**Keywords:** dispossession, documentary art, Russia's war on Ukraine, women's history, resilience, trauma

\*\*\*

In her text on the U.S. war in Vietnam, the art historian Mignon Nixon spoke of artists (Yayoi Kusama, in particular) in reflecting on the phenomenon of "degrading masculinity" brought about by the evidence of the atrocities of war. She justifies this process as a return to the anxieties of the early Cold War "nuclear mentality" and the representation crisis linked to it.[1] Each epoch and each place has its own anxieties. However, what sorts of flashbacks in the above

---

[1] Mignon Nixon, "What's love got to do, got to do with it? Feminist politics and America's war in Vietnam," ed. Melissa Ho, *Artists Respond: American Art and the Vietnam War, 1965–1975* (Princeton: Princeton University Press, 2019), 343.

terms did we experience over the past eight years while witnessing the trauma of the war in East Ukraine, which later escalated throughout the country on February 24, 2022? The eight years of grinding war in Ukraine's Donbas region presented society with a quantum leap in all available perceptions and interpretations, which were and continue to be shaped by fear, but also struggle for a redefinition of the very concept of power. If we revisit the cultural landscape of those years, which now read as both preface and warning to the atrocities committed post-February 2022, it is possible to detect a steadily growing feeling of uncertainty and disbelief already widespread throughout every region of the country. Peoples' daily confrontations with survival inside of broader uncertainties and power shifts during wartime were a point of reflection that Ukrainian artists consistently dwelt upon, and attempted to document in various forms.

Nixon's stance is on the crimes of the war that are caused and covered by the hyperbolized dominating masculinity, as an ontology transported right from the early 1950s, that was nothing more than appearance, its effects not more than a "farce."[2] But what about a Ukrainian society in the years from the outset of the first invasion and occupation of Crimea, Luhansk, and Donetsk in 2014, those eight long years in which Ukraine did not attack, and still does not mount any offensive outside of its own territory, but defends itself in a complex geopolitical confrontation? Is there a certain representation crisis occurring here, and how does it affect the work of artists, particularly those working with critical topics such as feminism and female histories?

In times of crisis, a woman is often depicted as a kind of "woman-warrior" endowed with both the power of emancipation and tools of defense. As art historian Linda Nochlin proposed, "Like the woman warrior, the term 'woman' fights back, and resists attempts to subdue its meaning or reduce it to some simple essence, universal, natural, and above all, unproblematic."[3] The collapsing of both roles—woman and warrior—into one another through social and gender performance, holds the key place in Ukrainian society in a time of austerity and the encroachment of liberties, leaving little or no space for the expression of one's individual vulnerabilities.

Feminist art specific to Ukraine, therefore, becomes even more concerned with depicting a strong female subject. The focus is on the agency of the female body as a fortress resistant to the shocks of an uneasy social reality. Strength here is also defined as a yarn which goes through generations of those who, ultimately, are thought to have become accustomed to uncertainties, as well as

---

[2] Nixon, "What's love got to do, got to do with it?," 343.

[3] Linda Nochlin, *Representing Women* (New York: Thames and Hudson, 1999), 35.

rapid and sporadic transformations beginning with the traumatic events of the twentieth century: the fall of the Iron Curtain, and the dissolution of the Soviet Union; this sense extends to the twenty-first century as well, in the violent events of the Maidan Revolution of Dignity in 2013-14 which slid into the Russian war on Ukraine.

In one of my previous published texts, "The Documentary Turn in New Ukrainian Art," I focus on the relation between visual art and documentary practices.[4] I analyze artists as filmmakers and photographers, and photographers and filmmakers as artists in an attempt to find unifying strategies that might allow for working with different artistic media using cross-disciplinary methods to record reality. The main notion is that the Ukrainian art field has been experiencing a "documentary turn" since 2014, brought on by revolution and war, producing an urgent need to document political reality and social turbulence, in order to fulfill the wider social urge to understand and interpret a changing reality.

In this text, I aim to explore the extremes to which the notion of "documentary art" can reach, i.e., where is the uniting—or divisive—point between document and fiction in art? This pushing of the boundaries between recording and interpretation is the essential feature in the development of any genre. At the intersection of imagination and political event, the stories narrated by artists obtain another dimension, as they transcend the line between the desired and the real, and modify shared visions of the traumatic events that they comment on. Here, I will consider different types of documents, both conventional and unconventional, including narration, archive, and the human body, that each describe and envelop lived experience.

My question here is to what extent is art *per se* documentary? What is the thin border that divides documentary art from art that concerns itself with social matters (e.g., socially and politically engaged art)? In search of answers to these questions, in this chapter, I focus on the practices of female artists who speak about history that is ongoing and that manifests through dispossession, which I hold is the defining experience of Ukrainian society since 2014. Here, public endurance is projected into personal experience, and vice versa: private traumas are extrapolated to the turmoil that Ukrainian society has survived in recent years, and continues to survive.

---

[4] Svitlana Biedarieva, "The Documentary Turn in New Ukrainian Art," ed. Svitlana Biedarieva, *Contemporary Ukrainian and Baltic Art: Political and Social Perspectives, 1991-2021* (Stuttgart: ibidem Press, 2021), 53–78.

The artistic practices prevalent in wartime Ukraine dating back to 2014 reflect what philosopher Judith Butler marks as two "valences" of dispossession, such as autonomy and dependency:

> Dispossession can be a term that marks the limits of self-sufficiency and that establishes us as relational and interdependent beings. Yet dispossession is precisely what happens when populations lose their land, their citizenship, their means of livelihood, and become subject to military and legal violence.[5]

Dispossession-as-loss is the underlying theme of many of the projects of recent years. It marks the generational rupture of post-Independence "coming-of-age" and describes the conditions in which the entirety of Ukrainian society persists against the annexation of wide swaths of Ukrainian territories. Internal migrations, forced by the war and the annexation of Crimea in 2014, found their reflection in the works of the artists who, firsthand, experienced the disconcerting effects of the conflict. These transformations affect the self-perception of both political and personal bodies that appear as documents of the time.

Butler, in her analysis of dispossession, echoes the book *The Dispossessed: An Ambiguous Utopia* (1974) by Ursula Le Guin (though she never directly refers to it), a science fiction novel where two twin worlds enter into a power struggle, caught within the ambiguous discrepancy between self-perception and colonial perception of one by the other.[6] While the inhabitants of one world consider themselves free and independent, liberated from the bounds of political co-dependency, the other world sees its twin primarily as a mining colony. The estrangement of the two worlds from one another is underscored by their different political structures, leading to the dispossession of the ambiguity between the oppressor and the oppressed, along with their intrinsic duality.

This early feminist critical utopia brings in strikingly familiar connotations for the ongoing Russian-Ukrainian conflict. When in 1991, the "twin worlds" of the Ukrainian and Russian Soviet republics fell apart, the Ukrainian society and state are forced to fight for economic and cultural independence, while the Russian society and state continue to alter the relationship between the two through the lens of old colonial clichés. At stake here is the hybridity of both

---

[5] Judith Butler and Athena Athanasiou, *Dispossession: The Performative in the Political* (Cambridge: Polity Press, 2013), 3.

[6] Ursula K. Le Guin, *The Dispossessed: An Ambiguous Utopia* (New York: Harper & Row, 1974).

worlds, where political history becomes personal history through the documentation and transmission of generational experiences, as in the stories told by Ukrainian artists. Butler's emphasis on the individual's performance of their gender finds its culmination in performative gestures in public spaces as the political foundation of the creation of societies: the "reiterative power of discourse to produce phenomena that it regulates and constrains."[7] For Ukrainian artists in wartime, the reconsideration (or retelling) of history as a personal record both transforms the present and prevents it from further postcolonial expropriation.

Here, I will speak of the work of three artists that trace female destinies through the turbulence of recent history. The ways in which history is inscribed into their biographies differ, depending on the artist's use of aesthetic and heuristic instruments, and the particular artistic media in which they work. The outcome is a traceable recording of a socially-conditioned estrangement that speaks through their art as a performative gesture, simultaneously advocating and striving for political change.

Sculptor and performance artist Maria Kulikovska uses her body as a document of the epoch, taking sculptural molds from her own figure. The project *Stardust* (2015), which she presented at the museum Mystetskyi Arsenal in Kyiv, interweaves the contemporary national military conflict into geolocation and the personal history of her family. Kulikovska addresses the Kerch Peninsula, where she was born and grew up, and as of the writing of this chapter is no longer the final outpost of Eastern Crimea on the border with mainland Russia, having been further occupied in 2022. Kulikovska dedicates her project to her grandmother, who fled to Crimea in the 1950s under persecution by the Soviet government:

> She, her husband, and my then 4-month-old mother ran to Crimea without documents, it was in 1956. As my grandmother told me, there was nothing in Crimea— except salted soils, sunburnt steppe, and the sea. No drop of drinking water, no fertile land, no trees. She, as many such migrants, brought steppe Crimea back to life after the war.[8]

---

[7] Judith Butler, *Bodies that Matter: On the Discursive Limits of Sex* (New York: Routledge, 1993), 2.

[8] Maria Kulikovska, quoted in Svitlana Biedarieva, "Crimea's amazing history told through art," *Hyperallergic*, no. 3 (May 2019); https://hyperallergic.com/498027/amazing-stories -of-crimea-art-arsenal/.

The artist interprets the map of the Kerch peninsula as she recreates its topography and landscape through its contours. She also uses casts of her body that recall Greek sculptures, referencing the Ancient Greek city in present-day Kerch named Panticapaeum, which was founded around the late 7th or early 6th century BCE. The sculptures are made from the same materials as the model of the peninsula, including metal, wood, different types of soil, fossils, cement, stone, dust, sand, iron oxides, and sea salt. Her small-scale recreation returns the peninsula back to Ukraine, serving as a recreation and re-annexation of the land that had been severed from the rest of the communal-national body, thus in her corporeal performance she prevents it from further falling into oblivion.[9] She writes:

> I was the first in my family to be born there. But almost the entire population of Kerch and Crimea are migrants, heroes who civilized the very special soil during thousands of years of its history. That is why this project is about People and Earth. People turn into the ground, into the landscape, and soil turns into humans.[10]

The story of Kulikovska's grandmother and her work as an agriculturist is central to the understanding of Kulikovska's decision to model her own body with soil, leaving an imprint on the family's genealogy, together with the geography of her imagined Crimean landscape. The copying of the body is the ultimate act of documentation, as well as a link to the corporeal replication of generations. By this act of historicized reproduction, Kulikovska opposes the very fact of dispossession; she denies the loss by symbolically merging her own image with that of what she sees as being a carrier of her family's history, and again with a third image—a replica of the geographical territory under dispute. Nostalgia is an important sentiment that enables the myth-making of primordial synthesis between humans and the Earth, even if people are acknowledged as initial strangers to the land.

Another project by Kulikovska, *President of Crimea* (2020), became a finalist in the Ukrainian Pavilion at the 56th Venice Bienniale. The conceptual content of the piece shows the figures of the artist, her mother, and her grandmother, each cast in bronze, hanging as bells in a metallic construction reminiscent of a ribcage. The sculptural portraits are double-faced, combining the figures of, respectively: the artist and her grandmother; the artist and her mother; two casts of the artist herself, connected with rude seams; and the artist in her

---

[9] Ibid.

[10] Maria Kulikovska, author's personal correspondence with the artist, April 17, 2019.

pregnancy. The yarn that connects the generations in this installation is the story of political violence, framed with reference to the individual artist's inability to return to Crimea due to its rapid political transformation under Russian occupation, and severe repressions against pro-Ukraine activists, conveyed through the tongues of the bells, which are made of police sticks. This intergenerational victimization and subjection to violence appear as outcomes of the annexation of Crimea. The artist artificially reconnects the family by inserting a reproduction of her body in place of absence, thus defying the redrawn borders that produced a gaping void between generations, cut apart by Russia's occupation of Crimea.

**Figure 1.1.** Maria Kulikovska. *President of Crimea.* 2020. Image courtesy of the artist.

Kulikovska's project for the Venice Biennale also included a display entitled *Constitution of the Autonomous Republic of Xena-Maria* (2020). This was a series of various bureaucratic forms that must be filled out and submitted to the occupying authorities by anyone seeking to leave Crimea and enter Ukrainian territory, covered with the artist's sketches, reminiscent of male and female genitalia. These images aim in a way to "bring to life" the deadly dry bureaucratic sheets that cover the abyss between territories and generations. "Xena" proceeds from "Ksenia" – the unofficial second name that the artist was given by her mother when she was born, but discovered much later, in 2010.[11] From that moment onward, she began to create several sculptural projects dedicated to Xena, searching for her identity and reunification with her doppelganger. The duality of two characters— the fictitious Xena and the real Maria—narrate an ambiguous story that highlights the link between myth and reality, bridging opposite sides of the gap between actual experience and the imaginary.

Linking the autobiographies and biographies of people close to one another into a single line of narrative is the subject of the project by the artist Alevtina Kakhidze in her performance *Through the War with Strawberry Andreevna* (2014). Her mother, a retired kindergarten teacher, nicknamed by her pupils Klubnika (Strawberry) Andreevna, lived in a small town located in the Donetsk Region occupied by pro-Russian forces (the so-called Donetsk People's Republic) in 2014.[12] From the very beginning of the war with Russia, until her untimely death, while crossing the border between occupied territory and Ukrainian land in 2019, she could not see her daughter in person. The artist took notes on their communication over the phone, and later incorporated them into a series of drawings and handwritten notes, representing an anxious, but at the same time, refreshing point of view of her mother's on the military violence surrounding her home. The eyewitness account in this story is important not only as it provides valuable insights into firsthand experiences of military conflict, but also because the evidence of the brutal struggle between two universes becomes clear: the quiet, hermetic life of Zhdanivka town in contrast to the violent invasion and grand-scale, alien terror brought on by the occupying pro-Russian forces.

---

[11] Maria Kulikovska, "Moia druga Xena IV"; https://ua.mariakulikovska.net/sculpture/my-second-xena-4. Accessed August 8, 2022.

[12] See also: Kateryna Iakovlenko, "The artist who 'made Donbas human': Alevtina Kakhidze on empathy and discrimination in eastern Ukraine," *Open Democracy* (July 29, 2019); https://www.opendemocracy.net/en/odr/alevtina-kakhidze-artist-donbas-ukraine/.

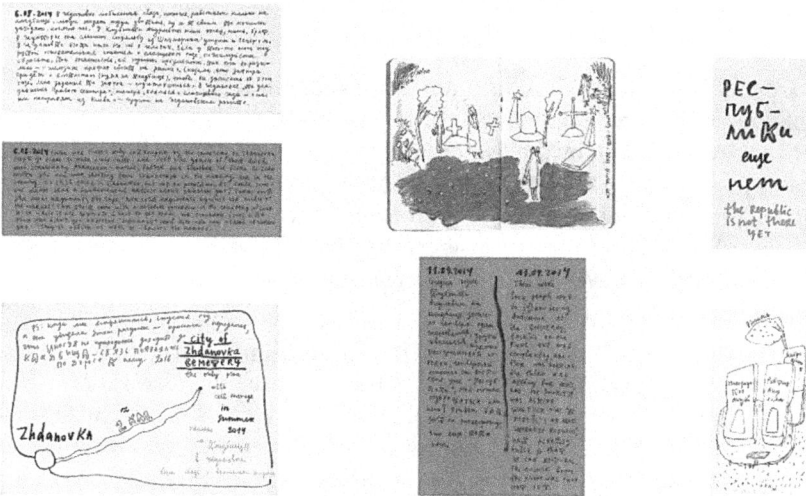

**Figure 1.2.** Alevtina Kakhidze. *Through The War With Strawberry Andreevna*, 2014-2019. Grynyov Art Collection.

In her drawings and post-it notes, Kakhidze gives us a glimpse into her mother's "diary" that the artist recorded as a day-to-day chronicle of war events and their impact on the daily life of the town and its inhabitants:

> 8/28/2014: I thought today I'd go to the cellar for the night. They bombed so heavily like it was in my yard. I didn't go and couldn't sleep until morning . . . The rain will finally put down the dust. And before the rain, the field with sunflowers was burning; they hit there. The smoke covered the entire Zhdanivka... And those were such good sunflowers . . . [13]

At times, the reported speech of Strawberry Andreevna interweaves with the direct speech of her daughter, who comments on her situation of isolation in a dangerous and uncertain environment, turning the report into a subjective narration:

> 9/9/2014: A monk died at the Zhdanivka cemetery from a shrapnel injury [ . . . ]. He lived there in a small monastery, in a chapel. At this point, Strawberry Andreevna decided to add: 'Nothing will happen to

---

[13] Alevtina Kakhidze, "Fear" (drawing), *Through the War with Strawberry Andreevna*, 2014, http://www.alevtinakakhidze.com/.

me, you got it, Alia?' And I realized that neither with tears, nor threats, nor trickery I will convince her to leave Zhdanovka.[14]

In Kakhidze's narration, it is, at times, impossible to distinguish the voices of the mother and the daughter, split by kilometers of distance and the political borderline, but united by the fear of the war and the shared feelings of anxiety and apprehension. This merging of identities, when the artist becomes the conduit of the personality of her family member, beyond merely her interpreter, is indicative of the necessity to transgress the dividing border – a symbolic act of reunification that never happened in real life, neither between mother and daughter, nor between territories.

It is noteworthy that the selection of the reports from "the frontline" follows a laconic pattern: Kakhidze cuts much of the text, bringing forward only brief insights into the everyday life of her mother, with a focus on the most tragic moments. This "less is more" approach serves as a literary trope for the metonymy of the text, and allows viewers to fill the void and revive Strawberry Andreevna as a fictitious, almost legendary, character that might be adorned with additional attributes and characteristics.

The search for continuity between generations in this project, which has already become a textbook example of Kakhidze's art, represents the unity between the quiet horror of dispossession, and the seemingly naïve perception of reality, as voiced by an elderly woman from a borderline town. It also shows the point of intersection between the analogous ways of narration, such as Kakhidze's drawings—and digital ways of fostering public discussion – such as the Facebook page of Strawberry Andreevna that the artist created in order to repost short dialogues with her mother, making her, in this way, a public personality. The distancing through time, especially our knowledge of the outcome of this tragic story, turns Kakhidze's reports into a chronicle of dispossession.

Yet the important questions here are whether and how narration can represent "real" events—and in what ways they occur in the mind of viewers as they learn a story through an engaged, compassionate, and subjective mediator. The relative nature of documentary narration is generally contested in visual art. It always oscillates between what an artist wants to say, their direct recording of the events, and the open possibilities for a viewer to relate to the image and bring to it their own interpretation.

The text-based conceptual project by Lia Dostlieva, *I Lied in a Visa Center* (2018), takes on another dimension of the intergenerational rupture of

---

[14] Kakhidze, "Not the End" (drawing), *Through the War with Strawberry Andreevna*.

dispossession: forced oblivion of family and background in favor of a successful, or at least a neutral, image in the eyes of surrounding people. In a seemingly simple project, Dostlieva discusses the position of a displaced "stranger" who travels out of Ukraine, and the subsequent stigmatization that such people experience due to the way their lives are shaped and rooted in military conflict.

Dostlieva takes her departure from a found text in a toilet stall at Martin-Gropius-Bau in Berlin that read: "I lied in a visa center about my parents. They are in Luhansk." The artist then realized that, as a refugee from Donbas, she shares these feelings of shame that prevent the protagonist from displaying her "unfavorable" milieu:

> I can imagine her daily routine in a foreign environment, thousands of miles away from the warzone, in a safe country, having to conceal her problems, to remain silent about them in order not to disturb happy people around her, not to display in public her wounds, not to be different from others.[15]

This self-identification led Dostlieva to create an installation that consists of a number of writings scattered on gallery walls with inscriptions that read: "I don't tell anyone I am from a country where the war is. I don't want them to look at me like I'm contagious." ; "My cat is always scared. I say that it's because it fell out of the window. But it's actually because of Grad shellings."; and, "I never go out to see the fireworks. I pretend not to enjoy them. The truth is that they sound too much like shelling."[16]

The power of stigma experienced by Ukrainian migrants from the occupied territories abroad before 2022 has the effect, in part, of providing the individual with an internalized and imaginary imperative by which to foreclose personal experience. The artist deconstructs and challenges these private statements of fear and exclusion by publicly displaying them on the wall, outside of the shameful and intimate enclosed space of a urinal. In not dissimilar ways akin to the cultural weight and catharsis that queer individuals face in the ritual of a "coming out" testimonial, the sensitivities and dangers of the moment of unveiling one's identity as a refugee abroad, amid safer conditions, is ironically the inverse of entering a "safe space," but is about making oneself vulnerable in order to claim ground. Giving up such secreted background identities, in

---

[15] Lia Dostlieva, *I Lied in a Visa Center*, 2018. https://www.liadostlieva.org/i-lied-in-visa-center/.

[16] Dostlieva, *I Lied in a Visa Center*.

turn, encourages others to open up, having the wider effect of ensuring stigmas are contested by moving them into the public domain.

In all the aforementioned examples, the symbolic dispossession of family or one's origins equals to the dispossession of identity. After all, Butler proposes that "We can only be dispossessed because we are already dispossessed," pointing out that human social interdependency establishes how vulnerable we are to social deprivation.[17] I believe she means that being human—or being a woman, as a particular case—already means being at risk of losing one's identity, together with the tangible phenomena that constitute it, such as land, belongings, family, or citizenship. Consequently, the necessity of reconstitution of these traumatic dispossessions emerges, and for this injury, art is one of the most effective remedies—not only for artists but for society too.

Art Historian Lucy R. Lippard proposes a notion of "multicenteredness" to describe our link to places by historical narratives of who lives or lived where, marking the intersections between culture, nature, and what Lippard calls "ideology," or what in contemporary conditions I would call "politics."[18] She emphasizes that multicenteredness does not denote multiculturalism, but rather marks the existing hybridity of any new place we enter and, therefore, become part of, including the preexisting and emerging political relationships inside of it. Speaking of identity as an intangible value, when entering into a situation of dispossession, one steps into a state of newly-acquired possession as well. One can also speak of nostalgia in this same sense, in that it is an intrinsic part of a utopian reconstruction of one's own self-documented livelihood.

The utopian and the documentary stances in Ukraine intersect within one notion–of dispossession—that is, the primary symbolic lens by which artists and their audiences in Ukraine have drawn shared meaning out of the national crises and revolutions renewals throughout the period of independence, since 1991. Ukrainian society regularly burns their hopes and expectations and rises them anew from ashes like a phoenix, and these cycles are reflected in the works by Ukrainian women artists especially, as their aesthetics are characteristic of their past and present and are tightly interwoven with the histories of their families. These personal and familial metamorphoses of identit(ies) are reflected in the process of estrangement produced by the territorial loss in Ukrainian society – and experienced as resulting alienation inside families (whether ideological or purely geographical). The most consistent feature across wartime works by the

---

[17] Butler and Athanasiou, *Dispossession*, 5.

[18] Lucy R. Lippard, *The Lure of the Local: Sense of Place in a Multicentered Society* (New York: The New Press, 1997), 7.

artists under discussion throughout this chapter takes form as a rupture in intergenerational history, often mirroring ruptures in Ukraine's territorial integrity. Thus, one might observe that the Russia-Ukraine war is a geopolitical conflict that has had bodily implications, as millions of living bodies have been uprooted and relocated from their homes. This sense of emancipation from previous generations and extended families, combined with a new sense of independence, brought about by dispossession, marks the construction of a political nation; however, it is reductive as well, closing off numerous possibilities of self-reflection through one's feeling of belonging. This hybrid situation poses a challenge for those trapped in it. They may exercise symbolic liberation through art's non-linear critique of politics, but are unable to overcome breaches in the fragmentation of everyday life.

The documentation of processes of dispossession in art helps transgress the limitations imposed by the political situation, and reunite scattered generations in performative gestures of belonging and continuity. Documentary Art gives means for reconciliation of the displaced, disconcerted, and expropriated narratives back into a coherent story—even when the final result, at times, is reminiscent of Kulikovska's die-cast bronze bells, merged together yet with a split still visible at the seams.

## Bibliography

Biedarieva, Svitlana. "Crimea's amazing history told through art." *Hyperallergic* (May 3, 2019). https://hyperallergic.com/498027/amazing-stories-of-crimea-art-arsenal/. Accessed November 11, 2022.

_____. "The documentary turn in new Ukrainian art." *Contemporary Ukrainian and Baltic Art: Political and Social Perspectives, 1991-2021.* Ed. Svitlana Biedarieva. New York: Columbia University Press, 2021.

Butler, Judith and Athena Athanasiou. *Dispossession: The Performative in the Political.* Cambridge: Polity Press, 2013.

_____. *Bodies that Matter: On the Discursive Limits of Sex.* New York: Routledge, 1993.

Dostlieva, Lia. *I Lied in a Visa Center* (2018). https://www.liadostlieva.org/i-lied-in-visa-center/. Accessed November 18, 2022.

Iakovlenko, Kateryna. "The artist who 'made Donbas human': Alevtina Kakhidze on empathy and discrimination in eastern Ukraine." *Open Democracy* (July 29, 2019). https://www.opendemocracy.net/en/odr/alevtina-kakhidze-artist-donbas-ukraine/. Accessed November 18, 2022.

Kakhidze, Alevtina. *Through the War with Strawberry Andreevna* (2014). http://www.alevtinakakhidze.com/. Accessed November 18, 2022.

Kulikovska, Maria. Author's personal correspondence with the artist. April 17, 2019.

Kulikovska, Maria. *President of Crimea. Proposal for the 56th Venice Biennale*, 2021.

_____. "Moia druga Xena IV," 2014. https://ua.mariakulikovska.net/sculpture/ my-second-xena-4. Accessed November 18, 2022.

Le Guin, Ursula K.. *The Dispossessed: An Ambiguous Utopia*. New York: Harper & Row, 1974.

Lippard, Lucy R. *The Lure of the Local: Sense of Place in a Multicentered Society*. New York: The New Press, 1997.

Nixon, Mignon. "What's love got to do, got to do with it? Feminist politics and America's war in Vietnam." Ed. Melissa Ho. *Artists Respond: American Art and the Vietnam War, 1965–1975*. Princeton: Princeton University Press, 2019.

Nochlin, Linda. *Representing Women*. New York: Thames and Hudson, 1999.

# Chapter 2

# Stasik: Problematizing Representations of Femininity in Wartime Ukraine Through Popular Music

Iryna Shuvalova

**Abstract**

This chapter offers a case study of the Ukrainian war veteran-cum-singer Anastasiia Shevchenko (Stasik), whose self-presentation on stage and beyond subverts the tropes of heteronormative femininity dominating Ukraine's contemporary popular music. The androgynous aspects of Shevchenko's stage persona, her readiness to reflect on violence and aggression through her music and lyrics, as well as her frank discussion of mental health and trauma, establish her gender presentation as non-conforming with the traditional understanding of femininity still dominating Ukrainian society today. More specifically, Shevchenko's contributions to the corpus of songs created post-2014 in response to the Russo-Ukrainian war disrupt the two narratives of femininity prevalent in these songs: that of a faithful mother and wife ("Beherynia"), and that of a fetishized female combatant whose subversive qualities are often neutralized by means of sexual objectification.

**Keywords**: Ukraine, Russo-Ukrainian war, popular culture, popular music, femininity, representation

\*\*\*

The outbreak of the Russo-Ukrainian war in the Donbas region of Ukraine in spring of 2014 has brought the gender roles in Ukrainian society into sharper focus.[1] The interlinking narratives of "militarism, masculinity, and heroism" have shaped the dominant discourse, largely relegating women to secondary

---

[1] Research for this chapter has been supported by the Canadian Institute of Ukrainian Studies John Kolasky Memorial Endowment Fund.

roles in society.[2] While the crisis caused by the war has led women to adopt some traditionally masculine roles, including their increased participation in the military, these changes have not consequently overridden the social status quo. However, in some cases, they have prompted the rethinking of traditional gender narratives, including through popular culture. In this chapter, I discuss one such disruptive voice that has emerged from the war in Donbas—that of the war veteran and singer Anastasiia Shevchenko, known by her stage name: Stasik.

The level of women's engagement in Ukraine's Armed Forces grew steadily after the war broke out in 2014 and continued to grow throughout the period before the mass escalation in 2022. In January 2020, for example, Ukraine's Ministry of Defense reported that over 31,000 women held military ranks in the Armed Forces (with ca. 26,000 more female civilian employees).[3] As of late 2019, this number constituted 22% of Armed Forces personnel and more than 11% of employees holding military rank.[4] The number had doubled since the start of the war, with the number of female officers increasing nearly threefold.[5] As of 2020, 13,500 women had been granted the status of participants in military action.

Nonetheless, women in the Armed Forces of Ukraine still faced substantial barriers. Although the number of positions open to women in the military had greatly increased in 2020 since the start of the war, and they were finally afforded some of the same privileges as men, women still routinely faced sexism and suffered from high rates of gender-based violence.[6] Indeed, the

---

[2] Olesya Khromeychuk, "Instrumentalisation of War History in Contemporary Memory Politics in Ukraine: A Gender Perspective," *EUXEINOS—Culture and Governance in the Black Sea Region* 10, no. 29 (2020): 27–46, 35.

[3] "Z Pochatku Viiny Kilkist Zhinok v Armii Zrosla Vdvichi," *Novynarnia*, March 6, 2021; https://novynarnia.com/2021/03/06/z-pochatku-vijny-kilkist-zhinok-v-armiyi-zrosla-vdvichi/.

[4] "Zhinok v Ukrainskii Armii Vzhe Ponad 20%—Minoborony," *Ukrinform*, December 17, 2019; https://www.ukrinform.ua/rubric-ato/2839911-zinok-v-ukrainskij-armii-vze-ponad-20-minoboroni.html.

[5] "Z Pochatku Viiny," *Novynarnia*, March 6, 2021.

[6] See: Tamara Martsenyuk, Ganna Grytsenko, and Anna Kvit, "The 'Invisible Battalion': Women in ATO Military Operations in Ukraine," *Kyiv-Mohyla Law and Politics Journal*, no. 2 (2016): 171–187; Marta Havryshko, "Chomu Suspilstvu Zruchno Bachyty Zhinku na Viini 'Beheryneiu,' a ne 'Heroineiu'?," *Hromadske Radio*, August 24, 2018; https://hromadske.radio/podcasts/undefined/obraz-zhinky-na-viyni-povilno-ale-zminyuyetsya-gavryshko; Olesya Khromeychuk, "Experiences of Women at War: Servicewomen During WWII and in the Ukrainian Armed Forces in the Conflict in Donbas," *Baltic Worlds*, no. 4

mobilization of women to fulfill the country's wartime needs in roles considered masculine before the war, did not mean that patriarchal societal attitudes had been effectively dismantled, but merely shifted the vision of "socially acceptable" femininity.[7] Moreover, even as greater inclusion and integration of women into the military was often advanced by politicians as part of the nationalist discourse, such inclusion only benefited a small group of women, disregarding those negatively affected either by the nationalist discourse or by the war.[8]

In Ukraine, the cultural narratives of war are gendered female through depictions of women in several stereotypical roles. Perhaps the most common representative model has positioned women as the passive feminine element embodied in mothers, wives, and daughters, reinforcing a domestic picture of the feminine in binary opposition to masculinity, the latter equated with the public functions of a soldier.[9] This set of social roles for women is often conflated with the "Berehynia" narrative. This figure, which even today still occupies a central position in both unofficial and official civic and state symbols, takes its name from a faux female Slavic pagan deity whose name literally means "the keeper" and who is ascribed with the attributes and communal tasks of a guardian. While rooted in the notion of the matriarchal heritage of ancient Ukraine, the contemporary Beherynia narrative underplays the notions of female power and authority, instead promoting motherhood and other roles coded as traditionally female and credited to the national cause at the expense of a woman's individual achievement.[10] Yet due to the growing numbers of women in Ukraine's armed forces after 2014, including in active service, alternative narratives were needed to reinterpret the stories of those women who did not conform with the prevalent hetero-hegemonic discourse. These narratives were forged through the rhetoric of exceptionalism, and aimed to highlight the rareness of women performing well in traditionally male roles as an unforeseen and unique instance brought on by war.[11] In the context

---

(2018): 58–70; Dariia Popova, "Viina, Natsionalizm ta Zhinoche Pytannia," *Spilne*, January 28, 2017, https://commons.com.ua/uk/vijna-nacionalizm-ta-zhinoche-pitannya/.

[7] Leila J. Rupp, *Mobilizing Women for War* (Princeton: Princeton University Press, 2015), 4.

[8] Popova, "Viina, Natsionalizm ta Zhinoche Pytannia," *Spilne*.

[9] Joshua S. Goldstein, *War and Gender: How Gender Shapes the War System and Vice Versa* (Cambridge: Cambridge University Press, 2003), 301–322.

[10] Oksana Kis, "(Re) Constructing Ukrainian Women's History: Actors, Authors, and Narratives," in *Gender, Politics and Society in Ukraine* (Toronto: University of Toronto Press, 2017), 152–179, 154–158.

[11] See Olesya Khromeychuk's analysis of the cases of Ukrainian fighter pilot Nadiia Savchenko and the Soviet sniper Ludmyla Pavlichenko in "Experiences of Women at War." This makes for an interesting comparison with Oksana Kis's examination of "the

of military conflict, where "war defines manhood, and soldiering is the ultimate expression of masculinity," [12] women taking up roles perceived as masculine are viewed as transgressors of the established gender order.[13] Women in the military often feel forced to prove that they have not lost their femininity, despite engaging in what is seen as a male pursuit.[14] In Ukraine, this has taken various shapes, such as beauty pageants for female soldiers,[15] or the inclusion of high heels as a part of full ceremonial dress.[16] Such symbolic gestures allow for the fetishization of "transgressive" women, which, in turn, serves to force them back into the heteronormative structures of desire and power relations.[17]

These two major narratives, that of the gender-conforming civilian "beherynias," and that of purportedly exceptional "gender transgressors" who perform as men, jointly ensure that women are "returned to the fold" of hegemonic femininities. Both narratives have dominated the corpus of popular songs created in response to the war in Donbas. The images of conventionally feminine women prevail, for example, in the female singer Eyra asking, in her song, "Who am I?" and then responding self-effacingly: "I'm a shadow of the hero".[18] Similarly, a male singer and songwriter, Volodymyr Burko, mobilizes the tropes of hegemonic femininity when he describes his idealized beloved back home "waiting [ . . . ], weeping, praying and watching over [ . . . ] children like a guardian angel."[19] Meanwhile, some voices present a more balanced vision, such as in the popular song "Ty pidbory zminyla na bertsi" (You traded your high heels for army boots) by Khrystyna Panasiuk, a regular volunteer at the

---

Great Woman" narrative in Ukrainian historiography, in which the state appropriates women's stories for its political purposes. See: Oksana Kis, "(Re) Constructing Ukrainian Women's History," 158–161.

[12] Khromeychuk, "Instrumentalisation of War History," 31.

[13] Caron E. Gentry and Laura Sjoberg, *Beyond Mothers, Monsters, Whores: Thinking About Women's Violence in Global Politics* (London: Zed Books, 2015), 6–7.

[14] Melissa S. Herbert, *Camouflage Isn't Only for Combat: Gender, Sexuality, and Women in the Military* (New York City: NYU Press, 1998).

[15] Havryshko, "Chomu Suspilstvu Zruchno Bachyty," 5:20.

[16] Rob Picheta and and Denis Lapin, "Ukraine to Give Female Soldiers 'More Comfortable' Heels After Sexism Controversy," *CNN*, July 8, 2021; https://edition.cnn.com/2021/07/08/europe/ukraine-female-soldiers-new-heels-scli-intl/index.html.

[17] Jeffrey A. Brown, *Dangerous Curves: Action Heroines, Gender, Fetishism, and Popular Culture* (Jackson: University Press of Mississippi, 2011).

[18] Eira, "Tin heroia," December 23, 2014; https://youtu.be/1tGAsfsa3wk.

[19] Volodymyr Burko, "Lyst do Kokhanoi," August 9, 2016; https://youtu.be/7qOq6JsbLp4.

Donbas frontline.[20] Panasiuk narrates the story of a female fighter who chose a uniform instead of a "delicate dress" and feels that she belongs in the trenches, where "there are no outsiders, everyone knows everyone" (nemaie chuzhykh, vsi svoi). Despite the presence of some women singers, the majority of popular war songs in Ukraine are still created and performed predominantly by men who deploy a heroic posture associated with the hypermasculine. The exceptions are few, including: Oleksandra Koltsova of the band "Krykhitka"; the pop singer Svitlana Tarabarova; and singers-songwriters such as Lesia Roi of the band "Teleri" and the aforementioned Khrystyna Panasiuk. While not all of these female performers embrace the overtly sexualized hyper-femininity that dominates the Ukrainian music business along with the global pop industry, their appearance and behavior largely invoke conventional femininity. Anastasiia Shevchenko stands in sharp contrast to these other women; a veteran, and singer known by her stage name "Stasik," she burst out into the Ukrainian media space in 2019 and audiences took notice.[21]

Shevchenko grew up in Kyiv and was part of the protests known as the Maidan Revolution or the Revolution of Dignity of 2013–2014. When in 2014, the war broke out in Donbas, she joined the army as a gunner (strilets) and a war medic, but eventually had to leave service due to health reasons. Back in Kyiv, she began the process of rehabilitation and readjustment to civilian life. Although involved in theater and performance before joining the army, she discontinued these activities upon her return, working instead as a TV presenter with the *Hromadske* channel on a show surveying Ukraine's cultural scene. In 2016 she released her first music video, "Cherez khmil" (Through the Hop Vines), a rendition of a Ukrainian folk song recorded under the name Anastasiia.[22] The song and the video reached a limited audience, accumulating ca. 12,000 views.[23] Over the next three years, despite continuing her training in Ukrainian traditional folk singing (perfecting a technique used in "Cherez khmil"), Shevchenko did not publish any original material. Her breakthrough came in 2019 when she released three original songs and music videos. This material,

---

[20] Khrystyna Panasiuk, "Ty Pidbory Zminyla na Bertsi," May 7, 2016; https://youtu.be/K2 a8IAgwo7Q..

[21] Shevchenko's first song, "Cherez khmil," a rendition of a folk tune, appeared in 2016 along with an accompanying music video, but failed to attract attention.

[22] Anastasiia, "Cherez khmil," November 15, 2016.; https://youtu.be/CjM957R_HiI. Accessed November 18, 2022.

[23] "'Prohrama Albert': Anastasiia Shevchenko pro Zelenskoho, Vtratu Zdorovia na Viini i Korysnu Propahandu." *Hromadske.* May 20, 2019; https://hromadske.ua/posts/programa -albert-anastasiya-shevchenko-pro-zelenskogo-vtratu-zdorovya-na-vijni-i-korisnu-propagandu. Accessed November 18, 2022.

produced under her new stage name of "Stasik," thrust Shevchenko into the media spotlight and earned her a wide and quickly growing fan base.

The first of these three songs, "Bii z tinniu" (Fighting My Shadow), is a reflection on mental health and identity struggles.[24] The second one, "Nizh" (A Knife), deals with anger and rejection.[25] The third song that brings Stasik particular recognition is her "Kolyskova dlia voroha" (A Lullaby for the Enemy), in which she sings overtly about the war in Donbas for the first time.[26] The video is complete with embedded Russian subtitles. In her song, Stasik addresses Russian fighters directly, promising them the prospect of eternal sleep in the Ukrainian land of the Donbas region that they desire to possess. Yet even after her unquestionably successful 2019 debut, Shevchenko did not utilize the opportunity to dedicate herself fully to a career in music. Although she continued to perform live, she followed her initial breakthrough with a year-long absence of new material. In October of 2020 she returned with a 2-minute-long track "Ne vidvod ochei" (Don't turn your gaze away) commemorating the explosion at the Chornobyl nuclear plant, but then fell silent again.[27]

To date, Shevchenko only has released five songs, four of them under the name of Stasik. Nonetheless, the significance of her cultural impact should not be underestimated: "In just three songs [as of September 2019 — I.S.], she paved a new path in the cautious and sterile Ukrainian pop music, [. . .]. Turns out, that it [Ukrainian music—I.S.] can be uncomfortable, painful, traumatized, dangerous, frank and beautiful at the same time," writes the music critic Dania Panimash.[28] However, Shevchenko's transgressive self-presentation as a woman, a veteran, and a performer was just as visible as her musical originality. Young and unconventional, a self-professed "hipster,"[29] the singer stirred popular imagination and provoked a flood of conflicting responses to her work. She replied by refusing to atone for her "unwomanly" pursuits as a former combatant by constructing a compensatory narrative of conventional femininity. Instead,

---

[24] STASIK, "Bii z Tinniu," June 20, 2019; https://youtu.be/VKKoXq_IXYQ.

[25] STASIK, "Nizh," April 18, 2019; https://youtu.be/5RgJoMXU1u0.

[26] STASIK, "Kolyskova dliaVoroha," September 19, 2019; https://youtu.be/40WD9RDAMVc.

[27] STASIK, "Ne Vidvod Ochei. Sounds of Chornobyl," October 26, 2020; https://youtu.be/2ASD0QZJtgc. On February 27, 2022, at the time when this chapter was being prepared for publication, Stasik recorded a new track "Byi" ("Fight") reacting to the escalation of the war. See STASIK, "Byi," February 27, 2022; https://youtu.be/K4LV4AjDbqk.

[28] Dania Panimash, "Khto Taka Stasik—Ukrainska Spivachka, za Iakoiu Varto Stezhyty," *Slukh*, September 20, 2019; https://slukh.media/texts/who-is-stasik/.

[29] Sofiia Pylypiuk, "Khto Taka Stasik? Nastia Shevchenko pro Teatr, Viinu ta Muzyku," *The Village*, December 23, 2019; https://www.the-village.com.ua/village/culture/culture-interview/292553-hto-taka-stasik.

the identity she continues to portray is much more complex. While Stasik's stage persona is recognizably feminine, hers is the version of femininity that is unflinchingly frank, devoid of gloss and frills, occasionally violent, and oftentimes distinctly uncomfortable for the viewer.

Shevchenko's very stage name Stasik could be seen as gender non-conforming, as it is a diminutive typically used for boys (usually, a short form of the male name "Stanislav"). However, the singer herself interprets "Stasik" as a short form of her given name Anastasiia.[30] The name is somewhat ironic in that it conveys the expectations of cuteness and quaintness, which are then dismantled completely by Shevchenko's self-presentation onstage. As one of the critics noted, "Stasik [sounds like someone who] ought to be playing in a sandbox, bring good grades (piatirky) home from school and have tea with jam, all the while being lovingly interrogated by grandma."[31] Yet, this is far from the image Shevchenko conveys: "If something needs to be cute about me, let it be my name," reacts the singer in a characteristically tongue-in-cheek way.[32] Instead, the femininity she presents is replete with what might be perceived as contradictions within a heteronormative model, yet for Shevchenko are simply multiple aspects of her nuanced understanding of herself. It is channeling this self that, according to the singer, is the primary driving force behind her creative work. She insists that Stasik is "neither an alter-ego, nor a name of a musical project,"[33] but "nakedness"[34] and an attempt to communicate the most urgent questions on her mind, hoping these will resonate with other people.[35] "Stasik is me when I have something to say," asserts the singer.[36]

Visually and sonically, Shevchenko refuses to align herself with one version of femininity. Instead, she carves out a multilayered symbolic space. On stage and in life, the singer combines her buzzcut with feminine dresses just as effortlessly as she does with track suits.[37] In her music videos, particularly in

---

[30] Sashko Polozhynskyi, "Stasik pro 'Kolyskovu dlia Voroha,' Viinu i Chesnist u Muzytsi," October 17, 2019; https://youtu.be/uh79BRFNO3s.

[31] Panimash. "Khto Taka Stasik."

[32] Polozhynskyi, "Stasik pro 'Kolyskovu dlia Voroha.'"

[33] Taisiia Kudenko, "Muzychna Vykonavytsia, za Iakoiu Varto Stezhyty Nastupni 20 Rokiv: Stasik," *Cosmopolitan Ukraina*, November 1, 2019; https://www.cosmo.com.ua/muzichna-vikonavicya-za-yakoyu-varto-stezhiti-nastupn-20-rokv-stask/.

[34] Iryna Krasutska, "Stasik pro Te, iak Vona Proishla ATO, Teatr, Telebachennia I Stala Ukrainskoiu Sinéad O'Connor," *Yabl*, July 18, 2019; https://yabl.ua/2019/07/18/stasik.

[35] Artem Risukhin, "Pro Tvorchist, Demsokyru, Bardasha i Kolektsiiu Nozhiv. Ris na Bis. Vypusk 10," March 18, 2020; https://youtu.be/47uyMZAr1Ec.

[36] Pylypiuk, "Khto Taka Stasik?"

[37] Anastasiia Shevchenko (@hardbride), https://www.instagram.com/hardbride.

"The Knife" ("Nizh"), she alternates convulsive, jerky movements seemingly inspired by Japanese Butoh with graceful, almost ballet-like dance sequences.[38] In nearly all of her songs, harsh electronic beats co-exist with archaic folk-style vocals. Stasik does not shy away from the violent sound and imagery, continuously re-examining her own trauma. The contemplative minimalist soundscape of "Lullaby for An Enemy" stands in eerie contrast to the song's lyrics that are fashioned as a death spell. In the second half of the song, this precarious balance is violently disrupted by the whining, pulsating sound imitating artillery shelling. In the video, we see Shevchenko in her white dress strikingly outlined against the black earth, painfully convulsing in an epileptic fit—one of the posttraumatic symptoms she admits to experiencing in real life.[39] Shevchenko's use of violent sound and imagery is no mere antics aiming for shock value. When asked—as she often is—why she chooses such a "shocking and harsh form" for her creative work, Stasik responds: "because I'm delving into difficult matters."[40] She describes Ukrainian popular music as "not ready to bite,"[41] i.e., not ready to deal with complex social issues, including those brought about by the war.

**Figure 2.1.** STASIK, Image still from music video "The Knife" ("Nizh"), 2019. Shared with permission from the artist.

---

[38] STASIK, "Nizh."

[39] Polozhynskyi, "Stasik pro 'Kolyskovu dlia voroha.'"

[40] Krasutska, "Stasik pro Te, Iak Vona Proishla ATO."

[41] " 'Prohrama Albert': Anastasiia Shevchenko pro Zelenskoho."

Indeed, Stasik stands out not only in Ukraine's musical milieu, but also among her fellow veterans, thanks to the frankness with which she discusses the mental and physical toll that her military service took on her. Defying the misogynistic trope of a hysterical woman, Stasik asserts her right to speak of pain and trauma openly and emotionally. In a 2016 public appearance at a veterans' event, she spoke onstage about a range of health issues that she had experienced while serving in Donbas, and continues to experience upon her return, including such socially taboo symptoms as problems with her urinal tract, gynecological issues, and low libido due to mental health medications.[42] Through her creative approach and frankness, she aims to serve as a role model for wider society, hoping that her own readiness to discuss traumatic experiences will help other people break the social conventions that limit dialogue, awareness, and human connection. According to Stasik, she wants her viewer to think: "If she can let herself weep, mourn (pobyvatysia) and experience some terrible emotions as deeply as possible, then, probably, I'm also allowed to do that."[43]

Shevchenko takes a strong stance on women's rights and equality issues, even though she refuses to speak for all women: "I can only speak on behalf of [one] specific woman—myself."[44] Her 2021 Instagram post features Stasik among the participants of the women's rights march in Kyiv (known as "Marsh rivnosti" (The Equality March).[45] In the photos, she can also be occasionally spotted wearing a t-shirt with an image of a vulva[46] created by the artist Mariia Kulikovska in her project "Flowers of Democracy."[47] While many of the ways in which she presents herself could be interpreted as queerness, Stasik denies belonging to the LGBTQI+ community and avoids even positioning herself in public as a strong ally. Although in her teens she once worked as a bartender in

---

[42] "'Prohrama Albert': Anastasiia Shevchenko pro Zelenskoho."

[43] Kateryna Iakovlenko, "Anastasiia Shevchenko, Stasik: 'Muzyka Nikomu Nichoho ne Vynna'," *LB.ua*, December 17, 2019; https://lb.ua/culture/2019/12/17/445000_anastasiya_shevchenko_stasik_muzika.html.

[44] Olha Litskevych, "Spivachka Stasik: 'Zapytuvaty Veterana pro Viinu – Tse Iak Pytaty Maloznaiomu Liudynu pro Seks'," *Iod Media*, November 13, 2019; https://iod.media/article/spivachka-stasik-zapituvati-veterana-pro-viynu-ce-yak-pitati-maloznayomu-lyudinu-pro-seks-3547.

[45] Anastasiia Shevchenko (@hardbride), "Za Vashu I Nashu Svobodu, Liubi," March 9, 2021.

[46] Anastasiia Shevchenko (@hardbride), September 16, 2018.

[47] Maria Kulikovska, "Confronting Violence Against Women… Using the Female Form," *CBC*, November 11, 2015; https://www.cbc.ca/arts/interruptthisprogram/maria-kulikovska-flowers-of-democracy-1.3306232.

one of Kyiv's prominent gay clubs, Andy Bar[48] and showcases her pictures from Tel Aviv and Berlin Gay Pride Parades in her Instagram feed,[49] she skirts the issue almost awkwardly in her 2019 interview. When asked about her attitude to the LGBTQI+ community ("Iak ty vidnosyshsia do . . . ?"), Shevchenko responds, "Niiak ne vidnoshusia," which could mean both "I have no position [on this]" or, alternatively, based on the word's second common meaning in casually spoken Ukrainian, "I don't belong [to this community] in any way."[50] However, Stasik does go on to explain that she is supportive of the community's rights and freedom of expression. Inclusion is an important issue for Shevchenko, and she highlights this in various ways: for instance, by ensuring that all of her performances are dubbed into sign language.

Stasik frequently speaks up about the role women play at the Donbas frontline, as well as the difficulties and discrimination they experience there. She insists that "a woman does not have a separate path in war," emphasizing that, in her experience, she has seen both men and women being well or poorly suited for military roles.[51] Shevchenko stresses that the differences due to personal capacities and disposition play a greater role in determining one's suitability for military service than one's sex or gender. She admits that her own time at the frontline started out tough: "For the first few weeks, they [male soldiers—I.S.] were destroying me morally. [ . . . ] [But eventually,] they agreed that I was also 'a bro' (bratan) and following that, treated me with great respect, [calling me] 'our Nastia,' 'our mouse,' 'our little sister.'"[52] In a different interview, though, Shevchenko highlights how even when accepted, a woman is often still discouraged from fighting on par with men: "[Male soldiers might tell you:] 'You are our berehynia. You are a good sniper, but maybe you better sit it out over there [in safety].'"[53] The singer insists that both men and women feel equally scared and uncomfortable at war, yet in addition to this, women are forced to prove and defend their basic right to participate in combat: "Being a woman at war is the same as being a man at war, aside from the fact that from time to time, [men] get in the way of your fighting [zavazhaiut voiuvaty]."[54]

---

[48] Pylypiuk, "Khto Taka Stasik?"

[49] Anastasiia Shevchenko (@hardbride), July 28, 2019; Anastasiia Shevchenko (@hardbride), June 28, 2019

[50] Risukhin, "Pro Tvorchist, Demsokyru."

[51] Iakovlenko, "Anastasiia Shevchenko, Stasik."

[52] Pylypiuk, "Khto Taka Stasik?"

[53] "STASIK: Ia ne Mesiia, Muzyka dlia Mene – Tse Prosto Sposib Zvernennia," *BBC News Ukraine,* October 14, 2019; https://youtu.be/f1rfxHuhAAg.

[54] "STASIK: Ia ne Mesiia, Muzyka dlia Mene – Tse Prosto Sposib Zvernennia," *BBC News Ukraine.*

**Figure 2.2.** STASIK, Image still from music video "Lullaby for the Enemy," 2019. Shared with permission from the artist.

Ukrainian mainstream media outlets have struggled to make sense of Stasik's unconventional self-presentation. While the independent media and their audience in social networks reacted to Shevchenko's work with excitement, her coverage in the mass press has oscillated between framing her as exotic and underplaying what is perceived as her eccentricity. "Stasik is a sensual, delicate, but also strong and robust girl," begins one article that attempts to locate Shevchenko within the space of conventional femininity.[55] "So, we should not expect from you any touching elements (zvorushlyvosti) in your next video?" asks another interviewer, almost rhetorically.[56] "Will you sing about romantic love?" echoes yet another journalist.[57] At the same time, the independent media have welcomed Stasik's presence in the Ukrainian music business as a breath of fresh air: "Instead of the sleek, carefree dancing ubiquitous in Ukrainian pop music, she wraps herself up in plastic bags, swallows them whole, then puts on wings made, literally, of meat—causing reactions ranging from disgust to wonder."[58] Shevchenko's "Lullaby for the Enemy" has also sparked the outrage of the conservative Russian media, but mostly due to the song's politics, not the singer's self-expression. Tsargrad TV published a piece

---

[55] Iakovlenko, "Anastasiia Shevchenko, Stasik."

[56] Krasutska, "Stasik pro Te, Iak Vona Proishla ATO."

[57] Litskevych, "Spivachka Stasik: 'Zapytuvaty Veterana pro Viinu.'"

[58] Panimash, "Khto Taka Stasik."

entitled: "A Vicious 'Lullaby for the Enemy' [Imbued] with Black Magic Has Caused Delight in Ukraine."[59] The outlet describes the song as "full of viciousness and hate towards Russians," while Russia's Federal News Agency misquotes Tsargrad's publication—likely intentionally—narrowing and directing Stasik's supposed hate against "the republics of the Donbas."[60]

While individual cases of transgressive femininities are gaining visibility in Ukraine's public space, they are unlikely to affect the dominant heterohegemonic discourse alone, without the allyship of wider networks of activists, legislators, and institutions. Nonetheless, celebrity figures like Stasik can still contribute in important ways to unmaking taboos around the experiences of women soldiers and veterans, as well as civilian women. The "Berehynia" and other stereotypes discussed at the beginning of this chapter continue shaping how the wider society in Ukraine understands the roles considered socially acceptable for women during wartime. Performances pushing against the prevalent attitudes towards gender and femininity in Ukrainian society also open up spaces of dialogue that can be transformative for healing and rebuilding a more inclusive future for the country, including in the aftermath of the recent escalation of the conflict after February 24, 2022. Stasik's role as not only a performer, but a female war veteran now back on the front line, is significant in this sense, as it opens possibilities for global understandings of women's experiences in the Russo-Ukrainian war, while her gender divergence injects a distinctly feminist lens into the hypermasculine discourse around the conflict. Her public discussions of mental health, female anger, and the role of women at war also constitute an important contribution to making these issues visible in the Ukrainian public space and changing how they are discussed. As Stasik herself puts it, "People are much more complex than we think. [ . . . ] We like pretty things, but we need genuine things."[61] At the same time, Stasik's reluctance to engage in public advocacy on behalf of women or the LGBTQI+ community in Ukraine is a testament to the fact that, while the Russo-Ukrainian war rages on with a vengeance, queerness, femininity, and patriotism in Ukraine are yet to be reconciled.

---

[59] "Zlobnaia 'Kolybelnaia Vragu' s Chernoi Magiiei Vyzvala Vostorg na Ukraine," *Tsargrad TV*, September 24, 2019; https://tsargrad.tv/news/greta-blin-zlobnaja-kolybelnaja-vragu-s-chernoj-magiej-vyzvala-vostorg-na-ukraine_218364.

[60] "Ukraintsev Privela v Vostorg Agressivnaia 'Kolybelnaia dlia Vraga' ot 'Veterana ATO'," *RIA FAN*, September 24, 2019; https://riafan.ru/1214554-ukraincev-privela-v-vostorg-agressivnaya-kolybelnaya-dlya-vraga-ot-veterana-ato.

[61] "'Prohrama Albert': Anastasiia Shevchenko pro Zelenskoho."

## Bibliography

Anastasiia. "Cherez khmil." YouTube video. November 15, 2016. https://youtu.be/CjM957R_HiI.

Brown, Jeffrey A. *Dangerous Curves: Action Heroines, Gender, Fetishism, and Popular Culture.* Jackson: University Press of Mississippi, 2011.

Burko, Volodymyr. "Lyst do Kokhanoi." YouTube video. August 9, 2016. https://youtu.be/7qOq6JsbLp4.

Eira. "Tin heroia." YouTube video. December 23, 2014. https://youtu.be/1tGAsfsa3wk.

Gentry, Caron E., and Laura Sjoberg. *Beyond Mothers, Monsters, Whores: Thinking About Women's Violence in Global Politics.* London: Zed Books, 2015.

Goldstein, Joshua S. *War and Gender: How Gender Shapes the War System and Vice Versa.* Cambridge: Cambridge University Press, 2003.

Greta, Blin. "Zlobnaia 'Kolybelnaia Vragu' s Chernoi Magiiei Vyzvala Vostorg na Ukraine." *Tsargrad TV.* September 24, 2019. https://tsargrad.tv/news/greta-blin-zlobnaja-kolybelnaja-vragu-s-chernoj-magiej-vyzvala-vostorg-na-ukraine_218364.

Havryshko, Marta. "Chomu Suspilstvu Zruchno Bachyty Zhinku na Viini 'Beheryneiu,' a ne 'Heroineiu'?" *Hromadske radio.* August 24, 2018. https://hromadske.radio/podcasts/undefined/obraz-zhinky-na-viyni-povilno-ale-zminyuyetsya-gavryshko.

Herbert, Melissa S. *Camouflage Isn't Only for Combat: Gender, Sexuality, and Women in the Military.* New York City: NYU Press, 1998.

Iakovlenko, Kateryna. "Anastasiia Shevchenko, Stasik: 'Muzyka Nikomu Nichoho ne Vynna.'" *LB.ua.* December 17, 2019. https://lb.ua/culture/2019/12/17/445000_anastasiya_shevchenko_stasik_muzika.html.

Khromeychuk, Olesya. "Experiences of Women at War: Servicewomen During WWII and in the Ukrainian Armed Forces in the Conflict in Donbas." *Baltic Worlds* 4 (2018): 58-70.

———. "Instrumentalisation of War History in Contemporary Memory Politics in Ukraine: A Gender Perspective." *EUXEINOS—Culture and Governance in the Black Sea Region* 10, no. 29 (2020): 27–46.

Kis, Oksana. "(Re) Constructing Ukrainian Women's History: Actors, Authors, and Narratives." In *Gender, Politics and Society in Ukraine.* Toronto: University of Toronto Press, 2017.

Krasutska, Iryna. "Stasik pro Te, Iak Vona Proishla ATO, Teatr, Telebachennia i Stala Ukrainskoiu Sinéad O'Connor." *Yabl.* July 18, 2019. https://yabl.ua/2019/07/18/stasik.

Kudenko, Taisiia. "Muzychna Vykonavytsia, za Iakoiu Varto Stezhyty Nastupni 20 Rokiv: Stasik." *Cosmopolitan Ukraina.* November 1, 2019. https://www.cosmo.com.ua/muzichna-vikonavicya-za-yakoyu-varto-stezhiti-nastupn-20-rokv-stask/.

Litskevych, Olha. "Spivachka Stasik: 'Zapytuvaty Veterana pro Viinu – Tse iak Pytaty Maloznaiomu Liudynu pro Seks.'" *Iod Media.* November 13, 2019. https://iod.media/article/spivachka-stasik-zapituvati-veterana-pro-viynu-ce-yak-pitati-maloznayomu-lyudinu-pro-seks-3547.

_____."Maria Kulikovska: Confronting Violence Against Women... Using the Female Form." *CBC.* November 11, 2015. https://www.cbc.ca/arts/interruptthis program/maria-kulikovska-flowers-of-democracy-1.3306232.

Martsenyuk, Tamara, Ganna Grytsenko, and Anna Kvit. "The 'Invisible Battalion': Women in ATO Military Operations in Ukraine." *Kyiv-Mohyla Law and Politics Journal* 2 (2016).

Panasiuk, Khrystyna. "Ty Pidbory Zminyla na Bertsi." YouTube video. May 7, 2016. https://youtu.be/K2a8IAgwo7Q .

Panimash, Dania. "Khto Taka Stasik–Ukrainska Spivachka, za Iakoiu Varto Stezhyty."*Slukh.* September 20, 2019. https://slukh.media/texts/who-is-stasik/.

Picheta, Rob, and Denis Lapin. "Ukraine to Give Female Soldiers 'More Comfortable' Heels After Sexism Controversy." *CNN.* July 8, 2021. https:// edition.cnn.com/2021/07/08/europe/ukraine-female-soldiers-new-heels-scli-intl/index.html.

Polozhynskyi, Sashko. "Stasik pro 'Kolyskovu dlia Voroha,' Viinu i Chesnist u Muzytsi." YouTube video. October 17, 2019. https://youtu.be/uh79BRFNO3s.

Popova, Dariia. "Viina, Natsionalizm ta Zhinoche Pytannia." *Spilne.* January 28, 2017. https://commons.com.ua/uk/vijna-nacionalizm-ta-zhinoche-pitannya/.

_____." 'Prohrama Albert': Anastasiia Shevchenko pro Zelenskoho, Vtratu Zdorovia na Viini i Korysnu Propahandu." *Hromadske.* May 20, 2019. https:// hromadske.ua/posts/programa-albert-anastasiya-shevchenko-pro-zelenskogo-vtratu-zdorovya-na-vijni-i-korisnu-propagandu.

Pylypiuk, Sofiia. "Khto Taka Stasik? Nastia Shevchenko pro Teatr, Viinu ta Muzyku." *The Village.* December 23, 2019. https://www.the-village.com.ua/ village/culture/culture-interview/292553-hto-taka-stasik.

Risukhin, Artem. "Pro Tvorchist, Demsokyru, Bardasha i Kolektsiiu Nozhiv. Ris na Bis. Vypusk 10." YouTube video. March 18, 2020. https://youtu.be/47uyMZ Ar1Ec.

Rupp, Leila J. *Mobilizing Women for War.* Princeton: Princeton University Press, 2015.

Shevchenko, Anastasiia (@hardbride). Instagram channel of Anastasiia Shevchenko. https://www.instagram.com/hardbride.

STASIK. "Bii z tinniu." YouTube video. June 20, 2019. https://youtu.be/VKKoXq_IXYQ.

_____. "Byi." YouTube video. February 27, 2022. https://youtu.be/K4LV4AjDbqk.

_____."STASIK: Ia ne Mesiia, Muzyka dlia Mene – Tse Prosto Sposib Zvernennia." *BBC News Ukraine.* YouTube video. October 14, 2019. https://youtu.be/f1rfx HuhAAg.

_____. "Kolyskova dlia Voroha." YouTube video. September 19, 2019. https:// youtu.be/40WD9RDAMVc.

_____. "Ne Vidvod Ochei. Sounds of Chornobyl." YouTube video. October 26, 2020. https://youtu.be/2ASD0QZJtgc.

_____. "Nizh." YouTube video. April 18, 2019. https://youtu.be/5RgJoMXU1u0.

_____."Ukraintsev Privela v Vostorg Agressivnaia 'Kolybelnaia dlia Vraga' ot 'Veterana ATO.'" *RIA FAN.* September 24, 2019. https://riafan.ru/1214554-ukraincev-privela-v-vostorg-agressivnaya-kolybelnaya-dlya-vraga-ot-veterana-ato.

_____."Zhinok v Ukrainskii Armii Vzhe Ponad 20%—Minoborony." *Ukrinform.*

December 17, 2019. https://www.ukrinform.ua/rubric-ato/2839911-zinok-v-ukrainskij-armii-vze-ponad-20-minoboroni.html.

_____. "Z Pochatku Viiny Kilkist Zhinok v Armii Zrosla Vdvichi." *Novynarnia.* March 6, 2021. https://novynarnia.com/2021/03/06/z-pochatku

## Chapter 3

# "We felt that the country was in the stage of a rough cut . . ." : Vernacular Documentation, Political Affect and the Ideological Functions of Catharsis

Nataliya Tchermalykh

### Abstract

In March 2014, I attended the first screening of *Euromaidan: Rough Cut*—a collective documentary chronicle of the Ukrainian Maidan Revolution. Quite unexpectedly, the event ended with an improvised mourning ritual for deceased Maidan protesters. Observed in the film, this ritual then transcended the screen and spread through the audience, stimulating an experience similar to a "collective catharsis." What are the reasons for such a strong affective response to a visual document, capturing the fluidity of still unfolding revolutionary events? This paper considers both the documentary and its screening as invaluable research sites, allowing us to study ethnographically the uncertainties preceding and accompanying the reification of (new) ideological narratives. By discussing the multifaceted understanding of cathartic experiences in the complex processes of group-building, truth-finding and justice-making, this paper considers new directions for anthropological understanding of collective catharsis, as it is experienced in post-industrial democratic societies.

**Keywords**: Maidan revolution, documentary film, political affect, catharsis

\*\*\*

### Introduction

It is early spring 2014. After a long wait, I sit myself uncomfortably on the one remaining seat in the back row of a fully packed screening hall. I am at Dom Kino, a symbolic space for the Ukrainian cinema industry, in fact it is a shabby Soviet-style building that still belongs to the Union of Ukrainian Filmmakers, or to what remained of this Soviet organization, so powerful in the past. That night, Dom Kino was expecting a full house: it was the opening ceremony of Docudays, the only, and therefore the biggest, international documentary film festival in Ukraine. The cinema hall was hot and suffocating, overcrowded, around me, hundreds of voices went on and on in endless discussions. *Maidan, Yanukovych, Crimea, Putin, Donbas...* From the snatches of conversations, one could sense the vibrations of the revolution still in the air. Kyiv city center smelled like fire and ashes, and Khreschatyk avenue was buried under tons of flowers in memory of the victims — one hundred protesters killed overnight by unidentified snipers.

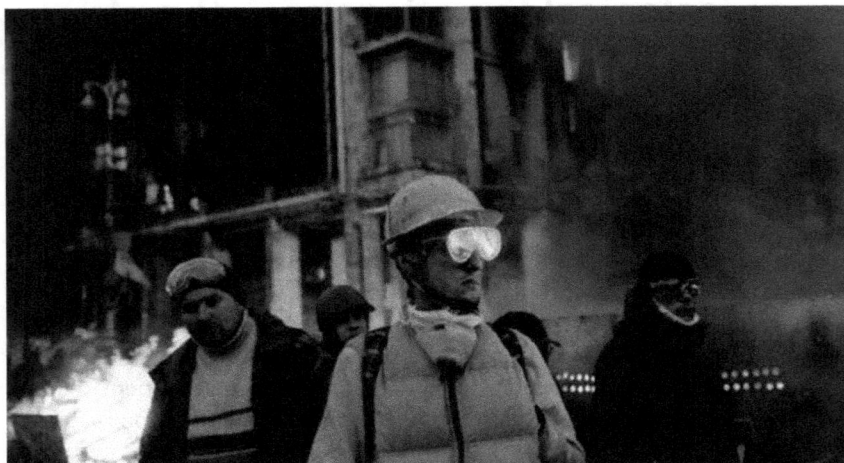

**Figure 3.1.** Roman Bondarchuk, Yulia Gontaruk, et al. 2014. *Yevromaydan. Chornovyy Montazh.* Image. Source: Public Domain.[1]

Suddenly, the lights went out. The conversations stopped: something was happening on the screen. A man stands motionless, looking odd: a construction helmet on his head, a gas mask dangling on his neck, his eyes covered by protective goggles, reflecting the vivid glow of fire. In the background, a city in flames. The shaky camera fixes his face for a while, as he looks intently at something beyond our view, as though oblivious. The otherworldly sounds turn into the melody of a Ukrainian ballad, accompanied by a crackling of fire — suddenly interrupted by a loud explosion.

And then the screen turned black: it was over. It was just a brief trailer for the festival, not the film itself.[2] But something changed. The suffocating air

---

[1] More images can be found online on the artists' webpages.

[2] Roman Bondarchuk, Yulia Gontaruk, Kateryna Gornostai, Andrey Kiselyov, Roman Liubyi, Andriy Lytvynenko, Aleksey Solodunov, Dmitry Stoykov, Oleksandr Techynskyi,

suddenly became electric, and everybody seemed hypnotized by the image of this man, deeply shell-shocked by the violence in the streets of Ukraine throughout the Winter of 2013. The audience in the Dom Kino cinema hall that evening in March 2014 was shell-shocked, just like us, after months of violence. The screening was about to begin.

This paper is dedicated to the documentary film *Euromaidan: Chornovyi Montaj* (*Euromaidan: Rough Cut*, 2014), which is a collective chronicle of civil protest on Kyiv's Maidan Nezalezhnosti Square (Independence Square). The film is the collaborative work of 10 young Ukrainian filmmakers, who produced a full-length documentary from their combined footage that they had each captured by camera while participating in the revolution. The resulting film debuted at the opening of *Docudays*, which is the largest and oldest Human Rights Film Festival in Ukraine.[3] More than "rough," it was rather a "rushed cut," since the footage was collected and edited in the months just prior to the festival. As Roman Bondarchuk, one of the filmmakers, put it: "We still didn't know what Maidan actually was. We felt that the country was at the stage of a rough cut as well."[4] Yet another contributor stated: "It was not a rough cut, but a completed film [ . . . ] The term 'rough cut' here was only a concept, a metaphor."[5]

After the film was over, I saw people standing up, crying, hugging each other and chanting the national anthem in unison: a pure moment of collective "effervescence," as Durkheim would term it. I myself left the cinema hall with the same mixed feelings each time. On the one hand, I was, as many festival guests were, mesmerized by the moving images on the screen and affected by the unique atmosphere of unity in the screening hall. But, on the other hand, I was stunned by the ideological homogeneity and the evident coherence of the narrative about the events that were at stake. This narrative seemed to materialize *sui generis*, almost from nowhere, as if I was witnessing the perceptible and visible effects of an invisible chemical reaction. How could one explain it?

---

and Volodymyr Tykhyy. *Yevromaydan. Chornovyy Montazh (Euromaidan: Rough Cut).* Documentary. Docudays, 2014. Film, Vimeo: https://vimeo.com/89969382. Trailer, YouTube: https://www.youtube.com/watch?v=wWzocCL1Owg.

[3] Viktoriia Khomenko. "Euromaidan: Rough Cut." *Docudays.ua.* Blog post. December 1, 2016; http://docudays.ua/eng/2016/news/kino/euromaidan-online-docu-space/.

[4] All translations from Russian and Ukrainian are mine, if not stated otherwise.

[5] Kateryna Hornostay and Roman Bondarchuk. "Rozmova z Katerynoyu Hornostay ta Oleksandrom Bondarchukom." (Interview with Kateryna Hornostay and Oleksandr Bondarchuk). *Hromadske telebachennya.* December 20, 2014; https://www.youtube.com/watch?v=MDa8zL8XAR0.

This paper is an attempt to find an answer to this question, by discussing how the process of vernacular documentation of political events contributes to the construction of fragile political communities, while being relentlessly captured in broader historical developments. The uniqueness of *Euromaidan: Rough Cut* as a cinematic and ethnographic source lies in its fragmented and unfinished structure, which reflects the consolidation of a strong political narrative of post-Maidan Ukraine. In this film, the refraction of competing political narratives is not retroactively suppressed in the name of a coherent recounting of the events, serving an ideological purpose, but remains its constituent element, visible and ready to be analyzed.

The first part of the article follows the structure of the chronicle and examines the role of vernacular visual documentation in contemporary activism. The construction of a collective visual archive, I argue, ensures the transformation of unstable activist networks towards a more clearly defined political community, sharing the same vision of political events. In the second part of the article, I interrogate the notion of *catharsis*, focusing on a ritual of collective mourning that followed the screening. Drawing on recent understandings of catharsis in psychology, aesthetics and law, I examine what has been lost in recent interdisciplinary developments, bringing to the forefront a complex relationship between cathartic experiences and forms of ideological reification in reference to Girard René and Bertold Brecht. [6] Finally, I dwell on the role cathartic experiences may play in the processes of justice-seeking and justice-making.

## Maidan: The Events

The film *Euromaidan: Rough Cut* begins in a conventional way. On the black screen, a brief sentence appears, situating the film's events: "The protest started on 21 November 2013 as a response to the Ukrainian government's decision to suspend the process of signing the Association Agreement between the EU and Ukraine . . ." This abrupt decision by President Yanukovych and Prime Minister Azarov, who instead signed an alternative agreement with Russia, signified a 180-degree turn towards a pro-Russian path, and was widely interpreted as a loss of Ukrainian sovereignty.

In reaction, street protests erupted in Kyiv's central square, Maidan Nezalezhnosti, now known worldwide simply as "Maidan." After the first violent crackdowns on protesting students by the *Berkut* (Ukrainian Riot Police), the movement expanded and gained popularity among the wider public from heterogeneous

---

[6] René Girard, *Violence and the Sacred* (Baltimore: Johns Hopkins University Press, 1979). Bertolt Brecht, *Brecht on Theatre: The Development of an Aesthetic* (New York: Farrar, Straus and Giroux, 1964).

political backgrounds, stretching from the ultranationalist right to the liberal left; activists from remote regions of Ukraine traveled to Kyiv to join the protests. On the weekends, the number of protesters reached over a million. Demonstrators occupied Kyiv's city hall and called on Yanukovych to resign.

As demonstrations gave way to rioting, the president signed a series of laws restricting the right to protest, and hundreds of thousands took to the streets in response. Bloody clashes between police and protesters ensued, with dozens injured on each side. Protesters occupied the justice ministry in Kyiv, and the parliament hastily repealed the anti-protest measures.

The protests reached a climax during mid-February. On February 20, 2014, violence in Kyiv escalated dramatically, with police and government security forces firing on crowds of protesters. In total, more than 100 people were killed and 2,500 injured in these clashes. In the early morning of February 21, the riot police retreated. Immediately after, protesters gained control of the presidential administration and the private estate of Yanukovych, who by that time had fled the country for Russia.

The bloodiest week in Ukraine's post-Soviet history concluded on February 21, 2014, with the opposition leaders calling for early presidential elections and the formation of an interim government. The parliament responded by approving the restoration of the 2004 constitution, thus reducing the power of the presidency. The next day, the Ukrainian parliament impeached Yanukovych, replacing his government with an oppositional one. The protests on Maidan officially reached their end, but some demonstrators stayed in the place till mid-Summer 2014. In May, the Ukrainian businessman Petro Poroshenko, nicknamed "Chocolate King" for his success in the sugar industry, was elected president: a handover between post-Soviet oligarchical elites. Using the pretext of the preparations for Independence Day, celebrated in Ukraine on the 22nd of August, the last camps on Maidan were liquidated.

The Maidan Revolution induced multidirectional geopolitical processes, evolving around the Ukrainian state, processes that modified patterns of governance in the post-Soviet region and the contours of Ukrainian sovereignty. On the one hand, the Association Agreement with the European Union and the instauration of a visa-free regime with Schengen countries liberalized the human and commodity circulation to and from Ukraine. On the other hand, the occupation and annexation of the Crimean Peninsula by the Russian Federation in the South militarized boundaries between Russia and Ukraine. The creation of self-proclaimed separatist para-republics in the East, and the still ongoing military operation in response devastated the region, provoking internal displacement and massive emigration of disenfranchised Ukrainian citizens. In 2015-2021 there were several diplomatic, military and judicial attempts to prosecute those responsible for the human losses and pacify the Eastern region, however, all of them remained inconclusive.

### "And what if we all gather on Maidan?"

In Ukraine, the revolutionary events are believed to have been started by a tweet, circulated on the night of the 20th of November 2013 by a famous oppositional journalist, Mustafa Nayem. Nayem, following Yanukovych's rejection of the Association Agreement with the European Union, proposed: "And what if we all gather on Maidan?" During one single night, his question was retweeted more than 3,000 times. Through the almost immediate creation of the hashtag #Euromaidan that functioned as a magnet, Maidan Nezalejnosti, the main square of Kyiv, became the center of urban occupation and rapidly acquired a parallel cyber-dimension. It expanded simultaneously "online" and "offline," and both processes of occupation—physical and cognitive— were tightly connected.

Just as Judith Butler wrote about the Occupy Wall Street movement (in "Bodies in Alliance and the Politics of the Street"), in Kyiv likewise, "politics (was) already in the home, or on the street, or in the neighborhood or indeed in those virtual spaces that are unbound by the architecture of the public square."[7] While people gathered physically on Maidan, a geographical space with its physical signs — the occupied Christmas tree, the digital clock of the Trade Union Building, the marble columns of the Central Post Office, inscribed with slogans. Demonstrators also gathered virtually on and around #Euromaidan, where those signs were represented by their digital footprints, traces, and duplicates: photos, short videos, ironic *demotivators*, visual and textual *memes*, *hashtags* and slogans.

The rapid, almost immediate, crystallization of a vast political agenda, symbolically associated with a particular urban center with a long protest history, was achieved in part by virtue of new digital technologies. While the outcome of the (physical) protest was unpredictable and could be lost at any moment, its virtual emanation enunciated an optimistic accomplishment of the events: Maidan was a disputed place, whereas #Maidan was not.

### Vernacular Documentation, Virtual Worlds and the Construction of Political Collectivities

The creation of revolutionary images was a key part of the protest culture, and some activists carried video cameras attached to their bodies 24 hours a day, 7

---

[7] Judith Butler, *Notes Toward a Performative Theory of Assembly* (Cambridge, MA: Harvard University Press, 2015); https://doi.org/10.4159/9780674495548-003.

days a week, and were involved in a continuous micro-broadcasting of live material through social media platforms. The first days of the protest gave birth to a new form of Ukrainian political journalism: an alternative online channel HromadskeTV was created. These journalists reported the news not through traditional "pieces to camera" with a microphone, but through real-time comments to streamed footage, coming from cameras on their smartphones, heads or helmets. This strategy of narrated information flow was counterbalanced by the uninterrupted streaming of surveillance camera footage from the central streets, provided by independent websites. Out of this feast of "rough" and "cooked" pieces of freely circulating authorless images, each person could reconstruct their own patchwork of revolutionary reality, of knowledge and action.

Ethnographer Jeffrey S. Juris, analyzing the dynamics of the *#Occupy Everywhere* movement in Boston, proposes to distinguish the cultural logic of networking from the logic of aggregation. The former, as Juris puts it, orients actors toward building horizontal ties, using the circulation of information, direct democratic decision making and networking. The latter is "an alternative cultural framework" that involves the aggregation of many individuals in concrete physical spaces.[8] Whereas networking logic requires a praxis of communication and coordination on the part of collective actors that are already constituted, the logic of aggregation involves the coming together of actors qua individuals, and their subsequent integration (or not) to the collectivity.[9]

Following my observations of the Maidan protests, I would argue that the dynamics of transformation between the two interconnected processes — the networking and the aggregation, in Juris' terms — is underpinned by the relatively new logic of vernacular (self-) documentation in a digital format. It is a cognitive and an agentive practice, aimed at the construction of a visual archive of evidence that ensures the transformation of unstable activist networks towards a more clearly defined community, sharing the same vision of a political event. To document, to photograph, film, stream, broadcast, edit, and later support, comment and share — means to recognize, to hope, to believe, to memorize, to show, to tell and to forget. The images that the community produces become the boundary markers for a new collective subjectivity.

---

[8] Jeffrey S. Juris, "Reflections on #Occupy Everywhere: Social Media, Public Space, and Emerging Logics of Aggregation." *American Ethnologist* 39 (2), 2012: 259–79. https://doi.org/10.1111/j.1548-1425.2012.01362.x.

[9] Juris, "Reflections on #Occupy Everywhere," 259–79.

### Towards an Anthropology of Technologically Mediated Emotions and Affect

One could presuppose that one of the (new) premises of the formation of this collective subjectivity is the development of strong emotional ties with the revolutionary visuals. That revolutionary events lead to the formation of a group identity, based on a range of experiences, including the emotional responses to imminent or remote events, is well known. But emotional ties are formed, surely, not only because of the wide circulation of those images in the social media and the press, but also, and perhaps more importantly, because of the activists' personal participation in their creation since the advent of social media.

In a recent article "Memory, body, and the online researcher: Following Russian street demonstrations via social media," Patty Gray describes her emotional responses to remote ethnographic experience as follows: "I was surprised [ . . . ] that, even though I was witnessing the Moscow protests remotely, I had had a similar kind of sensual experience: the goose bumps, the tears, the adrenaline. I was witnessing something extremely compelling that I wanted to document, and I desperately wanted to be present, 'be *there*,' even if only virtually. Although I could not be physically in the space of Moscow's streets, my virtual presence was actually satisfying in a bodily way."[10]

As this testimonial shows, cyberspace can be considered not only as a space where information is shared and exchanged, but also where emotional responses and sensual experiences may take place — which is perhaps one of the main reasons why social media are so attractive for large audiences. It is time to consider anthropologically the role of *technologically mediated emotions* — ones that arise or are sustained through the immersion in virtual worlds—and are to a much larger extent practiced symbolically, then physically, in order to include them in the general mapping of collective actions that tie a society together.

We all use social media as a tool that helps us to shape reality as we would like it to appear. The beautiful image, especially when taken from a favorable angle and slightly retouched to dramatize its effect, allows us to overcome the frustration we feel towards the things we merely "have." We crave the delights of publicly *displaying* what we have, our "possessions" including our perceptions. Children, animals, remote landscapes, lovers and frothy cappuccinos . . . The joy of being next to them seems to intensify progressively

---

[10] Patty A. Gray, "Memory, Body, and the Online Researcher: Following Russian Street Demonstrations via Social Media." *American Ethnologist* 43, no. 3 (2016): 500–510; https://doi.org/10.1111/amet.12342.

as they become parts of our personal archives and reach great heights as soon as someone else sees, approves, prizes them and by doing so, includes them in the landscape of their own desire. At this very moment, they come intensively into being, becoming truly ours.

Why couldn't one transpose the same mechanism to the way we construct a political reality? A similar futuristic enchantment, emanating from the haze-covered images of protest, permits us to shorten the distance toward the political spaces which have not yet come into being. In this way, the process of direct, even compulsive documentation in contemporary activism becomes particularly meaningful. It is a cognitive act and a gesture, a virtual effigy that represents the fragile, inchoate community which is being established. The viability of this community depends, among other things, on its ability to document itself on mobile devices.

### The Christmas Tree and Vertov's *Kinopravda*

*Maidan: Rough Cut* begins with no images: only white letters on the black screen. For a fraction of a second, we are immersed in the complete darkness and silence of a cinema hall. Then, almost immediately, the viewer's eye is overwhelmed by a flow of colorful, fuzzy images, similar to the aesthetics of unedited footage, realized with an amateur hand-held camera. This initial contrast between monochrome and color sequences marks the rhythm, but also the main tension of the chronicle, that lies between an "objective" description, briefly summarized in static, factual intertitles, and the dynamics of the visual "phrases" that follow.

The first *kino-novela* of the chronicle in Ukrainian, "Volya abo Smert" (Freedom or Death) realized by Volodymyr Tyhyi stands in the tradition of Dziga Vertov's *Kinopravda. The word Kinopravda* is a conceptual neologism deriving from the Russian *kino*, or cinema, combined with the word for truth: *pravda*. It reflects the avant-gardist experiments in documentary film-making that were practiced in 1920 in the USSR and inspired Jean Rouch and Edgar Morin's *cinéma-verité* in the 1960s. In "Ethnography in/of World Systems," one of the most cited essays of the history of the discipline, Marcus mentioned Vertov's "Man with the Movie Camera" as "the de facto ethnographic media" and "an excellent inspiration for multi-sited ethnography," capturing an interesting transnational afterlife of the Russian avant-gardist project.[11]

---

[11] G. Marcus, "Ethnography in/of World Systems: The Emergence of Multi-sited Ethnography" *Annual Review of Anthropology* 24 (1995), 96.

**Figure 3.2.** Roman Bondarchuk, Yulia Gontaruk, et al. 2014. *Yevromaydan. Chornovyy Montazh*. Image. Source: Public Domain.

To a certain extent, the new technological quantum leap of the twenty-first century can be compared to the early Soviet aesthetic breakthrough. What can David Kaufman, alias Dziga Vertov, one of the Soviet film pioneers, tell us about the interplay between the latest digital technologies and the formation of new social movements and their ideologies? Vertov considered modern cinema as a product of the technological progress that liberated the filmmakers from cumbersome equipment, leading the way to the revolutionary transformation of the regime of vision. "I am kino-eye, I am a mechanical eye. I, a machine, show you the world as only I can see it," wrote Vertov in 1929:

> Now and forever, I free myself from human immobility, I am in constant motion, I draw near, then away from objects, I crawl under, I climb onto them. I move apace with the muzzle of a galloping horse, I plunge full speed into a crowd, I outstrip running soldiers, I fall on my back, I ascend with an airplane, I plunge and soar together with plunging and soaring bodies. Now I, a camera, fling myself along their resultant, maneuvering in thechaos of movement, recording movement, starting with movements composed of the most complex combinations.[12]

One of the first and purest forms of modernist hope is that technological progress and formal experimentation are undeniably linked with the

---

[12] Dziga Vertov, *Kino-Eye: The Writings of Dziga Vertov* (Berkeley: University of California Press, 1984), 17.

forthcoming "social progress."[13] Is this belief a reality, or no more than an optical illusion?

The first episode of *Euromaidan: Rough Cut*, "Volya abo Smert" (Ukrainian: Freedom or Death) indeed offers us an explosion of movement. The camera shakes and jumps from one face to another, as the human crowd flows to Maidan — as if it was passed from hand to hand. It follows people climbing up to the top of the 5-meter-high metal carcass of the Christmas Tree, traditionally erected in the very center of Maidan around mid-November. Balancing dangerously at its very top, the camera offers a bird's-eye panorama on hundreds of people transforming the universal Christmas symbol into a revolutionary one by redecorating it with banners, slogans, portraits and Ukrainian flags. Online, a hashtag #yolka (Russian: pine tree) was created to honor this carnivalesque effigy and disseminate its image widely. A new year, and may be, a new era, was about to begin. Today, while analyzing the visual product obtained by virtue of cutting-edge digital technologies, appropriated by the protest movements — GoPro cameras, internet micro-broadcasting and 360-degree VR video — one can trace there a Vertovian logic of the ultimate modernization of vision, consisting in Vertov's words of "swimming with the tide" of moving human bodies, as if this camera-body alliance could reveal a hidden nature of the "movement," understood not only as a kinesthetic motion, but also as a form of social organization.

### Lenin's Fall: Chronicles of a Divisive Ritual

During the first 25 minutes of the film, the narrative easily shifts from political discussions to everyday conversations, while the camera focuses on the mechanical gestures of volunteers and faces of ordinary people on the Maidan, documenting their diverse activities in the camp — and revealing the generational, class, gender and political heterogeneity of the protestors. I would like to particularly emphasize a subtle, yet politically sharp episode by Kateryna Gornostai, "Zub Lenina" (Ukrainian: Lenin's tooth), which is dedicated to the so-called "fall of Lenin" — the incident that happened on the 8th of December 2013 in the very center of Kyiv, when demonstrators destroyed the marble statue of Lenin that had stood there since 1946. It was the first episode of a whole series of *Leninopads* (sometimes translated from Ukrainian as *Leninfalls*) — acts of collective and individual destruction of the Lenin statues that "went viral" throughout Ukraine in 2013-2014.

---

[13] Donna Haraway, *A Cyborg Manifesto: Science, Technology, and Socialist-Feminism in the Late Twentieth Century. Simians, Cyborgs, and Women* (New York: Routledge, 2013); https://doi.org/10.4324/9780203873106-17.

As if Gornostai's camera were sensitive enough to apprehend the long-term consequences of the statue's downfall, she observes debates that divided people of different generations and origins who had witnessed the event. Sitting on a bench, an old man cries, repeating, "This is not human . . . ," soon after, a woman in her late fifties, carrying a dachshund, expresses her sadness, due to the fact "Lenin looked at her everyday on this street as she passed by on her way to school." Meanwhile, in the background, masked youngsters destroy the granite statue with hammers; others, wrapped in Ukrainian flags, chant paradoxical slogans, such as "Down with oligarch commies!"— while two elderly men discuss what they should put there instead of Lenin: one suggests Stepan Bandera (a Ukrainian nationalist leader of the Second World War) and the other, perhaps a memorial to the Holocaust?

It all ends with a dialogue between Gornostai (whose voice we hear behind the camera) and an apparently drunk, middle-aged man in tears, who argues vehemently with the protesters gathering around the fallen Lenin. Notwithstanding the fierceness of his disagreement, he fails to explain precisely his reasons, saying enigmatically: "I told them who they are . . . Their truth is only their truth." Before leaving, he stares at the camera with eyes full of tears, smiles and unexpectedly whips out a pistol from his pocket: "If they try to beat me, they'll know . . ." and then gently bids farewell to the young filmmaker: "Thank you, my daughter."

Recalling that crucial day in a joint interview, the memories of two members of the *Euromaidan: Rough Cut* crew seem to diverge. While Gornostai remembers, justifying her commitment: "This place was a point of convergence of different energies. There were people who were happy that it happened and those who were profoundly shocked," Bondarchuk reveals: "We missed the very moment of Lenin's downfall. When we arrived at the end, and found there a kind of *pagan bacchanalia,* my sound man said that he would not document it—and I agreed with him." This diversity of opinions among the filmmakers reveals a crucial dichotomy in the strategies of exploration of social reality: a further immersion and engagement with a controversial material, or on the contrary, the exclusion of it from the field of vision. Exclusion that finally influences and shapes the aesthetic and discursive contours of the final visual product. In the first episodes, this strategic difference in positionality is still observable through the alternative standpoints that the authors take, while engaging with their subjects.

### Filming the Violence of Others

After the first 30 minutes of the film, its modality changes dramatically: an almost palpable shift in the visual regime occurs. All the diverse themes, including political and personal divergences over the events, merge into one visual flux — the witnessing of violence. It seems that its magnetic spectacle adjusted the very lenses of the documentarists: close-up portraits of the activists speaking about their commitments were replaced by the narratives of the violent clashes with the *Berkut*, the riot police, burning cityscapes, strident sounds and sparks of explosions.

It is interesting to note that in the fragmented structure of the documentary, the shift doesn't occur between two separated episodes, directed by different authors, but in the very middle of one of them, called "Masha's peaceful protest." This is a second short film by Gornostai, which follows a young Ukrainian woman working as an English teacher in a secondary school in Kyiv's suburbs. First, we see Masha on her way back home from the square, discussing politics with her friends, fellow students, and strangers on the streets. Then, in a blink of an eye, we see the first violent clashes: barricades in fire, smoke and fumes everywhere and suffocating people — the camera turns and meets the gaze of a woman wearing a gas mask and a white medical uniform with a big red cross on her cap. After a few instants, we recognize Masha, the schoolteacher.

In an interview that Gornostai gave me, she said that she recognized Masha by accident, while filming the clashes—and decided to rebuild the plot of her short film around this coincidence. A coincidence that emphasized visually the shift in the gender dimension of the protest, by contrasting two close-up portraits of the same young woman (Masha's smiling face, vividly discussing politics, and her unrecognizable face, covered with a medical mask and blended in the crowd of volunteers).

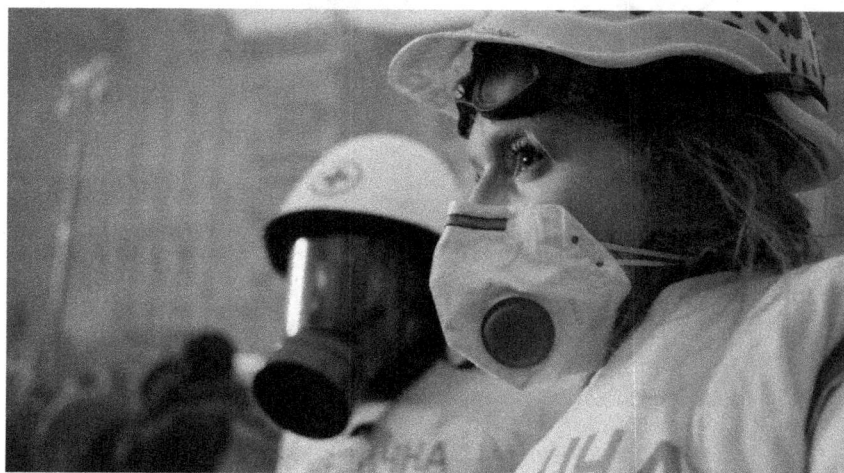

**Figure 3.3.** Roman Bondarchuk, Yulia Gontaruk, et al. 2014. *Yevromaydan. Chornovyy Montazh.* Image. Source: Public Domain.

The gendered logic of urban violence captured in Masha's story replicates the logic of war, which almost invisibly, and yet inevitably, restrains the repertoire of active roles available to female subjects. Here, a young woman who started as a political activist, within a time frame of one month (and Gornostai's film lasts less than 5 minutes) "naturally" changes her role, becoming a nurse who helps those wounded and injured in battles. Of the entire chronicle, "Masha's peaceful protest" is the last film that is not exclusively dedicated to the urban clashes and the last one that has as its central figure a woman.

As if it was meant to illustrate and reiterate this schism by cinematic means, the next episode, "Searching for a leader" by R. Bondarchuk, follows the fuzzy process of on-the-spot decision-making, carried out exclusively by men gathering around the barricades. The fighters casually exchange opinions in different Ukrainian dialects as well as in Russian, trying to decide when and whether they should attack the riot police congregating around the square. "You've locked yourself in here. Get the girls out!," a middle-aged man in a military uniform utters persuasively: "Every girl—get them out of here—it's the only way out. If there is panic, it'll be fuckin' slaughter." There is something almost medieval in this scene, in which men decide on the march of events, in the darkness of a winter night, their faces irradiated only by the light of the bonfires.

**Eyes with Dilated Pupils**

**Figure 3.4.** Roman Bondarchuk, Yulia Gontaruk, et al. 2014. *Yevromaydan. Chornovyy Montazh.* Image. Source: Public Domain.

All of the following episodes share a common aesthetic: "Sense? Damned if I know" by A. Kiselyov, "Cobble by Cobble" by R. Lyubyi and "All Things Ablaze" by O. Techinsky. The spectacle of urban clashes, the sounds of grenades and rough masculine voices, abrupt gestures, Molotov cocktails, burning tires, smoke and the black helmets of policemen. The object of documentation also shifts almost seamlessly — from an observant and participating eye, which captures and inquires in heterogeneous forms of micro-politics, it becomes an "eye with dilated pupils." The eye that tries to distinguish its subjects under their black masks and behind the curtain of fumes, but fails to do so, hypnotized by the violence of the riots.

"All Things Ablaze," the final episode of the series, showing the last and most violent days of the protests, is the longest of all. It exposes a spiral of clashes that accelerate in rhythm from one scene to another, as though inevitably leading to a climax: the chaotic images of the tragedy that started on the night of February eighteenth and splattered a peaceful city with blood. In one single night, over one hundred protesters were killed by unidentified snipers: the victims have been posthumously officially named *Nebesna Sotnya*—the Heavenly Hundred.

**Figure 3.5.** Roman Bondarchuk, Yulia Gontaruk, et al. 2014. *Yevromaydan. Chornovyy Montazh.* Image. Source: Public Domain.

The final events of that day are omitted from the film, perhaps because the majority of Kyivans had deserted Maidan by evening. The city center was closed off and encircled by the aforementioned incumbent Viktor Yanukovych's riot police forces (*Berkut*), as was the metro system. Taxi drivers demanded astronomic sums from those who ventured to reach the central square. On the Maidan itself there remained only a handful of orthodox priests, a few doctors, and men and women willing to fight with or without arms. The latter became the prime target of snipers who were standing on high buildings, surrounding the Square. Snipers who were, mysteriously, later erased from the official investigation reports conducted by Ukrainian government during the two post-revolutionary Presidential administrations, Petro Poroshenko (2014-2019) and Volodymyr Zelenskyy (2019-present).

## The End of the Screening

In the cinema hall of Dom Kino, there is barely enough space for people to move: people stand between rows and sit by the screen, as if intentionally replicating the crowd on the Maidan during the protest days. We are watching the last scene of "All things ablaze," which takes place on the day that followed the massacre. It is quite emblematic: on Maidan, by then as full of people as it had been during its first days, the camera follows closed and open black coffins, carried by thousands of hands, and covered with the national blue and yellow flag or the black and red flag of the Ukrainian insurgent army.[14]

*Euromaidan: Rough Cut* ends with the sounds of the song *Plyve kacha po Tysyni* (Ukrainian: Duck Swims on the Tysyna)—a traditional polyphony, performed a cappella by seven male voices, a polyphony belonging to a rare and sophisticated repertoire (Pikkardiyska Tertsiya 2002). Known previously only by a circle of connoisseurs, *Plyve kacha po Tysyni* became nationally famous following February 2014 as a requiem for Maidan's *Heaven Hundred*. This song is sung in one of the Carpathian dialects, barely understandable to the average native speaker from Central Ukraine.[15] It narrates an imagined dialogue between a son who predicts his own death to his mother, alternating

---

[14] The Ukrainian Insurgent Army (UPA, *Ukrayins'ka Povstans'ka Armiya*) was a Ukrainian nationalist paramilitary army that fought against the Soviet troops in Western Ukraine. Aiming at the foundation of the independent Ukrainian state, the UPA was for some time allied to Nazi Germany and provided support for the military occupation of Eastern European borderlands. Despite succinct attempts of Ukrainian historiographers to absolve the UPA of war crimes, the recently declassified archival documents bring evidence on their involvement in ethnic cleansing of Jewish and Polish populations. See: Jared McBride, "Peasants into Perpetrators: The OUN-UPA and the Ethnic Cleansing of Volhynia, 1943–1944." *Slavic Review* 75, no. 3 (2016): 630–54.

These findings, however, remain confined within the international academic circles, and have not yet stimulated a significant debate at the national level, where the "heroic narrative" of the UPA soldiers remains central, See: Oksana Myshlovska, "Establishing the 'Irrefutable Facts' about the OUN and UPA: The Role of the Working Group of Historians on OUN-UPA Activities in Mediating Memory-Based Conflict in Ukraine." *Ab Imperio* 1 (2018): 223–54.

[15] The Lemko dialect.

with a refrain where pain and tragedy ooze, emphasized by the complex grammar of the dialect:

> — Mamko j moya, ne lay meni / Zalayesh my v zlu hodynu / Sam ne znayu, de pohynu /
> Hey, pohynu ya v chujim krayu / Hto j my bude braty yamu? / Hey, vyberut my chuji lyudy / Tsy ne jal' ty mamko bude?

> Please don't be mad with me, oh mother. You will scold me in bad times; I don't know where I shall die. I shall die in a faraway land. But who will dig my grave?
> Other people will. Will you take pity on me, oh dear mother?[16]

And the voice of the mother replies, interpreted by the same male choir:

> — Hey, yak by j meni synku ne jal' / Ty j na moyim sertsyu lejav . . . /
> Hey, plyve kacha po Tysyni . . .

> How could I not take pity on you, oh son? You are the one who laid on my heart.
> A duck swims on the river Tysyna . . .

On the screen, thousands of people gather on the square and all sob their hearts out — and so do most of the public around me in the cinema hall. As a ritual of collective mourning is unfolding on the screen something very similar happens in front of it. At this moment, the meaning of the expression "the Opening Ceremony" seems to regain its archaic sense, and a high-definition screening of real events begins to acquire mythological dimensions. The hall is transformed by means of the half-forgotten magic of cinematography — the same that made people run out of the first film screening, organized by the Lumières Brothers — into a ritualistic space of sacrifice, where uninhibited tears flow on both sides of the screen.

When the cinema lights turn on, the song does not stop: Mariana Skadovska (a Ukrainian folksinger) appears onstage, standing in front of the film screen and is holding a hand-pumped organ. There is also a magical quality to her unexpected "materialization" onstage. Without interruption, she goes on singing *Plyve kacha*, this time adding her female voice to the male choir previously heard in the film. The entire audience in the cinema hall stands up.[17] Then, almost without letup, she follows her solo requiem with a coda: the

---

[16] All translations here from Ukrainian into English are by the author.

[17] A similar performance by Mariana Sadovska, "Plyve kacha." YouTube. March 8 2014; https://www.youtube.com/watch?v=8ZFdtFTJfkg.

Ukrainian national anthem. Everybody sings with her. Somebody shouts: "Glory to the Heroes!" Everybody responds almost unanimously: "Glory to Ukraine!"[18] The spontaneous exchange of revolutionary and nationalist slogans among the audience goes on for a while in the still-dark cinema hall. The lights go out and the public starts to leave the place, still under the effect of emotional arousal. The screening is a flawless, unconditional success.

As I leave the cinema hall, I find myself standing alone in front of an incongruently large mirror, so distinctive of Soviet architecture. An endless flow of images and questions crowd my mind: why had the diversity of the protest, so intelligently reflected in the multivocal structure of the film, finally culminated in its viewers chanting the national anthem — a performance of unquestionable loyalty to the state? Why and when exactly did this reification of Ukrainian nationalist narrative happen? During the years that followed, my thoughts have very often come back to *Dom Kino* and this experience, in my numerous discussions and debates about Ukrainian politics. I was thinking especially about the very moment of emotional catharsis, when the ritual of collective mourning transcended the level of representation and spread in the cinema hall. It seemed to consolidate irrevocably the interpretation of the events in a unique narrative. Does it mean that *catharsis* may bear a particular ideological function?

### Interdisciplinary Attempts to Understand Catharsis

*Katharsis* (from κάθαρσις, purification, purgation), an ancient medical term, was used metaphorically by Aristotle in *Poetics* to describe the necessary purification from strong emotions of pity and fear experienced by the audience at the end of a tragedy.[19] Inasmuch as this mixture of feelings is concerned, the so-called "cathartic experience" seems to describe accurately the ways according to which humans deal with pain, trauma and violence, actual or represented.

Due to its enigmatically universalizing dimension, the concept has traveled across epochs and disciplines, acquiring new interpretations and elaborations. As an observable phenomenon, catharsis can be ranged in three broad categories of understanding: psychological, aesthetic, and anthropological. However, even in the recent scholarly literature it is often mentioned that there is no exhaustive definition of what *catharsis* is. Let's face it: there is always

---

[18] These nationalist salutations were used by UPA (Ukrainian Insurgent Army, supra note) during World War II. In 2014, they had become the central slogans of the Maidan Revolution. Nevertheless, there have been a part of pro-Maidan Ukrainians, including myself, who distanced themselves from using them as everyday greetings.

[19] Aristotle, and Anthony Kenny. *Poetics*. Oxford World Classics, 2013.

something mysteriously indescribable about catharsis, that escapes proper scientific categorization.

Since Aristotle, Western aesthetics has been preoccupied with the effect that a scenic representation of fictional or historical events has on its spectators. In aesthetics, catharsis can be defined as the emotional arousal or affective state that occurs when the audience identifies itself fully with the events that are represented on stage — and might be communicated, for example, by a collective standing ovation.[20]

In experimental psychology—the discipline that deployed maximal efforts to "capture" catharsis — it is described as a complex phenomenon, having two aspects. One is cognitive-emotional and consists of the contents of consciousness during the re-experiencing of an emotional event; the second is physical, or somatic-emotional, and consists in a discharge of emotions in tears, laughter or angry yelling. Its effects can also be observed through such physical reactions as "goosebumps," or an accelerated heart rate, which appear when humans experience an unexpected aesthetic or emotional arousal.[21]

In psychotherapeutics that focuses on its healing effects, the notion of catharsis has merged — to the extent that they are used interchangeably — with that of abreaction. Abreaction designates the narrative or performative process of bringing forgotten or inhibited material from the unconscious into consciousness, with concurrent emotional release and discharge of tension and anxiety.[22]

Both initially stemming from the Aristotelian conception of catharsis-as-purification, its understanding in psychology and aesthetics has evolved in two different directions. If understood in the aesthetic sense, catharsis relates to the experience of the spectator, when the events are narrated or performed by the other(s). In the therapeutic sense, catharsis relates to the experiences that occur when the events are narrated or performed by the self, and the other(s)

---

[20] Eva Schaper, "Aristotle's Catharsis and Aesthetic Pleasure," *The Philosophical Quarterly* (1950-) 18, no. 71 (1968): 131–43; https://doi.org/10.2307/2217511; Alan Paskow, "What Is Aesthetic Catharsis?," *The Journal of Aesthetics and Art Criticism* 42, no. 1 (1983): 59–68. https://doi.org/10.2307/429947.

[21] For a foundational study in this particular area of psychoanalytic research, see: Michael P. Nichols and Melvin Zax, *Catharsis in Psychotherapy* (New York: Gardner Press, 1977).

[22] This latter therapeutic understanding was elaborated by legal scholars, who argue that public trials, e.g., the truth and reconciliation commissions (TRCs) bear a "cathartic function" for the community of victims, achieved through a verbalization of their grievances. Here, the "cathartic function" is based uniquely on the subject-oriented understanding of catharsis, and overlooks the performative, theatrical aspects of trials, where complex social relations come into play.

play the role of the audience. This distinction is not pertinent for an anthropological understanding, that tends to think beyond the polarizing differentiation of the self and the other, presenting empirical evidence of when the two may come to unity in a self-transcendental, or transformative experience, involving both the therapeutic and the performative, unfolding at the individual and the social level.

To escape this definitional conundrum, it is important to move away from the debates about what catharsis is and when exactly it occurs, and address the question of what catharsis *does*, both to the self and to the society. There are at least three, not mutually exclusive, instances that are worth thinking of: catharsis as therapy, as (self-)transcendence, and as transformation. Whereas there is a recognized lack of operational definition of catharsis in anthropology, I would argue that an eventual return of interest within the discipline could contribute to an effective bridging of the two distinct lines of thought, that is, the psychological and the aesthetic. This will provide conceptual tools to understand the occurrences and functions of catharsis in modern, non-ritualized social arenas.

Helen Bamber, one of the first therapists to enter the Bergen-Belsen Nazi concentration camp, has provided the world since with an extraordinary account of her own cathartic experience, as mediated by a theatrical performance. In her memoir, she recalls a play performed by and for Holocaust survivors from the recently-liberated camp. The play depicted a typical Jewish family whose everyday domestic evening gathering is suddenly interrupted by Nazi officers who intrude into the home and kill the mother. Bamber writes:

> I have never seen anything so effective, despite the crudity of the stage and the performance, writes Bamber. It was raw and so close to the experience of the audience. There was never any applause.
> Each time was like a purging.[23]

The total absence of applause is something that connects Bamber's poignant account to my experience of the screening of *Euromaidan: Rough Cut*, where too the cathartic moment of collective effervescence obliterated the traditional clapping. In modern autonomous spaces, designated for cultural consumption, the final applause marks the end of the fictional time — what Coleridge has wittily described as the "willing suspension of disbelief" and the return to the ordinary. One may hypothesize that there was no applause in both settings because there was no moment of such a suspension: the narrated events and

---

[23] Helen Bamber quoted in Richard Kearney, "Narrative Imagination and Catharsis," *Kronos* 43, no. 4 (2017), 194.

the audience shared a syncretic temporal regime that was neither entirely fictional, nor historical. To put it differently, the performances in Bergen-Belsen and Dom Kino did not feel *as if* they were real, but actually *were* real for their audiences.[24]

In post-revolutionary Kyiv, this moment of historical/fictional liminality, preceded the moment of what I have described as *ideological reification*. Through the mimetic enactment of a collective mourning — that was not a traditional ritual, but rather a "bricolage" in a Levi-Straussian sense — unfolding on the screen and in the cinema hall, the bounded social arena of people sharing similar aesthetic tastes and tools came apart and was "automatically" embedded into a wider one — the whole Ukrainian nation, permeated by a solidifying consensus about its contours. This moment was the epitome of the political and ideological transition, marking the shift in the way Ukrainians imagine themselves as a nation.

## Anthropological Understandings of Catharsis

In his classical *Violence and the Sacred*, that is the first substantial attempt to present an anthropological model of catharsis, René Girard goes back to Aristotelian theories to analyse the mysterious benefits that accrue to the community upon the death of a human *katharma* (also known as *pharmakos*) — the surrogate victim, chosen haphazardly, and whose sacrifice produces reconciliation inside a polarized society.[25] For Girard, Greek tragedy springs from earlier mythic and ritual forms and provides exceptional material to observe what he calls "the logic of sacrifice," that he considers universal. In his vision, any cathartic action is structurally similar to the catharsis of the sacrificial ritual.

According to this model, sacrifice prevents the escalation of violence by the substitution of a victim who can be killed or injured without triggering a revenge: "Society is seeking to deflect upon a relatively indifferent victim, a 'sacrificial' victim, the violence that would otherwise be vented on its own members."[26] The emotional release and affective "healing" that humans share at the end of a well-structured tragedy, and that in fact constitutes catharsis, is the most rudimentary form of processing the arbitrariness of violence and

---

[24] For an extended discussion on history and catharsis in populations that have experienced extreme political violence, See: Martha Minow, *Between Vengeance and Forgiveness: Facing History After Genocide and Mass Violence* (Boston: Beacon Press, 1998).

[25] Girard, *Violence and the Sacred*, Ibid.

[26] Girard, *Violence and the Sacred*, 4.

injustice, and quite counterintuitively implies reconciliation and restoration of societal harmony.

The sacrificial logic plots the structure of the classic tragedy, which is narratively based on ritualistic and cathartic relics. This powerful narrative script ensures the longevity and, arguably, the universal validity of tragedy as one of the most significant narrative forms. The reliance on violence as the "mechanic engine" of plot construction activates a strong, yet predictable script that is based on a simplifying, reductionist logic. "When the shaman draws forth from his patient an object he identifies as the sickness itself, writes Girard, he is transferring and transforming this mythical interpretation into yet another form—*that of a small, insignificant object.*"[27] Similarly, the cathartic experience decreases the effects of violence by multiple operations of semantic substitution, leading to the resolution of forces that individuals perceive as violent and unjust.

A similar logic of escalation could have been observed on the Maidan and extracted from the *Euromaidan: Rough Cut* footage. In the final segment, which is entitled "All Things Ablaze," Techynsky's camera, semi-blinded by the glow of sun and snow, seems to move chaotically, evading bullets, running around and shooting with groups of armed men. At some point, the cadency of events captured by its "eye" is so rapid, that only death seems to be a valid cause to interrupt its suffocative race. The violence literally becomes the "moving engine" leading and orienting the cameras.

Even now, with a certain distance, it is still striking to observe how the documentary narration whose objectiveness was supposed to be determined by a precise timeline and only direct, camera-in-hand documentation, follows a very classical structure. Similarly to a Greek tragedy, it has its *prologos*, introducing the circumstances, several episodes of *parodos*, capturing the plurivocality of the revolutionary events, underscored by a crescendo of clashes, leading to a tragic *exodus*, coinciding with a moment of sacrifice, where the public experience a collective affect — the *catharsis*, that strikes a final chord in the spiral of violent events depicted onscreen.

The last sequence of Techynsky's film begins with two sentences:

> On February 18-20 the city center saw violent clashes between protesters and the police, resulting in the brutal crackdown and killing of one hundred people. Most victims were shot by snipers in the heart or in the

---

[27] Girard, *Violence and the Sacred*, 287.

head. Two days later, the fourth president of the country, Viktor Yanukovych, fled the country for Russia.[28]

There is, surely, a temporal connection between those two events, but it is still (and will always be) unclear if one can establish a link of causality between the two. However, when it comes to collective memory, a temporal connection is often interpreted as causal. Today, with several years, many people believe — and the plot of the film in a way reiterates this belief visually —that the regime of Yanukovych ran to its end precisely because a hundred Maidan activists had sacrificed their lives.

On a larger scale, the post-Maidan Ukrainian nation tends to imagine itself as a community of those who recognize the essence of the Maidan massacre as a sacrifice in the name of a construction of a different, less authoritarian, less oligarchic and more "modern" state. When watching the film, one ends up having the feeling that the Maidan deaths were not meaningless: after their sacrifice, the "evil" fled the country and the balance of forces was symbolically restored. The deeply emotional cathartic effect of mourning them collectively made this conclusion unquestionable.

However, there is a paradox between the concept of a modern democratic state and the notion of a societal balance built upon a symbolic sacrificial paradigm. According to Girard's model (and this is precisely where its limitations show) sacrificial rites are measures against violence that take place in societies without stateness or those without centralized authority. In "modern cultures" there are no sacrificial rites, since they have been reframed by or delegated to the judicial systems, where violence is "enacted by a sovereign authority specializing in this particular function."[29] In Girard's teleological understanding of social evolution, the establishing of a legal system substitutes and gradually erases *catharsis* as a form of reconciliation. Indeed, the exact opposite may be observed in contemporary Ukraine, where catharsis as an elementary and most immediate form of dealing with violence coexists and is deeply enmeshed with more elaborated forms of justice-seeking and justice-making, achieved through both domestic and international means.

In March 2014, I had a chance to discuss the festival screening of *Euromaidan: Rough Cut* with my students, who had also been in the audience. They shared

---

[28] See the episode "All Things Ablaze," by Oleksandr Techynskyi, in Bondarchuk, Roman, Yulia Gontaruk, Kateryna Gornostai, Andrey Kiselyov, Roman Liubyi, Andriy Lytvynenko, Aleksey Solodunov, Dmitry Stoykov, Oleksandr Techynskyi, and Volodymyr Tykhyy. *Yevromaydan. Chornovyy Montazh (Euromaidan: Rough Cut)*. Documentary. Docudays, 2014. https://vimeo.com/89969382.

[29] Girard, *Violence and the Sacred*, 16.

with me their emotional responses towards what they had seen: some of them confessed that they almost felt shivers running up and down their spine while watching the film. However, not all of them defined this communal experience as positive. One girl, Marichka, acknowledged to me that she was disturbed by the "regulating power" of the experience that she had undergone in the cinema hall: she realized that she was not able to escape, and automatically repeated the gestures — and even emotions — of those who stood around her: standing up, singing the anthem and crying. Afterwards, as she told me, she felt a mixture of sorrow and shame.[30]

Hearing about being driven by an external force is supposed to be nothing strange for a social anthropologist, and yet in practice, it was quite a disturbing experience. Experimental psychologists have observed that the cathartic experience can be so disruptive and cognitively unusual for a human being that it is sometimes described as an experience of a *different self*, external to someone's consciousness.[31] The "automatism" of this momentous change of scale is due to, perhaps, the main physiological characteristics of catharsis, implying the merging of intellectual and emotional responses to an event in a totalizing experience of affect, that involves the so-called "precognitive" body. Classical anthropology alludes that these holistic experiences may be culturally translated as possession by the spirits, or "the whisper of gods." The prescriptive capacity of rituals implies that nonparticipation in these events can bring harmful consequences: those who become possessed and yet fail to follow the instructions of the gods will fall ill or become insane.

Marichka's description is quite close to what I felt myself. Today, with distance, I can confess that the emotional "mixture" I experienced also involved the feeling of shame. Despite my sympathy towards the filmmakers, my activist path, my sincere tears and the lump in my throat I feel every time I hear *Plyve Kacha*, I felt ashamed of my strong, almost uncontrollable physiological reactions towards a nationalism that I don't necessarily defend intellectually, and yet I too was driven by these slogans and songs, as one can be driven by the movement of a crowd. Perhaps an even more disturbing component of this feeling of shame came from an acute presentiment, that this shared collective experience was not a starting point in a long process of justice-making for the massacre, but it's very end — and justice will never be achieved for the victims. I experienced catharsis, but it did not purify me.

---

[30] All names of my interlocutors have been anonymized, except for the filmmakers.

[31] Nichols and Zax, *Catharsis in Psychotherapy*, Ibid.

In the 1980s, anthropologists debated whether rituals channel genuine emotions or provide a space for their codified and socially controlled expression.[32] What our common film-viewing experience suggests to me is that there might be no contradiction between the two. In fact, our feeling of disarray may have come from the observation of our genuine emotions of sorrow, unleashed by the cathartic experience, which immediately came to be controlled, or "captured" by a conventional script of devotion to the state.

This observation chimes with the critique formulated by Bertold Brecht, a Marxist thinker and theatre playwright, who vigorously opposed the notion of "Aristotelian catharsis," as a sort of a simplistic, ready-made resolution for powerful feelings of injustice, communicated by a scenic performance.[33] In his own dramas, Brecht attempted deliberately to subvert the effect of catharsis, leaving significant emotions unresolved on the stage. Brecht reasoned that the absence of catharsis would require the audience to challenge the dominant ideology and to take political action in the real world.[34] The unexpectedly ritualistic dimension of the ending of the Opening Ceremony for Docudays in 2014 didn't leave any unresolved questions: the *pathos* of our mutual cathartic experience, stimulated by the logic of violence and sacrifice, had neutralized the *phronesis* — the imperative for truth-finding.

### Un-cathartic Attempts at National and Supranational trials

Today, seven years after the Maidan deaths, and despite an internationally supervised investigation, none of the cases of sniper shooting has been resolved judicially in a satisfactory way. Justice for the killing of protesters has remained elusive and marred by procedural delays, constant reorganizations of investigative bodies, numerous vague dismissals and self-recusals of judges. A set of controversial "memory laws" were unilaterally passed in April 2015 heavily regulating and restricting all public discussion and activity concerning the Soviet past and especially the period of the Second World War.[35]

The turn of the twenty-first century has instilled new hope in technology, namely the advancement of citizen-driven accountability in response to the

---

[32] Saba Mahmood, "Rehearsed Spontaneity and the Conventionality of Ritual: Disciplines of Şalat," *American Ethnologist* 28, no. 4 (2001): 827–53; https://doi.org/10.1525/ae.2001.28.4.827.

[33] Brecht, *Brecht on Theatre.*

[34] Angela Curran, "Brecht's Criticisms of Aristotle's Aesthetics of Tragedy," *The Journal of Aesthetics and Art Criticism* 59, no. 2 (2001): 167–84.

[35] John-Paul Himka, "Legislating Historical Truth: Ukraine's Laws of 9 April 2015," *Ab Imperio* 21 (2015).

violent states. The Ukrainian Revolution has arguably produced the largest digital archive of evidence of state-driven violence, that happened at the very center of a European city in front of dozens of cameramen, smartphones and security cameras. In 2019 *New York Times* published a minute-by-minute, inch-by-inch reconstruction of the events, co-realized by a Brooklyn-based architectural bureau and Ukrainian activists who utilized artificial intelligence platforms to synchronize the enormous quantity of footage.[36] It is accessible in open source and was accepted as evidence by the Ukrainian court.[37] However, the large amount of available digital footage and data in open source did not lead to a faster and more efficient investigation. The central location of the events has complicated the ballistic expertise, as most bullets disappeared from the crime scene, visited daily by thousands of people. At the very least, the Maidan Revolution has produced a sort of "evidential entropy" in which it has become more apparent in light of recent escalation of war that more evidence in the post-revolutionary years did not produce a better or clearer path for justice.

In 2019, the integral Maidan "super-case" contained a total of 1,973 victims, 89 accusations of murder, 193 suspects, and as many as 9,500 witnesses, including the former President Yanukovych, testifying by videoconference from a Russian court. All the court hearings were broadcasted on YouTube in real time, as were the events on Maidan — however, they were met with much less public interest, generating only several thousand views. Alevtina, an investigative journalist who covered the protests and the trials, told me that "the legal proceedings got lost in their spectacularity. With time, even journalists lost interest in them. This is all too complicated, no one can really follow. The hearings appear crowded, but in the audience, there are only those who are directly concerned: the accused, the victims, and their families."[38] As becomes evident from this testimony, the final trials, and the legal process more generally, did not generate any societal catharsis, neither in a narrative form of truth-telling, nor in a performative form of spectacle.

By the end of 2019, the trial of five former members of the Berkut, accused of the most dramatic shootings that happened on February 20, 2014, rendered in the closing scenes of *Euromaidan: Rough Cut* was close to delivering a final decision. The ending of the trial was quite unexpected, though: prior to the final

---

[36] Mattathias Schwartz, "Who Killed the Kiev Protesters? A 3-D Model Holds the Clues," *The New York Times,* May 30, 2018; https://www.nytimes.com/2018/05/30/magazine/ukraine-protest-video.html.

[37] http://maidan.situplatform.com.

[38] Anonymous correspondence with the author.

decision, all five accused were deported to uncontrolled territories in eastern Ukraine, as part of the exchange of detainees agreed during the peaceful negotiations in Minsk earlier that year. To complicate matters even further, some of these policemen later returned to Ukraine, illustrating the deadlocks of individualized criminal culpability, especially when processes of justice-making are enmeshed in mixed regimes of peace and war.

On December 11, 2020 the Prosecutor of the International Criminal Court (ICC), Fatou Bensouda, released a statement in which she announced that the necessary criteria for opening international investigations into the situation in Ukraine had been met.[39] Her declaration was founded upon "three broad clusters of victimization: crimes committed in the context of the conduct of hostilities; crimes committed during detentions; and crimes committed in Crimea" that were sufficiently grave to warrant investigation by ICC, both in quantitative and qualitative terms.[40] The very fact of dividing victimization into clusters made evident the judicial effort to make sense of the multi-dimensionality of injustice faced by post-Maidan Ukrainian society. This model combines authoritarian, state-driven violence with elements of international armed conflict, conducted "by proxy," and involving local civilian populations and non-state actors, fighting on both sides — and is analogous to the reconfiguration of sovereignties at the Russian-Ukrainian border and beyond, by sea and air.

Bensouda's statement did not mention an important international incident that happened in the Ukrainian airspace in July 2014, namely the downing of an aircraft, flying from Amsterdam to Kuala-Lumpur with 298 passengers, including 80 children on board. All of them were killed by a surface-to-air Buk missile, launched from a territory controlled by the separatists. In 2015 the Netherlands initiated the creation of an *ad hoc* international tribunal, established through the UN system for those responsible for the shooting. Whereas the resolution to establish such a tribunal gained a majority at the UN Security Council, it was subsequently vetoed by the Russian Federation, who bears this right as one of the five "permanent members" of the UNSC.

The Netherlands decided to pursue the investigation domestically and launched a procedure at the European Human Rights Court, to establish facts of human rights violation. The case was thereafter fully investigated by the Dutch court at the Hague, which is coincidentally only a 10-minute drive from

---

[39] Fatou Bensouda, "Statement of the Prosecutor, Fatou Bensouda, on the conclusion of the preliminary examination in the situation in Ukraine," December 11, 2020, Office of the Prosecutor. International Criminal Court; https://www.icc-cpi.int/news/statement-prosecutor-fatou-bensouda-conclusion-preliminary-examination-situation-ukraine.

[40] Bensouda, "Statement of the Prosecutor."

the headquarters of the International Criminal Court. After a year, these proceedings have reached an impasse, as the Russian constitution does not allow the extradition of the alleged offenders to third countries, and the Netherlands High Court does not have jurisdiction over Russian citizens, who are the main suspects in the case. If the ICC investigation of Ukraine reaches trial, it will be the first instance of international justice on the territory of the former USSR. However, if the Russian government refuses to cooperate, the ICC procedure would risk a similar impasse as the one launched by the Netherlands at the international level.

However, the process of truth-finding itself is entrapped in a complicated pattern of multiple, contested sovereignties, that are in their turn tied up in knots of overlapping, and sometimes conflictual, national and international jurisdictions, indicative of the global processes that followed the dissolution of the USSR and the end of the Cold War era. It is evident that, notwithstanding the collected evidence of various political crimes, in Ukrainian society, there has not been a real, articulated demand for a judicial way to restore societal harmony. On the one hand, one can hypothesize that the Ukrainian society has found other ways to ask for forgiveness for a hundred deaths, through multiple collective cathartic expressions of mourning, including the ones that I witnessed in the cinema hall. On the other hand, it seems that a belief in a possibility of a fair trial is not part of the Ukrainian, and more broadly, post-Soviet legal imaginary, that is defined by multiple failures of national and international legal institutions to achieve collective justice over this territory. When placed in this context, the improvised mourning ritual that a small fracture of the urban, middle-class Ukrainian intelligentsia performed in a cinema hall does not appear so illogical, or "archaic."

## Conclusion

This article, inspired by the screening of *Euromaidan: Rough Cut* examines an experimental documentary film ethnographically, recounting very recent revolutionary events, and proposes an anthropological interpretation of a collective cathartic experience of mourning for the deceased protestors that happened after the screening. The first part of the article follows the structure of the film and describes how vernacular visual documentation, alongside networking and aggregation, in reference to Jefferey S. Juris' concepts, contributes to the construction of emerging political communities by mediating a sense of belonging through the production of affectively charged images. In the second part, I turn to the anthropological reconsideration of *catharsis*, understood in reference to Bertold Brecht and René  Girard as a complex psycho-social phenomenon, that implies the merging of intellectual and emotional responses to an event in a totalizing experience, implying therapeutic, transcendental and transformational effects. Arguing against Girard's simplistic model of catharsis, that is rooted in human sacrifice and presents catharsis as a *rudimentary form* of dealing with violence in pre-modern societies, I use the example of contemporary Ukraine to show that cathartic experiences belong to a cultural repertoire of more elaborated forms of social organization and justice-making. This observation complexifies the existent literature on political emotions and affects and urges to recognize the ambivalence of catharsis as an anthropological phenomenon, that, on the one hand, helps individuals and communities to process immediate traumatic experiences, and on the other hand, may serve *ideological reification,* conferring an affective dimension to processes of narrative unification, accompanying ideological transformations.

## Bibliography

Aristotle, and Anthony Kenny. *Poetics.* Oxford, New York: Oxford University Press, 2013.

Bensouda, Fatou. "Statement of the Prosecutor, Fatou Bensouda, on the conclusion of the preliminary examination in the situation in Ukraine." Report. December 11, 2020. Office of the Prosecutor. International Criminal Court. https://www.icc-cpi.int/news/statement-prosecutor-fatou-bensouda-conclusion-preliminary-examination-situation-ukraine.

Bondarchuk, Roman, Yulia Gontaruk, Kateryna Gornostai, Andrey Kiselyov, Roman Liubyi, Andriy Lytvynenko, Aleksey Solodunov, Dmitry Stoykov, Oleksandr Techynskyi, and Volodymyr Tykhyy. *Yevromaydan. Chornovyy Montazh (Euromaidan: Rough Cut).* Documentary. Docudays, 2014. https://vimeo.com/89969382.

Brecht, Bertolt. *Brecht on Theatre: The Development of an Aesthetic.* New York: Farrar, Straus and Giroux, 1964.

Butler, Judith. *Notes Toward a Performative Theory of Assembly.* Cambridge, MA: Harvard University Press, 2015. https://doi.org/10.4159/9780674495548-003.

Curran, Angela. "Brecht's Criticisms of Aristotle's Aesthetics of Tragedy." *The Journal of Aesthetics and Art Criticism* 59, no. 2 (2001): 167–84.

Girard, René. *Violence and the Sacred.* Baltimore: Johns Hopkins University Press, 1979.

Gray, Patty A. "Memory, Body, and the Online Researcher: Following Russian Street Demonstrations via Social Media." *American Ethnologist* 43, no. 3 (2016): 500–510. https://doi.org/10.1111/amet.12342.

Haraway, Donna. *A Cyborg Manifesto: Science, Technology, and Socialist-Feminism in the Late Twentieth Century. Simians, Cyborgs, and Women.* New York: Routledge, 2013. https://doi.org/10.4324/9780203873106-17.

Himka, John-Paul. "Legislating Historical Truth: Ukraine's Laws of 9 April 2015." *Ab Imperio* 21 (2015).

Hornostay, Kateryna and Roman Bondarchuk. "Rozmova z Katerynoyu Hornostay ta Oleksandrom Bondarchukom." (Interview with Kateryna Hornostay and Oleksandr Bondarchuk). *Hromadske telebachennya.* December 20, 2014; https://www.youtube.com/watch?v=MDa8zL8XAR0.

Juris, Jeffrey S. "Reflections on #Occupy Everywhere: Social Media, Public Space, and Emerging Logics of Aggregation." *American Ethnologist* 39, no. 2 (2012): 259–79. https://doi.org/10.1111/j.1548-1425.2012.01362.x.

Kearney, Richard. "Narrative Imagination and Catharsis." *Kronos* 43, no. 4 (2017): 182-196.

Khomenko, Viktoriia. "Euromaidan: Rough Cut." *Docudays.ua*. Blog post. December 1, 2016; http://docudays.ua/eng/2016/news/kino/euromaidan-online-docu-space/.

Mahmood, Saba. "Rehearsed Spontaneity and the Conventionality of Ritual: Disciplines of Şalat." *American Ethnologist* 28, no. 4 (2001): 827–53.https://doi.org/10.1525/ae.2001.28.4.827.

Marcus, G. "Ethnography in/of World Systems: The Emergence of Multi-sited Ethnography." *Annual Review of Anthropology* 24 (1995): 95-117.

McBride, Jared. "Peasants into Perpetrators: The OUN-UPA and the Ethnic Cleansing of Volhynia, 1943–1944." *Slavic Review* 75, no. 3 (2016): 630–54. https://doi.org/10.5612/slavicreview.75.3.0630.

Minow, Martha. *Between Vengeance and Forgiveness: Facing History After Genocide and Mass Violence*. Boston: Beacon Press, 1998.

Myshlovska, Oksana. "Establishing the 'Irrefutable Facts' about the OUN and UPA: The Role of the Working Group of Historians on OUN-UPA Activities in Mediating Memory-Based Conflict in Ukraine." *Ab Imperio* 1 (2018): 223–54. https://doi.org/10.1353/imp.2018.0008.

Nichols, Michael P. and Melvin Zax. *Catharsis in Psychotherapy*. New York: Gardner Press, 1977.

Paskow, Alan. "What Is Aesthetic Catharsis?" *The Journal of Aesthetics and Art Criticism* 42, no. 1 (1983): 59–68. https://doi.org/10.2307/429947.

Pikkardiyska, Tertsiya. *"Plyve Kacha Po Tysyni."* *Eldorado*, Track 6. Rostok Records, 2002.

Rouch, Jean, and Edgar Morin. *Chronique d'un été*. Documentary. Éditions Montparnasse, 1961. http://journals.openedition.org/lectures/7825.

Sadovska, Mariana. "Plyve kacha." YouTube. March 8 2014; https://www.youtube.com/watch?v=8ZFdtFTJfkg.

Schaper, Eva. "Aristotle's Catharsis and Aesthetic Pleasure." *The Philosophical Quarterly* (1950-) 18, no. 71 (1968): 131–43. https://doi.org/10.2307/2217511.

Scheff, Thomas J., and Don D. Bushnell. "A Theory of Catharsis." *Journal of Research in Personality* 18, no. 2 (1984): 238–64. https://doi.org/10.1016/0092-6566(84)90032-1.

Schwartz, Matthathias. "Who Killed the Kiev Protesters? A 3-D Model Holds the Clues." *The New York Times* (May 30, 2018). https://www.nytimes.com/2018/05/30/magazine/ukraine-protest-video.html.

Vertov, Dziga. *Kino-Eye: The Writings of Dziga Vertov*. Berkeley: University of California Press, 1984.

Wellenkamp, Jane C. "Notions of Grief and Catharsis among the Toraja." *American Ethnologist* 15, no. 3 (1988): 486–500. https://doi.org/10.1525/ae.1988.15.3.02a00050.

Chapter 4

# Between Time of Nation and Feminist Time: Genealogies of Feminist Protest in Ukraine

Olga Plakhotnik

Maria Mayerchyk

## Abstract

This paper offers our view on genealogies of Ukrainian feminisms within the time frame 2008-2018. Using an analytic lens of temporality and contesting the Western-centered model of "waves" in the classification of the feminist movements, we explore interconnections between feminisms, nation-state, neoliberalism, coloniality, war, sexuality, and hetero-cis-normativity. Two key concepts of our framework – *feminist time* and *time of nation* – stem from critical theorizing of temporality within a feminist critique of war. The paper's argument is organized around such crucial moments within the studied period as the occurrence of activism evoking *feminist time* in the late 2000s and its disappearance again during the Euromaidan events of 2013-2014. Instead, new feminist activism of *time of nation* emerged and eventually dominated the feminist scene. We conclude that by 2018, the whole set of meanings around "feminism" and "nation" has shifted in Ukraine, thus enabling resignifications and new discursive conformations.

**Keywords**: feminism, nationalism, temporality, Ukraine, postsocialism, Eastern Europe

\*\*\*

In 2003, in the paper titled "Lost between the Waves? The Paradoxes of Feminist Chronology and Activism in Contemporary Poland" Agnieszka Graff stated:

> Polish feminism can be viewed through a series of paradoxes. It is a movement that began its growth by denying its own existence; it uses third wave tactics to achieve goals typically associated with the second

wave of feminism; it exists in a cultural climate of backlash—but this backlash was not preceded by any feminist gains. Finally, as I have tried to show, the political position of anyone involved in the struggle for women's rights in Poland is a paradoxical one.[1]

This ironic conclusion made us think that paradoxes and inconsistencies in the development of Polish (as well as Ukrainian) feminisms are the results of applying the Western classification and periodization of the feminist movement to Eastern Europe. The paradoxes, therefore, are not the immanent characteristic of East European feminism; they occur when the feminist protest (grassroots movements and academic discourse alike) in the postsocialist regions is analyzed through the progressivist model of waves. As a result, we see a set of contradictions, opacities, inconsistencies that unavoidably lead to the conclusion about the backwardness of East European feminisms that must "catch up" with the West. Not in correspondence to the historical facts, this conclusion nevertheless dominates the global feminist discourse. For example, a study of feminism by a Ukrainian scholar has concluded as follows:

> The arrival of the *Feminist Offensive* [in 2010] can be said to signal the *completion* of the formative stage of the women's movement in Ukraine, which now has a *full spectrum* of women's organizations, from the most conservative (traditionalist) to the most radical (anarcho-feminist), including a large segment of feminist groups of the liberal type.[2]

The statement stems from the idea of the upward progress in feminist development. According to this assumption, the women's movement's formation can be completed by exhausting all its known and predefined forms. Interestingly enough, the feminist scene changed in 2014 (*Feminist Ofenzyva* dissolved while some new feminist projects appeared) but the application of the Western taxonomies and "waves" framework to Ukrainian feminism persisted, producing new paradoxes. For example, the authors of the "Invisible Battalion" project stated that women-warriors on the front line of the military conflict in the eastern part of Ukraine pursue a feminist agenda that is typical for the

---

[1] Agnieszka Graff, "Lost between the Waves? The Paradoxes of Feminist Chronology and Activism in Contemporary Poland," *Journal of International Women's Studies* 4, no. 2 (2003): 114.

[2] Oksana Kis, "Feminism in Contemporary Ukraine: From 'Allergy' to Last Hope," *Kultura Enter*, no. 3 (2013). https://www.academia.edu/4890934/Feminism_in_Contemporary_Ukraine_From_Allergy_to_Last_Hope. The author, Oksana Kis, meant *Feminist Ofenzyva*—a grassroots initiative analyzed in the next sections.

"first wave."[3] Does it mean that Ukrainian feminism is progressing back-to-front when the alleged "first wave" comes after the alleged "second wave"? How then do they interplay with the alleged "third wave" (which, as they say sometimes, often fails)?[4]

To propose an alternative view on the genealogies of feminisms in Ukraine, we develop a methodological framework that weaves together the analytic lens of temporality with some ideas from the postcolonial feminist critique. More specifically, we rely upon the segment of postcolonial theorizing, which keeps in a critical focus both colonialism and nationalism, particularly in a postsocialist setting.[5] Two key concepts of our analytic framework—*feminist time* and *time of nation*—stem from critical theorizing of temporality within a feminist critique of war.[6] They are explored in detail in the next section.

The departure point of our investigation is an influential study by Tatiana Zhurzhenko of how feminist discourses in Ukraine participated in the nation-building process.[7] We further elaborated on this line and analyzed how feminisms—and *what* feminisms—intervene in the nation-building orientation and establish a new vision of the future. This paper is a genealogical sketch of feminism in Ukraine between 2008-2018 (that is, the next decade after

---

[3] Our notes are from the presentation by Anna Hrytsenko at the International workshop "Gender and Military Conflicts" organized by the Heinrich Boell Foundation, Lviv, March 9, 2017.

[4] Maria Dmytrieva, FemTalk Presentation. October 19, 2017. Insight LGBTQ NGO Facebook Post. https://www.facebook.com/insight.ngo/videos/1817742665196704.

[5] See: Claudia Snochowska-Gonzalez, "Post-Colonial Poland—On an Unavoidable Misuse." *East European Politics & Societies* 26, no. 4 (2012): 708–23. See also: Leela Gandhi, *Postcolonial Theory: A Critical Introduction* (New York: Columbia University Press, 1998). For a discussion of race see: Vera Šídlová, "Viewing the Post-Soviet Space Through a Postcolonial Lens: Obscuring Race, Erasing Gender," Master of Arts in International Relations and European Studies, Budapest: Central European University, 2013, http://www.etd.ceu.hu/2013/sidlova_vera.pdf; Claudia Snochowska-Gonzalez, "Post-Colonial Poland—On an Unavoidable Misuse," *East European Politics & Societies* 26, no. 4, (2012): 708–23; https://doi.org/10.1177/0888325412448473.

[6] See: Victoria Hesford, "Securing a Future: Feminist Futures in a Time of War," *Feminist Time Against Nation Time: Gender, Politics, and the Nation-State in an Age of Permanent War* (Lanham: Lexington Books, 2008), 169–84.

[7] Tatiana Zhurzhenko, "Ukrainian Feminism(s): Between Nationalist Myth and Anti-Nationalist Critique," *Vienne: IWM Working Paper* 4, 2001; http://iiav.nl/epublications/2001/UkrainianFeminism.pdf; Tatiana Zhurzhenko, "Vpisyvayas' v Diskurs Natsional'nogo: Ukrainskiy Feminism ili Feminism v Ukraine?" *Gendernye Rynki Ukrainy: Politicheskaya Economiya Natsional'nogo Stroitel'stva (Gendered Markets of Ukraine: Political Economy of Nation-Building)* (Vilnius: EHU-Press, 2008), 38–72.

Zhurzhenko's study had been completed). Particular attention has been paid to how feminisms interconnect with nation, state, neoliberalism, coloniality, war, sexuality, and hetero-cis-normativity. Reflecting upon our participation in queer feminist activism, we seek to produce the situated knowledge from within the studied communities and to find an analytic language for researching feminisms in the region, which is typically designated through the "geotemporal" categories of Eastern Europe, post-soviet, postsocialism or Global South.[8]

## Notes on Methodology

Within the conceptual framework of temporality, we define time of nation and feminist time as different modes of thinking and acting that envision and bring into being different futures. *Time of nation* is a linear historical time that relies upon the idea of progress and development: a movement from what is disapprovingly marked as outdated, backward, non-productive, slow, and utopian (but sometimes, paradoxically critiqued as too complicated, tangled, incomprehensive for "ordinary people") towards what is typically approved as progressive, productive, successful, triumphal, and popular among the masses. Feminisms that produce and are productive of the time of nation predominantly struggle for gender equality meaning equal access of women to positions already occupied by men. Thus, the aim of inclusion and visibility of women in the power structures takes over the potential critique of the structures as such. The fight for access to the highest political positions, big business, "Europe," military, and barricades is rooted in the socio-political and economic systems of nation-states, so it does not leave room for critique of the institutions of power and resistance to the systemic hierarchies, neoliberalism, colonialism, and other mechanisms of global inequalities. [9]

---

[8] The term "geotemporal" is from: Joanna Mizielinska, "Travelling Ideas, Travelling Times: On the Temporalities of LGBT and Queer Politics in Poland and the 'West,'" *De-Centring Western Sexualities: Central and Eastern European Perspectives* (Farnham: Ashgate, 2011), 85–106.

[9] During the Euromaidan protests 2013–2014, barricades and other sites deemed "important" were restricted to women. See: "Ukrainian Feminism at the Crossroad of National, Postcolonial, and (Post)Soviet: Theorizing the Maidan Events 2013-2014." *Krytyka.com*. November 2015. https://krytyka.com/en/articles/ukrainian-feminism-crossroad-national-postcolonial-and-postsoviet-theorizing-maidan. Also see: Maria Mayerchyk, "On the Occasion of March 8th/ Recasting of Meanings." Translated by Natalia Godun, edited by Kelly Iacobazzy and Oleh Kotsyuba. *Krytyka.com Blog*. 2014. https://krytyka.com/en/articles/do-8-bereznya-pro-pereplavku-smysliv.

Wartime activates time of nation dramatically. Victoria Hesford calls this temporality "an emergency time of nation and war" where "emergency suggests a direct means of response, which leaves no time for either analysis, forecasting, or prevention. It is an immediate protective reflex rather than a sober quest for long-term solutions."[10] A side-effect of this urgency is that some issues are privileged at the expense of others that are ostensibly less relevant, "not timely" enough. Recent activist debates on a new law draft on same-sex partnerships legalization in Ukraine is a good example of such logic. So far, the property-related rights are substantially privileged in the discussions, while adoption of a partner's children is deemed less important and "untimely" because it can put the entire same-sex partnerships legislation on hold. This case indicates whose rights (in terms of gender, class, race, citizenship, and sexuality) are neglected by the law project and who pays the price for such "justice." It is important to understand that a "proper" time for "others" is always legitimized from the privileged position; it happens only when the political demands of the "others" have already been appropriated, commodified by the neoliberal power, and have become complicit with it. What is happening today with many feminist and LGBT claims in Ukraine illustrates how the time of nation reinforces the dominant system under cover of human rights rhetoric.[11]

*Feminist time* occurs beyond the boundaries of linear time; sometimes, it is designated as mixed/hybrid time because the very idea of linear progressive time has been contested here. Is it progress to destroy local cultures and cosmologies? Is it progress to kill the planet, its flora and fauna? Is it progress to improve and complicate mechanisms of surveillance and control of the population? Is it progress to concentrate resources and wealth in the hands of the constantly diminishing share of people on the Earth? Is it progress to develop various systems of mass destruction? Which societies are considered more progressive—those where prisons are massive, for example, as in the U.S.?[12] Or other societies where jails are fewer in number or absent? Societies which grow their military forces and attack other states, or those which are free from armies? Which future do we strive for, and where do we want to move?

---

[10] Hesford, "Securing a Future," 176.

[11] For more on the dilemmas of human rights discourse within LGBT activism, see: Olga Plakhotnik, "Imaginaries of Sexual Citizenship in Post-Maidan Ukraine: A Queer Feminist Discursive Investigation." Ph.D. Thesis, Milton Keynes: The Open University, 2019. https://doi.org/10.21954/ou.ro.0000f515 .

[12] A fifth of all incarcerated on the planet are jailed in the U.S., according to Roy Walmsley, World Prison Population List 2018 (twelfth edition). https://www.prisonlegalnews.org/news/publications/institute-criminal-policy-research-world-prison-population-list-2018/.

And—is there a connection between the logic of success, security, and progress on the one hand, versus violence and war on the other?

Feminist time stands for a temporality that focuses not on achieving access to the dominant position but on dismantling the structures of domination or finding a way to live beyond them. This is about organizing a world according to other principles than oppression and colonization, success, and progress. Feminist time does not enquire how to overcome racism in the society that engendered racism and slavery; it seeks to build a society where racism and slavery are impossible.[13] It is concerned not about how to win a war in a world where wars are permanent but how to build a world where war does not make any sense. Differently put, feminist time is directed not to victory and success but rather to a "queer art of failure," in Halberstam's words, or "degrowth": the process of searching for the adequate concept continues. Finally, feminist time requires and sets up a new, "perhaps, utopian" ethics.[14] Contrasting to the aims of time of nation that are comprehended as potentially achievable, initially imagined in terms of being feasible and realistic, feminist time is "a struggle without end, a process of endless becoming-other than dominant models, rather than the attainment of recognizable positions and roles that are valued."[15]

In our study, the distinction between time of nation and feminist time presumes simultaneity and co-existence of two modes of temporality as well as the possibility to combine them both in a feminist activist agenda. Our aim is not to create a binary opposition but to delineate a conceptual framework for analyzing the feminist debates, movements, and resistance in Ukraine within the one-decade period 2008-2018. Following an understanding of genealogy as "history of the present," the following three sections circumscribe three key moments (snapshots) in the development of feminist discourses through the analytic lens of temporality.[16]

---

[13] Judith Halberstam, *The Queer Art of Failure* (Durham: Duke University Press Books), 2011.

[14] Victoria Hesford and Lisa Diedrich, eds. *Feminist Time Against Nation Time: Gender, Politics, and the Nation-State in an Age of Permanent War* (Lanham, MD: Lexington Books, 2008), 12.

[15] Elizabeth Grosz, "The Time of Thought." In *Feminist Time Against Nation Time: Gender, Politics, and the Nation-State in an Age of Permanent War*, edited by Victoria Hesford and Lisa Diedrich (Lanham: Lexington Books, 2008), 52.

[16] For "history of the present" see: Michel Foucault, *Society Must Be Defended: Lectures at the College de France*. Translated by David Macey (New York: Picador), 2003.

## Moment One: Time of Nation Interrupted

According to Zhurzhenko, before 2008 (the starting point of our study), individuals rather than collectives used "feminist" self-nomination in Ukraine. The flourishing activism aimed at women's rights and gender equality was ideologically inscribed into the discourse of nation-building: "Borrowed from Diaspora women's organizations, the idea of the primacy of Ukrainian statehood became the ideological basis for the emerging Ukrainian women's movement." [17] This position was justified by another scholar, Marta Bohachevsky-Chomiak, who insisted that nationalism and feminism in Ukraine are "two sides of the same coin" that leads to independence for the nation and emancipation for women. [18] Both Bohachevsky-Chomiak and Zhurzhenko used the term "national feminism" to designate this discursive formation; we call this: feminism evoking the time of nation.

Long-lasting domination of time of nation in feminist discourse was interrupted around 2008-2010 by the occurrence of a new activism that proposed a new vision of the feminist agenda. We analyze it using the case of two Kyiv-based groups, FEMEN and *Feminist Ofenzyva*. This choice is determined by our positionality in the field: we had become closely familiar with FEMEN in the course of our study at that time, and were personally involved in Feminist Ofenzyva. [19] Being acutely aware of the limits and biases of our positionality that prevented us from seeing other activism in other regions of Ukraine, we consider the two analyzed groups as a case in point for the main argument of our study. [20]

The case of FEMEN is particularly interesting for analysis because the group received fierce, sometimes merciless criticism from women's NGOs and

---

[17] Tatiana Zhurzhenko, "Ukrainian Feminism(s): Between Nationalist Myth and Anti-Nationalist Critique." *Vienne: IWM Working Paper* 4 (2001). http://iiav.nl/epublications/2001/UkrainianFeminism.pdf .

[18] Martha Bohachevsky, "Natsionalism ta Feminism—Odna Moneta Spil'noho Vzhytku." (Nationalism and Feminism are the Same Coin). *Yi: Nezalezhnyi Cul'turolohichnyi Chasopys*, 17 (2000): 4–13.

[19] Maria Mayerchyk and Olga Plakhotnik. "The Radical FEMEN and The New Women's Activism." *Krytyka* 10, no. 11-12 (November 2010): 157-158. https://krytyka.com/en/articles/radical-femen-and-new-womens-activism.

[20] In another publication, we analyze one more case of activism that evoked feminist time—the *Svobodna* collective, See: Maria Mayerchyk and Olga Plakhotnik. "Mizh Kolonial'nistiu i Natsionalismom: Henealohii Feministychnoho Aktyvismu v Ukraini (Between Coloniality and Nationalism: Genealogies of Feminist Activisms in Ukraine)." *Feminist Critique.com*. July 2019. https://feminist.krytyka.com/ua/articles/mizh-kolonialnistyu-i-natsionalizmom-henealohiyi-feministychnoho-aktyvizmu-v-ukrayini.

gender/ feminist communities. One of the reasons why FEMEN were denied being called feminists is that their form of activism —"sextremism," in their definition — did not fit Western taxonomies, so it could not be recognized as feminist at all. This discrepancy looks the most striking when FEMEN's famous performances (slim young women stripped their breasts and wrote protest slogans on their bodies) are analyzed through the concept of *sexism*. As a result, the glamorously looking bodies of activists were typically recognized as an unambiguous manifestation of sexism. What matters, however, is that the concept of sexism was coined within a feminist critique of capitalist bio-politics and Western history of fashion and consumption.[21] Being used for the analysis of feminism in Eastern Europe, it entails a conclusion about the "fictitious" feminism of FEMEN as if their activism reinforces the patriarchal objectification of women's bodies. This idea has significantly dominated feminist discourse in Ukraine and beyond. The Ukrainian article about FEMEN in Wikipedia states that "the *real* feminist organizations criticized FEMEN's actions and consider them *discrediting* the feminist movement."[22]

We are not commenting on a chauvinism of the quoted statement but would like to note that the same "feminist movement" also lamented someday to be discredited by LGBT activism and, recently, by the transgender agenda.[23] Instead, we want to stress the important aspects of FEMEN's activism that slip away from the lens of sexism: the protest was performed by precarious bodies of young women in a poor country who lived without stable jobs or income and were subjected to police brutality and constant cyber-violence. Since these post-Soviet bodies inherited the memory of women's life beyond the Western-type industry of beauty and fashion, the glamour of FEMEN had totally different meanings. Importantly, these bodies were used not for the sale of goods but to convey critical political statements. After all, it was one of the first civil initiatives that publicly refused to support the legitimacy of President Yanukovych. When in 2011, the President announced a press conference to answer questions from civil society, many feminist- and gender-equality organizations did send their queries (which were partly ignored by the

---

[21] Sandra Lee Bartky, "Foucault, femininity, and the modernization of patriarchal power." *Writing on the body: Female embodiment and feminist theory* (New York: Columbia University Press), 1997.

[22] FEMEN. Wikipedia page. Accessed November 19, 2019: https://uk.wikipedia.org/wiki/FEMEN

[23] For example, in the ground rules of the *Feminist UA* community on Facebook, analyzed later in this paper, any support of transgender activism is prohibited because it is considered a misogynist practice. *Feminism.UA Facebook Group*. Main Page. Accessed October 1, 2021: https://www.facebook.com/groups/feminism.ua/about/.

President and partly commented formally), thus legitimizing the status quo of the power regime. FEMEN, on the contrary, came to the central square in Kyiv with the only eloquent question drawn on the piece of cardboard "Where did you so fucking come from?" (Figure 4.1). The activists commented: "We don't have any other questions for the current President."[24]

**Figure 4.1.** Activist of FEMEN with a placard on Maidan Nezalezhnosti. Source: © Ivona.bigmir.net portal. [25] Reproduced with permission.

As we argued elsewhere and are convinced still, the postcolonial feminist lens would allow reading FEMEN's activism in a more nuanced way, at least their activity before 2013 when they were forced to flee from Ukraine after a series of physical attacks on activists and the brutal police search in their office.[26] In our view, FEMEN should be analyzed through the lens of post-Soviet temporality, which was invaded by the neoliberal capitalist economy together with the newly emerged neo-patriarchal model of women's body. When mobilized politically for the feminist struggle (notably, with zero budget, especially at the beginning), this body model produced an explosion-like effect. Though this was not recognized by the main part of the feminist communities, Ukrainian

---

[24] *Ivona.ua.* "Femen Yanukovycha: Otkuda ty takoi py?" (Femen to Yanukovych: where are you from?). News Post. February 25, 2011. https://ivona.ua/shou-biz/novosti/5277925-femen-janukovichu-otkuda-ty-takoj-pi.

[25] The image is reproduced here with permission from ivona.bigmir.net portal.

[26] Mayerchyk and Plakhotnik, "The Radical FEMEN and The New Women's Activism," 147.

and international alike, we see FEMEN's activism as subversive and provocative. While not all their performances align with the logic of feminist time, FEMEN had created a precedent for such a way of thinking and acting in Ukraine.

The fate of *Feminist Ofenzyva* turned out differently.[27] Founded in 2010 as a radical separatist feminist initiative, the group actively participated in the street protest actions and organized feminist rallies in Kyiv on March 8 supplemented by a "feminist week"—a series of public events, including cinema festivals, conferences, women's art exhibitions and workshops, and so on.[28] But in contrast to FEMEN, the political activism of *Feminist Ofenzyva* was consistently pushed out of public space by the media as well as the mainstream NGOs pursuing a gender equality agenda. The article about *Feminist Ofenzyva* in Wikipedia was deleted in 2015 because, as Wikipedia's administrators commented, the page has a "doubtful significance." According to Wikipedia's politics, the page must refer to sources that are different from the website of the organization: "The importance of the *Feminist Ofenzyva* has not been proved by the independent, trustworthy sources. Most of the references lead to the organization's website." A sheer scarcity of media reports about the group means that the mainstream media mostly ignored *Feminist Ofenzyva*. While the notice about *Feminist Ofenzyva* was restored in Wikipedia in 2017 owing to the efforts of several ex-activists of the group, such a fate in media space is telling. We assume it to be a result of the *Feminist Ofenzyva's* agenda that often transgressed time of nation through the critique of the nation-state, for example, "Stop covering inequality by traditions" or "Church and state, it's time for separation" slogans.[29]

In sum, FEMEN and *Feminist Ofenzyva* were very different groups aimed at different missions, acting from different political positions, and pursuing different activist strategies. But exactly their activism has formed a starting momentum for feminist time in Ukraine, not the "completion of the formative stage of the women's movement in Ukraine," as the earlier quotation suggested. Notwithstanding the differences, the groups had a substantial commonality: they were among the first conformations of stable feminist collective solidarities in contrast to rather individual feminist positionality, which prevailed earlier.

---

[27] In the Halychyna regional dialect of Ukrainian the word *ofenzyva* signifies an attack or fight.

[28] See more about *Feminist Ofenzyva. Website. Wordpress.com.* https://ofenzyva.wordpress.com/. For more about Feminist Ofenzyva and their "Women's Work Unit" workshop, See: Olenka Dmytryk, " 'I'm a Feminist, Therefore . . . : ' The Art of Gender and Sexual Dissent in 2010s Ukraine and Russia." *Journal of Soviet and Post-Soviet Politics and Society (JSPPS)* 2, no. 1 (2016): 137–78.

[29] Mayerchyk, "On the Occasion of March 8th/ Recasting of Meanings."

They were also among the first initiatives that refused to follow the lead of the mainstream NGOs and assimilate/ negotiate with the state: writing and signing petitions, teaching government authorities how to avoid sexism in their rhetoric, collaborating with state institutions, and advocating legislative reforms, especially these that reinforced the punitive power of the state. They were among the first grassroots initiatives that were not substantially rooted in the Western grant economy, so their positionality and activist strategies were not dictated directly by the politics of donor organizations.[30] Finally, for some coincidence (or not), both groups ceased their activity in Ukraine by the end of 2013.

New challenges for Ukrainian feminisms emerged following the events of Euromaidan (2013–2014) that lasted for almost three months and went through both peaceful and violent phases. It was a dynamic process, concluding with the fall of President Yanukovych's regime. Being closely followed by the annexation of Crimea by the Russian Federation and the war in the eastern part of Ukraine, it signifies the beginning of dramatic political transformations in society, including feminist communities.[31]

### Moment Two: Euromaidan as a "Lost Opportunity" for Feminist Time

We have borrowed a "lost opportunity" phrase from the art exhibition of the same name by David Chychkan. The project was exhibited at Visual Culture Research Center in 2017 and sought to express the artist's belief that Euromaidan has turned out to be a "lost opportunity" of society to envision and articulate a new political-social order in Ukraine. Soon after the opening, the exhibition was attacked and vandalized by a neo-Nazi group. In line with the artist's point, we consider the "lost opportunity" motto relevant to Ukrainian feminism, too. Feminist activism of Euromaidan that started with radical left-wing oriented claims has gradually turned back to the bosom of the nation-state during the about three months of the protest. In the course of the Euromaidan events, feminist time stopped; instead, a new activism of time of

---

[30] We elaborate on the relations between NGO-ized and grassroots activisms and the grant economy in "Uneventful Feminist Protest in Post-Maidan Ukraine: Nation and Colonialism Revisited." In *Postcolonial and Postsocialist Dialogues: Intersections, Opacities, Challenges in Feminist Theorizing and Practice,* edited by R. Koobak, M. Tlostanova & S. Thapar-Björkert. (New York: Routledge, 2021), 121-137. https://doi.org/10.4324/9781003 003199-11

[31] Despite the absence of the word "war" in the official titles of what was occurring in the eastern part of Ukraine beginning in Spring 2014 (namely, "anti-terrorist operation," "the military conflict," etc.), we use the word "war" because it corresponds to our political positionality and personal experience.

nation emerged and eventually dominated the field. While we have analyzed the dynamics of feminist temporality during Euromaidan in more detail elsewhere, in this paper, we focus on two extreme points: feminist initiatives at the beginning (November 2013) and the end (February-March 2014) of Euromaidan.[32]

It is not widely known that within the first week of the protest in 2013, several feminist and leftist actions took place at the Euromaidan venue. There is evidence that all of them were attacked by men from the ultra-right groups:

> **27 November.** Activists of social movements and independent trade unions have joined together to hold such slogans as "Freedom, Equality, Sisterhood"; "Europe Means Equality"; "Who fears gender, should not go to Europe"; "Organize trade union instead of praying the European Union"; "Glory to the Ratio" (mocking a nationalist greeting "Glory to the Nation" that already has been heard from everywhere). [33] Then an accusation of provocation has been voiced out loud from the Euromaidan's podium. As a result, a group of ultra-right men calling themselves "security of Euromaidan" pulled out the placards from their holders' hands and displaced activists from the square by force.

> **28 November.** About 30 masked thugs from the conservative party "Right sector,"[34] armed with tear gas sprayers and shouting "Glory to the nation, death to enemies!" attacked a women's rights street action that was taking place under the slogans "European salaries for Ukrainian Women" and "Europe means paid maternity leave."[35]

---

[32] Mayerchyk and Plakhotnik, "Ukrainian Feminism at the Crossroad of National, Postcolonial, and (Post)Soviet: Theorizing the Maidan Events 2013-2014."

[33] The slogans "Glory to Ukraine, glory to heroes!" and "Glory to the nation, death to enemies!" were created in the Ukrainian Insurgent Army—a Ukrainian nationalist paramilitary and later partisan army during World War II. Before Euromaidan, the slogans were mostly used by right-wing nationalist groups. During and after Euromaidan, they have become popular greetings amongst the broader patriotically oriented population in Ukraine. This process of legitimation was finalized in August 2018 when "Glory to Ukraine, glory to heroes!" became the official greeting of the Ukrainian military.

[34] "Right Sector" (*Pravyi Sektor* in Ukrainian) is a far-right Ukrainian nationalist political party that originated in November 2013 as a paramilitary confederation at the Euromaidan protest in Kyiv where its members fought against the armed police.

[35] Kravchuk, Yustyna. "Pro Tyh Hto 'Sie Rozbrat' na Maidani/On Those Who 'Sow Discord' on Maidan." June 12, 2013. *Krytyka.com*. https://krytyka.com/ua/community/blogs/pro -tykh-khto-siie-rozbrat-na-maydani.

**Figure 4.2.** Feminist action on Euromaidan, November 27, 2013.
Source: © Internet portal *Racurs*.[36] Reproduced with permission.

After this evidence was published, some readers wondered whether the attackers were actually provocateurs whose aim was to discredit Euromaidan. We ask a different question: how did it happen that the massive part of the

---

[36] Notably, the publication's title "At Euromaidan, clashes have happened because of far too sophisticated placards" points to the publisher's ironic disapproval of the feminist action and sympathy for the attackers. November 27, 2013. *Racurs.ua.* Blog News Post. https://racurs.ua/ua/n18878-na-ievromaydani-stalasya-sutychka-cherez-zanadto-rozumni-plakaty-foto.html.

Euromaidan protesters did not condemn these attacks? On the contrary, some public intellectuals admonished feminist activists to refrain from their ostensibly untimely claims not to provoke right-wingers, not to "sow discord" on Euromaidan (this is why the paper by Justyna Kravchuk is ironically entitled "On those who 'sow discord' on Maidan").

The slogans held within the disrupted actions are indicative of the political positionality that underpinned feminist activism during the first week of Euromaidan. However, in the course of the protest, this positionality did not strengthen and a resolute dissociation from the ultra-right agenda did not happen. Quite the opposite, this feminist positionality has been minimized, rolled down, and veiled; eventually, feminisms at Euromaidan have become inscribed to the "emergency time of nation." The launch of the group *Zhinocha Sotnya* (Women's Squad) became a climactic event within this process. [37] Though it was initiated by feminists of various political views, including leftist, anarchist, and lesbian activists, the groups as such consciously followed the principle "to not irritate ultra-right groups" and declared that "political views of any members of *Zhinocha Sotnya* are their private affair." [38] In doing so, *Zhinocha Sotnya* positioned itself as apolitical or politically neutral. It was also notable that the group "did not position itself as a feminist" for "strategic reasons." [39] It did not explicitly aim to introduce women's rights principles to "segments of the population previously reluctant to embrace feminism." [40]

The methodological framework of our study enables another perspective on *Zhinocha Sotnya's* claims for political neutrality. To begin with, using the "squad" wording in their name, the group inscribed itself into the militarized structure of Euromaidan and thus legitimized the dominant militarized

---

[37] While several Women's Squads were active at the final stage of the Euromaidan events, our analysis is focused on the "Women's Squad named by Olha Kobylyanska," which was established by a group of self-identified feminists. For the sake of brevity, we refer to this organization using "Zhinocha Sotnya" as shorthand.

[38] *Zhinocha Sotnya*. Facebook Page. https://www.facebook.com/pg/zhinocha.sotnya/about/?ref=page_internal .

[39] Olesya Khromeychuk, "Gender and Nationalism on the Maidan." In *Ukraine's Euromaidan. Analyses of a Civil Revolution,* edited by David R. Marples and Frederick V. Mills. (Stuttgart: Ibidem-Verlag 2015), 128.

[40] Sarah D. Phillips, "The Women's Squad in Ukraine's Protests: Feminism, Nationalism, and Militarism on the Maidan." *American Ethnologist* 41, no. 3 (2014), 415. https://doi.org/10.1111/amet.12093.

discourse.[41] On their Facebook page, *Zhinocha Sotnya* was visualized using folklore motifs (female figures with long plaits dressed in embroidered shirts and wearing red boots) combined with such attributes as military helmets, whips, Molotov cocktails, batons, etc. Also, *Zhinocha Sotnya's* members widely promoted an idea to rework a traditional nationalist greeting "Glory to heroes!" into "Glory to heroines!" as more concordant to gender equality principles. Notably, they did not problematize either the first part of the greeting —"Glory to Ukraine!"— or another variant, "Glory to the nation, death to enemies!" Finally, women's self-defense classes were the most popularized (and popular indeed) activity of *Zhinocha Sotnya*. But how did such opposing discourses as a critique of violence and operationalization of violence coexist in the group's agenda? As feminist scholarship on militarization has argued, the very idea of "defense" is produced through and productive of the normalization of violence.[42]

These observations lead us to the conclusion that *Zhinocha Sotnya* was neither an apolitical nor a neutral organization. The entire group's agenda — claims for women's access to (all) military structures and venues, self-defense classes, rejection of the feminist self-naming for the sake of attracting masses, uncritical use of the right-wing slogans — reproduced the time-of-nation discourse. All these elements fit neatly with prioritizing the nation-state and seeing women as an essential part of the nation-building project. The absence of attempts (and refusal to recognize the importance of such attempts) to detach themselves from the right-wing ethos of Euromaidan but, instead, their cooperation with ultra-right structures and forms of protest pumped blood into the increasing right-wing discourse of Euromaidan. Hence, *Zhinocha Sotnya* did not oppose but rather contributed to the hegemony of time of nation, simultaneously supporting and legitimizing the right-wing turn in Ukraine. The fact that the military commandant of Euromaidan has publicly approved the launch of *Zhinocha Sotnya* — something that is an object of the group's pride — serves to be an additional argument in favor of this conclusion.

Not to confuse the reader: the ultra-right groups did not dominate Euromaidan in terms of numbers; this was proved by the numerous quantitative surveys. But the surveys could not measure discursive domination

---

[41] *Sotnya* (squad) stands for the unit division in the Ukrainian Cossacks male-only military structure that existed in the early modern times and was reconstructed at Euromaidan.

[42] See, for example, Cynthia Enloe, *Globalization and Militarism: Feminists Make the Link* (Rowman & Littlefield, 2016); and "Theory Talk #48: Cynthia Enloe on Militarization, Feminism, and the International Politics of Banana Boats." *Theorytalks.org.* May 22, 2012. http://www.theory-talks.org/2012/05/theory-talk-48.html.

of the right-wing ideology that presumes heroization of men's militaristic parades, sacralization of victims, mythologization of barricades, justification of violence, and dehumanization of a newly produced "enemy." As it was initially shown by Ukrainian scholars Anastasiya Ryabchuk and Maria Mayerchyk, the minoritarian of right-wing discourse eventually seized the logic and strategies of civic resistance and dominated Euromaidan.[43] In line with this conclusion, we argue that this happened not without the support of *Zhinocha Sotnya*, among other groups and units. As a result, feminist time disappeared, melting away during the three months of the Euromaidan events. In the context of growing violence and then war, a new militarized discursive formation of the emergent time of nation has produced a new understanding of rightness and justice, which literally swept away much slower anti-nationalist, anti-colonial, anti-capitalist, anti-hierarchical feminist approaches and visions.

### Moment Three: Feminist Complicity with Nationalism and Militarization

After the occupation of Crimea, a war broke out in the eastern part of Ukraine and continues until now. What kind of response to these events has been developed by the already prevailing feminism evoking time of nation? Firstly, after Euromaidan feminism became more popular; self-identified feminist groups became massive and more visible in public space. This contrasted with the situation in the mid-2000s when feminist discourse existed as a self-identification of individuals but not collectives.[44] In our view, one of the reasons why previously marginalized self-identification has gradually transformed into something like the mainstream is the recasting of meanings with respect to feminism. Almost non-alternative domination of the time-of-nation paradigm has produced new meanings and shadows of feminism that brought about its complicity with the nation-building process and patriotic mobilization of the population for the war. Two cases analyzed below exemplify two aspects of such

---

[43] Maria Mayerchyk, "Seizing the Logic/ A World Without Women." Translated by Vladislava Reznik. *Krytyka.com Blog.* 2014. https://krytyka.com/en/articles/zakhoplennya-lohik-svit-bez-zhinok ; Anastasiya Ryabchuk, "Right Revolution? Hopes and Perils of the Euromaidan Protests in Ukraine." *Debate: Journal of Contemporary Central and Eastern Europe* 22, no. 1 (2014): 127–34. https://doi.org/10.1080/0965156X.2013.877268.

[44] Tatiana Zhurzhenko, "Vpisyvayas' v Diskurs Natsional'nogo: Ukrainskiy Feminism ili Feminism v Ukraine?" *Gendernye Rynki Ukrainy: Politicheskaya Economiya Natsional'nogo Stroitel'stva (Gendered Markets of Ukraine: Political Economy of Nation-Building).* Vilnius: EHU-Press, 2008: 38–72. Also see: Tatiana Zhurzenko, "Ukrainian Feminism(s): Between Nationalist Myth and Anti-Nationalist Critique." *Vienne: IWM Working Paper* 4 (2001). https://www.academia.edu/3312252/UKRAINIAN_FEMINISM_S_BETWEEN_NATIONALIST_MYTH_AND_ANTI_NATIONALIST_CRITIQUE.

complicity: a "nationalist feminist" positionality in feminist communities and the instrumentalization of feminism by the war machinery.

The Euromaidan events boosted the popularity of the particular self-designation used explicitly by individuals and collectives: "nationalist feminism." *Feminism UA*, the largest feminist online community on Facebook that grew with accelerating speed after 2014, is a case-in-point.[45] Notably, the group justifies its collective identity as follows:

> We are a postcolonial state, a postcolonial nation, so we can't escape nationalism... Not a nationalism, but the *bil'shovytskyi* imperialism has led Ukrainian feminism to the dead end, which has strangled both feminism and nationalism.[46] That is why we should not refuse nationalism but claim it back. We must take it back from the right radicals and re-appropriate it. I propose a placard for the next rally: "Feminism is the Ukrainian national idea."[47]

While the reference to postcoloniality is typical in the "nationalist feminist" narratives, we are not asking whether Ukraine *is* a postcolonial state and the ongoing war between Ukraine and Russia *is* an anti-colonial struggle. Instead, we are more concerned with what a rhetoric of postcoloniality *does* in the Ukrainian feminist discourse, what symbolic-material effects it produces. In this regard, we rely on postcolonial feminist scholarship and corresponding feminist critique in Central and Eastern Europe, which stresses that the uncritical application of postcolonial rhetoric (i.e., when it is used to signify a status of the nation-state, not an analytic tool) often opens the door to right-wing nationalistic projects.[48] We conclude that the *Feminism UA* community uses the label of postcoloniality in the sense of the geopolitical status of the nation-state but hardly as a framework for feminist analysis. Otherwise, the community would be more concerned with the solidarity of women and other vulnerable groups across the front line *to stop* the war instead of aligning with the nationalist obsession about *winning* the war.

---

[45] By November 2021, the *Feminism.UA* community had united more than 12,000 members. See: *Feminism.UA Facebook Group.*

[46] *bil'shovytskyi* (Ukrainian) refers to the adjectival form of Bilshovyk.

[47] An anonymized Facebook comment in *Feminism.UA*, March 2017. Following the ethical assumptions of Internet-mediated research, we use only quotations from public domains and anonymize them. All the translations from Ukrainian into English in the quoted materials are ours.

[48] Gandhi, *Postcolonial Theory: A Critical Introduction*; Šídlová, "Viewing the Post-Soviet Space Through a Postcolonial Lens: Obscuring Race, Erasing Gender." ; Snochowska-Gonzalez, "Post-Colonial Poland—On an Unavoidable Misuse."

Another case of instrumentalization of feminism by the war machinery is an "Invisible Battalion" project about women in the Ukrainian military taking part in the war in the eastern part of Ukraine. This large-scale project includes documentary films, mobile photo exhibitions, and a sociological study focused on "an issue of integration of women to the military" and aimed at the promotion of "visibility of women and recognition of their equal contribution in comparison with men."[49] The rhetoric of visibility and recognition is particularly telling about the project's positionality since, in Hesford's words, feminist claims for equal representation "collapse into the mythologizing that structures the temporality of nation at war," meaning that such feminist politics become "indivisible from those of the nation-state."[50] In this regard, an epigraph that opens the "Invisible Battalion" research report is telling:

> I know a girl who rescued wounded soldiers under the fire in Illovaysk when most of the men were hiding in a cellar.[51] If a wife, or a mother, or a sister, or a daughter desire to defend our values and our territory, nobody can forbid this.[52]

From our perspective, the choice of an epigraph is not a random pattern. From the very outset, the quotation produces a romanticized gendered time of the nation and, typically for this temporality, constructs women through kinship, matrimonial status, and reproduction. Though the study criticizes inequality and exclusion of women, and the consecutive advocacy campaign really helps *some* women in *some* military structures, it does not prevent the project from being a part of the political economy of war. As Daria Popova wrote, "the initiative to include more women and other minorities into war may definitely be successful inasmuch as it can be easily inscribed into the nationalist discourse."[53] Referring to Nira Yuval-Davis's prominent study, Popova noted that a launch of a "people's army" which includes both men and women facilitates legitimating the state government and particular regimes of

---

[49] Tamara Martsenyuk, Hanna Hrytsenko, and Anna Kvit, "'Nevydymyi Bataliyon': Uchast' Zhinok u Viys'kovykh Diyah v ATO." ('Invisible battalion': Women Taking Part in ATO Military Action) Kyiv: Ukrainian Women's Fund UWF), 2016: 1. http://ekmair.ukma.edu.ua/handle/123456789/7746.

[50] Hesford 2008, 175.

[51] Illovaysk is a town in Ukraine where the bloodiest battle happened in Summer 2014.

[52] Martsenyuk, Hrytsenko, and Kvit, "'Nevydymyi Bataliyon': Uchast' Zhinok u Viys'kovykh Diyah v ATO." ('Invisible battalion': Women Taking Part in ATO Military Action), 1.

[53] Daria Popova, "Viyna, Natsionalism ta Zhinoche Pytannya (War, Nationalism and A Women Question)." Commons 10 (2016). https://commons.com.ua/uk/vijna-nacionalizm-ta-zhinoche-pitannya/.

power.[54] The inclusion of women can also be a strategy for recruiting the population to the military. By means of heroization and romanticization of women at war, the "Invisible Battalion" project also contributes to the production of the national politics of grief that defines whose death is grievable (female warriors) and whose is not (women who remain on the occupied territory).[55]

Finally, focusing on the visibility and representation of women in the army, the project does not leave room for critique or, at least, analytic attention to the military structures as such. For example, the study report includes pictures and testimonies of female warriors from the *Aidar* Battalion, the unit known for its close connections with neo-Nazis. The international human rights watchdog organization Amnesty International accused the *Aidar* Battalion of committing war crimes, including abductions, unlawful detention, theft, extortion, and possible executions.[56] These aspects are omitted in the study as if the participation of women in particular military formations renders these very structures above suspicion.

## Conclusion

In this paper, we propose a sketch of genealogies of Ukrainian feminisms within the time frame 2008-2018. Looking at the feminist scene through the analytic lens of temporality and contesting the progressivist Western-centered model of "waves" in the feminist movement, we organized our argument around three moments. Firstly, we show how, around ten years ago, the long-lasting domination of time of nation in Ukrainian feminism was interrupted by the occurrence of new activism evoking feminist time. In the first part of the chapter, we analyzed how a starting momentum for a feminist time was formed in particular by such groups as FEMEN and *Feminist Ofenzyva*. Secondly, we examine how, in the course of the Euromaidan events of 2013-2014, feminist time disappeared from public discourse for a while; instead, new feminist activism of time of nation emerged and eventually dominated. It appeared that feminist initiatives born on Euromaidan did not oppose but rather contributed to the hegemony of time of nation, simultaneously supporting and legitimizing

---

[54] Nira Yuval-Davis, *Gender and Nation*. SAGE, 1997.

[55] Judith Butler, *Precarious Life: The Powers of Mourning and Violence* (New York: Verso, 2004); *Frames of War: When Is Life Grievable?* (New York: Verso, 2009).

[56] Amnesty International, "Ukraine must stop ongoing abuses and war crimes by pro-Ukrainian volunteer forces." September 8, 2014. https://www.amnesty.org/en/latest/news/2014/09/ukraine-must-stop-ongoing-abuses-and-war-crimes-pro-ukrainian-volunteer-forces/.

the right-wing turn in Ukraine. Thirdly, in the aftermath of Euromaidan, the explicit "feminist *and* nationalist" collective positionality, as well as feminist projects inscribed in the nationalist ideology, massively appeared on the activist and scholarly scene. Never before the feminist discourse was so popular in Ukraine; never before the combination of feminism and militarized nationalism was so much normalized in public discourse. In our view, the whole set of meanings around "feminism" and "nation" has shifted in Ukraine after Euromaidan, thus enabling new discursive conformations.

Notwithstanding the significant domination of the nationalist feminist discourse, complicity with nationalism is not the only feminist response to the right-wing political turn and anti-colonial war. Feminist initiatives that pursue both anti-nationalist and anti-colonial political agendas do exist in Ukraine. We consider them to constitute a relatively new form of feminist activism: "uneventful protest," as we call it, borrowing the term from Elżbieta Korolczuk and Kerstin Jacobsson's study of urban activism in Central and Eastern Europe. It designates activism that is "low-key, small-scale, and initiated by individuals or small, informal groups, and little discussed in the mass media and public discourse."[57] Being typically omitted by Western scholarship and barely visible in the framework of Western aid grant economies, this activism evokes feminist time through its simultaneously anti-nationalist and anti-colonial, anti-militarist, anti-racist, and anti-capitalist agenda.[58] This gives us hope that resistance and resilience are possible even in such an extremely troubling time as that we live in Ukraine today.

### Acknowledgments

This chapter was previously published in *Feminist Circulations between East and West (German: Feministische Zirkulationen zwischen Ost und West).*[59] We are thankful to Frank & Timme Publishing House for permitting us to reprint it here. We also owe our gratitude to all colleagues and comrades who commented on this study during our presentations in the Fulbright Program office in Kyiv in April 2017 and the *Queer Necropolitics* Summer School in Uzhgorod in August 2019.

---

[57] Jacobsson and Korolczuk, "Mobilizing Grassroots in the City: Lessons for Civil Society Research in Central and Eastern Europe." 130.

[58] Mayerchyk and Plakhotnik, "Uneventful Feminist Protest in Post-Maidan Ukraine."

[59] Maria Mayerchyk and Olga Plakhotnik, "Between Time of Nation and Feminist Time: Genealogies of Feminist Protest in Ukraine." *Feminist Circulations between East and West / Feministische Zirkulationen zwischen Ost und West.* A. Bühler-Dietrich, ed. (Berlin: Frank & Timme Verlag 2019), 47-70.

# Bibliography

Amnesty International. "Ukraine must stop ongoing abuses and war crimes by pro-Ukrainian volunteer forces." September 8, 2014. https://www.amnesty.org/en/latest/news/2014/09/ukraine-must-stop-ongoing-abuses-and-war-crimes-pro-ukrainian-volunteer-forces/.

Bartky, Sandra Lee. "Foucault, femininity, and the modernization of patriarchal power." *Writing on the body: Female embodiment and feminist theory.* New York: Columbia University Press, 1997.

Bohachevsky, Martha. "Natsionalism ta Feminism—Odna Moneta Spil'noho Vzhytku." (Nationalism and Feminism are the Same Coin). *Yi: Nezalezhnyi Cul'turolohichnyi Chasopys,* 17 (2000): 4–13.

Butler, Judith. *Precarious Life: The Powers of Mourning and Violence.* Verso, 2004.

_____. *Frames of War: When Is Life Grievable?* New York: Verso, 2009.

Dmytrieva, Maria. FemTalk Presentation. October 19, 2017. Insight LGBTQ NGO Facebook Post. https://www.facebook.com/insight.ngo/videos/1817742665196704.

Dmytryk, Olenka. " 'I'm a Feminist, Therefore . . . :' The Art of Gender and Sexual Dissent in 2010s Ukraine and Russia." *Journal of Soviet and Post-Soviet Politics and Society (JSPPS)* 2, no. 1 (2016): 137–78.

Enloe, Cynthia. "Theory Talk #48: Cynthia Enloe on Militarization, Feminism, and the International Politics of Banana Boats." *Theorytalks.org.* May 22, 2012. http://www.theory-talks.org/2012/05/theory-talk-48.html.

_____. Globalization and Militarism: Feminists Make the Link. New York: Rowman & Littlefield, 2016.

FEMEN. Wikipedia page. Accessed November 19, 2019. https://uk.wikipedia.org/w/index.php?title=FEMEN&oldid=24675624.

*Feminism.UA Facebook Group.* Main Page. Accessed October 1, 2021. https://www.facebook.com/groups/feminism.ua/about/.

Foucault, Michel. *Society Must Be Defended: Lectures at the College de France.* Translated by David Macey. New York: Picador, 2003.

Gandhi, Leela. *Postcolonial Theory: A Critical Introduction.* New York: Columbia University Press, 1998.

Graff, Agnieszka. "Lost between the Waves? The Paradoxes of Feminist Chronology and Activism in Contemporary Poland." *Journal of International Women's Studies* 4, no. 2 (2003): 100–116.

Grosz, Elizabeth. "The Time of Thought." In *Feminist Time Against Nation Time: Gender, Politics, and the Nation-State in an Age of Permanent War,* edited by Victoria Hesford and Lisa Diedrich. Lanham: Lexington Books, 2008: 41–56.

Halberstam, Judith. *The Queer Art of Failure.* Durham: Duke University Press Books, 2011.

Hesford, Victoria. "Securing a Future: Feminist Futures in a Time of War." In *Feminist Time Against Nation Time: Gender, Politics, and the Nation-State in an Age of Permanent War,* edited by Victoria Hesford and Lisa Diedrich. Lanham, MD: Lexington Books, 2008, 169–84.

Hesford, Victoria, and Lisa Diedrich, Eds. *Feminist Time Against Nation Time: Gender, Politics, and the Nation-State in an Age of Permanent War.* Lanham, MD: Lexington Books, 2008.

*Ivona.ua.* "Femen Yanukovycha: Otkuda ty takoi py?" (Femen to Yanukovych: where are you from?). News Post. February 25, 2011. http://ivona.bigmir.net/showbiz/stars/306585-FEMEN-Janukovichu--Otkuda-ty-takoj-pi.

Jacobsson, Kerstin, and Elżbieta Korolczuk. "Mobilizing Grassroots in the City: Lessons for Civil Society Research in Central and Eastern Europe." *International Journal of Politics, Culture, and Society* 33 (2020): 125–142. https://doi.org/10.1007/s10767-019-9320-7 .

Khromeychuk, Olesya. "Gender and Nationalism on the Maidan." In *Ukraine's Euromaidan. Analyses of a Civil Revolution,* edited by David R. Marples and Frederick V. Mills. (Stuttgart: Ibidem-Verlag 2015), 123–146.

Kis, Oksana. "Feminism in Contemporary Ukraine: From 'Allergy' to Last Hope." *Kultura Enter,* 3 (2013). https://www.academia.edu/4890934/Feminism_in_Contemporary_Ukraine_From_Allergy_to_Last_Hope.

Kravchuk, Yustyna. "Pro Tyh Hto 'Sie Rozbrat' na Maidani/On Those Who 'Sow Discord' on Maidan." June 12, 2013. *Krytyka.com.* https://krytyka.com/ua/community/blogs/pro-tykh-khto-siie-rozbrat-na-maydani .

Kristeva, Julia. "Women's Time." *Signs* 7, no. 1 (1981): 13–35.

Martsenyuk, Tamara, Hanna Hrytsenko, and Anna Kvit. "'Nevydymyi Bataliyon': Uchast' Zhinok u Viys'kovykh Diyah v ATO." ('Invisible battalion': Women Taking Part in ATO Military Action) Kyiv: Ukrainian Women's Fund (UWF), 2016. http://ekmair.ukma.edu.ua/handle/123456789/7746 .

Mayerchyk, Maria. "On the Occasion of March 8th/ Recasting of Meanings." Translated by Natalia Godun, edited by Kelly Iacobazzy and Oleh Kotsyuba. *Krytyka.com Blog.* 2014. https://krytyka.com/en/articles/do-8-bereznya-pro-pereplavku-smysliv.

———. "Seizing the Logic/ A World Without Women." Translated by Vladislava Reznik. *Krytyka.com Blog.* 2014. https://krytyka.com/en/articles/zakhoplennya-lohik-svit-bez-zhinok (Accessed 16 November 2019).

Mayerchyk, Maria and Olga Plakhotnik. "The Radical FEMEN and The New Women's Activism." *Krytyka* 10, no. 11-12 (November 2010): 157-158. https://krytyka.com/en/articles/radical-femen-and-new-womens-activism.

———. "Ukrainian Feminism at the Crossroad of National, Postcolonial, and (Post)Soviet: Theorizing the Maidan Events 2013-2014." *Krytyka.com.* November 2015. https://krytyka.com/en/articles/ukrainian-feminism-crossroad-national-postcolonial-and-postsoviet-theorizing-maidan.

———. "Mizh Kolonial'nistiu i Natsionalismom: Henealohii Feministychnoho Aktyvismu v Ukraini (Between Coloniality and Nationalism: Genealogies of Feminist Activisms in Ukraine)." *Feminist Critique.com.* July 2019. http://feminist.krytyka.com/ua/articles/mizh-kolonialnistyu-i-natsionalizmom-henealohiyi-feministychnoho-aktyvizmu-v-ukrayini.

———. "Between Time of Nation and Feminist Time: Genealogies of Feminist Protest in Ukraine." In *Feminist Circulations between East and West / Feministische Zirkulationen zwischen Ost und West,* edited by A. Bühler-Dietrich. (Berlin: Frank & Timme Verlag, 2019), 47-70.

_____. "Uneventful Feminist Protest in Post-Maidan Ukraine: Nation and Colonialism Revisited." In *Postcolonial and Postsocialist Dialogues: Intersections, Opacities, Challenges in Feminist Theorizing and Practice,* edited by R. Koobak, M. Tlostanova & S. Thapar-Björkert. (New York: Routledge, 2021), 121-137. https://doi.org/10.4324/9781003003199-11

Mizielinska, Joanna. "Travelling Ideas, Travelling Times: On the Temporalities of LGBT and Queer Politics in Poland and the 'West.'" *De-Centring Western Sexualities: Central and Eastern European Perspectives.* Farnham: Ashgate, 2011.

Phillips, Sarah D. "The Women's Squad in Ukraine's Protests: Feminism, Nationalism, and Militarism on the Maidan." *American Ethnologist* 41, no. 3 (2014): 414–26. https://doi.org/10.1111/amet.12093.

Plakhotnik, Olga. "Imaginaries of Sexual Citizenship in Post-Maidan Ukraine: A Queer Feminist Discursive Investigation." Ph.D. Thesis, Milton Keynes: The Open University, 2019. https://doi.org/10.21954/ou.ro.0000f515 .

Popova, Daria. "Viyna, Natsionalism ta Zhinoche Pytannya (War, Nationalism and A Women Question)." Commons 10 (2016). https://commons.com.ua/uk/vijna-nacionalizm-ta-zhinoche-pitannya/

*Racurs.ua.* Blog News Post. November 27, 2013. https://racurs.ua/ua/n18878-na-ievromaydani-stalasya-sutychka-cherez-zanadto-rozumni-plakaty-foto.html.

Ryabchuk, Anastasiya. "Right Revolution? Hopes and Perils of the Euromaidan Protests in Ukraine." *Debate: Journal of Contemporary Central and Eastern Europe* 22, no. 1 (2014): 127–34. https://doi.org/10.1080/0965156X.2013.877268 .

Šídlová, Vera. "Viewing the Post-Soviet Space Through a Postcolonial Lens:

Obscuring Race, Erasing Gender." Master of Arts in International Relations and European Studies, Budapest: Central European University, 2013. http://www.etd.ceu.hu/2013/sidlova_vera.pdf.

Snochowska-Gonzalez, Claudia. "Post-Colonial Poland—On an Unavoidable Misuse." *East European Politics & Societies* 26, no. 4 (2012): 708–23. https://doi.org/10.1177/0888325412448473.

Walmsley, Roy. World Prison Population List 2018 (twelfth edition) http://www.prisonstudies.org/sites/default/files/resources/downloads/wppl_12.pdf (Accessed 16 November 2019).

Yuval-Davis, Nira. *Gender and Nation.* SAGE, 1997.

*Zhinocha Sotnya.* Facebook Page. https://www.facebook.com/pg/zhinocha.sotnya/about/?ref=page_internal

Zhurzhenko, Tatiana. "Ukrainian Feminism(s): Between Nationalist Myth and

Anti-Nationalist Critique." *Vienne: IWM Working Paper* 4 (2001). http://iiav.nl/epublications/2001/UkrainianFeminism.pdf .

_____. "Vpisyvayas' v Diskurs Natsional'nogo: Ukrainskiy Feminism ili Feminism v Ukraine?" *Gendernye Rynki Ukrainy: Politicheskaya Economiya Natsional'nogo Stroitel'stva (Gendered Markets of Ukraine: Political Economy of Nation-Building).* Vilnius: EHU-Press, 2008: 38–72.

# Chapter 5

# "As Never Before": The Body and Revolution in the Ukrainian Worlds of Natalka Husar and Lesia Khomenko

Jessica Zychowicz

**Abstract**

This chapter explores representations of the female body, gender, and class by two women artists: an American-born Canadian-Ukrainian (b. 1951) and a Kyiv-born Ukrainian (b. 1980). Husar and Khomenko are from different generations, different countries, and different "waves" of feminists if one examines them from the standpoint of the representational politics of their works' embedded social contexts. Yet there are many similarities: Khomenko, like Husar, utilizes the human form in large-format paintings of groups of people and crowds; both artists place objects and stylistic details in their paintings from the visual diction of "local" Ukrainian early Soviet modernism, late socialist realism, and the "global" pop idiom of television, print, mass media, and fast fashion of the consumption patterns of working-class men and women. Both look "outside" at the unfamiliar, and at lived memory, producing a unique language of Ukrainianess: the Soviet generations and the aesthetics of that era, are reworked as a backdrop for their depictions of the human form. Both artists paint bodies and portraits of faces, mediating their own, individual historical and geographical connections to the people inside the paintings. The circumstances of the people in these paintings would, in their everyday appearances, seem to be "obsolete" — they are themselves outsiders: impoverished, poor, working-class women, gay, mafiosi, and even a "has-been" as Husar names one of her heroines. By examining time, place, and identification with Ukrainianness as both heritage in the case of Husar, and a new generation's aesthetic turn in-between two revolutions (Orange and Maidan), in the case of Khomenko, I conclude that the post-Soviet context is best understood as a global condition. Through close readings, theoretical framing, and archival context, this chapter argues for an alternative to the reductivism of "progress" as a mandated category, where queer identities and feminist identities come to stand for the right of the individual to define themselves and their own set of values. What shared features do places and times considered "contemporary" merit in these terms with regard to concepts of freedom? Are these similar or different qualities to the "universal community" in Natalka Husar's comment of 1984 on her own artistic task, with regard to the concept of "contemporary Ukraine" as it was not in 1998, but how it is perceived in light of concepts of freedom today?

**Keywords**: revolution, aesthetics, post-Soviet, historiography, Canadian-Ukrainian, feminism, socialist realism

***

In 1984, during a conference on Canadian-Ukrainian culture, the American-born Canadian-Ukrainian painter Natalka Husar (b. 1951), then thirty-three years old, remarked:

> I was born American, raised Ukrainian and my status is Canadian — a hyphenated consciousness reinforced by anger and guilt, and, of course, there is going to be evidence of this in my work....Nevertheless, I am in it for life. I do art because I have to. The content is always very specific, usually biographical. Sometimes, if I am lucky, the concept is universal . . . I depict the universal characteristics of human nature specifically through Ukrainian people because I am Ukrainian, and therefore I see myself in my work. Only by confronting that which I hate can I resolve my guilt and see that which I love.[1]

When asked by a participant in the audience: "Would Natalka Husar consider the audience for her paintings to be the Ukrainian or the universal community?" she responded: "The universal community."[2] What could possibly be meant here by the universal community? And what might Husar be telling us that we might perceive in her paintings, with regard to history, and the people in them — are these people capable of revealing to us some "truth" that we, in our individual understandings of ourselves in relation to history, cannot access on our own?

In 1989, a decade before her untimely and tragic death, famed literary scholar and feminist from Kyiv, Solomea Pavlychko, found herself in Edmonton, Canada as a visiting professor at the University of Alberta where she began working on an anthology that would bring together literary voices from Ukraine and the Canadian-Ukrainian diaspora. The resulting volume is graced with not

---

[1] Natalka Husar, "The Relevance of Ethnicity to the Artist's Work: Personal Perspectives." In *Visible Symbols: Cultural Expression Among Canada's Ukrainians,* edited by Manoly R. Lupul (Edmonton: Canadian Institute of Ukrainian Studies, 1984), 37.

[2] Ibid., 43.

one, but two Introductions, the first penned by Pavlychko. Being from Ukraine and having lived through the turbulent decade of the 1990s after the fall of the Soviet Union, she inscribes a specific moment, but does so by positioning the texts in the volume and their Ukrainian authors within a concept of time marked by gender: "the return, after a long period of silence or some puzzling boycott of socialist realism, of women." The end of the Soviet Union, for her, is a revolutionary paradigm that means overcoming "the most optimistic era of Ukrainian history," of everything "saccharine" that "spawn[s] terrible fantasmagorical plots, a world without dawn or hope." From the old world of Soviet utopianism, new processes of *world-ing* take its place, in which the Red Army brigades' and their officers' promises wither away into the fading backdrop of marching bands and parades that now deliver "a pessimistic minor key, an interest in the dark side of consciousness."[3]

The second Introduction to the volume is by the Canadian-Ukrainian writer and scholar Janice Kulyk Keefer. She remarks that the primary difference between the authors from Ukraine and those from Canada are the latter's striving to articulate their ethnos and histories vis-à-vis a dominant mainstream, a task that requires "transformation." This task relies on subject-position, though it is not dependent upon it, as it is "indispensable for any artist: that of being both within and outside of a formative community, of being free to observe, analyse, and judge as you will, without the kind of censorship so often exacted by blind loyalty to 'our own.'" In her view, pointing out injustices, contradictions, hypocrisy, and cruelty is the crucial task of the writer and the artist, who for her are interchangeable. Kulyk Keefer addresses her Introduction to Canadians "of whatever background" and sets before all readers a great challenge to understand not only a place, but another sense of time: "of discovering something of what it is like to live in contemporary Ukraine — the hopes and frustrations, the continuing shock of the old and the comparable shock of a runaway and often hostile "new."[4] This sense of time is revolutionary time, a break from teleological narratives under the spell of the USSR; it is time stripped from organized labor, hierarchical public/private divides, and production quotas. It is all free time, all time outside of the public domain; it is a woman's time, embodied time.

---

[3] Solomea Pavlychko, "Introduction." In *Two Lands, New Visions: Stories from Canada and Ukraine*, edited by Janice Kulyk Keefer and Solomea Pavlychko (Regina: Coteau Books, 1998), iv, iii.

[4] Janice Kulyk Keefer, "Introduction." In *Two Lands, New Visions: Stories from Canada and Ukraine*, edited by Janice Kulyk Keefer and Solomea Pavlychko (Regina: Coteau Books, 1998), xii-xiv.

And with this "new" sense of time is mapped a new Ukraine. This charting of history is defined by the term "contemporary Ukraine," mirrored at the end of both Introductions, tethered to 1991. Pavlychko writes:

> "As never before" — these are the words used most frequently to characterize contemporary Ukraine as well as its literature. Indeed, Ukrainian life is, as never before, dramatic, dynamic, multifaceted, and creatively and intellectually stimulating. The atmosphere of liberty and constant change that has lasted for years now is inebriating as never before.[5]

What shared features do places and times considered "contemporary" merit? Are these similar or different qualities to the "universal community" in Natalka Husar's comment of 1984 on her own artistic task, with regard to the concept of "contemporary Ukraine" as it was not in 1991, but how we perceive it today in 2021?

Natalka Husar would later travel with Janice Kulyk Keefer to Ukraine in 2005, where the latter would write a collection of texts, and the former create a series of paintings, published together as *Foreign Relations/Burden of Innocence*.[6] On one level, this return to their parents' homeland would seem to revert to traditional values in an act of cultural preservation and heritage work, at odds with the break from the Soviet past taking place at the same time. Yet the distance and temporal removal of their familial emigration out of "the old country" as well as their lives lived in Canada, as Canadians, makes them outsiders to the community in contemporary Ukraine, in Kulyk Keefer's sense, "free to observe, analyse, and judge as you will." Is it possible that the "contemporary," more than Ukraine or Canada, is the universal community, the global condition for which their art strives?

In 2007, shortly after 2005, the year Natalka Husar was traveling in Ukraine and working on the paintings that would later become *Burden of Innocence*, the painter Lesia Khomenko (b. 1980) was mounting her series *Dacha's Madonnas*, featuring large-format canvases of elderly women with robust figures working in the fields. The citation of the socialist realist pastoral harvest scenes of the prior century was clear, but the clothing, colors, and perspectives in the paintings introduced to Ukrainian art something "new." This something was not new, in essence, but newly visible: in Pavlychko's sense, the return of women, old rural women, invisible women, to the platform of "contemporary" art. Lesia Khomenko, from Kyiv, is a founding member of the R.E.P. Group, a non-hierarchical affiliation of approximately twelve artists who found common

---

[5] Pavlychko, "Introduction," viii.

[6] Janice Kulyk Keefer and Natalka Husar, *Foreign Relations/Burden of Innocence* (Ukraine: Rodovid, 2009).

ground after the Orange Revolution in their growing interest in exploring public spaces, post-Soviet aesthetics, and theories and practices of direct democracy.[7]

Husar and Khomenko are each from different generations, different countries, and different "waves" of feminists if one examines them from the standpoint of the equally progressive, yet divergent, representational politics of their works' embedded social contexts. Yet there are many similarities between these two painters. Khomenko, like Husar, utilizes the human form in large format paintings of groups of people, crowds; both artists place objects and stylistic details in their paintings from the combined — clashing —visual diction of "local" Ukrainian early Soviet modernism, late socialist realism with the "global" pop idiom of television and print, mass media, and fast fashion in the consumption patterns of working-class men and women. Khomenko, like Husar, is an artist looking "outside" at what is unfamiliar to her, but within reach of living memory, couched in a familiar but inaccessible language of Ukrainianess: her parents' Soviet generation and the aesthetics of that era, reworked as a backdrop for their living memories. Husar, by contrast, encounters the Soviet ghost differently — by looking at its contours wherever the Ukraine that her parents left appears as a backdrop for understanding the people she painted on her travels in Ukraine.

Both artists paint bodies and portraits of faces, but as "outsiders" they do so with a great deal of distance in mediating the connection to the people inside the paintings. Characters appear and reappear within and across series; rarely are individuals named, rather the titles of the paintings frame their larger social fabric with irony, humor, even sarcasm. *Dacha's Madonnas*, for example, is at once an elevation of the field laborer to holy icon, a recognition of women's work as the backbone of the Ukrainian family food chain, an inversion of the church's role in policing proper conduct for women, and an interrogation of conformist standards of beauty (subjects are in indiscreet poses with buttocks facing the viewer, bent wrinkly knees, etc.). By bringing these two artists together in a closer exploration of their work, we can identify a few additional shared features along with those named above. The layers of time referents in their paintings mark decline and yet introduce a dynamism that opens up space for reflection on the reductivism of "progress" as a mandated category, rather than individually defined set of values. The circumstances of the people in their paintings would, in their everyday appearances, seem to be "obsolete" — they are themselves outsiders: impoverished, poor, working-class women, mafiosi, and even a "has-been" as Husar names one of her heroines. The

---

[7] R.E.P. Group (Revolutionary Experimental Space), *R.E.P.: Revolutionary Experimental Space: A History*, edited by Lada Nakonechna, translated by Larissa Babij, Mariana Matveichuk, Weronika Nowacka, Anastasiya Osipova, and Olena Sheremet (Berlin: The Green Box, 2015).

everyday, as subject, is reclaimed from the dregs of socialist realism providing the backdrop for these painters' historical commentary on the post-Orange revolutionary moment, layered over post-1991. The once second/first world and bipolar Cold War are set in relief against globalization.

## Dead Artists' Paints — A Visual Language for Time

For Natalka Husar, "to paint history is to paint the truth." Husar's and Janice Kulyk Keefer's aforementioned trip to Ukraine took place just after the Orange Revolution, which entailed peaceful mass demonstrations in public spaces against election fraud in the presidential elections. The outcome of the journey, like the revolution, was fruitful. Kulyk Keefer produced several texts and a cycle of poems under the heading *Foreign Relations*, which were published together in a book featuring Husar's series of paintings she created, *Burden of Innocence*. These many sized paintings were exhibited in Canada by the McMaster Museum of Art from November 2009 until 2011. Husar painted the works in the series using what she calls "dead artists' paints":[8] tubes of heavy metal pigments, most too toxic for today's market standards, that she collected in street markets of Ukraine, or by negotiating with local museums. A close-up color photograph of these corrugated, chipped, and rusty tubes of paint lines the inside of the published book. The names of the colors in Cyrillic on the tubes are only partially visible, due to the oxidation processes eating away at the label over what appears to be decades. These metal capsules double as a mirror of the defunct, dilapidated, hulking Soviet metal structures everywhere in Ukraine in the 2000s, as well as a frame, an ersatz door, into Husar's passage into and through the scenes she encounters and reimagines.

The curator of the McMaster Museum, Carol Podedworny, has written of Husar's relationship to painting in the context of the genre of "history painting" in post-revolutionary France, when painters left the studio and focused not on grand narratives, but humble everyday life instead of classical, mythological, or religious scenes. She compares Husar's preoccupation with the ordinary to Goya, Daumier, and Hogarth, but adds that "Husar's Ukraine is seen from the outside in, through eyes of someone brutally honest and in despair." The critical agenda is to develop further the language of painting for a "current artistic vocabulary," while also "to create a critical thematic response for the record of a State in its current social, political, and cultural moment."[9] Husar's published notes that accompany the series *Burden of Innocence* describe it as

---

[8] Husar, "Burden of Innocence." In Kulyk Keefer and Husar, *Foreign Relations/Burden of Innocence*, 14.

[9] Carol Podedworny and Gerta Moray, et. al. *Husar Handbook* (Macdonald Stewart Art Centre: ABC Art Books Canada, 2010), 30, 29.

"a history play in three acts." Act I, "Nurse and Stew," features the artist in her dual avatars as a nurse and stewardess; Act II, "Trial" includes the group of paintings called *Soviet Priesthood*, of burly men who look like they have stepped out of a series of mugshots, and whose brutal masculinity speaks of a world mired in corruption and lawlessness, where the individual struggle for honor necessarily takes on Shakespearian magnitude. The third and last Act is "Banquet" and the grand finale is the painting *Looking at Art* (2009) in which the artist's alter-egos Nurse and Stew serve empty platters to a cadre of characters from the other paintings: a young girl impacted by Chernobyl now grown up, a leather-clad bald man, and an overwrought "has-been" whose expression is unequivocally Husarian — captured so as to rest forever on canvas in that indistinguishable state between laughter and sobs. Such is the history of Ukraine.

While traveling in Ukraine, Husar collected various photographs, prints, and folk paintings along the way. Husar has spoken about these found images as ghosts: "Hanging in my studio as I was painting my own work, these anonymous portraits felt like ghosts of innocents from a bygone era."[10] These "ghosts" come to populate the project, appearing almost as interlopers in the series' intertextual references between the other characters and their environments. A detailed pencil sketch of a photograph of a boy soldier is smuggled into this "contemporary" art series by the subversive hand of Husar and given the title *Soldier* (an anonymous portrait from the 1940s). We are not given any information about him, but can see from the star on his uniform he was in the Red Army. Later, in another painting there is another young boy of approximately the same age, roughly ten years old, but he is wearing all black and the title is simply *Boy in Uniform* (an anonymous portrait from early twentieth-century Ukraine). The weary expression on his face, formal stance, and shaved head indicate that he may also be a soldier, or a revolutionary; the latter is more likely the case, given the background of the image, which is pastoral and split evenly between a blue sky and yellow-green earth — a way of organizing the sight plane of the canvas that mirrors the stripes of the Ukrainian flag and its sky-over-grain. A third boy, also roughly ten, appears in a different painting in a new guise: an adidas tracksuit and clenched fist, at the edge of a traffic jam in a rain-soaked village road at night. Stew and Nurse are in the background with a babusia (grandmother) figure selling weights on a home scale on the side of the road. The small mafia-soldier boy stares at us; he could be from a Shevchenko painting, or recently released from prison. His face portends a difficult future, a life of hardship ahead in a world gone bad. Husar's despair is felt most clearly in the faces of these children, whose innocence becomes not only Ukraine's burden, but the burden of the painter to bring to

---

[10] Quoted by Stuart Reid in Podedworny, Moray, et. al. *Husar Handbook*, 41.

light what came before her — the dead artists, whose deaths left no evidence of revolution, only the admission of loss. The "ghosts" Husar refers to hover over the most defining historical event of these territories of the twentieth century: the Bolshevik revolution and the Soviet experiment, which left millions and millions interned, starved, imprisoned, and dead. Artists were the first to go.

What makes the intertextual elements of the series especially powerful is that the point where the references cross is in the found portraits, and it is at these points precisely that the "world" of Husar's imagination becomes most *Ukrainian.* A young girl-child in the found painting *Maiden by the Well* (anonymous folk portrait, early twentieth century) conjures up a key moment in history: after the folk romanticism of the nineteenth century, but during or just before the targeting and killing of rural Ukrainian peasants in the Soviet dekulakization campaign and the stifling of national expression under Stalinism. The repetition of this image in the pastoral painting *Seedspitter* (2006-08) of a young woman in a short leather skirt and boots in a garden is styled after the folk artist Kateryna Bilokur. Bilokur's artistic associations with Ukraine were brave, as they were largely forbidden in the 1930s-40s, as well as her successful struggle, against the will of her father, to continue drawing. The citation of Bilokur in Husar's scene could only be one of prostitution (the car leaving the scene in the background, and the ironic title). This scene, also in reference to the nineteenth-century "found portrait" of the maiden by the well, can be read as Husar's commentary on the timelessness of an issue as stemming from patriarchal control over young women. Patriarchal control over women mirrors the state's control over artists. And in this version of affairs, a state that no longer has any reason to support or justify artistic expression, the girls wind up prostitutes and the boys mafiosi.

Husar reveals by omission the time gaps in history. All of the found images are images of children, save for one: *Ukraine and Me* (2007). The backdrop of this painting is a folk-style painting on linen from the early twentieth century. Husar's two alter-egos, Nurse and Stew, cling to each other on a bridge. In the foreground a woman in a peasant-style dress crosses the bridge; her two-dimensional round features match the socialist realist painting common to the style of the artists surrounding Mykhailo Boichuk in the 1920s, including Olenka Pavlenko, whose famous painting *Long Live 8th of March!* (1930-31) depicted a crowd of rural women in peasant dress with red flags. The woman in Husar's painting is left at the end of the bridge, alone, with no one behind her; it is almost as though the original, unknown, artist of the painting had been waiting for Husar to fill in the rest of the picture. The effect is also of a "ghost," but this time Husar herself is the ghost rather than the person depicted in the found image. By adding her own likeness in dual form in the painting, in her own style, she also adds her artistic signature: reconfirming her right to exist as an artist, as a woman, as a woman-artist in all guises.

The fact of mass execution of Ukrainian artists in the 1930s, beginning with Boichuk and his followers, is pinned onto the painting in the form of Husar's grammar, which reveals the time gap between the original and the present tense. Moreover, Husar's addition showing herself in dual roles is her gift to what others have written about as "difficult heritage," as otherness, in her own Canadian context, where to be Ukrainian and female has not only meant being perceived as "alienated and rebellious" under an Anglo gaze, but within the Ukrainian immigrant community as "guilty of rejecting traditional restraints and values, and of succumbing to the vulgar and superficial in the Canadian lifestyle."[11] If we return once more to this painting to "read" it not as an artifact of where Husar found it, in Ukraine, but as if it were found in her more immediate context, in hyphenated Canadian-Ukraine, the representational qualities will shift. This gap in place mirrors the time gap. This painting could then be said to resemble those precious remnants among families in Canada that are displayed in their homes as the few prized possessions that were taken by their ancestors to the "new country." Of nominal or no value, even mass-produced, these folk paintings stand in for the story of immigration to Canada that, not unlike the propaganda of early Soviet socialist realism, also demanded certain roles from women at different points in time.[12]

Historian Frances Swyripa in *Wedded to the Cause: Ukrainian-Canadian Women and Ethnic Identity 1891-1991,* takes a long-range view of Canada and Ukraine as intertwined civic projects in which women take up the social positions available to them at different points in time on either side of the ocean:

> With the consolidation of organized community life and the hardening of ideological lines between the wars, the question of community influence over individuals grew in importance as nationalist and progressive elites sought to popularize their perceptions of what was best for Ukraine and for Ukrainians in Canada... Now military and political defeat and the insecurity of national-cultural life in the homeland necessitated motivating individuals in the interests of group survival and duty to Ukraine.[13]

Yet her study also shows a continuous struggle by women for discursive power that transcends the bounds of nation: "Whether cultivated and exploited by community elites (male or female) as part of a political message, or

---

[11] Frances Swyripa, *Wedded to the Cause: Ukrainian-Canadian Women and Ethnic Identity 1891-1991* (Toronto: University of Toronto Press, 1993), 64.

[12] For a more expansive history of women's roles including their depiction in Soviet socialist realism during and after the Second World War, see: Maria Bucur and Nancy W. Wingfield, *Gender and War in Twentieth-Century Eastern Europe* (Bloomington and Indianapolis: Indiana University Press), 2006.

[13] Swyripa, *Wedded to the Cause,* 102.

expressing spontaneous grassroots emotions, the images, roles, and myths created about and for Ukrainian-Canadian women over the past century said relatively little about their lives . . . But the images, roles, and myths created about and for Ukrainian-Canadian women said a great deal about the way Ukrainian-Canadians at elite and grassroots levels saw themselves, and about the way they identified women with the issues and concerns of their group."[14] Husar inherits these myths, takes them to Ukraine, then spits them out again in a new form. She does this from her own unique subject position—but also in a more universal commentary on the social conditions of being a woman in art. As Podedworny writes: "there is no sweet and syrupy nostalgia for a homeland here. Husar is pissed off and she is kicking the shit out of history."[15]

**Figure 5.1.** Natalka Husar, "Ukraine and Me," From the Series *Burden of Innocence*, 2007. Oil on early 20th century Ukrainian folk painting, sewn on linen, 62 x 77 cm. Shared with permission of the artist. Photo credit: Michael Rafelson.

An illicit self takes form throughout Husar's paintings, where deeper taboos against which one defines oneself surface: ethnicity, belonging, fear, and love, including self-love too often demarcated as a last priority for the virtuous Ukrainian woman, for whom self-sacrifice is supposed to equal virtue. This visual vocabulary is bolstered by a fellow traveler, a sister in arms: the poetic language of Janice Kulyk-Keefer's *écriture féminine*. The poem *"Ars Grammatica"*

---

[14] Ibid., 19.

[15] Podedworny, Moray, et. al. *Husar Handbook*, 37.

opens the section of the collection *Foreign Relations* entitled "¡Pomaranchevo / Orange!":

> ... To name this country
> in any alphabet but Cyrillic
> is to speak in a condition
> of transliteration, yes, but also of
> translation, which is another word for error,
> as in wandering, *errare*. Not just words,
> but the very letters from which words are stitched,
> pure symbols as those letters be, refuse to pose, connect
> like petals at their base, becoming flower. Instead,
> they sting, not prettily, like the bees
> that puzzle Cranach's cupid,
> holding up the plundered honeycomb,
> but bites that rasp and scorch,
> swelling the skin on which they're inked:
> УКРАЇНА—[16]

The poet's voice here is alienated, like Husar, from the medium; where to speak as a Canadian-Ukrainian is everywhere already "a condition of translation." The alphabet, like dead artists' paints, does not simply transport meaning between eras or places, but recreates them, and in so doing, introduces "another word for error"— experiment, subversion, transgression — or revolution, perhaps. The act of "wandering" itself, and especially as a woman, involves stealing back one's freedom outside the boundaries of family, work, church, home, and hearth. This is not only the perpetual position of the nonconformist female, but also that of the perceptive writer or painter. The Canadian-Ukrainian author and feminist Myrna Kostash, a contemporary of both Janice Kulyk Keefer and Natalka Husar, has likened the position of being an outsider to being "an ethnic" in Canada, e.g., "Baba Was a Bohunk" from 1977. In one of her autobiographical reflective essays, entitled "Domination and Exclusion: Notes of a Resident Alien," she drives at the double-edged sword of daring to speak about ethnicity as a subversive concept in Canadian society: "They give me a place to stand, from which to launch salutary barbs, critiques, *and* visions, but there is a price to pay. In trying to reconcile all the elements of my alienation into a critical whole, I discover new marginalities and new exclusions. Such is the dance of the dialectic!" She reclaims this outsider status not only for herself and her own identification as a writer and "as an ethnic, a

---

[16] Kulyk Keefer, "Foreign Relations." In Kulyk Keefer and Husar, *Foreign Relations/Burden of Innocence*, 16.

feminist, and a socialist," but for anyone willing to venture a critique of the status quo. She accomplishes this through giving back history to the marginalized: ". . . the history of social movements also reveals to us the capacity of the outsider to fight back against marginality, pain, and inconsequence"[17] Kulyk Keefer's reference to Lucas Cranach the Elder's painting of Cupid complaining to Venus after being stung by the honeybees from which he had stolen their honeycomb is a similar twist on the idea of emancipation. Words are "pure symbols" and bites that "rasp and scorch" the tattooed serf's hand; the words of the feminist poet are the tools of the master's house. Yet both, and especially in combination with the paintings of the feminist artist, the meanings in the images and the text are opened up to new possibilities.

The eponymous image from the series *Burden of Innocence* features the portrait of a small girl on the shoulders of a burly man smoking a cigarette, likely her father. She is sucking her finger, a gesture repeated from an earlier painting *Pandora's Parcel to Ukraine* (1993). Like in the earlier painting, and in the depiction of the other children throughout Husar's works, the expression on the girl's face is overwise, self-protected, determined. The artist and several critics have commented on these finger-sucking girls as the survivalists of a post-Chernobyl world. The allegorical condition of emergency is here elevated through the figure of a child combined with "the outsider": ethnic or otherwise. Here the mafioso man's cigarette burns as the background burns red — he is an anti-hero cast in a moment of heroism — possibly carrying a small child away from the flames of a society in peril. The bows on the girl's head are Soviet-era *bantiky* traditionally worn by schoolgirls to school on official state holidays, most importantly on September first, or "Day of Knowledge." The artist presents a picture of mixed despair and hope for the fate of a nation: where knowledge cannot emancipate, it becomes a burden. Is it better to be innocent? Or to know, and carry on knowing, even if one is condemned to repeat the same mistakes?

Cranach's cupid is also Eve —"the plundered honeycomb," the original sin, after which all else is divided into knowns and forbidden unknowns. Meeka Walsh, writing in reference to the critic Barry Schwabsky: "like modernist and conceptualist antecedents, contemporary painting holds that 'a painting is not only a painting but also the representation of an idea about painting' thus abstract and representational are no longer opposed (as they were in the Soviet era), in both cases, he says, 'the painting is not there to represent the image, the

---

[17] Myrna Kostash, "Domination and Exclusion: Notes of a Resident Alien." In *Ethnicity in a Technological Age,* edited by Ian H. Angus (Edmonton: Canadian Institute of Ukrainian Studies Press, 1988), 57.

image exists in order to represent the painting.'"[18] The young girl is a future Ukraine that is survivalist and discordant, emerging from relegation to a "second world" status. This Ukraine is "the contemporary" that Husar reaches for, but cannot fully grasp for it does not exist anywhere. And in this failure to fully know Ukraine, or be known, there is a window through which the generations can finally admit to one another's time and place: as being truly nowhere, but for the bravery and intent toward self-invention from exactly where one stands, as Kostash declared in 1985: "in the action of the dissident alien *in this place.*"[19]

**Figure 5.2.** Natalka Husar, "Burden of Innocence," From the Series *Burden of Innocence,*
2007. Oil on rag board, 22 x 21 cm. Shared with permission of the artist.
Photo credit: Michael Rafelson.

## Embodied Memory

Artist Lesia Khomenko could also be said to be "kicking the shit out of history," but from a different viewpoint. She is a generation younger than Husar and was born and raised in Kyiv. Where Husar's characters in the "new" Ukraine are

---

[18] Meeka Walsh in Podedworny, Moray, et. al., *Husar Handbook,* 127.

[19] Full quote, from the paper delivered by Myrna Kostash in October 1985 at the University of Alberta "Second Wreath Conference" organized and about women, feminism, and activism in Ukraine: "This new consciousness does not stop with multiculturalism, which accepts the social hierarchy, nor with conservation. It proposes a struggle for a social existence based on humanizing relations. Those of us engaged in the development of this new consciousness may have begun with our particular ethnoculture, with ancestral memory, with historical grievances but we end in the action of the dissident alien *in this place.*" Kostash, "Domination and Exclusion: Notes of a Resident Alien," 57.

ultimately filtered through her eyes, which peer through the shadow of the immigrant experience, and of the challenge of being a female and an intellectual; by contrast, a kind of smuggling of knowledge between places and times, like knowledge between mothers and daughters, Khomenko's "new" in post-revolutionary Ukraine is positioned differently. For the artist living in Ukraine, daughter of Soviet artists, hers is a dismantling of the systematic "rules" governing public space, public conduct, time, and the professions, including the management of labor vs. leisure. For example, in the painting *Personal Vocation*, it is clear that these are the bodies of the working classes emptied of their ideological content —"set free" from their appropriation by the past regime. We cannot tell whether the figures are working or at leisure. Their poses do not conform to any expectations: they could be workers working, workers at leisure, pensioners daydreaming, thinking, or exercising. Diagonal lines shift the composition in a gravity-defying visual display of a circus or gymnastic pyramid. The bodies could not possibly stand up in this configuration in actual life; this is not socialist realist representation of reality; it is socialist realism reimagined. The appropriation of forms into a kind of playful free-fall lends the pastel color schemes, not unlike the hues of Husar's dead artists' paints, a certain significance: these hues were not chosen or arranged by the artist; they are the inherited backdrops of the environments she co-inhabits with the people in the paintings, people who lived through the Soviet era, some still holding Soviet passports, and who populate Ukraine as it actually exists, today. In the context of the post-Maidan Decommunization Laws introduced in Ukraine in 2015, Khomenko's playful gestures in the idiom of earlier sots-art propaganda lend her work an immediacy to the artistic legacy of the language of propaganda/censorship as material for critical reflection.

Enter the Ukrainian flag. As in Husar's found folk portrait of the small rural boy dressed in black, Khomenko also displays the flag as a backdrop — as it might have appeared in its most subversive placement by artists killed in the previous century: in its classical association with sky over grain. The citation of the body in front of this background also clearly evokes the pastoral Ukrainian peasant from socialist realism of the past century. Here we see a new take on the iconic painting *Bread* (1950) by Tatiana Yablonska, where the happy faces of harvesters spare no irony in the wake of the manmade famine (Holodomor) under Stalin in the 1930s. Khomenko goes a step further. The view of the backside of this "Madonna" positions audiences for a literal take on conception; the body, from which all life springs forth, is posed for everyone's contemplation. Like Husar, Khomenko's Ukraine is carnivalesque and post-revolutionary. Voluptuous flesh and muscle recline and stretch while working. Her protagonists are Caravaggio rearranged into unposed and deliberately "incorrect" stances, even "unflattering" in the traditional language of painting, and brashly rude in terms of social mores or religious morals. No figures of authority, neither

Soviet bureaucrat nor royal, could find a flattering portrait of themselves among her cast of casual outsiders, who are, by any measure, everyday working-class Ukrainians. In the genre of history-painting, Khomenko, like Husar, also uses titles and irony to challenge the idea that history belongs to the few, and therefore should be somehow represented only by portraits of happy peasants, neatly arranged for the oppressive gaze of the landholder, or the state.

**Figure 5.3.** Lesia Khomenko, *Personal Vocation*, 2010-11.
Shared with permission of the artist.

**Figure 5.4.** Lesia Khomenko, From the Series *Dacha's Madonnas*, 2004-07.
Shared with permission of the artist.

Each in their own respective idioms, Husar and Khomenko both explore themselves as artists and the role of art in its relationship to power, a relationship in which the body takes central stage as the oldest material for the language of art. Memory in these works is intensely personal — and both painters present subversive interstices through which the generations pass knowledge, once forbidden, about the cruelty wreaked upon everyday people, in this instance, people living on the territories of Ukraine during and after the Soviet experiment. The role of painting becomes a commentary on death and renewal, as much as it is an object capable of linking the generations in their different experiences of upheaval. The body stands as a testament to the fleeting nature of life, and the loss of knowledge with the loss of life as the opposite of the artists' task as creator, life-giver. These two painters are both intensely concerned with corruption and decay in the post-Soviet period, yet in their large format canvases and their citation of the body, they accomplish more than just reactionary statements against the Soviet regime, or how they imagine it, as both experience that era mostly as outsiders (Husar due to her place, Canada; and Khomenko due to her time, born in 1982 at the end of the communist regime).

Rather, both painters introduce and experiment with a language for alienation marked by their individual identity, which takes plural form: in collage, fragments, and intertextual references. In Khomenko's work, the Soviet workers' bodies are reframed in a baroque saturation of space and time into a compressed present tense. The 1960s pastel colors of advertising and fabrics add to the androgyny of her protagonists with large hands, feet, shoulders, even disproportionately so. These forms contrast with Husar's hypersexed feminine characters who seem to contort themselves into the straps and buttons of their tiny tank-tops and miniskirts, or the prickly necks of the mafia men who seem to burn with frustration, "oligarchs in waiting," Husar has called them, "yet without any real clout." These are the men who kill to be more than men, demigods of a broken palace. They are not androgynous at all in their pursuit of dominion, nor godly, more like Gogolian devils. And that is exactly the point. Husar, like Khomenko, is playing with archetypes. The common denominator is that all of their archetypes give viewers a glimpse of Ukraine with the effect of being "outside looking in." This is not because either artist is fully outsider/insider — and what these categories could fully mean in terms of ethnicity, gender, class, and nation will always be unresolved; rather, this is because this can only ever be the view of an artist in a constant revolutionary state-of-affairs.

In Kulyk Keefer's poem "Looking At Art," dedicated to Husar's painting of the same title, the poet addresses the artist:

> Oh artist who, with polished tongs
> and rubber gloves;
> with downcast gaze
> or double-crossing eyes,
> concocts a seating plan
> for multitudes, then crams
> the mess of meaning in a dish
> compact, divided as an egg[20]

---

[20] Kulyk Keefer, *Foreign Relations/Burden of Innocence*, 85-86.

Here, Husar's alter egos of the nurse and stewardess are serving dinner to the protagonists of the young girl, now grown, a painted lady "has-been" and a mafia-man, but the platters are empty. This is Judy Chicago's dinner party in negative, where the artist is captive to her imagination and its possibilities. The scene also references Husar's early porcelain culinary sculptures from 1977 featuring gendered commentary through Canadian-Ukrainian cultural foodways: *Veroniky Varenyky* ; *The TV Dinner Sviat Vechir*; and *After All That, Supper*. These works found resonance in the North American context among feminist works of this period, such as Martha Rosler's *Semiotics of the Kitchen* (1975). Feminist theorist Cynthia Enloe's *Bananas, Beaches, and Bases: Making Feminist Sense of International Politics*, published in 1990, reflects on the militarization of society in the global military buildup of the post-World War II order. She has written elsewhere of the symbolism of a Heinz promotional *Star Wars* soup can as an artifact of a globalism that "may reveal a gendered military system that is more political than it is cultural," and can "show just how politically constructed any national or international culture is." Uncertainty, more than consensus, among the decision-makers within the constructed order "may reveal tension, contradiction, and confusion," along with "ambivalence, that is, both men and women with mixed feelings." She: "Masculinity-privileging militarization, however, can survive, even thrive, on mixed feelings."[21]

Is Husar's *Last Supper* a sacrificial ritual warning a Ukrainian or Canadian farewell before the resurrection . . . or an invitation to a beheading? Whose art is this? Who is imagined by whom?

> Cigarette unraveling, a luscious
> orchid strangling a wrist. One book
> of unstruck matches and this silver dish:
> this mirror in a foreign language.[22]

Here in the poem are two mirrors, not only the silver dish, but also "the book." The enjambment of the line after "book" links it to the final line, and, in combination with "this silver dish," doubles other doubles in the painted scene. The nurse and stewardess twins, the latter with two expressions at once, in motion, conjure up the Judeo-Christian duality of Saint/Sinner, especially in the yellow star-like points and halo-like sheen covering the nurse's head. The "double" in Slavic lore and literature is also there as a mocking devilish element. The "mirror in a foreign language" is the immigrant's daughter, always in

---

[21] Cynthia Enloe, "How Do They Militarize a Can of Soup?" *Maneuvers: The International Politics of Militarizing Women's Lives* (Berkeley: University of California Press, 2000), 109.

[22] Kulyk Keefer, "Looking at Art," *Foreign Relations/Burden of Innocence*, 86.

translation, but never fully translated. The doubled state of existence is one of permanent exile that artists have long had to negotiate, whether Bulgakov's Master with his cat, or Gogol's farmer's wife with a conniving little devil before serving varenyky on Christmas Eve. Kulyk Keefer's book of poems is the matchbook on the table, ready to ignite new ideas in a new generation, like the "book of unstruck matches," or be ignited and consumed.

**Figure 5.5.** Natalka Husar, "Looking at Art," From the Series *Burden of Innocence*, 2007. Oil on rag board, 81 x 102 cm. Shared with permission of the artist. Photo credit: Michael Rafelson.

## The "Contemporary" in Contemporary Ukraine

Husar's and Khomenko's individual Ukrainian worlds depend on rejecting the grand-scale historicism of *nation* and *people* as giant categories, or propagandistic tools, handed down to them from the past century. Rather, they both focus on the everyday, framing what is "contemporary" about the present, as they experience it. The way out of repeating the Soviet past, for them, is both content and form in the language of painting, a language that shares some features in each of their individual activation of its Ukrainian idioms, some of the specifics of which we have noted throughout this chapter.

But what can these painters offer to the wider landscape of visual culture? What is the sociopolitical context of art in Ukraine today, and how does it inform our global present condition, a condition marked by war, mass protest, and a pandemic? Is there any hope left? The answer is yes: Husar and Khomenko's bold and frank critiques of society, of history, and of gender. The body becomes the figure for painting itself; the subsumption of time into an act for which the artist must be present. They interpolate continuities across the times and places represented in their works that can be recognized as distinctly Ukrainian, but also have a universal meaning connected to the broader language of revolutionary emancipation, especially for women.

Where the idea of "the contemporary" in their works pivots on the concept of emancipation, it is, in turn, part of a world that is not just in perpetual crisis but is always changing; this differs from modernism or post-modernism, which are rooted in a progressivist linear time, but links aesthetic language to historical turn as a procedure of recovering lost agency for women. Ukraine's historical trajectory is punctuated with dramatic change from the post-1991, and post-Orange Revolutionary moment of 2007, to the moment after the Revolution of Dignity in 2013-14. Hito Steyerl has remarked on the institutional setting of art in developing countries more recently, that, "every contemporary oligarch loves contemporary art."[23] Ukraine's attempts to decentralize institutions since 1991 have been met with the monopolization of private enterprise and corruption in public institutions, including state museums. The outcome of these changes has meant that private galleries far outpace state funding for independent art initiatives, and the structure of old elites still maintains a grip over talent acquisition and access to resources. For the rural, working-class, young, women, and minorities, the situation for arts mirrors broader inequities in labor relations across the professions. A few words on feminist activism are in order if we are to fully understand the landscape not only of Husar and Khomenko's biographies as artists on different sides of the ocean, but the extent to which their work depicting women in Ukraine is subversive (and in a not unimportant sense "contemporary" with regard to global movements for feminist and LGBTQI+ rights reaching a peak in the mid-2000s and continuing today).

Arts and media production in Ukraine have become an important resource for discussions concerned with a range of feminist issues from the #ЯнеБоюсьСказати / #IaNeBoiusSkazaty (I'm not afraid to say) campaign against domestic violence (a counterpart to the #MeToo movement), to wikis,

---

[23] Hito Steyerl, "Politics of Art: Contemporary Art and the Transition to Post-Democracy," *e-flux Journal*, no. 21 (December 2010). https://www.e-flux.com/journal/21/67696/politics-of-art-contemporary-art-and-the-transition-to-post-democracy/

blogs, and publishing portals.[24] Human rights discourse in education, communications, and civic inclusion aim to counter social stigmas in wider society, including where false attitudes toward women and other gender minorities as vulnerable subjects serves to marginalize. Recent feminist art initiatives in Ukraine converge with these efforts. For example, a large retrospective exhibit in 2018 in Kyiv, called *A Space of One's Own*, in reference to Virginia Woolf. Spanning the twentieth and twenty-first centuries and co-curated by Tatiana Kochubinska and Tetiana Zhmurko, the exhibit featured works by hundreds of women artists past and present. The public program included scholars and an anthology of contemporary texts and images by and about women artists and authors, edited by Kateryna Iakovlenko, entitled *Chomu v ukrains'komu mystetstvi ie velyki khudozhnytsi* (Why There are Such Great Women Artists in Ukrainian Art).[25] Ukraine's activists who identify as women and/or feminists do not ascribe to a single unified strand of feminism and are as diverse as are the mediums and topics of its creative communities.

Museums and other exhibit spaces provide rare opportunities for researchers and the public to engage difficult and controversial subjects both at home and abroad. In recent years, the Revolution of Dignity in 2013-14, the occupation of Crimea, and Russia's war in Donbas since 2014, then large-scale invasion in 2022 have had a profound effect on the arts. An example is *At the Front Line: Ukrainian Art 2013-2019*, curated by Svitlana Biedarieva and Ania Deikun, exhibited in 2019 in Mexico City and in 2020 in Winnipeg, Canada, which included seminars, talks, guided tours, and an academic anthology.[26] Artifacts and pieces in the exhibit were by artists who have been engaged in activism and research for several years in East Ukraine. Participants addressed the role of art exchanges in the face of war and how to protect the voices and works of artists in exile from the occupied territories.

Ukrainian art has gained wide visibility both domestically and abroad since the Maidan Revolution of Dignity in 2013-14, which provides additional opportunities for education in facing gendered, ethnic, and social differences in processes of assimilation/rejection of memories of the Soviet past. Examples of mutual tolerance and solidarity-building across national lines within

---

[24] Tamara Martsenyuk and Sarah D. Phillips, "Talking about Sexual Violence in Post-Maidan Ukraine: Analysis of the Online Campaign #IamNotAfraidToSayIt," *Sexuality & Culture* 24, no. 3 (2020), 1-20.

[25] Kateryna Iakovlenko, ed., *Chomu v ukrains'komu mystetstvi ie velyki khudozhnytsi* (Kyiv: PinchukArtCentre, 2019).

[26] Svitlana Biedarieva, ed., *Contemporary Ukrainian and Baltic Art: Political and Social Perspectives, 1991-2021* (Hanover: Ibidem Press, 2021).

creative communities have included authors who publish in both Ukrainian and Russian; have included individuals who exhibit with members of the Russian, Belarusian, and Polish feminist movements; and Ukrainian professional artists who have boycotted funding or speak Ukrainian in virtual invitations from Russian state-backed museums, including the prestigious Garage Museum, of which its partnerships include institutions based in the West.[27] More projects that bring together artists, activists, and scholars dedicated to cultivating critical perspectives on women's lived experiences can shed light on Ukraine's dual challenges of restoring sovereignty in Donbas and Crimea, while pressuring lawmakers to respond to social demands in protecting civil rights.

On 14 April 2021, President Volodymyr Zelenskyy enacted a National Human Rights Strategy, or Decree No. 119/2021. The law includes "prevention and countering discrimination" and "ensuring equal rights and opportunities for women and men," along with military veterans and internally displaced persons.[28] The law aims to uphold treaties within the EU-Ukraine Association Agreement in order to "contribute to the implementation of Ukraine's UN Sustainable Development Goals until 2030, and improve the position of Ukraine in international human rights rankings."[29] Since 2010, international human rights monitoring groups have traced a regression in the implementation and reinforcement of laws protecting women by measuring, among other indicators, rising rates of domestic violence in Ukraine.[30] The severity of this problem was made more acute over the period of the war beginning in 2014 (before its escalation in 2022); a period in which more than 1.5 million were displaced from the Ukraine-Russia military combat zones and separatist-occupied territories.

Despite these difficulties, or, possibly because of them, women's and LGBTQI+ movements in Ukraine continue to grow; for example, the 8 March 2020 Women's March and Kyiv Pride March now each draw more than two thousand

---

[27] For an example, see Nikita Kadan, "Buduvaty ruiny." (Building Ruins). Lviv Municipal Art Centre with Garage Museum Moscow. Artist Talk. December 19, 2020. lvivart.center YouTube Channel. https://www.youtube.com/watch?v=xb3KeqqDEQ0.

[28] *Sluha narodu,* "President of Ukraine Approves the National Human Rights Strategy," *Sluha narodu.com.ua.* News Blog Post. April 20, 2021. https://sluga-narodu.com/en/president-of-ukraine-approves-the-national-human-rights-strategy/.

[29] *Ukrinform,* "President of Ukraine Volodymyr Zelensky Signed Decree No. 119/2021 to Enact the National Human Rights Strategy," *Ukrinform.net.* News Post. February 7, 2021. https://www.ukrinform.net/rubric-society/3214900-zelensky-enacts-national-human-rights-strategy.html.

[30] Tamara Martsenyuk, *Chomu ne varto boiatysia feminizmu?* [Why fear feminism?] (Kyiv: Komora, 2019).

participants annually, compared with a few dozen when they began a decade ago. Several studies document these changes in the context of the mixed reception of feminism in wider society in Ukraine.[31] Recent gains include the signing of an Anti-Discrimination Law adopted in 2012 and amended in 2014. The law was again revisited in 2016, after the Maidan Revolution of Dignity, in the context of the UN Human Rights Office of the High Commissioner.[32] The law was expanded and included schedules for implementing a future National Human Rights Strategy. This led to some progress toward pluralizing Ukrainian society, but new challenges have appeared, including in the form of disinformation campaigns, many stemming from the Russian Federation, as well as online organizing of "anti-gender" and "anti-feminist" campaigns by far-right groups in Ukraine, the EU, and globally.[33]

Lesia Khomenko's artistic response to the demonstrations that took place on the Maidan starting from 1 December 2013 involved drawing portraits of passersby on individual sheets of paper placed over black carbon paper. She described the tent city of the Maidan encampment as a "small scale new model of a utopian state," noting how all services there operated twenty-four hours a day, on a volunteer basis, and everything was free of charge. She writes: "I decided to test whether the artist may be a part of this exchange? And if the

---

[31] Oksana Kis, "Ukrainian Women Reclaiming the Feminist Meaning of International Women's Day: A Report About Recent Feminist Activism," *Aspasia* 6, no. 1 (March 2012): 219-32. Olena Hankivsky and Anastasiya Salnykova, eds., *Gender, Politics, and Society in Ukraine* (Toronto: University of Toronto Press, 2012). Also see: Tamara Martsenyuk, *Gender dla vsikh: vyklyk stereotypam (Gender for All: Against Stereotypes)* (Kyiv: Osnovy, 2017). Olga Plakhotnik and Maria Mayerchyk, "Ukrainian Feminisms and the Issue of Coloniality," Virtual Public Presentation. University of Alberta, Edmonton: December 11, 2020. Jessica Zychowicz, *Superfluous Women: Feminism, Art, and Revolution in Twenty-First Century Ukraine* (Toronto: University of Toronto Press, 2021). *UN Women*, Annual Report 2019-2020. https://www.unwomen.org/en/digital-library/annual-report.

[32] UN Human Rights Office of the High Commissioner, "Committee on the Elimination of Racial Discrimination: The Report of Ukraine," August 12, 2016, https://www.ohchr.org/EN/NewsEvents/Pages/DisplayNews.aspx?NewsID=20370&LangID=E.

[33] Atlantic Council, "Meeting the Moment: Shaping the Future: 2018/2019 Annual Report," https://www.atlanticcouncil.org/wp-content/uploads/2019/09/Atlantic-Council-Annual-Report-2018%E2%80%932019.pdf. Human Rights Watch, "Ukraine: Events of 2019," https://www.hrw.org/world-report/2020/country-chapters/ukraine#. Amnesty International, "Annual Report 2019: Eastern Europe and Central Asia," https://www.amnesty.org/en/latest/campaigns/2020/04/air2019-eeca/. . Jessica Zychowicz, "Ukraine Hosts Most Successful LGBTQ Event in the Nation's History, but New Challenges Appear," *Wilson Center Kennan Institute. Ukraine Focus Blog*, August 2 2019. https://www.wilsoncenter.org/blog-post/ukraine-hosts-most-successful-lgbtq-event-the-nations-history-new-challenges-appear.

artist is needed at all in this situation."[34] Further to her response, which she links to "historical consciousness and mythologizing," she decided to make portraits of "members of Maidan" offering to give them away as gifts. Visiting the Maidan daily, she made one hundred and seventy-one portraits, giving some away and retaining others. The outcome was exhibited in Ukraine along with the carbon copies, which are a palimpsest collage of faces. The "ghost" of history peers through the layers and layers of pages, leaving their trace in a composite that is androgynous and collective — there is nobody here, only the face of an unknown future. Walter Benjamin's angel of history descends upon the revolution of the twenty-first century, terrifying with unknowns: as Ukraine's future would soon collide into a war with Russia, upon Putin's invasion and occupation of Crimea, Luhansk, and Donetsk.

The "contemporary" marks time. Here in Khomenko's drawings time appears out-of-joint in the visage of the collective anonymous. Like the dead artists' paints of a century ago, the pencil captures images of individuals who can be assumed neither alive nor dead.

**Figure 5.6.** Lesia Khomenko, *Drawing on Maidan* Series, 2013-2014.
Shared with permission of the artist.

---

[34] See: Lesia Khomenko. Artist Personal Website. https://www.lesiakhomenko.com/. https://www.lesiakhomenko.com/drawing-on-maidan.

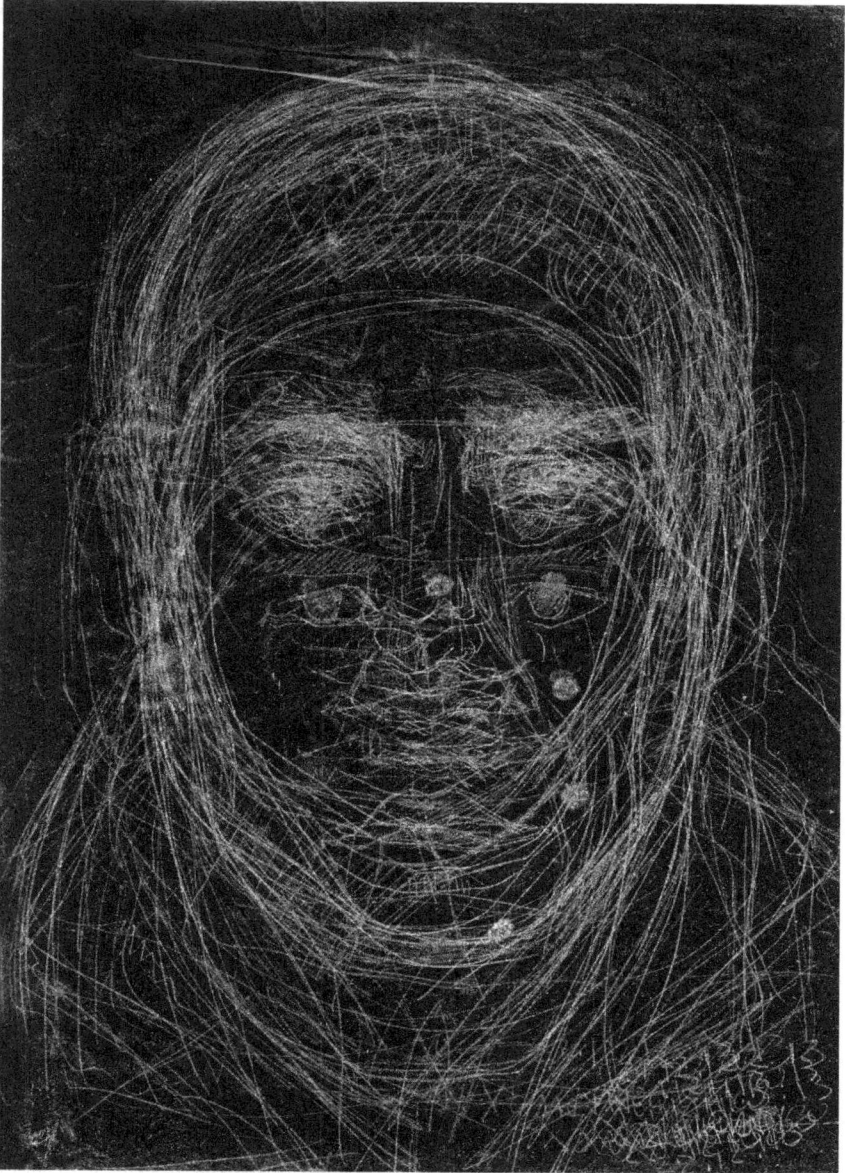

**Figure 5.7.** Lesia Khomenko, *Drawing on Maidan* Series, 2013-2014.
Shared with permission of the artist.

**Figure 5.8.** Lesia Khomenko, *Drawing on Maidan* Series, 2013-2014.
Shared with permission of the artist.

Husar's poet-companion text is composed in the same place, half a decade earlier in 2007. Reread in the context of the events of 2013-14, it appears just as relevant — indeed "contemporary" of both moments. The prognosis offers no easy end. There are no heroes. There are no identifiable traces of us/them, here/there, yesterday/today. Maidan becomes a universal chronotope. Every revolution in this place and time encompasses all previous and future revolutions, everywhere:

The Eyes of Maidan[35]

That photograph of an old woman,
her face a map worn through at the creases,
her mouth a whole alphabet of pain
and patience. Anonymous, snapped
at one of the vigils, day or night, to keep
pressure on the powers-that-be, to keep
world's pale eyes trained where, any moment,
tanks might spell out their mandate
in a mash of blood and bone.
...

[35] Kulyk Keefer notes that in the original publication of the poem this is the title of a photograph from Kyiv by Vasyl Artiushenko.

What is it turned to, face
Rough as hemp, eyes
Deep-dug as graves? Who
Looks back at her?
Who sees?

The only person left in the poem is the viewer, whose only way out of repetition is remaining vigilant in daring to see the repetition, not only of others, of themselves, but of Ukraine and its ghosts, *as never before:*

> I more than ever live through what's going on around me. And how I want to turn off the television when they broadcast the regular sessions of parliament! It's hard to bear when, before our eyes, everything's lurching to the right. I see it and understand it clearly, but at the same time I sense the mood around me or feel irritated by the indifference of others. Besides, in writing these letters about what's going on, I am doomed to thinking always the same thoughts: Why is it like this? What for? And what next?

– Solomea Pavlychko, December 4, 1991, Kyiv. Translated by Myrna Kostash.[36]

## Bibliography

Atlantic Council. "Meeting the Moment: Shaping the Future: 2018/2019 Annual Report." Report https://www.atlanticcouncil.org/wp-content/uploads/2019/09/Atlantic-Council-Annual-Report-2018%E2%80%932019.pdf.

Amnesty International. "Annual Report 2019: Eastern Europe and Central Asia." Report. https://www.amnesty.org/en/latest/campaigns/2020/04/air2019-eeca/.

Bucur, Maria and Nancy W. Wingfield. *Gender and War in Twentieth-Century Eastern Europe.* Bloomington and Indianapolis: Indiana University Press, 2006.

Biedarieva, Svitlana, Ed. *Contemporary Ukrainian and Baltic Art: Political and Social Perspectives, 1991-2021.* New York: Columbia University and Ibidem Press, 2021.

Enloe, Cynthia. "How Do They Militarize a Can of Soup?" *Maneuvers: The International Politics of Militarizing Women's Lives.* Berkeley: University of California Press, 2000, pp. 1-34.

Hankivsky, Olena, and Anastasiya Salnykova, Eds. *Gender, Politics, and Society in Ukraine.* Toronto: University of Toronto Press, 2012.

Husar, Natalka. *Natalka Husar: Burden of Innocence* (artist's book). Ukraine: Rodovid Press, 2009.

Human Rights Watch. "Ukraine: Events of 2019." Report. https://www.hrw.org/world-report/2020/country-chapters/Ukraine. Accessed November 17, 2021.

---

[36] Solomea Pavlychko, *Letters from Kiev*, edited by Bohdan Krawchenko, translated by Myrna Kostash (Edmonton: Canadian Institute of Ukrainian Studies Press, 1992), 136.

Iakovlenko, Kateryna, Ed. *Chomu v ukrains'komu mystetstvi ie velyki khudozhnytsi.* [*Why There are Such Great Artists in Ukrainian Art*]. Ukraine: PinchukArtCentre, 2019.

Kadan, Nikita. "Buduvaty ruiny." [*Building ruins*]. Lviv Municipal Art Centre with Garage Museum Moscow. Artist Talk. December 19, 2020. https://www.youtube.com/watch?v=xb3KeqqDEQ0.

Khomenko, Lesia. Artist Personal Website. https://www.lesiakhomenko.com/.

Kis', Oksana. "Ukrainian Women Reclaiming the Feminist Meaning of International Women's Day: A Report About Recent Feminist Activism", *Aspasia* Vol. 6 (2) (2021): 2012, pp. 219-32.

Kostash, Myrna. "Domination and Exclusion: Notes of a Resident Alien." [first edition in "Second Wreath" Conference at University of Alberta, October 1985]. *Ethnicity in a Technological Age*, Ed. Ian H. Angus. Edmonton: Canadian Institute of Ukrainian Studies Press, 1988, pp. 57-66.

Kulyk Keefer, Janice. *Foreign Relations/Burden of Innocence* (artist's book). Ukraine: Rodovid Press, 2009.

Kulyk Keefer, Janice and Solomea Pavlychko, Eds. *Two Lands, New Visions: Stories from Canada and Ukraine*. Regina, Saskatchewan: Coteau Books, 1998.

Lupul, Manoly R., Ed. *Visible Symbols: Cultural Expression Among Canada's Ukrainians*. Edmonton: Canadian Institute of Ukrainian Studies Press, 1984.

Martsenyuk, Tamara "Ukrainian Societal Attitudes towards the LGBT Communities," in Olena Hankivsky and Anastasiya Salnykova, Eds., *Gender, Politics, and Society in Ukraine*. Toronto, University of Toronto Press, 2012.

_____. *Chomu ne varto boiatysia feminizmu?* (Why Fear Feminism?). Kyiv: Komora, 2019.

_____. Gender dla vsikh: vyklyk stereotypam. (Gender for All: Against Stereotypes). Kyiv: Osnovy, 2017.

Martsenyuk, Tamara and Sarah D. Phillips. "Talking About Sexual Violence in Post-Maidan Ukraine: Analysis of the Online Campaign #IamNotAfraidToSayIt," *Sexuality & Culture* 24, no. 3 (2020): 1-20.

Moray, Gerta; Carol Podedworny; Stuart Reid; Dawn Owen; Meeka Walsh. *Husar Handbook*. Macdonald Stewart Art Centre / ABC Art Books Canada, 2010.

OHCHR, "Committee on the Elimination of Racial Discrimination the report of Ukraine," https://www.ohchr.org/EN/NewsEvents/Pages/DisplayNews.aspx?NewsID=20370&LangID=E. 12 August 2016.

Pavlychko, Solomea. *Letters from Kiev*. Edited by Bohdan Krawchenko. Translated by Myrna Kostash. Edmonton: Canadian Institute of Ukrainian Studies Press, 1992.

Plakhotnik, Olga and Maria Mayerchyk. "Ukrainian Feminisms and the Issue of Coloniality." Virtual Public Presentation. University of Alberta, Edmonton: December 11, 2020. https://www.ualberta.ca/canadian-institute-of-ukrainian-studies/news-and-events /seminars/2020/december/maria-mayerchyk-and -olga-plakhotnik--ukrainian-feminisms- and-the-issue-of-coloniality.html

R.E.P. Group (Revolutionary Experimental Space). *R.E.P.: Revolutionary Experimental Space: A History*, Ed. Lada Nakonechna. Transl. Larissa Babij,

Mariana Matveichuk, Weronika Nowacka, Anastasiya Osipova, and Olena Sheremet. Berlin: The Green Box, 2015.

*Sluha narodu.* "President of Ukraine Approves the National Human Rights Strategy." *Sluha narodu.com.ua.* News Blog Post. April 20, 2021. https://sluga -narodu.com/en/president-of-ukraine-approves-the-national-human-rights -strategy/.

Steyerl, Hito. "Politics of Art: Contemporary Art and the Transition to Post-Democracy," *e-flux Journal,* no. 21 (December 2010), https://www.e-flux.com/journal/21/67696/politics-of-art-contemporary-art-and-the-transition-to-post-democracy/.

Swyripa, Frances. *Wedded to the Cause: Ukrainian-Canadian Women and Ethnic Identity 1891-1991.* Toronto: University of Toronto Press, 1993

*Ukrinform.* "President of Ukraine Volodymyr Zelensky signed Decree No. 119/2021 to enact the National Human Rights Strategy." *Ukrinform.net.* News Post. February 7, 2021. https://www.ukrinform.net/rubric-society/3214900-zelensky-enacts-national-human-rights-strategy.html.

UN Women. Annual Report 2019-2020. https://www.unwomen.org/en/digital-library/annual-report.

UN Human Rights Office of the High Commissioner. "Committee on the Elimination of Racial Discrimination: The Report on Ukraine," August 12, 2016. https://www.ohchr.org/EN/NewsEvents/Pages/DisplayNews.aspx?NewsID=20370&LangID=E.

Zychowicz, Jessica. *Superfluous Women: Feminism, Art, and Revolution in Twenty-First Century Ukraine* (Toronto: University of Toronto Press, 2021).

_____. "Ukraine Hosts Most Successful LGBTQ Event in the Nation's History, but New Challenges Appear." *Wilson Center Kennan Institute. Ukraine Focus Blog.* August 2, 2019, https://www.wilsoncenter.org/blog-post/ukraine-hosts -most-successful-lgbtq-event-the-nations-history-new-challenges-appear.

# III.
## On Crossing Borders: Past as Litmus of Freedom of Expression

# Chapter 6

# "No Need for Genius—Good Taste is Enough": Conditional Permission on Women's Professional Art Practices in the Kingdom of Poland in the Nineteenth and Early Twentieth Centuries

Joanna Dobkowska-Kubacka

**Abstract**

This chapter analyzes the conditions under which women gained social consent for professional activity in creative fields in the nineteenth-century Kingdom of Poland. I argue that it was largely the result of a specific combination of sociopolitical and economic circumstances following the defeat of the armed uprisings for independence. After the November Uprising of 1831, women were given the green light to pursue literature, although attempts were made to limit their activities to specific literary genres. After the January Uprising of 1864, when many upper-class women faced the necessity of earning a living, art appeared as one of the pathways. I argue that social and economic factors determined not only the mere fact of women practicing art professionally, but also influenced what female artists created, and how. I attempt to reconstruct the social expectations of female artists based on their gender in the 19th and early 20th centuries.

**Keywords**: women's history, nineteenth century, female artists, Kingdom of Poland, feminism, equal rights movement

*** * ***

Can a woman create? This dilemma was discussed frequently in the nineteenth-century Polish press, usually in conjunction with a debate over the female nature: its limitations and predispositions. In contemporary research this question recurs in the version "Could a woman create?" Social consent is crucial to artistic activity, as Linda Nochlin noted in her famous essay *Why Have There Been No Great Women Artists?*[1] She pointed out from a historical perspective that the artist's profession has always been associated with a certain class and gender affiliation. It is the society that decides who is allowed to perform the role of an artist, in what circumstances, and on which conditions. The so-called artist is also a social role conditioned by certain social structures (systems of education, patronage, exhibition, distribution, critic, etc.). The case of female artists in the nineteenth-century Kingdom of Poland can be considered as evidence supporting this thesis. The social, political and economic circumstances determined the very right of women to practice art professionally. Shifting circumstances also had a strong impact on what Polish women created and how they did it. Social and economic factors decided on what genres women chose to turn their attention, or better said, what genres were available to female artists, which compositions were favored, etc. In this study, I argue that the public approval of women's professional art practices was, to a critical extent, a consequence of the lost armed uprising for independence.[2]

As agreed at the Congress of Vienna in 1815, the Kingdom of Poland was to be united with the Russian Empire by a personal union, but to retain its autonomy. In practice, the Kingdom became a part of the Russian Empire. The diminishing and subsequent elimination of promised autonomy, accompanied by a policy of Russification and repression, was at the root of both uprisings in 1831 and in 1863. They were lost. Polish society, especially the gentry, suffered acute political and economic consequences from these defeats. Nonetheless, these consequences also had a decisive impact on women's social position, offering them the opportunity to take on new activities. Among these activities was the professional practice of art. Allowing women to engage in it was part of a campaign carried out by Polish elites after 1864 to find gainful employment for ladies, with the intention of helping to solve economic problems.

This campaign was conducted predominantly in weekly magazines. In the Kingdom of Poland, the Polish press played a pivotal role, replacing many public institutions. Due to the Russification policy of the Tsarist government, Poles at the time were gradually being eliminated from public education, administration and the judiciary institutions – generally from all offices of civil

---

[1] Linda Nochlin, *Why Have There Been No Great Women Artists* (London: Thames & Hudson, 2021).

[2] Portions of this text are drawn from my doctoral research, which concerns the campaign for women's labor rights in professional work in the nineteenth century Kingdom of Poland.

service. But the press, although strictly censored, could still publish in Polish. Even despite these restricted conditions, it became a bastion of national identity and reflected the life of a society that was not represented in official state institutions. Contemporaries of one another noticed and commented on this phenomenon, e.g. Eliza Orzeszkowa, a writer who enjoyed significant respect in Polish society. She noted in 1885 that the press was the only medium for public opinion by which it could express itself on most of the social issues of the day, and the primary instrument for promoting one's viewpoint.[3] The Polish press, therefore, had a major impact on the propagation of ideas, the formation of new attitudes, and the evolution of people's mindset on various issues. Its influence was limited to the gentry and intelligentsia, thus I have chosen to focus and narrow my research to these classes as well. Based on my analysis of archival press publications, it is possible to observe distinct changes occurring in the attitude of Polish society towards the issue of women's professional work, including the professionalization of the artistic sphere. The correlation between public opinion expressed in the press and the character of Polish women's artistic activity is also noticeable. Thus I have attempted to reconstruct the social expectations of female artists based on their gender.

Most statements in the nineteenth-century Polish press, especially in the first half of the century, claimed that not only the role of women in society as wives and mothers, but above all their female nature in the biological and psychological sense excluded them from any serious artistic activity. It was to be God's plan that humans should live in a dichotomous order. This order was manifested in gender divisions and gender-specific fundamental features. According to this essentialist approach, the "male sphere" was reason, while the female one was "heart."

Men were granted rationality, an intellect, and the ability to create abstract concepts. Women were denied intellectual predispositions; their specialty was "feeling." Within the framework of the traditional world order based on the gender dichotomy, women and men were given separate characteristics. Different tasks resulted from these characteristics, and the traditional role of woman was justified precisely in her own nature. Therefore any changes to this dichotomy, conservatives argued, would harm both society and women. This worldview was dominant in nineteenth-century Polish society, not only among the upper classes. It was also propagated (it is still propagated) by the Catholic Church.

---

[3] Eliza, Orzeszkowa, "Polki." *Kwestia kobieca w Europie,* edited by Teodor W. Stanton (Warszawa: Wydawnictwo Przeglądu Tygodniowego, 1885), 288.

This fundamental, supposedly divinely-sanctioned polarity served as a strong argument for the proponents of preserving the traditional gender status. They stressed that women's professional work went against nature. They emphasized the threat which a woman's professional life supposedly posed to their spousal and maternal duties. While more or less keeping up appearances and referring to the well-being of the family, for which a woman's professional work would create undesirable competition, the fight was in fact aimed at keeping a dichotomous world order. Conservatives opposing women's work had in mind most of all intellectual employment. In regards to the question of women entering into manual occupations, the resistance was much weaker, or it even did not exist at all. While women's access to prestigious intellectual professions—art included—met with strong resistance, paid physical work seemed to protectors of the family totally acceptable. Regarding these phenomena, Maria Ilnicka, the editor of the popular women's magazine *Bluszcz*, pointed out the hypocrisy. She asked the opponents of women's intellectual work who had argued that it took a woman away from her family and hurt her children, what they thought was happening to the children of the seamstresses who used to spend their whole day in a factory: "If you say that it [woman's intellectual work] takes a woman away from the family, that it tears her away from the most sacred work of motherhood, then it would be necessary to say at the same time who is raising the child of a modiste who spends her whole day in a shop, who is taking care about the child of a seamstress chained to a needle or a machine in a sewing room [ . . . ?]."[4] The job of a seamstress, regarded very low on the ladder of social prestige, poorly paid at rates on the verge of starvation, as Ilnicka rightly pointed out, was not controversial at all and was even considered quite suitable for a woman. Since it is not about the very obstacle in taking care of the family, and not about work as such, why, Ilnicka further asks, should anyone force a woman "to do the least profitable work, what right does anyone have not to let an intelligent and educated human being use her mind?"[5] Ilnicka was firmly of the opinion that if a female gender is granted the right to work in manual occupations, then the same permission should also apply in the case of professions based on intellectual work. With no income other than the money that she earned from writing and editing, Ilnicka had a personal interest and investment in protecting just such a right.

Referring to God and nature, Polish conservatives tried hard to preserve male exclusivity in all areas of intellectual activity, and this included art, which was understood at that time as an intellectual field. Apart from the sphere of the

---

[4] Maria Ilnicka, "Słówko o emancypacji kobiet." *Bluszcz*, no. 10 (1867): 38-39.

[5] Ibid.

intellect, however, there was another indispensable component of artistic activity, namely creativity. Women were also to be deprived of this in the conservative criticism of the time. For example, in 1874, Henryk Struve announced in the magazine *Kłosy* that a woman's nature is inherently more passive than creative.[6] Adolf Dygasiński, a novelist and publicist, believed the same: "The female intelligentsia, which is not creative, but conscientious and repetitive of others, constantly needs impulses, models and encouragement . . . It will not produce anything on its own."[7] The female gender, then, in these conservative conceptualizations was therefore incapable of invention; it could only copy manifestations of male genius. A woman should remain a muse, inspiring artists with her beauty and charm. She was also irreplaceable as an audience, again because of her "nature," which made her highly sensitive to beauty. A woman was predisposed to admire beauty in art, landscape, flowers etc. Sensitive, yes. But not creative.

Delicacy was also seen as an innate feminine feature and consequently attributed to all female activity. In the case of the evaluation of women's art, however, delicacy was positioned as the opposite of power. The deficit of power was logically associated with weakness and was supposedly accompanied by timidity and shyness. In the context of art, these features were not understood as modesty, but as belying a lack of courage. According to the critics, such lack of courage supposedly also predispositioned women to imitate male artists. Consequently, women were perceived as creatively dependent. Maria Dulębianka, a painter and social activist, discussed the female artists' alleged creative dependence, without denying the legitimacy of this accusation. She explained the situation not by recourse to supposed "feminine nature," but by living circumstances. She wrote in 1903: "The conditions in which a woman lives make her least independent as possible and thus least creative as possible."[8] According to critics, women artists tried to make up for this lack of creativity and lack of impetus by painting with meticulousness and an excessive focus on detail.[9] Here, again without denying the legitimacy of the accusation, the line of defense of female art ran in two directions. On the one hand, the passion for detail could be given a positive spin because details are also worth an artist's

---

[6] Henryk, Struve, "Udział kobiet w sztukach pięknych." *Kłosy*, no. 456 (1874): 199-201.

[7] Adolf Dygasiński, "Myśli o stanowisku kobiety ze względu na wychowanie społeczne." *Świt*, no. 23 (1884): 374.

[8] Maria Dulębianka, "O twórczości kobiet." *Głos kobiet w kwestii kobiecej*, edited by Maria Wiśniewska (Kraków: Stowarzyszenie Pomocy Naukowej dla Polek im. J.I. Kraszewskiego, 1903), 194.

[9] Antoni Nowosielski, "O przeznaczeniu i zawodzie kobiety." *Tygodnik Ilustrowany*, no. 166 (1862): 217.

attention and appreciation. On the other hand, focus on the minuscule was seen as another effect of upbringing and living conditions. Maria Dulębianka did not question women's marked tendency to concentrate on details. However, she believed that the traditional role of women (domestic chores, raising children) developed a specific way of perceiving the world. Women were accustomed to noticing and remembering numerous details, but they failed at constructing a vision of the whole. According to Dulębianka, if one's living conditions and educational context change, this so-eagerly criticized feature of female creativity will disappear, just like women's supposed artistic and creative dependence on men.

Within the framework of the traditionally understood world order, women did, however, have an opportunity to engage in some artistic professions, such as becoming an actress, singer, pianist or dancer. Nineteenth-century public opinion considered the stage to be a suitable place for women, but only for some women; in their case, the problem of a professional career did not arouse pro-family emotions, because actresses, dancers etc., were morally suspicious by definition and were not understood to be fit wives and mothers. The conflict between the calling to raise a family versus practice a profession did not concern them. Above all, however, the acceptance of the aforementioned artistic activities as viable pathways for women was based on their reconstructive and not creative character. Singers, pianists, actresses, etc., performed the works of male composers and playwrights. Their art was based on the best possible rendering of the author's idea, or possibly interpretation, and so became permissible because the attribution at its root sanctioned male creativity; in the eyes of the male-dominated cultural apparatus, it did not threaten or suggest an attack on the position of a man as creator.

When writing about the artistic activity of Polish women in the nineteenth century, it is necessary to address the issue of amateur practices and the relationship between professionalism and amateurism in the context of female art. Women's aspirations to become professionals in the field of art were in opposition to the then socially accepted amateur practice of art by ladies. The framework of the traditional "salon" education, which applied in the upbringing of nearly every upper-class girl in Poland consisted of learning foreign languages, music, drawing and often watercolor painting (despite attempts to reform education to make it more applicable in the wider labor market). A parallel phenomenon occurred in many other European countries. On the one hand, this kind of "artistic touch" was supposed to emphasize a maiden's sensitivity, subtlety and ensure her a successful marriage. On the other hand, it contributed to treating women's creativity as amateurism and dilettantism. It was a well-known fact that ladies amused themselves with painting. Their more or less successfully executed pictures were not taken seriously as art. These pejorative clichés had to be confronted by professional pioneer women artists, who usually had to navigate significant shortages in their own professional preparation, as compared with male artists.

At this point, it is also important to make a distinction between creativity and art. Art is a social activity, and it can occur only when it is received. This is the implication of the notion of "artist" as a social role. Meanwhile, creativity can be defined as an individual action. This distinction is important in the context of women's art. It was not until female artistic activity moved out of the private sphere that was traditionally assigned to women into the public, male sphere, that nineteenth-century critics began to recognize their accession to the realm of art.

Despite the columnists who attributed to women a lack of intellectual and creative predispositions, the dynamic growth of Polish women's artistic aspirations could be observed in the Kingdom of Poland as early as the 1840s. Initially, this growth mainly occurred in the field of literature. This phenomenon received some social support due to a specific combination of political and cultural factors. The defeat of the November Uprising in 1832 was followed by the Great Emigration of Polish intellectuals and writers, mostly to Germany and France. This in turn caused soon a demand in the Kingdom of Poland for artists "on the spot." At the beginning of the 1840s, attempts intensified to revive Polish culture and break it out of the stagnation in which it had fallen, due to the lost uprising and the post-revolt Russian government repressions. The circles involved in the awakening of Polish artistic life treated almost every creative activity, especially in the field of literature, as a contribution to the national culture. [10] Even in the case of *ouvrés* far from outstanding, critics believed that it was their patriotic duty to motivate authors to continue their efforts and not to discourage them if such criticism were to cause them severe distress. They, therefore, supported good intentions and mobilized debutants to continue their work and to improve it (including men and women alike, because women also wanted to fill this gap in artistic activity). With this support, however, also went attempts to limit women's creativity to defined areas corresponding to "female nature." Thus women were granted the right to try their hand at poetry, as well as to write didactic novels containing a moral message for readers. Ideally, it was widely held that the female author should combine literary ambitions with a woman's "natural" vocation of child-rearing. Society perceived literature for children and young people not so much as a creative, but rather as an educational activity, for which a woman, as a mother

---

[10] For example, those concentrated around *Biblioteka Warszawska*, a literary and scientific monthly magazine founded in 1841.

(real or potential) was appointed by nature. According to contemporary critics, children's literature was the most fitting field in which a woman who wanted to write books could excel.[11] Such literature was to have not only a pedagogical character, but also to be characterized by emphasizing sentiment and a certain infantilism with which to better influence young readers. Sentimentality and infantilism fit well with female nature, as it was traditionally understood. Women were thought to acquire these features from Godin order to facilitate contact and communication with children. Thus two interconnected activities were considered inseparable from one another in society: pedagogical literature and teaching, both of which became the professional specializations of Polish women from the gentry and intelligentsia at the time.

Polish women writing educational books for children and teenagers in the 1840s could refer to Klementyna Tańska-Hoffmanowa, a writer highly respected in Polish society. Hoffmanowa made her debut in 1819 and thus became the first Polish woman to make a living from writing. She wrote guidebooks and novels for girls. She also worked in a female school. In her opinion, girls should be well prepared for the role of mother, wife and housekeeper. They must also be patriotic and religious. Hoffmanowa did not support movements for female emancipation, however, she set an example for many Polish women wishing to combine pedagogical activity with literature.

In the second half of the nineteenth-century, the literary profession was already widely recognized as appropriate for women, and so was not the source of much controversy. Most female writers still wrote so-called "minor literature" for children, but some of them dared to write novels for adults. The books of Eliza Orzeszkowa, for example, enjoyed great recognition. Orzeszkowa's novels entered the Polish canon, as did the poetry of Maria Konopnicka. At the turn-of-the-century further outstanding figures of Polish literature met their debute: Gabriela Zapolska, novelist and playwright, and Zofia Nałkowska, novelist.

The next historical milestone that deeply impacted Polish women's professional artistic activity was the January Uprising. Its defeat in 1864 led to the bankruptcy of many Polish landowners. Their fall was mostly the result of Russian repressions of Polish life and society, and the punishment for participation in the uprising was very severe, often involving exile to Siberia and the confiscation of property. But the economic conditions after the uprising also changed, largely due to the enfranchisement of the peasants, which the Tsarist government carried out throughout the Kingdom of Poland at this time. Landowners could no longer count on a free labor force. Numerous

---

[11] Adam Pług, "Wspomnienie pośmiertne o Paulinie Krakowowej." *Kłosy*, no. 870 (1882): 134.

lords and petty nobles sold their estates and migrated to cities. These changes forced many gentlewomen to face the necessity of earning their living and so they started desperately on the path of seeking a job. Columnists noticed that ladies looking for gainful employment were in an extremely difficult position. Most of them tried to become governesses, but supply in the teaching profession quickly exceeded demand. Literature did not provide enough income to live on. The narrow range of paid activities suitable for and accessible to ladies became an acute sociopolitical problem. It was necessary to find other income sources. Women who aspired to prestigious intellectual professions were often accused of inappropriate ambition and immorality, but manual occupations did not arouse much resistance (on the contrary, conservatives considered them appropriate for the female gender); given this juxtaposition between intellect and manual work, many Polish columnists and social activists thought that the perfect compromise had been found: craftsmanship. It was promoted as a suitable manual occupation for women in need. Many private artisan female schools were then established. Among the upper-class, it even became a fashion for young women to learn a craft. However, it soon turned out that most of the female "new artisans," as they were called, could not cope with the labor market. Their time-consuming and laborious products did not withstand the competition: the products of the guild craftsmen were superior, as these men were much better trained. There were also factory products available on the market that were much cheaper than craftsmen's products. Amid this dynamic, the educational fashion once again shifted to the applied arts, causing another flood of schools and courses for women. These schools were often started by women themselves, which provided an additional income opportunity for them.

Thus the practice of art appeared to impoverished upper-class women as one of the few options to make money.[12] As in the case of literature, here columnists also tried to find a compromise between women's aspirations and conservative worldviews by once again manipulating their skillset and specialization based upon essentialist gender ideas. Nineteenth-century experts on the "female nature," ascribed to women innate manual skills which were given by God to enable good housekeeping. Women were also stated to have an aesthetic sense, which supposedly helped them in their task of pleasing men. This aesthetic sense was of course deemed insufficient to create any lasting or meaningful

---

[12] Publicists who postulated this were Edmund Nałęcz and Wojciech Gerson (also an artist and teacher). See: Eduard Nałęcz, "Zawodowa praca kobiet." *Tygodnik Ilustrowany*, no. 15 (1895): 237-238; Eduard Nałęcz, "Nasze pionierki w dziedzinie sztuki." *Tygodnik Ilustrowany*, no. 24 (1896): 462-463; Wojciech Gerson, "Praca kobiet w sztukach pięknych, plastycznych i obrazowych." *Świt*, no. 16 (1885): 123.

artwork, but was just enough of a sense by which to make things appear somehow "prettier." Thus women had been granted the right to take care of their own beauty (by fashion, cosmetics) and ambience (interior decoration, decoration of objects, etc.), consequently, applied art was to become a female specialization within the field of art.

While there were strong attempts to limit women's professional expansion exclusively to the manual sphere, the main battle of emancipation was fought over access to gainful intellectual labor, including the right to practice professionally the so-called pure arts (painting, sculpture), understood at the time as intellectual activity. For Polish women in the nineteenth century, access to practicing these art forms was far more difficult than work in the applied arts. But there were attempts to find them a niche there. Female nature was thought to be deeply religious. This view was shared by many women; one can refer here to the statements of writer and philosopher Eleonora Ziemięcka or editor and writer Maria Ilnicka. They were convinced that the characteristic features of feminine nature were idealism and deep religiosity.[13] Therefore, critics like Edmund Nałęcz proposed religious painting as an avenue for women with artistic aspirations.[14] In the Kingdom of Poland in the second half of the nineteenth century, Bronisława Wiesiołowska and Maria Łubieńska, inter alia, specialized in religious painting. Founded by the latter, *Zakład św. Łukasza* employed only women and consisted of four "departments," one of which was the department of religious paintings for churches.[15] It is very likely that the authorship of many anonymous paintings from the second half of the nineteenth century that are scattered around Polish churches should be attributed to women.

However, Polish female painters of the discussed period mostly painted portraits. Anna Bilińska, who specialized in portraits, enjoyed the great recognition of her contemporaries. The most famous of her works, a turning point in Bilińska's career, was *Self-portrait* which was awarded a medal at the *Salon de Paris* in 1887. Afterwards, she enjoyed a successful international career, won many prizes, and received many commissions, not only from Polish patrons.

---

[13] Elonora Ziemięcka, *Myśli o wychowaniu kobiet* (Warszawa: F. Spies i Spółka, 1843), 15-16; Maria Ilnicka, "Kobieta i książka." *Bluszcz*, no. 38 (1867): 153.

[14] Edmund Nałęcz, "Nasze pionierki w dziedzinie sztuki." *Tygodnik Ilustrowany*, no. 24 (1896): 462-463.

[15] Danuta Czapczyńska-Kleszczyńska, "Maria Magdalena Łubieńska (1833-1920) – artystka wyemancypowana." *Sacrum et Decorum*, no. 4 (2013): 9-13.

**Figure 6.1.** Anna Bilińska-Bohdanowicz, *Self-portrait,* 1887. Oil on canvas, National Museum in Kraków. Source: Public Domain.[16]

Portrait specialists Emilia Dukszyńska-Dukszta and Maria Nostitz-Wasilkowska also enjoyed considerable recognition in the Kingdom of Poland.

---

[16] Anna Bilińska-Bohdanowicz, Public domain via Wikimedia Commons, https://commons. wikimedia.org/w/index.php?curid=123373.

The specialization in portraiture among female painters from the second half of the nineteenth century was viewed by contemporary columnists as yet another manifestation of women's nature. In this instance, the identified feminine qualities comprised assets such as the ability to give the picture a cozy, warm atmosphere; or the ability to establish emotional contact with the portrayed person, which resulted in a closer capture of the model's personality on canvas. The most important aspect of this specialization, however, seems to have been financial: it was easier to obtain commissions for portraits than for other genres, and thus also easier to earn money through this activity.[17] It was also less problematic for women to create portraits instead of e.g., historical compositions; in the former artists only had to picture one, at most two persons.

The fact that Polish women did not usually paint the multi-figure historical compositions that were typical for academism and highly valued by critics at the time belied a common objection to women's art.[18] It served as an argument that there was no female predisposition toward the creation of true art. Polish nineteenth-century critics understood the painting as an "artistic poem," which should contain a clear message and present a story. They evaluated painting on the basis of how well the painter fulfilled the task of rendering ideas on canvas. Illustrating the subject, idea, imagined scene, etc., was evidence of the artist's inventiveness; the same testimony was not obtained by the practice of so-called imitative genres, i.e., portrait, landscape, still life. Polish critics, rewarding the narrative element in art, highly rated and considered it to be the most prestigious multi-figure historical compositions, which they called "great topics" (wielkie tematy) and "serious painting" (powa ne malarstwo). It is apparent even in their reports from exhibitions in the order in which they discussed the presented paintings. Without undertaking to paint historical compositions, the female painters condemned their work as being perceived by Polish critics as inferior. During the period under discussion, supporters of women's emancipation in the field of art constantly hoped that female artists would eventually take up historical compositions. The choice of genres entailed consequences for the artist's professional position, and if historical

---

[17] This aspect of women's creative activity is also raised in Maria Poprzęcka, "Boznańska i inne." *Kobieta i kultura: kobiety wśród twórców kultury intelektualnej i artystycznej w dobie rozbiorów i w niepodległym państwie polskim*, edited by Anna Żarnowska and Andrzej Szwarc (Warszawa: DiG, 1996), 175 – 187.

[18] The exception is Mgadalena Andrzejkowicz-Buttowt who did create historical compositions.

subjects were deemed appropriate, could remove the stigma of amateurism from female art.[19]

Despite such hope, Polish female artists (except Magdalena Andrzejkowicz-Buttowt) did not generally undertake to paint the multi-figure compositions which at that time were so highly regarded by critics. This wide pattern of a version to historical themes illustrates just how closely the specificity of women's artistic themes in the second half of the nineteenth century were related not only to economic issues, but also to education. Women also did not paint multi-figure compositions because they lacked technical preparation in this area.[20] They painted what they had the opportunity to learn. In the case of the visual arts, it was difficult to make up for the lack of formal education on one's own. Whereas, in the case of literature, self-education was of much more help. This difference was noticed by columnists supporting emancipation.[21]

To undertake historical painting, an academic education was necessary. To attempt the "Great Topics" required thorough professional preparation: anatomy lessons, naked model studies, studies of the human body in motion. This was the most important element of the curriculum in fine arts academies, but at the time, academies of fine arts were either closed to women in general (which was the case in Poland), or open (for example, in Spain) under certain conditions, which meant that women could not attend the most advanced levels of art studies (the very classes of naked model study and of composition). Naturally, this fact had consequences not only for the topics undertaken by women, but also for the level of their professional skills. Polish private art schools for female students provided very limited training, in comparison to the curriculum in academies. Graduates of these schools simply painted what and how they could. There was, however, for a determined Polish woman with artistic aspirations, an opportunity to study the naked model. One could go to France and enroll in the so-called free academies (for example, Académie Julian, a private school which admitted both men and women). But that solution was an expensive remedy. Besides, for many women artists, there were still moral barriers. A "decent female" had a great problem with nudity – both someone else's and her own; women were brought up in such a way that nudity discouraged them from figure studies. The artist had to break through this reluctance.

---

[19] Edmund Nałęcz, "Nasze pionierki w dziedzinie sztuki." *Tygodnik Ilustrowany*, no. 24 (1896): 462-463.

[20] This aspect was also raised in Joanna Sosnowska, *Poza kanonem: sztuka polskich artystek 1880-1939*, (Warszawa: Instytut Sztuki Polskiej Akademii Nauk, 2003), 115-149.

[21] Ibid.

In general, female artists also showed their subject in a tight frame. Conservative critics, such as Henryk Struve, perceived this choice as another manifestation of the feminine nature, which was tasked with introducing intimacy, subtlety, a focus on details, etc., and at the same time, unable to gain the power and momentum typical for male nature and male works.[22] Meanwhile, this tendency was also linked to educational shortcomings in composition skills.

Public fine art academies eventually opened their doors to women at the beginning of the twentieth century, but by that time, historical painting was out of fashion. The corresponding increase in consistently higher evaluations of women's painting by critics in the early twentieth century is also connected with the fact that the canon of academic painting – the hierarchy of topics – clearly lost its force and then ceased to apply at all.

Since the qualities attributed to a woman were to be reproductive, not creative; passive and not active, the woman who creates— and what is more, does it well, was perceived as an unnatural creature—neither male nor female. According to conservative critics, female art, due to its feminine nature, will always bear the stigma of imitation and weakness. Thus a work of high artistic value, which was difficult to depreciate despite its female authorship, had to be masculine in character – its creator was attributed either with the denial of her femininity or its inborn lack. The most famous and valued "male women artist" of her time was Rosa Bonheur, a French painter and sculptor, known especially for her naturalistic paintings depicting animals. Discussing her work, critics emphasized Rosa's male psyche and behavior, her quasi-male appearance, including her short hair, her fondness for male clothing (she had official permission from the police to wear trousers) and so on. On Polish soil, the quintessential example of painting which emerged from a brush held by a woman and to which a masculine character was constantly attributed, was the work of Anna Bilińska. After Bilińska won the silver medal at such a prestigious exhibition as the Paris Salon, the high value of her works remained undisputed for Polish critics. It was not appropriate to describe the works of the medalist as weak, imitating, without momentum, etc. But, if they were very good, they had to be masculine. Critics' statements on Bilińska's works repeatedly used this term. Much was written about this artist's "male" courage and about the

---

[22] Henryk Struve, "Udział kobiet w sztukach pięknych." *Kłosy,* no. 455 (1874): 187-188.

"male power" of her brush.[23] The contemporary critic, Czesław Jankowski believed that: "Bilińska's talent was primarily male."[24]

The "masculine" character of the outstanding feminine work manifested itself not only in the field of fine arts, but also in literature. When Wacław Szymanowski wrote about Narcyza Żmichowska in 1855, he highly valued her abilities. In his opinion, her talent was far superior to that of other women who tried their hand at poetry. Immediately after these words of recognition, an explanation follows: "In this female body, the male soul was burning."[25] According to Szymanowski, Żmichowska was an exception. In her case, the denial of nature could be regarded as heroism and a sacrifice made on the altar of genius.

According to the Polish male critics of the day, when a woman, therefore, does not want to abandon her creative ambitions, she runs the risk of losing her feminine qualities. As soon as she becomes an outstanding artist, she stops being a woman (but she does not become a man, either). For those who did not feel ready for a similarly radical step, the "middle" skill level remained the only one open to them: the class of artistic craftswomen. It was this level with which many female artists of the second half of the nineteenth century were content.[26] The male critics, in their designation of "masculine qualities" did not extend access to the woman artist to their own male privilege, rather they simply erased her gender in order to appropriate her individual talent for the male gender and its hegemony over artistic life.

At the end of the nineteenth century, a key narrative trend about women artists that challenged believers in the essential feminine nature, gained in importance and even began to dominate in the Polish press. This heroic narrative exposed hardships and struggles which brave female students experienced at the early stages of their careers. This new emphasis on the tenacity of professional women served to break the stereotypes that served as social masks for inequality in all-too-rare examples of successful scientists like Maria Skłodowska-Curie, as well as in some of the first professional female

---

[23] For example, see: Seweryna Duchińska, "Listy z Paryża." *Kłosy*, no. 1152 (1887): 60-61; Sęp. "Z Warszawy." *Biesiada Literacka*. No. 16 (1892): 194-195.

[24] Czesław Jankowski, "Na malarskiej niwie." *Tygodnik Ilustrowany*, no. 174 (1893): 263.

[25] Wacław Szymanowski and Aleksander Niewiarowski. *Wspomnienia o Cyganerii warszawskiej* (Warszawa: Czytelnik, 1964), 215.

[26] This issue was also raised by Maria Poprzęcka in "Problemy feministycznej historii sztuki." *Kobieta i edukacja na ziemiach polskich w XIX i XX wieku*, vol. 2, edited by Anna Żarnowska and Andrzej Szwarc (Warszawa: DiG, 1992), 267-279.

artists. [27] By contrast, it became recognized that the majority of females involved in intellectual work, including art, were able to overcome a great amount of adversity thanks to their individual talent, willpower, determination and faith in the progress of humanity. Again the case of Bilińska, a medal winner at the Paris Salon, was very meaningful here. She served as an example in arguments which upheld that a woman could achieve such lofty goals and professional successes, but also served as an example of just how much such success could cost, given the prevailing social system she endured. The death of the thirty-six-year-old Bilińska was then interpreted as the result of the financial difficulties in which she had struggled and which put her health at risk. If Polish society had facilitated the work of a talented person, no matter her gender, Bilińska might not have become terminally ill and died prematurely. She may have created many other outstanding paintings for the glory and benefit of Polish culture – this was the meaning of the text that the poet Maria Konopnicka, embittered by her own struggle for financial stability, wrote and published in *Kraj*.[28] She bluntly accused an insensitive, conservative society of this painter's premature death. Konopnicka wrote dramatically about how cold Bilińska's workplace was, because the artist had not had enough money for heating, how she had to save on food and very often was hungry etc. The young painter, however, did not give up, strove for success and managed to do so: "she ran to the very top – and she fell down there."[29] Also, the later husband of Bilińska, Antoni Bohdanowicz, recalled the very difficult time of Bilińska's life before she became famous.[30] A painter and friend of Bilińska, Józef Chełmoński, said of her in 1893: "a true martyr and art priestess."[31]

The year 1904 can be considered a symbolic *caesura* in the situation of female artists in the Kingdom of Poland. It is the date of the establishment of the School of Fine Arts in Warsaw, where women and men were equally admissible. Thus, the beginning of the twentieth century marks the end of the first pioneering stage of women's struggle for admission to the Parnassus. The generation with artistic ambitions that began its career in the Kingdom of Poland after 1904 acted under altogether different conditions – both institutional

---

[27] Edmund Nałęcz, "Nasze pionierki w dziedzinie sztuki." *Tygodnik Ilustrowany*, no. 24 (1896): 462-463.

[28] Maria Konopnicka, "Luźne kartki." *Kraj*, no. 19 (1893): 5-7.

[29] Ibid, 6.

[30] Antoni Bohdanowicz, *Anna Bilińska, kobieta, Polka i artystka w świetle jej dziennika i recenzyj wszechświatowej prasy*, (Warszawa: Bohdanowicz, 1928), 102.

[31] Ibid, 103.

and mental – as compared with the women who sought to become professional artists in the nineteenth century.

My primary research interest and focus here has been on the dominating significance of social and economic conditions of women's activity, including their artistic creativity. I believe, taking into consideration all discussed factors, institutional and social obstacles, difficulties in fulfilling their artistic potential, that it is justified to look at the art of Polish women in the period under discussion not so much in terms of artistic value, but pioneering merit. These women have built the tradition of Polish female artistic activity. Such a tradition was more difficult to create in visual arts than in literature, because of the organization of the educational system in Poland after the uprisings. But it is only thanks to this artistic tradition, however unfinished it was when it ended, that made possible the appearance of outstanding Polish artists in the twentieth century, such as Zofia Stryjeńska, Tamara Łempicka (de Lempicka) or Magdalena Abakanowicz.

## Bibliography

Bohdanowicz, Antoni. *Anna Bilińska, kobieta, Polka i artystka w świetle jej dziennika irecenzyj wszechświatowej prasy.* Warszawa: Bohdanowicz, 1928.

Czapczyńska-Kleszczyńska, Danuta. "Maria Magdalena Łubieńska (1833-1920) – artystka Wyemancypowana." *Sacrum et Decorum*, no. 4 (2013): 9-32.

Duchińska, Seweryna. "Listy z Paryża." *Kłosy*, no. 1152 (1887): 60-61.

Dulębianka, Maria. "O twórczości kobiet." *Głos kobiet w kwestii kobiecej.* Ed. Maria Wiśniewska. Kraków: Stowarzyszenie Pomocy Naukowej dla Polek im. J.I. Kraszewskiego, 1903: 163-197.

Dygasiński, Adolf. "Myśli o stanowisku kobiety ze względu na wychowanie społeczne." *Świt*, no. 23 (1884): 373-374.

Gerson, Wojciech. "Praca kobiet w sztukach pięknych, plastycznych i obrazowych." *Świt*, no 16 (1885): 123-124.

Ilnicka, Maria. "Słówko o emancypacji kobiet." *Bluszcz*, no. 10 (1867): 38-39.

_____. "Kobieta i książka." *Bluszcz*, no. 38 (1867): 153-154.

Jankowski, Czesław. "Na malarskiej niwie." *Tygodnik Ilustrowany*, no. 174 (1893): 263.

Konopnicka, Maria. "Luźne kartki." *Kraj*, no. 19 (1893): 5-7.

Nałęcz, Edmund. "Zawodowa praca kobiet." *Tygodnik Ilustrowany*, no. 15 (1895): 237-238.

_____. "Nasze pionierki w dziedzinie sztuki." *Tygodnik Ilustrowany*, no. 24 (1896): 462-463.

Nochlin, Linda. *Why Have There Been No Great Women Artists.* London: Thames & Hudson, 2021.

Nowosielski, Antoni (Antoni Jaksa-Marcinkiewicz). "O przeznaczeniu i zawodzie kobiety." *Tygodnik Ilustrowany*, no. 166 (1862): 215-217.

Orzeszkowa, Eliza. "Polki." *Kwestia kobieca w Europie*. Ed. Teodor W. Stanton. Warszawa: Wydawnictwo Przeglądu Tygodniowego, 1885: 280-296.

Pług, Adam. "Wspomnienie pośmiertne o Paulinie Krakowowej." *Kłosy*, no. 870 (1882): 133-135.

Poprzęcka, Maria. "Problemy feministycznej historii sztuki." *Kobieta i edukacja na ziemiach polskich w XIX i XX wieku*, vol. 2. Eds. Anna Żarnowska and Andrzej Szwarc. Warszawa: DiG, 1992: 267-279.

Poprzęcka, Maria. "Boznańska i inne." *Kobieta i kultura: kobiety wśród twórców kultury intelektualnej i artystycznej w dobie rozbiorów i w niepodległym państwie polskim*. Eds. Anna Żarnowska and Andrzej Szwarc. Warszawa: DiG, 1996: 175-187. Sęp. "Z Warszawy." *Biesiada Literacka*, no. 16 (1892): 194-195.

Sosnowska, Joanna. *Poza kanonem: sztuka polskich artystek 1880-1939*. Warszawa: Instytut Sztuki Polskiej Akademii Nauk, 2003.

Struve, Henryk. "Udział kobiet w sztukach pięknych." *Kłosy*, no. 455 (1874): 187-188.

_____. *Kłosy*, no. 456 (1874): 199-201.

Szymanowski, Wacław and Aleksander Niewiarowski. *Wspomnienia o Cyganerii warszawskiej*. Warszawa: Czytelnik, 1964.

Ziemięcka, Eleonora. *Myśli o wychowaniu kobiet*. Warszawa: Spies i Spółka, 1843.

# Chapter 7

# Fighting for Ourselves: Iconography of the Body in Polish Women Artists' Works After 1945

Magdalena Furmanik-Kowalska

Małgorzata Jankowska

### Abstract

The aim of this chapter is to present selected works of the most outstanding Polish female artists after World War II. It is also to point out characteristic motifs of body iconography in Polish women art. The subject of this research are all artworks in which the body is a main subject, and not only feminist art, which Izabela Kowalczyk aptly splits into three stages: feminist interventions—the 1970s and partly the 1980s; feminist criticism of the 1990s; and post-feminist art at the turn-of-the-20th and 21st centuries. In this paper, we identify the following four issues: postwar trauma reflected in deformed/crippled bodies; the fight for subjectivity and the Polish People's Republic through feminist theories and the body in Polish reality; The Third Republic of Poland and female sexuality in battles for Others' bodies; and conflicts with religious and political conservatism involving bodies as tools of activism.

**Keywords**: women's art, iconography of the body, corporeality, contemporary Polish art, revolution, subjectivity, female sexuality

*\*\*\**

In 1991, the Polish adaptation of the American artist Barbara Kruger's famous 1989 poster that featured the slogan "Your Body Is a Battleground" appeared on the facade of the Ujazdowski Castle, housing the Centre for Contemporary Art in Warsaw. Its small-format version went up all over the capital, sparking a social debate on reproductive rights and sex education in state schools. Two years later, the conservative PiS (Prawa i Sprawiedliwosci) government, bound by an agreement with the Catholic Church, passed an anti-abortion bill that permitted termination only in the case of severe and irreversible fetal abnormality, pregnancy endangering the woman's life, or pregnancy resulting from rape. In October 2020, the pro-Catholic ruling party further tightened abortion laws, paying no heed to public opinion, which ignited a wave of protests across the country. The slogan coined by Barbara Kruger was topical once more, and the black-and-white female face with red inscriptions running across it returned to the streets of Warsaw as a symbol of women's fight for their basic rights.

Widespread patriarchal and radical politics and religious fundamentalism of the late twentieth century can also be observed in Poland; and in the twenty-first century, Polish women find themselves needing to continue the struggle for the right to decide the legislation of their bodies.[1] The battle for the body is, at the same time, a battle for female identity in a postmodern world. According to Zygmunt Bauman, a body is conceptually "a prominent part of the reflexive project of the self."[2] It is no longer, as it was in nineteenth-century romanticism, a husk holding consciousness or soul, but an integral part of being, having become the primary locus for where sociocultural interactions take place, and where control over those interactions is established and reinforced.[3] Unsurprisingly, issues explored by numerous women artists in their work, including those who would rather not be called feminists, encompass ideas of "womanhood," "the female body" and the social roles that women occupy in society. Their creative outputs are rarely presented within this context, however, and there have been thus far very few scholarly publications discussing art on these themes created by Polish women in a comparative perspective.

A pioneering work on this subject accompanied the *Sztuka kobiet* [Women's Art] show staged at the Galeria Bielska in Bielsko-Biała. Rather than simply cataloguing displayed works, the book offers a compilation of texts discussing feminist art in Western Europe and the United States, as well as performs a critical analysis of the oeuvres of Polish women artists, featuring contributions by Polish art critics and historians, including: Maria Hussakowska-Szyszko, Kazimierz Piotrowski, Magdalena Ujma, Agata Jakubowska, Bożenia Czubak and Agnieszka Rayzacher.[4] Among other observations, the publication indicates dissimilarities between the Western and Polish receptions of feminism in art.

---

[1] Manuel Castells. *Siła tożsamości* (*The Power of Identity. The Information Age: Economy, Society and Culture, vol. 2*) (Warszawa: PWN, 2009), 43.

[2] Giddens, *Nowoczesność i tożsamość*, 297.

[3] Giddens, *Nowoczesność i tożsamość*, 296.

[4] Jolanta Ciesielska and Agata Smalcerz, eds., *Sztuka kobiet (Women's art)* (Bielsko-Biała: Galeria Bielska BWA, 2000).

Despite the book's valuable contribution to knowledge about Polish women in art, it took another five years for the first monograph on contemporary art written by a women to be published. This book is Agata Jakubowska's *Na marginesach lustra: Ciało kobiece w pracach polskich artystek* [At the Margins of the Looking Glass: The Female Body in Polish Women Artists' Works].[5] A range of critical articles by Izabela Kowalczyk also appeared at the time in the online journal *Artmix* and the feminist periodical *Ośka*. Some of these articles were reprinted in 2010 in *Matki-Polki, Chłopcy i Cyborgi... Sztuka i feminizm w Polsce* [Polish Mothers, Boys and Cyborgs . . . Art and Feminism in Poland].[6] Both publications bring into focus the processes of constituting corporeality and sexuality through artistic practice. Defining femininity is also the subject of Kowalczyk's essays, printed in the exhibition catalog accompanying the exhibition *Gender Check: Femininity and Masculinity in the Art of Eastern Europe*[7] staged in Vienna in 2009 and in Warsaw in 2010. The relationship between socialist realism and women[8] is further investigated by Ewa Toniak. She is also the editor of the volume entitled *Jestem artystką, we wszystkim, co niepotrzebne: Kobiety i sztuka około 1960 roku* [I Am an Artist in Everything that is Unnecessary: Women and Art around 1960].[9] The eventful year 2011 saw the appearance of a few key texts, such as the monumental work *Artystki polskie* [Polish Women Artists],[10] edited by Agata Jakubowska, containing articles by a number of Polish women researchers[11] as well as a comprehensive catalog of works and biographies of women artists active from the nineteenth century

---

[5] Agata Jakubowska. *Na marginesach lustra. Ciało kobiece w pracach polskich artystek (In the margins of the mirror. The female body in the works of Polish artists)*, (Kraków: Wydawnictwo Universitas, 2005).

[6] Izabela Kowalczyk. *Matki-Polki, Chłopcy i Cyborgi... Sztuka i feminizm w Polsce (Polish Mothers, Boys and Cyborgs ... Art and Feminism in Poland)*, (Poznań: Galeria Miejska Arsenał, 2010).

[7] Izabela Kowalczyk, "The Ambivalent Beauty." In *Gender Check: Femininity and Masculinity in Art of Eastern Europe*, edited by Bojana Pejić (Wien: Museum Moderner Kunst Stiftung Ludwig Wien, 2009), 40-59.

[8] Ewa Toniak, *Olbrzymki: kobiety i socrealizm (Giants: Women and Socialist Realism)*, (Kraków: Korporacja Ha!art, 2008).

[9] Ewa Toniak, ed. *Jestem artystką, we wszystkim, co niepotrzebne. Kobiety i sztuka około 1960 roku (I am an artist in everything unnecessary. Women and Art around 1960)*, (Warszawa: Neriton, 2010).

[10] Agata Jakubowska, ed. *Artystki polskie (Polish Women Artists)*, (Warszawa: PWN, 2011).

[11] The book contains articles by Agnieszka Morawińska, Anna Markowska, Maria Poprzęcka, Agata Jakubowska, Karolina Puchała-Rojek, Joanna M., Ewa Małgorzata Tatar, Ewa Toniak, Joanna Turowicz, Magdalena Ujma.

through the present day. All of these publications have created a solid foundation for further research on art produced by Polish women artists. With the exception of *Gender Check*, these texts are available exclusively in Polish. The only publication in English is the exhibition catalog *Architectures Of Gender: Contemporary Women's Art In Poland*,[12] which accompanied a show at New York's Sculpture Center in 2003.

This article offers a review of selected artworks created by Polish women artists active after the Second World War, and points out some characteristic motifs that have shaped, over time, the iconography of the body in Polish women's art. Yet the subject of this research is more far-reaching than feminist art alone, which has been aptly divided by Izabela Kowalczyk into three stages: feminist interventions of the 1970s and partly 1980s; feminist critique of the 1990s and post-feminist art at the turn of the twentieth and twenty-first centuries, covering as well the creative output of those female creators who have positioned the body as the central focal point of their work.[13] We have differentiated the following four areas:

1. Postwar trauma reflected in deformed/crippled bodies.

2. The fight for subjectivity and the Polish People's Republic through feminist theories and the body in Polish reality

3. The Third Republic of Poland and female sexuality in battles for Others' bodies

4. Conflicts with religious and political conservatism involving bodies as tools of activism

Employing a chronological approach to this material what follows here will facilitate the presentation of various developments in artistic approaches to the body within the context of the social and cultural changes that have occurred in Poland in times of political transformations and regime change.

### Postwar Trauma: Deformed Bodies, Crippled bodies

Zoom back to the end of WWII: the time-consuming process of reconstruction is launched in Poland, and survivors face the need to come to grips with their stories, seeking salvation and recovery from the trauma of war. Among them,

---

[12] Aneta Szyłak, ed. *Architectures of Gender: Contemporary Women's Art In Poland*. Exhibition Catalogue (New York: Sculpture Center, 2003).

[13] Izabela Kowalczyk, "Od feministycznych interwencji do postfeminizmu" (From feminist interventions to post-feminism), *Matki-Polki, Chłopcy i Cyborgi . . . Sztuka i feminizm w Polsce* (Poznań: Galeria Miejska Arsenał, 2010), 11-20.

there are two women artists of Jewish descent: Erna Rosenstein (1913 – 2004) and Alina Szapocznikow (1926 – 1973). As early as 1946, the former produces a series of works aiming to depict and commemorate dramatic scenes from the German occupation, in, for example, her piece *Ghetto*. The vivid colors of this bold expressionist painting draw attention to death and suffering through the deformed bodies of murdered children, and the pain of their mourning parents. Thick black contours enable the artist to simplify human figures, adding a universal dimension to them. She paints a contemporary pieta, creating one of the most poignant artworks of the entire postwar era. Severed heads in this painting will keep reappearing in Rosenstein's work. The motif dominates *Screens*, 1951, a surrealistic portrait of the artist's parents, who were killed by the Nazis during the war. It will also return in their depictions made in 1979: *Dawn*, and *Midnight*.[14]

A head almost totally separated from its torso appears in *Little Mirror* (1951). A largely simplified and slightly deformed face in profile, painted in blue, is looking at its reflection in the mirror, which shows the portrait of a smiling blonde woman. The painting offers an intriguing reversal of an established configuration – it seems to be the obverse of Dorian Gray's story.[15] The surrealistic scene captures the viewer's attention with its ambiguity, posing a number of questions. If the mirror reflects the real self, is the face in it the face of a person of internal or merely external beauty? Is the blue figure, apparently sad, smiling to herself internally? Or is it the other way round? Or, perhaps, may the blue body represent a body affected by trauma – like the blue figures in Andrzej Wróblewski's paintings? Possibly it is a body bearing the mark of past experience, but still holding an internal spark of hope and joy revealed in the timid smile of the person in the mirror. Could this be a female version of the myth of Narcissus, a different interpretation of which is suggested by Julia Kristeva? The philosopher claims that self-love and delight in one's inner self – symbolically represented as looking into the mirror – is a prerequisite for the development of subjectivity.[16] "Some worldly things flow through me and I

---

[14] For more information see: Alison M. Gingeras, ed. *Erna Rosenstein: Once upon a time.* Exhibition Catalogue (New York: Hauser and Wirth Publishers, 2020); Dorota Jarecka and Barbara Piwowarska, *Erna Rosenstein: Mogę powtarzać tylko nieświadome (Erna Rosenstein: I Can Only Repeat Unconsciously)*, (Warszawa: Fundacja Galerii Foksal, 2014).

[15] *The Picture of Dorian Gray* is a novel by Oscar Wilde which depicts a story of a young man who remained eternally young and beautiful, yet his true face was shown in a painting hidden from others.

[16] Julia Kristeva, *Histoires d'amour* (Paris: Denoël, 1983); Agata Jakubowska, *Portret wielokrotny dzieła Aliny Szapocznikow (Multiple portraits of the work of Alina Szapocznikow)*, (Poznań: UMA Press, 2008), 140-141.

make them real," claimed Rosenstein, emphasizing the autobiographical aspect of her work.[17] For this reason, even if some of her works may appear to be purely abstract, e.g., *Disintegration* (1966), they should be viewed as surrealistic visions and in connection with her earlier pieces.

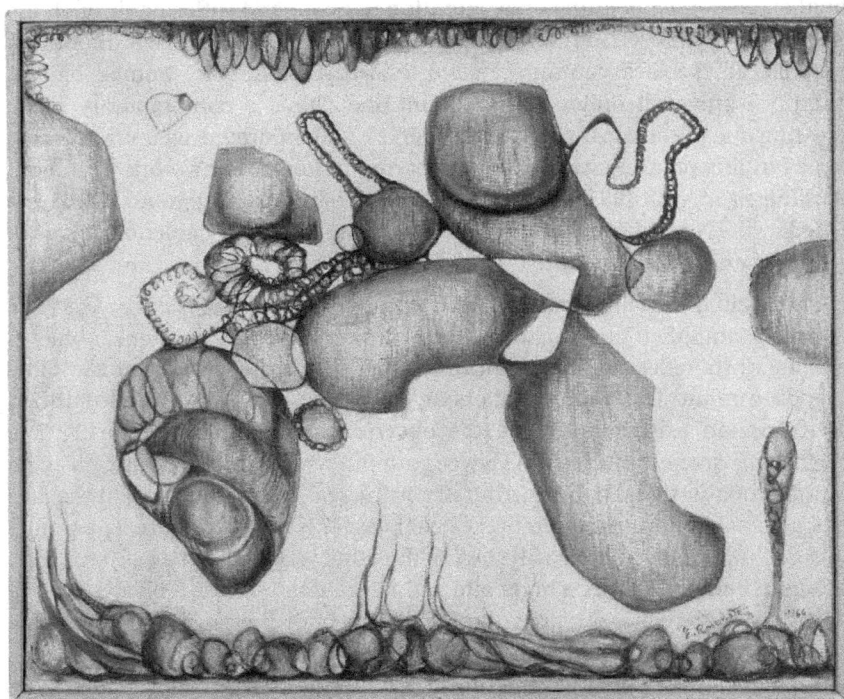

**Figure 7.1.** Erna Rosenstein, *Disintegration,* 1966, mixed media on canvas, 60 x 70 cm. Private Collection.© Archive of Wejman Gallery.

This linear, monochromatic painting dominated by blue reveals soft organic forms, bringing to mind human internal organs as well as underwater worlds of invertebrates or microbes seen under a microscope. Writhing ovoid shapes divide, multiply, disintegrate, while giving rise to new forms. Bodies break down so that new life may appear.

Organic forms are also meaningfully prominent in Alina Szapocznikow's creative output. In 1959, the artist made a series of sculptures interpreted as flower women, entitled: *Bellissima I; Bellissima II; Rose* and *Rambling.* She transformed simplified female bodies into plant-like shapes. In these works,

---

[17] Zbigniew Taranienko, ed. *Erna Rosenstein: Rzeczy, ślady, papiery z szafy (Erna Rosenstein: Things, traces, papers from the closet),* (Łódź: Galeria 86, 2002), 42.

women have no arms or calves, which, on the one hand, seems to evoke antique classical figures; but on the other hand, the exuberance and structural aspect of these sculptures repudiate such a reference. According to Agata Jakubowska, Szapocznikow's monographist, the artist: "( . . . ) not only stylistically but also in her attitude towards the object, i.e. female body, more closely approaches ( . . . ) the baroque or neo-baroque perspective."[18] Her pieces depict lushness and highlight female biological sensuality, but they also remind us of death and transience. In them, deformation and beauty permeate one another.

Jakubowska points out that by using the popular metaphor of woman-as-flower, the sculptor in her work is able to both "analyze and be immersed in the analyzed."[19] The researcher interprets her creative output in the context of the feminist debate on beauty and the power of seeing. She maintains that:

> Szapocznikow transformed the female body but without refining it or uncovering its 'true' facets, which is often the case in feminist art. She changed it into a grotesque object, an entity that disregards limits, contours that restrict bodies, pre-established stable figures.[20]

In 1963, the artist moved permanently to Paris where she got in touch with the Nouveau movement. In the wake of the Réalisme movement, which left a mark on her work, Szapocznikow experiments with unusual materials, including ready objects, and casts sculptures in plastic, which is described by Izabela Kowalczyk as "attempts at a veristic representation of corporeality."[21] In 1967, she creates one of her most recognizable pieces, *Multiple Portrait*. It is made up of four fragments of the human face featuring the mouth, placed one upon another. Each is cast in polyester in a different color, from near-black via dark-blue to flesh-colored, and then mounted on a piece of rock imitating female breasts. The multiplied physiognomy reflects the complex nature of womanhood. But the faces have no eyes, as in the 1959 pieces with missing extremities. The artist cannot see, but she can speak. Against the patriarchal culture that determines the power of seeing, which here has been taken away from the woman, she can express herself through her body. "Write with the body," demanded Hélène Cixous in *The Laugh of the Medusa*. The artist casts pieces of her own body that are evidently feminine – bellies, thighs, mouths, breasts – in order to transform them into innovative sculptures, such as: *Illuminated Lips* (1966), *Fetishes* (1970), *Dessert I* (1970-1971), *Dessert III* (1971)

---

[18] Jakubowska, *Portret wielokrotny dzieła Aliny Szapocznikow*, 143-144.

[19] Jakubowska, *Portret wielokrotny dzieła Aliny Szapocznikow*, 134.

[20] Ibid, 153.

[21] Kowalczyk, *Matki-Polski, Chłopcy i Cyborgi*, 89.

or *Tear* (1971). She records and fixes the impermanent and imperfect human body. The awareness of her own transitory nature intensifies when she is confronted with a lethal cancer. Her terminal illness marked her works. This was one of the reasons why she imprinted parts of her body and transformed them into artworks. Szapocznikow blurred many borders in her work, including the between high art and applied art, the public and the private, the solid and the brittle, beauty and deformation, elegance and kitsch.

### The Fight for Subjectivity and the Polish People's Republic through Feminist Theories and the Body in Polish Reality

The paradox of the 1970s was that women artists were present on the art scene, while at the same time absent from it. Many of them managed to carve out a niche for themselves in the art world, even if their activities were not in keeping with accepted trends and tendencies, and therefore were ignored. As the researcher Luiza Nader pointed out in her overview of conceptualism in the Polish People's Republic, the leading artistic movement in Poland at the time, conceptual art, steered clear of inquiring "about lust and constructs of subjectivity." [22] The era of the "Second Poland" was, however, full of contradictions and twists in the social and political context that frequently produced dramatic effects in art. [23] The solidarity of female textile workers who staged a strike in 1971, for example, in protest against privation, distress and overwork, and were disparaged as carrying little weight in political history and cultural memory, nevertheless proved successful at bringing pressure to bear upon the government, which reconsidered its decisions in raising food prices and slashing wages.[24] Written records demonstrate that weavers and spinners used a language that was pregnant with emotion and concern over their families, and the only form of physical aggression they displayed was showing naked buttocks to representatives of the authorities. In this narrative, the crucial role was served not by activism but by solidarity which developed at work – in the toilets, cloakrooms, and found its expression in resistance, or consistency in refusal to work. Contemporary literary women scholars point out that actions taken by Polish female activists, workers and communists exerted a stronger influence on emancipatory attitudes of some women artists than the inspiration derived from Western feminists. It is difficult to state

---

[22] Luiza Nader, *Konceptualizm w PRL* (*Conceptualism in the People's Republic of Poland*), (Warszawa: Wydawnictwo Uniwersytetu Warszawskiego, Fundacja Galerii Foksal, 2009), 11.

[23] "Second Poland" was a propaganda phrase used after 1970 used in official discourse to insist that the country was soon to achieve Western living standards.

[24] The strike occurred in February 1971 in the Julian Marchlewski Cotton Works, Łódź, with women comprising 80% of the staff; thirty-two plants across Łódź joined in.

positively if that was really so, but these events made anything look feasible. Investigating the literary output of Anna Świrszczyńska (1909-1984) who, a mature poet by the 1970s, announced that she needed to "create herself anew" by turning to her "problematic" body and its needs, Monika Rudaś-Grodzka suggests that the emancipatory power of this somatic turn in her poems, equivalent to the appropriation and reversal of the linguistic order, was rooted not only in the Western feminist theories, but very much in the attitudes of Polish activists, who encouraged her personal protestation against male dominance.[25]

New expectations harbored by women coincided with an economic boom (1971-1975), improvement in international relations ("opening to the West") and growing appetites for a new life among the Polish people. Within this context, the body and its imaginary occupied a significant role, setting out to reclaim some of its aspects, e.g., eroticism, which in official discourse were neither metaphorized in compliance with the patriarchal world, nor constructed in accordance with the rules imposed by those in power.

The diversionary and subversive character of actions undertaken by Polish women artists involved instituting a new iconography of images and forms of body representations, in which the body was construed in terms of sex and gender (performance acts). Vaginal motifs and autobiographical elements began to emerge. One of the leading women artists of the period was Natalia LL (1937-2022) – the "bad girl" of the Polish neo-avantgarde. As early as the late 1960s, the artist created a cycle of drawings entitled *Rima* (Gate), paving the way for female vaginal iconography later (1967-1968) and directing attention to human eroticism. Her colorful and expressive drawings contain recurring motifs, including male and female genitals: mons pubis in the form of a triangle in *Amazing triangle* and *Whirlwind*; and a vagina in *Burning Hole*, in *Rima*, and in *Explosion*. In 1968, Natalia LL started working on a cycle known as *Intimate Photography*, capturing on film sexual intercourse between a woman and a man—herself and her husband Andrzej Lachowicz. According to Anna Markowska, *Intimate Photography*, which the artist described as showing acts of elation and ecstasy with almost documentary precision (e.g., close-ups of genitals), drew inspiration from the aesthetics of pornography; however, unlike in the pornographic convention, no faces or emotions stirred by sex acts are visible in the work.[26] The photographs were displayed in the form of an

---

[25] Monika Rudaś-Grodzka, "*Parthenogeneza* w okresie menopauzy" (Parthenogenesis During Menopause). *Teksty Drugie: teoria literatury, krytyka, interpretacja*, no. 6 (2002): 77-79.

[26] Anna Markowska, "Amour fou w nieprzyjaznych dekoracjach" (Amour fou in hostile decorations). *Natalia LL: Secretum et Tremor*, edited by Ewa Toniak (Warszawa: Centrum Sztuki Współczesnej, 2015), 27.

installation, as *Intimate Photography* (1971) or *Natalia is SEX* (1974), of which only the former was accessible to the public at the PERMAFO gallery in Wrocław; even so, it was censored soon after the opening, despite viewers' tremendous enthusiasm.

Insistence on the right to represent one's body was driven by the desire for freedom in the political, as well as artistic senses. This objective could only be achieved by applying a language radically different from the one used by dominant tendencies in public speech, state and social rituals, etc. Women artists ridiculed prevalent styles and did not shy away from addressing such issues as sex, women's needs, or the situation of women in life and art; they were resolute and intransigent. They grew in power in spite of, or perhaps, because of the indifference and silence of art critics and theorists. Working in androcentric, often misogynist circles, women artists built a new iconography of female subjectivity and body: undecorated, free from lyrical poeticism, unrestricted by male models of representation. Świrszczyńska's output was described as pouring forth "like a volcano, like a rough sea, splashing like a fountain, intemperately and prodigally," blurting out whatever was prompted by her body, entangled in time, daily chores and wishes. The compulsion to distance herself from the male subject introduced new principles into her work, allowing the poet to act somatically, unashamed of her fascination with simple actions from which she derived pleasure, such as lying, yawning, screaming, dancing and sharing herself, and to reference her own body which hurts and bleeds, howls and yells in pain, but also "bursts with laughter" and "lifts the skirt" (displaying naked buttocks) to knock down established structures and the masculine symbolic order. [27] Natalia LL, the terrorist, disregarded any canons and seized the power and position available theretofore to the male subject alone. Closely approaching pornography, advertising and kitsch in the photographic cycle called *Velvet Terror* (1970), the artist challenges the viewer to a staring contest, confronting them with their own prejudices, desires and imagination. Seated on a throne, nude or provocatively dressed, Natalia LL assumes a position superior to the beholder, while her poker face of a haughty Madonna or countenance of a castrating Medusa seems to complete the process of taking primacy.[28]

The subversiveness and power in representations of women and the female body in Natalia LL's work located her close to feminist art, but the nature of this

---

[27] Rudaś-Grodzka, "*Parthenogeneza*," 74.

[28] Małgorzata Jankowska, *Jedna o wielu twarzach: Natalia Lach-Lachowicz, strategie i formy obecności* (*One with many faces: Natalia Lach-Lachowicz, strategies and forms of presence*). (Toruń: Wydawnictwo Naukowe UMK, 2018), 182.

relation was never obvious; although the artist joined the international feminist art scene, she never admitted to being a feminist.

Apart from being uncompromising, the work of women artists active in the 1970s was also full of mindfulness and compassion. Adopted forms of expression amounted to an intuited prognostication of "women's writing" (*écriture féminine*), as Hélène Cixous termed it, in that they counteracted the official construction of the image of women in the Polish People's Republic. Discussing body art in Central Europe, the globally-reknown critic, Piotr Piotrowski, has stressed that the sexist policies pursued by the government at the time were a mere reflection of the general problem of the "belittlement of women in Polish culture, a culture molded by Catholic tradition and its worldview and institutionalization."[29] Women's entanglement in power and cultural hierarchies is aptly pictured in Ewa Partum's (b. 1945) creative output, which, like that of Natalia LL, belongs to conceptual as well as feminist art, or, as the researcher Izabela Kowalczyk puts it: proto-feminist art. Still a student of the Łódź State High School of Visual Arts, Partum took to using a language that combined, according to Dawidek-Gryglicka, body and text in order to make "these two autonomous means into instruments for reacting to social and political realities" and introduced this transformed and "purloined" language to social discourse.[30] Partum's subversive practice directly aimed at the linguistic sphere, entering into a dialogue with the concrete poetry movement. Initiated and propagated in Poland by Stanisław Dróżdż, he described concrete poetry as a separate literary genre in which language and thought took a material form. However, in Ewa Partum's work, this materialization follows completely different rules. Her *poems*, as well as her actions and activities featuring her naked body, represent a cry for "herself—a position of her own, a position of a woman artist marginalised in a male-dominated world of art."[31]

Taking the linear structure of a poem as her starting point, the artist bursts it apart by filling in consecutive lines, for instance, with red imprints of her lips. This direct physical act of recording articulated speech highlights the connection between speech and body, not to be found elsewhere in concrete poetry of the day (acts of pronunciation were recorded in varied forms also by Natalia LL, e.g., in *Word*, 1971, and *YES*, 1972). Begun in 1972, *poems by ewa*

---

[29] Piotrowski, Piotr, "Ciało i tożsamość. Sztuka ciała w Europie Środkowej" (Body and identity: Body art in Central Europe). *Artium Quaestiones*, no. 14 (2003): 214.

[30] Małgorzata Dawidek-Gryglicka, *Historia tekstu wizualnego: Polska po 1967 roku* (*The history of the visual text: Poland after 1967*). (Kraków: Korporacja Ha!art and Wrocław: Muzeum Współczesne Wrocław, 2012), 472. The author examines Ewa Partum's work, among others, within the context of Helene Cixous' "women's writing."

[31] Dawidek-Gryglicka, *Historia tekstu*, 478.

remained faithful to poetic principles with their condensed content that consisted of letters and words, but also images, signs and gestures. The English word "poem" that Partum chose for her title is derived from the Greek *poíēma* and its meaning also encompasses creation/production, linking *poems by ewa* to a physical act of creation: pressing the lips, cutting hair and pasting it to a piece of paper, scattering letters in public space or the "haemo-poetic" breastfeeding of her daughter Berenika. *Poems* as a work begins from important moments compressed, creative activity that brings together the public as creating art, with the private sphere of creation—nursing, as well as simultaneously being a woman and being an artist. Agata Jakubowska pointed out that Ewa Partum "brought her female subjectivity into conceptual art,"[32] and her statements left no doubt as to the overwhelming nature of her need to establish her own position against dominant patterns of representation and exclusion and female objectivization in the fields of life and art: "intensified by the name *ewa* in the title of the cycle."[33] It seems that Partum came the closest to fulfilling the slogan formulated by America's radical feminists Carol Hanisch, Kate Millett and Shulamith Firestone, "the personal is political," because she used her body and its signs (imprint of lips) to express objection to, and disapproval of, any violence inflicted by the authorities and the social exclusion of women more broadly. Starting from the 1970s, her performance acts *Change* (1974; 1979); *Women, Marriage Is Against You* (1980); and the *Stupid Women* cycle (1981), were delivered naked in front of an audience, commanding viewers' attention and provoking interaction, as well as putting her image on display. It was controversial: a nude woman-artist asking for kisses, questioning the audience and attacking the stereotypical nature of the roles and attitudes ascribed to women e.g., marriage, old age. She brashly challenged the society and government of her time and place, which overtly marginalized and showed disrespect for women. Under martial law, Partum performed for the Solidarity Movement (the "Solidarity" Independent Self-Governing Trade Union), an all-Polish oppositional trade union defending civil liberties and labor rights; her action involved "writing" while naked and making prints of her red lips pronouncing consecutive speech sounds of the word "solidarity" next to the word written out and on display (*Hommage à Solidarność*, 1982). This piece also deals with the presence and impact of or, frankly, the absence of women in the discourse about the history of the Solidarity Movement, which is central to Poland's national identity with regard to the end of the PRL in 1989 (socialist

---

[32] Agata Jakubowska, "Usta szeroko zamknięte" (Mouth wide shut). In *3 kobiety: Maria Pinińska-Bereś, Natalia LL, Ewa Partum* (*Three women: Maria Pinińska-Bereś, Natalia LL, Ewa Partum*), edited by E. Toniak (Warszawa: Zacheta Narodowa Galeria Sztuki, 2011), 28.

[33] Jakubowska, "Usta szeroko zamknięte," 28-29.

People's Republic of Poland)—despite their contribution and commitment, the key role women played in this history has been disregarded to this day.

Women's art in the 1970s and 80s constituted a tool of resistance and a barricade against male dominance, even if the artists themselves did not resort to aggression or violence. In this context, intimacy was no longer a weakness, female fantasy was no longer hysteria, and protectiveness and empathy ceased to be viewed as a waste of time. Making art came to equal private or even intimate rites of passage in the form of on-camera actions/performances. From the late 1960s on, Teresa Gierzyńska (b. 1947) photographed/documented her life in a period she described as "apparent freedom," refusing to avert representations of her intimate life in her visual diary. She later used the collection she made to create a composite photographic cycle called *About Her*, some of the pictures were dedicated to erotic emotions, such as in *Little Caresses*, while others recorded the artist's frames of mind or experiences (*Calculating* 1979; *Sensual* 1981). Eroticism also offered a space of freedom to Teresa Tyszkiewicz (1953-2020). The artist wrote that narratives in her films oscillate between an "act of creation and destruction," in which soft and seemingly friendly substances are contrasted with an aggressive or provocatively positioned body. Corporeal iconography constituted itself where the active female body – in rituals, gestures, poses – met with external material attributes: high-heeled shoes, a massager; and organic substances: grain, pepper, glue, fur, lard, flour or root vegetables, some of which referred to female sexuality, vitality and procreation, as well as mass culture.[34] For Tyszkiewicz, her body was a medium that allowed her to experience reality in attempting to rationalize it. Her somatic films, *Day after Day* and *Seed* in 1980; *Image* and *Games* and *Breath* from 1981, are permeated by tenderness and eroticism of the artist burrowing herself in grain or wrapping herself in feathers. Slimy and fluffy substances in Tyszkiewicz's films pour down fingers or stick to legs; the resulting aesthetic corresponds with some of Natalia LL's statements that she wrote about in her theoretical essays: "absorbing outwardness," "the sliminess of the essence of life," or "the meaning of jelly." Stickiness and fluidity appear in this context as weapons in the struggle against androcentric rational art. An iconography of shared presence of bodies came with Teresa Murak's (b. 1949) work. Staged by the artist as soon as the early 1970s, processes of cultivating and sowing encompassed intimate, tender and patiently performed rituals in *Sowing/Cradle* in 1975 and *Watercress* in 1975. The swelling and sprouting of watercress in Murak's activities represented, according to Agata Jakubowska, an exchange "between two beings," and the body in direct tactile contact with the plant

---

[34] Teresa Tyszkiewicz, *Film poza kinem* (*Movies outside of the ciemna*), (Wrocław: Galeria Jatki PSP), 1981.

(Jakubowska writes that it was pulled out) functioned beyond cultural conditioning, e.g., by time, turning it into pure experience and "returning" to nature.[35] The plant's growing and spreading across a female body tells a story about closeness and about control over the situation at hand — an individual, corporeal and palpable experience of life's energy.[36]

### The Third Republic of Poland and Female Sexuality: Battles for Others' Bodies

The presence of a woman and her body, along with the "otherness" of that other body within the field of art undergoes a major transformation in the 1980s and 1990s.[37] According to Anna Markowska, the changes in the political system that occurred in 1989 unlocked "new areas of activity, a different accountability on the part of the creator, and divergent horizons." Markowska also claims that artists were given "an opportunity to air their critical opinions on the political situation" and could investigate "social issues such as justice, various identities, discrimination, exclusion and, in addition, confusion, abashment and being unable to find a place of one's own in daily life."[38] Exploitation of the body as a medium went into overdrive and, as Izabela Kowalczyk points out, the body became "viewed as an arena of experimentation, a territory affected by power games, an object of incessant innovation, as well as a platform for determining one's identity."[39] Critical art which markedly conditioned the choice of subjects that artists engaged meant the exploration of all kinds of exclusion, otherness and difference, the tabooed and the marginalized. Women and women's art were not separate from this discourse, but one of its main threads.

In the early 1990s, Poland saw an abundance of representations of women's/ artists' bodies. Some examples which speak to the above in terms of explorations of marginality can be found in Anna Janczyszyn-Jaros' (b. 1967) figure crawling along the pavements of Kraków in the 1994 film *To the City*, or in a nude Alicja Żebrowska (b. 1956) lying in a sarcophagus that has been warmed up to body temperature in her action *Fossilisation* in 1993; or in Katarzyna Kozyra's (b. 1963) self-portrait as Édouard Manet's Olympia in the 1996 film photograph *Olympia*; and in Barbara Konopka's (b. 1965) images of

---

[35] Jakubowska, *Na marginesach lustra*, 158-159.

[36] Jakubowska, ibid., 159.

[37] "Otherness" in this context refers to bodies excluded by modernist structures of representation because of age, gender or any kind of physical departure from the norm.

[38] Anna Markowska, "Transformacje w sztuce Polskiej po 1989" (Transformations in Polish art after 1989), *Sztuka i dokumentacja*, no. 13 (2015): 5. https://www.journal.doc. art.pl/pdf13/sid_13_transformacje_intro.pdf.

[39] Izabela Kowalczyk, *Niebezpieczne związki sztuki z ciałem* (*Dangerous ties between art and the body*), (Poznań: Galeria Miejska Arsenał, 2002), 9.

the human body made up of the physical and virtual forms (digital technologies), displaying an ephemeral identity in the 1998-1999 cycle *Iluminations: Online. Binary Man*. These and other pieces, such as Katarzyna Kozyra's *Blood Ties* in four photographs from 1995; or Alicja Żebrowska's 1994 *Original Sin: A Presumed Project of Virtual* and 1995-1997 piece *Noone: A World after the World* all stirred up controversy and aversion primarily because of the democratic system that was still under construction in Poland at the time. These artworks were part of a more general rising hope that included the issue of freer gender-sex identity (the "difference" factor, as Paweł Leszkowicz put it) as a key component of "discussions about the human condition and the meaning of freedom," but eventually failed. [40] Meanwhile, the female body retained its considerable power as a critical form for making accusatory gestures about morality, however, individualist and subjective such accusations are, the subject or the object onto which the blame was projected tended always to have a universal character. Still, there were some cases that left no doubt as to who was answerable. Ewa Partum's 1987 critical piece *Marital Disaster* addressed domestic violence and drew upon her own experience in depicting the artist's face beaten up. Kozyra's 1995 *Blood Ties* came to be understood as a response to the situation in Yugoslavia, where women were deeply entangled into violence brought on by broader political power structures. The cycle made up of four large-format photographs portrayed two naked young women — Kozyra and her sister — against the cross and crescent, symbols of humanitarian organizations. Katarzyna Górna's (b. 1968) photographic installation *Ten Virgins* in 1995 referred to the parable of the foolish and wise virgins in the Gospel of Matthew, and comprised photos of ten nude women in large format covered in paper dresses with ultrasound images and medical descriptions, revealing half of them were pregnant. *Ten Virgins* did not distinguish which of the women were foolish and which were wise. The work was produced in reaction to the tightening of state policies around Family Planning, Human Embryo Protection, and Conditions of Permission on the Abortion Act, alongside the mitigation of punishment for rape crimes introduced in 1993.

A distinct iconographic feature of the 1990s was the emergence of artworks fulfilling the assumptions of *HerStories*. The graphic and multimedia artist Izabella Gustowska (b. 1948) launched stories about women in the mid-1970s. Begun in 1975 and continuing until the mid-1990s as *Relative Features of Similarity II*, the initial cycle *Relative Features of Similarity* from 1975-1979 was dedicated to the iconography of womanhood. Gustowska assembled a unique female community using her own image, inclusive of both group and individual portraits, and nudes executed in various techniques and media. In Gustowska's

---

[40] Paweł Leszkowicz, "Sztuka i płeć," *Magazyn Sztuki,* no. 2 (1999): 88.

later works, the search for different representations of femininity is equated with mindfulness and the need for shared presence in the female world, as well as of summoning the absent. Solidarity and the idea of sisterhood, even if the artist did not use these terms, continued to shape the route for her consecutive projects.[41] For example, her 2008 project, entitled *SHE: media story*, took the form of a log documenting a physical and mental journey in search of "woman," which gradually evolves and becomes more and more explicit, culminating in the 2014 film *The Case of Josephine H . . .* This piece was inspired by Josephine, an artist who gave up her own career in order to support that of her husband, the re-known American painter Edward Hopper. Women in Gustowska's pieces are as authentic as they are virtual; this multidimensionality and elusiveness can be explained, in the artist's words, by "a naïve sense of otherness, sensibility, emotions, intuition, biology, instinct and, finally, a sense of power and independence." Further, she states she aims to "uncover sensuality, imagination, forgotten presentiments and worldly wisdom."[42] The urge to talk about women as a community is also a distinct feature in Anna Baumgart's work (b. 1966). From 1996 on, the artist made films nearly exclusively about women and femininity. Her protagonists speak about their feelings, their relationships with partners and children, and their struggles within various social roles due to the widespread patronizing attitudes towards their own sex. The frequently intimate and disturbing monologues in *Love Movies* (1997); *Mother* (1998); and *Who Says That?* (1998), framed by a severe aesthetic documentary style, testified to female determination and power, but also to the oppression and failures that women faced. Examining women's experiences, including her own, Baumgart created a pantheon of female figures: mothers, daughters, partners, victims of male, cultural and historical violence; rejected, abused, unsatisfied — the loving and the fighting. Baumgart stressed that her appearance in the films, including: *Real?/Bear* (2001); *Cranes Are Flying* (2001);

---

[41] The idea of sisterhood in post-war Poland was not considered to be a viable topic of research in the humanities, nor in artistic practice. This does not mean that women did not support one another. Female workers in the textile industries demonstrated particularly strong solidarity; for example, Anna Świrszczyńska dedicated herself to advocating for the lives of women burdened by violence and poverty. In Polish women's artistic practice, ideas of sisterhood continued to resonate into the new century, well after 2000. Artists and works include: Anna Baumgart; Anka Leśniak, *For Zofia* (2017), *Lost Element* (2016), *Fifi Zastrow* and *Acta est Fabula* (2015); Aleksandra Polisiewicz, *Pre-revolutionary landscape* (2015). In all of these works the women are described, quoted, and foregrounded through the memories of mothers, other female artists, and fellow women workers. Anka Leśniak notes how the artists impersonate others in order to become, for a while, a woman from the past. See: Zeic, Liliana (Piskorska), "Sourcebook," 2020–2021, Artist Website. http://lilianapiskorska.com/en/praca/sourcebook-ksiazka-zrodel-2/.

[42] Izabella Gustowska, ed. *Obecność III* (*Presence III*), (Poznań: Galeria ON, 1992), 1.

and *Ecstatics, Hysterics and Other Saintly Ladies* (2004); helped her to identify closely with her heroines as a "sister to the women performing in . . . films."[43]

**Figure 7.2.** Anna Baumgart, *Ecstatics, Hysterics and Other Saintly Ladies*, 2004, video still. / Zachęta - National Gallery of Art collection. © Anna Baumgart.

In the pieces that came later, compassion and the wish to recall absent and forgotten women rose to prominence, for instance, in *Fresh Cherries* (2010) and *Journey Diary* (2020), in which Baumgart stages a fragment of the life of Mieczysława Nogajewska, the owner of a photo parlour known as Foto-Elite established in Gdynia in 1928. In her latest film, *Miczika is Not Afraid of Airplanes* (2020), the artist spotlights the complex relations between the researcher and anthropologist Maria Antonina Czaplicka and Miczika, her female guide from the Evens community, reflecting on the problematic postcolonial relationship of the two women[44].

---

[43] Anna Baumgart, "'Imperatyw z Anna Baumgart rozmawia Adam Mazur" ('An Imperative by Anna Baumgar, interviewed by Adam Mazur), edited by Aniela Mucha. *Silo Tips website*. February 23, 2017. https://silo.tips/download/imperatyw-z-ann-baumgart -rozmawia-adam-mazur.

[44] Maria Antonina Czaplicka (1884-1921) was a Polish ethnographer, anthropologist and geographer. She studied anthropology at Bedford Women College and was the first female professor of anthropology at Oxford. She took part in research expeditions to

Women's art of the 1990s was characterized by a plurality of means and objectives. Sexuality and the right to pleasure were highlighted by works by figures like Ewa Kuryluk and Małgorzata Plata; exclusion on the basis of age and other factors in works by Katarzyna Kozyra; the erasure of boundaries between the private and the public or the critique of the commodification of women by Joanna Rajkowska and Zuzanna Janin); or various sorts of sex and post-sex imaginaries in pieces by Alicja Żebrowska and Barbara Konopka. All of these women artists broke boundaries with these leading motifs, although these were by no means the only subjects taken up by women debuting or continuing their experiments in the 1990s. A shared power arose from a common determination to build a new iconography for the creation of forms capable of nuancing, and unveiling what is imagined to be *female*.

### Fighting Against Religious and Political Conservatism: Bodies as Tools of Activism

The rise of democracy in Poland brought about a diversity of attitudes and views among women artists in the 1990s. They tended to explore personal identities shaped by female corporeality and spirituality – two elements of parallel importance. An increasing number of women artists chose to express themselves through performance art and other new media, frequently mixing them with traditional ones such as painting or sculpture. However, the variety of identities visualized in the rich iconography of the body at the time was also influenced by political changes, and especially conservative ideologies that later resurged and have continued to grow in prominence since 2005.[45] Still, even before the escalation of protest demonstrations in 2020, after the tightening of the abortion law by the government, Polish women artists continue to intensively revisit and investigate themes taken up earlier, in the 1990s, while introducing new ones aimed at mounting an allied resistance to the increasing oppression faced by women and sexual minorities.

In 2003, Katarzyna Kozyra (b. 1963) launched an art project called *In Art Dreams Come True,* comprising a dozen or so artistic actions, including performance acts, happenings and related videos and photographs.[46] As the

---

Siberia. During her expeditions Czaplicka obtained abundant scientific materials: interviews, photos, observations, and ceremonial artifacts.

[45] The 2005 parliamentary election was won by the Law and Justice party (PiS: Prawo I Sprawiedliwość) in Poland. Law and Justice then formed a coalition with other conservative and pro-Catholic parties, such as the League of Polish Families and Self-Defense.

[46] For the full documentation of the project, see: Katarzyna Kozyra, "In Art Dreams Come True: Cycle of Performances, Happening, and Films 2003-2006." Artist Personal Website. http://katarzynakozyra.pl/en/projekty/in-art-dreams-come-true/.

title indicates, she seized on the opportunity to fulfill her wishes and to impersonate, among other characters, an opera diva, a drag queen, Offenbach's Olympia, a cheerleader, and Snow White.[47] This seemingly innocent undertaking touches upon some crucial issues, bringing to the forefront socially-excluded or stigmatized populations, including transsexuals, as in *Tribute To Gloria Viagra: Birthday Party* (2005), or the physically different in *The Winter's Tale* (2005-2006). The artist plays with religious iconography referencing the figure of the Virgin Mary, Mother of God, for example, in the 2005 performance *Madonna, 2005.* The artist familiarizes viewers with bodies rejected by mainstream culture – those deemed too ample, too old, too small, or sexually ambiguous. She continues to pursue similar subject matter in the 1997 piece *Women's Bathhouse; Men's Bathhouse*, in 1999; and *Dance Lesson*, in 2001, questioning the definitions of womanhood and manhood.

Anka Leśniak (b. 1978) has made a valuable contribution to the discussion on the role of woman-as-artist. She produced prints by pressing her nude body against canvases in various shades of red, thus striking up a conversation with Yves Klein (b. 1928-1962), who once applied characteristically blue paint to his female models and pressed their bodies against canvas. His treatment of women's bodies as objects – artistic tools – is arraigned in Leśniak's work. In the making of *Prints* (2006), the artist employs her own body as both the object and the subject. She also abandons the cold associations with the color blue for a warm red, which in its most primitive imaginary is also symbolically tied to blood, the life-giving fluid considered by many cultures to be unclean and taboo.[48] A video of red imprints also appeared in the finale of the 2012 performance act *Take the Lipstick*, which involved the artist's body being covered by viewers with inscriptions in bright red. With her eyes closed, naked and helpless, Leśniak acts as the reverse of her two companions, who are clad in black robes imitating Muslim chadors or burkas, which conceal everything except for their eyes. The cultural contrast between women illustrates cross-cultural tensions between immigrants and local communities, especially regarding women's roles. The work indicates the various forms of "soft" oppression used against women that prevent them from self-representation. Red as the symbolic color not only of blood, but through this also of femininity, is exploited by consecutive generations of performance artists. It is often present in artworks created by Anna Kalwajtys (b. 1979) and Izabela Chamczyk (b. 1980). The former's red clothes are signifying elements. In a 2005 piece called *Womanist* she performed dressed in a specially

---

[47] Hanna Wróblewska, *Katarzyna Kozyra: In Art Dreams Come True* (Wrocław: Hatje Cantz, 2007), 71.

[48] David Gilmore, *Mizoginia, czyli męska choroba* (*Misogyny: The Male Malady*), translated by Janusz Margański (Kraków: Wydawnictwo Literackie, 2003), 43.

designed costume filled with raw meat, and the red top or dress she wore serve to imply her sex. Kalwajtys also covered her body in red paint in *Weapon-Isotope* in 2018 in response to oppression against women and animals, or nature in general, which is the main focus of her work.

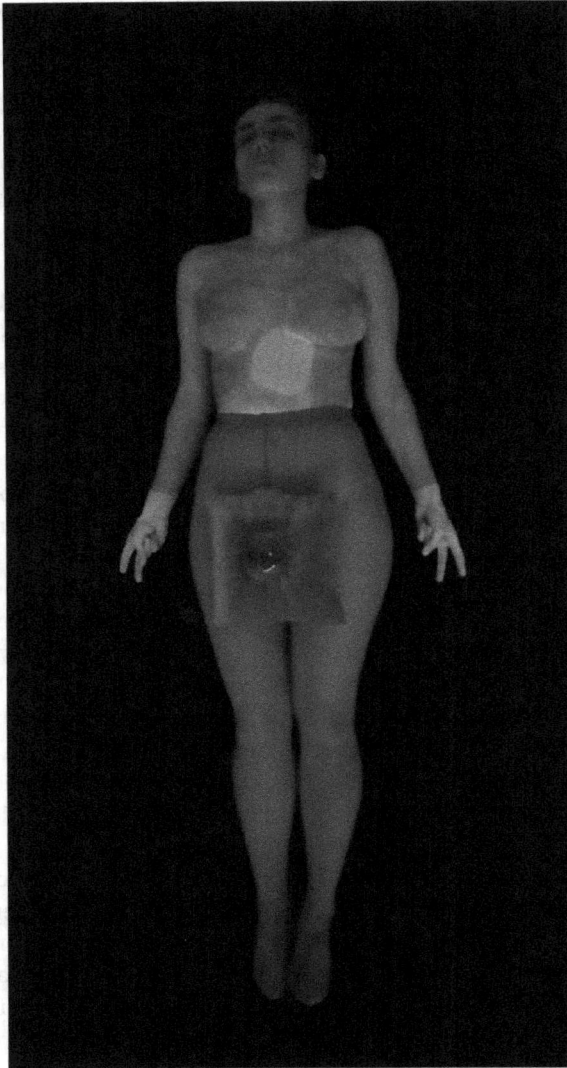

**Figure 7.3.** Anna Kalwajtys, *Weapon-Izotop*, 2018, video still.
Courtesy of the artist. © Anna Kalwajtys.

Izabela Chamczyk explores similar matters, however, it is the question of individual identity that is the core of her practice. Her projects combine painting and performance, relying on the symbolism of colors and their contrasts, for example, in: *I Look Good in Blue* (2011); *Fight for Myself* (2013); *Something In Something* (2015).

In the photographic series *To Love, and Give Birth to Children* (2008), created in collaboration with Epipactis, the artist deals with the politics of fertility and restricted availability of contraceptives imposed by conservatives and the Catholic Church. Marta Smolińska-Byczuk gives an accurate description of the piece, drawing attention to its baroque nature and use of irony:

> Like the Madonna, the nursing mother towers above the dolls but fails to provide them with love and care – she seems to be merely carrying out her duty. Motherhood is a burden and not joy – children are born wholesale, but there is no way they can be loved wholesale. There is only one pair of breasts and the mouths willing to suck it come in dozens. In traditional modern painting the breastfeeding Madonna evokes peace, affection and harmony, representing the strong bond between a mother and a child. In Chamczyk's photographs there is no bond between the woman and the offspring, while tenderness and intimacy have been replaced by narcissism and mental inaptitude of the young woman who just happens to be a mother.[49]

The conservatives in power in Poland encourage the public expression of aversion to LGBT+ people. Not surprisingly, women artists and curators act and create in ways that aim to oppose this exclusionary behavior. Liliana Zeic (formerly Piskorska, b. 1988) unites the roles of an artist and an activist. Her pieces embrace performance acts, installations, and photographs as she recounts the experience of non-heteronormative individuals being erased from the public sphere. In 2020, she created *Sourcebook*, an archive of the "non-normative Polish history of women."[50] The faces of her protagonists are obscured by straw rope—they disappear, except for their mouths and protruding tongues. Their bodies are a symbol of their sexuality, and the ropes – political and cultural oppression against lesbian people. In spite of this, they are struggling for their identity by stretching out their tongues in each other's directions to touch each other, if only for a moment.

---

[49] Marta Smolińska-Byczuk, "Urock macierzyństwa" (The charm of motherhood). *Artluk*, no. 1/210 (2022). http://www.artluk.com/eart.php?id=153.
[50] Zeic, "Sourcebook," Ibid.

Kozyra, Leśniak, Kalwajtys, Chamczyk and Zeic are but a few of Poland's many multimedia women artists who question the conservative idea of femininity. All these creators not only challenge accepted schemata but also fight to protect otherness. They put up resistance to the brutality of authorities towards minorities, the excluded and erased. Their bodies are used as tools in the struggle, while also reflecting their search for identity.

Since the 1950s Polish women artists have been treating the female body as a means of expression, allowing them to narrate their individual and collective *herstories.*[51] Their work can be seen as a mirror image of social and political changes, yielding direct insight into the problems and dilemmas that women confront on a daily basis. War against patriarchy continues to be waged, and although one would expect that by the early twenty-first-century history is long overdue for women's equality and unrestricted civil rights, yet this is regrettably not the case. Perhaps how far we still have to go in order to achieve a freer society, in Poland, is best illustrated by the events of October 2020. The moment that the Polish government tightened abortion laws, mass protests exploded all over the country, staged in every city and small town—regardless of the coronavirus pandemic. Nevertheless, the PiS ruling party was determined to carry out their intentions, leading to the tragic consequences of disenfranchisement of the majority voice of all women, young and old, who united together to demand their rights. The impact of the draconian abortion laws that continue in Poland, and have found a counterpart now in the U.S. in the overturning of Roe vs. Wade, cannot be underestimated.[52] Visual outcomes from the 2020 *Strajk kobiet,* or Women's Strike mass protests in Poland, include an artbook by the artist duo that created the main symbol that became a visual anthem for the protests, circulated in social media around the globe. The artists are Lejdis Luxus (Bożena Grzyb-Jarocka and Ewa Ciepielewska) and are associated with Wrocław in the 1980s. The iconic image they created which came to signify the Women's Strike lives on in Poland and can be seen in windows, on pavement in graffiti, and anywhere one dares to look. As an artistic communicative piece, the image is also an important record of this initial chapter of 2020 of solidarity-building in opposition to political and religious conservatives.[53]

---

[51] Herstory is a term created by feminists as an alternative to "history" to convey a female-centered historiography.

[52] Early in November, Iza, aged 30, died in Pszczyna, Poland because the tightened abortion law rendered doctors unable to help her.

[53] The artbook was presented at the *Wieża Bab 2* exhibition at Galeria Biała in Lublin, Poland on September 10–November 5, 2021.

**Figure 7.4.** Lejdis Luxus (Bożena Grzyb-Jarocka and Ewa Ciepielewska), pages of the artbook *Breaking News,* 2020. Courtesy of Biała Gallery in Lublin. © Bożena Grzyb-Jarocka, Ewa Ciepielewska and Biała Gallery.

Women artists have no choice but to keep fighting for themselves. Art can be used as a tool. It is hard not to agree with Anna Kalwajtys, who boldly claims: "Art is an indispensable voice that provokes people to think, to pose questions, to verify reality; it is a battlefield and expression of oppositions to unwanted reality, to injustice . . ."[54]

## Bibliography

Baumgart, Anna. "'Imperatyw' z Anna Baumgart rozmawia Adam Mazur" (An Imperative by Anna Baumgart, interviewed by Adam Mazur). Edited by Aniela Mucha. *Silo Tips website.* February 23, 2017. https://silo.tips/download/imperatyw-z-ann-baumgart-rozmawia-adam-mazur.

Castells, Manuel. *Siła tożsamości (The Power of Identity: The Information Age: Economy, Society and Culture, vol. 2).* Warszawa: PWN, 2009.

Ciesielska, Jolanta, and Smalcerz Agata, Eds. *Sztuka kobiet (Women's art).* Bielsko-Biała: Galeria Bielska BWA, 2000.

Dawidek-Gryglicka, Małgorzata. *Historia tekstu wizualnego. Polska po 1967 roku (The history of the visual text: Poland after 1967).* Kraków: Korporacja Ha!art, Wrocław: Muzeum Współczesne Wrocław, 2012.

---

[54] Anna Kalwajtys, *Anna Kalwajtys: Krawędź (Anna Kalwajtys: The Edge),* edited by Maksymilian Wroniszewski, translated by Katarzyna Podpora (Gdańsk: Academy of Fine Art in Gdansk & Wyspa Progress Foundation, 2019), 23.

Giddens, Anthony. *Nowoczesność i tożsamość (Modernity and Self-Identity: Self and Society in the Late Modern Age)*. Translated by Alina Szulżycka. Warszawa: PWN, 2007.

Gilmore, David. *Mizoginia, czyli męska choroba (Misogyny: The Male Malady)*. Translated by Janusz Margański. Kraków: Wydawnictwo Literackie, 2003.

Gingeras, Alison M., Ed. *Erna Rosenstein: Once Upon a Time*. Exhibition Catalogue. New York: Hauser and Wirth Publishers, 2020.

Gustowska, Izabella, Ed. *Obecność III (Presence III)*. Poznań: Galeria ON, 1992.

Jakubowska, Agata. *Na marginesach lustra. Ciało kobiece w pracach polskich artystek (In the margins of the mirror: The female body in the works of Polish artists)*. Kraków: Wydawnictwo Universitas, 2005.

_____. "Usta szeroko zamknięte" (Mouth wide shut). In *3 kobiety. Maria Pinińska-Bereś, Natalia LL, Ewa Partum (Three women: Maria Pinińska-Bereś, Natalia LL, Ewa Partum)*. Edited by Ewa Toniak. Warszawa: Zacheta Narodowa Galeria Sztuki, 2011.

Jakubowska, Agata, Ed. *Artystki polskie (Polish Women Artists)*. Warszawa: PWN, 2011.

_____. *Portret wielokrotny dzieła Aliny Szapocznikow (Multiple portraits of the work of Alina Szapocznikow)*. Poznań: UMA Press, 2008.

Jankowska, Małgorzata. *Jedna o wielu twarzach: Natalia Lach-Lachowicz, strategie i formy obecności (One with many faces: Natalia Lach-Lachowicz, strategies and forms of presence)*. Toruń: Wydawnictwo Naukowe UMK, 2018.

Jarecka, Dorota, and Barbara Piwowarska. *Erna Rosenstein. Mogę powtarzać tylko nieświadome (Erna Rosenstein: I can only repeat unconsciously)*. Warszawa: Fundacja Galerii Foksal, 2014.

Kalwajtys, Anna. *Anna Kalwajtys: Krawędź (Anna Kalwajtys: The Edge)*. Edited by Maksymilian Wroniszewski. Translated by Katarzyna Podpora. Gdańsk: Academy of Fine Art in Gdansk & Wyspa Progress Foundation, 2019.

Kowalczyk, Izabela. "The Ambivalent Beauty." In *Gender Check: Femininity and Masculinity in the Art of Eastern Europe*. Edited by Bojana Pejić. Wien: Museum Moderner Kunst Stiftung Ludwig, 2009, 38–45.

_____. *Niebezpieczne związki sztuki z ciałem (Dangerous ties between art and the body)*. Poznań: Galeria Miejska Arsenał, 2002.

_____. *Matki-Polki, Chłopcy i Cyborgi… Sztuka i feminizm w Polsce (Polish Mothers, Boys and Cyborgs . . . Art and Feminism in Poland)*. Poznań: Galeria Miejska Arsenał, 2010.

Kozyra, Katarzyna. "In Art Dreams Come True: Cycle of Performances, Happening, and Films 2003-2006." Artist Personal Website. http://katarzynakozyra.pl/en/projekty/in-art-dreams-come-true/

Kristeva, Julia. *Histoires d'amour.* Paris: Denoël, 1983.

Leszkowicz, Paweł. "Sztuka i płeć" (Art and gender). *Magazyn Sztuki*, no. 2, (1999): 88.

Markowska, Anna. "*Amour fou* w nieprzyjaznych dekoracjach" (*Amour fou in hostile* decorations). In *Natalia LL. Secretum et Tremor*. Edited by Ewa Toniak. Warszawa: Centrum Sztuki Współczesnej, 2015, 105–122.

_____. "Transformacje w sztuce Polskiej po 1989" (Transformation in Polish art after 1989). *Sztuka i dokumentacja* 13 (2015): 5. https://www.journal.doc. art.pl/pdf13/sid_13_transformacje_intro.pdf.

Nader, Luiza. *Konceptualizm w PRL (Conceptualism in the People's Republic of Poland)*. Warszawa: Wydawnictwo Uniwersytetu Warszawskiego, Fundacja Galerii Foksal, 2009.

Piotrowski, Piotr. "Ciało i tożsamość. Sztuka ciała w Europie Środkowej" (Body and identity: Body art in Central Europe). *Artium Quaestiones*, no. 14, (2003).

Rudaś-Grodzka, Monika. "Parthenogeneza w okresie menopauzy" (Parthenogenesis during menopause). *Teksty Drugie: teoria literatury, krytyka, interpretacja*, 6 (2002): 77-79.

Smolińska-Byczuk, Marta. "Urok macierzyństwa" (The charm of motherhood). *Artluk* 1, no. 210 (2022). http://www.artluk.com/eart.php?id=153.

Szyłak, Aneta, Ed. *Architectures of Gender: Contemporary Women's Art In Poland*. Exhibition Catalogue. New York: Sculpture Center, 2003.

Taranienko, Zbigniew, Ed. *Erna Rosenstein. Rzeczy, ślady, papiery z szafy (Erna Rosenstein: Things, traces, papers from the closet)*. Łódź: Galeria 86, 2002.

Toniak, Ewa. *Olbrzymki: kobiety i socrealizm (Giants: Women and Socialist Realism)*. Kraków: Korporacja Ha!art, 2008.

_____, Ed. *Jestem artystką, we wszystkim, co niepotrzebne. Kobiety i sztuka około 1960 roku (I am an artist in everything unnecessary: Women and Art around 1960)*. Warszawa: Neriton, 2010.

Tyszkiewicz, Teresa. *Film poza kinem (Movies beyond the cinema)*. Wrocław: Galeria Jatki PSP, 1981.

Wróblewska, Hanna. *Katarzyna Kozyra: In Art Dreams Come True*. Wrocław: Hatje Cantz, 2007.

Zeic, Liliana (Piskorska), "Sourcebook." 2020–2021. Artist Website. http://lilianapiskorska.com/en/praca/sourcebook-ksiazka-zrodel-2/.

Chapter 8

# Materiality, Maternity, and Ignorance: How Women Artists Faced Social And Economic Crises in 1990s Kyiv

Kateryna Iakovlenko

### Abstract

This chapter emphasizes the problem of ignorance in Ukrainian art in the late 1980s and early 1990s and explores women artists' practices through the lenses of materiality and maternity. Utilizing ideas from feminist theory and looking more deeply at Ukraine's art history, the author illuminates biographies of women artists who abandoned or postponed their artistic practice in the 1990s. Paying attention to the missing details in the history of Ukrainian art, the author touches upon essential issues in the history of culture, such as cultural memory, the connection between art and materiality, the problem of motherhood, and age.

**Keywords**: Ukraine, contemporary art, maternity, materiality, post-Soviet culture

\*\*\*

Interest in the history and archives of contemporary Ukrainian art arose with the advent of Ukrainian independence in the early 1990s. It was then revealed again with cultural resistance after the Maidan Revolution of 2013-2014 in close connection with a global archival turn. The emerging interest in the history of art and culture led to the creation of mostly private and institutional archival projects and initiatives predominantly based on digital representation. Among others available online are Open Archive; Open Archive of Ukrainian Media Art; PinchukArtCenter Research Platform; Ukrainian Unofficial Archive dedicated to non-official artists' practices of the mid-1950s — early 1990s, the archival project of Odesa and Kharkiv Art by Odesa Museum of Modern Art; and the emergence of the MOKSOP—Museum of Kharkiv School of Photography.[1]

---

[1] For Ukrainian art and criticism materials in open-access digital archives, see: *PinchukArtCentre Research Platform*, Kyiv, Ukraine, Official website. https://new.pinchuk

Moreover, an independent and nonprofit organization, The Method Fund, that emerged during 2013-2014 initiated a critical program and discussion entitled *Creating Ruin,* dedicated to reflecting upon Ukraine's institutional legacy and cultural and artistic heritage.[2]

The early 1990s were some of the most challenging times for art historians: this history is fragile and easily reframed each time it is revisited due to people's varied interests in the critic and their connections with artists, their unstable memory, and desire to "correct" this memory. Assessing the range of artists' works of the 1990s, some critics might argue that if no female names appear in museums and collections, those works by women are thus not of any interest or consequence. This logic and explanation, nevertheless, do not suit the situation with women artists' practice in Ukraine for many reasons. According to Griselda Pollock and Rozsika Parker, contemporary art historians need to reconsider all principles for evaluating works of art. Pollock and Parker argue that, instead of focusing on the concept of a masterpiece, it might be worth focusing on the contexts of production and conditions under which women artists lived and worked.[3] For example, by examining the artistic processes of the late 1980s — early 1990s, one can draw attention to a strong bias toward male artists. Male perspective and male figures —both critics and artists— are still dominant in Ukrainian art history, even if the situation has been changing consistently in recent decades. These days, several publications endeavor to shed light on the art of artists-women, their working conditions, and their opportunities. Among others, my article entitled " 'The Body' in the Art of Paryzkoii Komuny Street Group" in the book *The ParCommune: Place, Community, Phenomenon,* as well as the book *Why There Are Great Women Artists in Ukrainian Art,* offer critical descriptions of women participants of several Ukrainian art movements. Unfortunately, many are no longer practicing artists, and some names have been forgotten. What are the reasons

---

artcentre.org/en/research; *Open Archive,* Kyiv, Ukraine, Official website http://openarchive. com.ua/; *Open Archive of Ukrainian Media Art,* Official website http://mediaartarchive. org.ua/; *Ukrainian Unofficial Archive,* Official website, Kyiv and Lviv http://archive-uu.com/en; *Moksop Museum of Kharkiv School of Photography,* Official website, Kharkiv https://moksop.org/; there are also excellent holdings of materials from the cities of Kharkiv and Odesa in the archives of the Odesa Museum of Modern Art.

[2] An independent and nonprofit organization, *Method Fund,* initiated a critical program and discussion platform dedicated to reflecting upon Ukraine's institutional legacy and cultural and artistic heritage. The organization emerged during the Maidan Revolution of 2013-2014 and their project includes including open-access digital archives. See: *Method Fund.* "Creating Ruin Project." Official Website. Kyiv. https://creatingruin.net/.

[3] Rozsika Parker and Griselda Pollock, *Old Mistresses: Women, Art and Ideology* (New York: Pantheon, 1982).

behind the public's ignorance about female artists? This chapter will cast light on the reasons for the invisibility of and disregard for women artists; in particular, the material and social factors behind this blindness.

### "Baring of the Soul" and Early 1990s Social and Economic Crisis

Although the General Secretary of the Communist Party of the Soviet Union (March 1985 — August 1991), Mikhail Gorbachev, officially launched Perestroika in 1985, changes in society did not become visible until after the nuclear power accident at the Chernobyl reactor near Kyiv.[4] This tragic event catalyzed public distrust in the government and soured relations between Moscow and Kyiv. Along with this cultural upsurge, other processes increased social and national discontent. In August 1991, Ukraine proclaimed the Act of Independence, and in December 1991, Ukrainian citizens voted for this decision in an all-Ukrainian referendum. Due to the gradual liberalization and illegal trade, or grey economy, which took place in liminal zones such as flea markets, various Western publications on art, literature, and culture, in general, became increasingly available. These new sources of information could not fail to captivate the young artists who, at the time, found a breath of fresh air and a source of inspiration in them.

Political transformations brought about changes in the cultural infrastructure: in the USSR, each of the individual republics' cultural organizations were centralized and subordinated to Moscow; the newly independent countries thus started to restructure their cultural departments. As a result, cultural infrastructure underwent a mass redistribution of resources, causing an ever-greater financial crisis that only intensified in the first years of national independence.

Art historian and critic Alisa Lozhkina describes this situation as a temporary collapse. In her book *The Permanent Revolution*, she writes:

> After Ukraine gained independence, the state almost stopped buying works of art. As a result, even in the country's most important collection —the National Art Museum— a gap of three decades was formed. None of the state and private institutions currently have a demonstration art collection of this period. Instead, the works are scattered in numerous

---

[4] Oksana Barshynova and Olena Martynyuk, "Ukrainian Art of the Independence Era: Transitions and Aspirations," in *From "the Ukraine" to Ukraine: A Contemporary History 1991—2021*, edited by Matthew Rojansky, Georgiy Kasianov and Mykhailo Minakov (Berlin and New York: Ibidem and Columbia University Press, 2021).

private collections in Ukraine and abroad; some of them are irretrievably lost.[5]

In the 1990s, artists could no longer count on the support of the state and official art institutions. As a result, some of them started experimenting with the media, whereas others left the profession or put their artistic careers on hold, relying on other sources of income.

This symbolic turn to artistic experiments is best illustrated by the early artistic practice of the artists Ilya Chichkan [6] and Oleksandr Hnylytskyi [7] frequent visitors to the flea market in Kyiv (now Bulvarno-Kudryavska Street). The objects they found at the flea market often became elements of their artworks or a part of the artists' style. Hnylytsky, for example, found elements of his installations *The Moon Cowboy (1991)*, as well as the curved mirrors that served to create special effects in the video *Funfair Mirrors: Tableau Vivant* (1993), which he filmed with his curator, Natalia Filonenko [8] and the artist Maksym Mamsikov. [9] These artists belonged to the Parcommune squat, an artistic community that existed in Kyiv until 1994. It is from the history of squatting and the works by these artists that art today is often begun, emphasizing the factor of uncontrolled freedom, expressiveness, "baring of the soul" and talent. [10] When describing expression in paintings, researchers often provide examples by focusing on how artists created their works. For example, Oleg Holosiy [11] painted with a broom; other artists created specific images by

---

[5] Alisa Lozhkina, *The Permanent Revolution: Art of Ukraine from the 20th–early 21st century* (Kyiv: ARTHUSS, 2019), 270.

[6] Ilya Chichkan (b. 1967, Kyiv) was born in an artistic family. He works in photography, video art, performance art, and installations. He has no formal schooling.

[7] Oleksandr Hnylytskyi (b. 1961, Kharkiv – d. 2009, Kyiv) graduated from the workshop of monumental painting at the National Institute of Art in Kyiv. He worked in painting, installation, and video art and was co-founder of the Institution for Unstable Thoughts, a non-commercial art organization, as well as an eponymous artistic duo.

[8] Natalia Filonenko (b. 1960, Kyiv) is a curator and art critic currently based in Canada. She graduated from a curatorial studies program at Bard College in New York and then worked as Director of Marat Guelman Gallery in Kyiv.

[9] Maksym Mamsikov (b. 1968, Kyiv) is an artist and a painter. He graduated from the Department of Graphics of the Ukrainian Academy of Art.

[10] Tatiana Kochubinska. "The Late Soviet Kyiv Bohemians: On the Significance of the Paris Commune Squat." In *The ParCommune: Place, Community, Phenomenon.* (Kyiv: Publish Pro, 2019), 12-17.

[11] Oleg Holosiy (b. 1965, Dnipropetrovsk – d. 1993, Kyiv) was a painter. He studied at the Department of Painting at the Kyiv State Art Institute. His works were exhibited abroad beginning in 1991, and he became the first Ukrainian artist to collaborate with a private

pointing a projector at the canvas and, literally, redrawing film images. Critics of these artists emphasize that their paintings often appear in a large format, which is why they can capture the viewer emotionally and physically. On the other hand, the materiality of this aspect is also quite natural and influential.

Art historian Tatiana Zhmurko emphasizes that 2 x 3 m (80 x 120 in) was also a "standard and widely used painting format in the USSR":

> The high-ceilinged buildings of the squat, first on Lenin Street, then on Paris Commune Street, allowed for it. The origins of this phenomenon can be traced either to the tradition of large narrative paintings or to the global practice of the new generation of painters, such as the Italian Transavantgardists and the German Neue Wilde. The format also dictated the character of the painting: expressive, dynamic, mostly done in one sitting. These works were often marked by non-finitism, which became an expression of freedom and authorial will in opposition to the completeness of Socialist Realist paintings.[12]

According to Zhmurko, the canvas format defines its nature: expressive, dynamic, and made chiefly in one session. Moreover, this style and type of painting stands in contrast to the Social Realist principle of regulated pictures and is a manifestation of creative freedom and authorial will.

However, what is meant by this freedom? Lack of commitment; free housing (squats); the opportunity to live out the stereotypes of the bohemian art movement? In her manifesto for the Secondary Archive Project, the Parcommune artist Valeria Troubina writes:

> We reminded ourselves of broken sluices through which flowed the fresh water of purification and transformation. There were many experiments, not only with painting but also with one's consciousness. The uncontrollable desire to understand ourselves and our work, to find something new in this experience literally tore each of us apart. We had a wonderful time, despite the ongoing chaos in the country. Everything was one continuous performance.[13]

---

gallery, Regina Gallery in Moscow. With the support of Regina Gallery he enjoyed a solo exhibition in 1991 at the Central House of Artists in Moscow.

[12] Tetiana Zhmurko, "A Few Words About Painting" in *The Parcommune: Place, Community, Phenomenon* (Kyiv: Publish Pro, 2019), 69.

[13] The Ukraine section of the *Secondary Archive project* was launched in February 23, 2022. However, all of the texts for the Ukraine section were produced in 2021. See: *Secondary Archive Project*. Valeria Troubina (b. 1966, Luhansk) is a painter based in Berkeley, California. She graduated from the Department of Theater and Decoration at

Tatiana Kochubinska argues that the analysis of Parcommune's art is mainly performed from the "mundane-revolutionary" perspective, where the artistic practice gets dissolved in the "warmth of cooking borscht." [14] This borscht metaphor shows how closely everyday life and artistic life, unfolding in the same space, were interconnected. However, even though the space was shared, there was an unspoken division: life belonged to artists-women, whereas art was supposedly given to the prerogative of male artists. However, the word "shared" is not quite appropriate here because artists-women were engaged primarily in the education of child-rearing and managing everyday life, while their husbands and partners were engaged in art and fun.

In the 1990s, when a new commercial market emerged, there were no rules for evaluating art other than those that served personal interests. Artists asserted their creative status when they demonstrated their involvement in bohemian life by investing their human and economic resources in holding parties, events, and home exhibitions. The desire to follow a bourgeois lifestyle was accompanied by a desire to assert one's difference from the ordinary people. Artists imagined the post-Soviet Kyiv as boring, gray, sad, and were accustomed to this vision of the city as one that was painfully familiar, so they tried to escape from this reality and manifest their difference from what they saw as uniformity among its inhabitants.

The Kyiv-born artist Taia Galagan recalls that buying staple goods was quite a challenge in the first years of independence; the clothing on sale, for example, appeared very depressing:

> We made it our rule to go there every Saturday and Sunday and fish out the most interesting items [. . . ] The raincoats of the Soviet-Chinese company "Druzhba" found on Male vintage avantgarde jackets: this was the pinnacle of fashion at the time. Also, cowboy boots, jeans bought from fartsovschiki [on the black market], bandanas, hats, caps, and other accessories. We bought and exchanged things. At one time, I shaved my temples, wore men's jackets and ties with brooches, which

---

the National Art Institute Kyiv. See: Valeria Troubina, *Secondary Archive Project*, Ukraine section curated by Oksana Briukhovetska, Kateryna Iakovlenko, Iryna Polikarchuk, and Kateryna Rusetska, Warsaw, Poland: Katarzyna Kozyra Foundation. February 23, 2022. https://secondaryarchive.org/?s=troubina&id=435.

[14] Tatiana Kochubinska, "The Late Soviet Kyiv Bohemians: On the Significance of the Paris Commune Squat," in *The ParCommune: Place, Community, Phenomenon* (Kyiv: Publish Pro, 2019), 12.

caused quite a surprise among my professors because no one at the Faculty of Arts dressed like that . . .[15]

In 1992, the young artists Natalia Radovinska and Victoria Parkhomenko created the installation *To Those Who Can Knit*.[16] They posted their photos in various knitted hats on a plaque, accompanied by instructions from a Soviet magazine on how a woman should wear knit hats. By mimicking Soviet models, they criticized everyday experience and ordinary reality, the lack of individualism and creativity, as well as the influence of the state on individual life. It is symbolic that none of them continued her career as an artist: Radovinska almost immediately tried her hand at becoming a stylist, while Parkhomenko moved on first to modeling, and then onward to the restaurant business. Parkhomenko's and Radovinska's artwork might have been ironic, but this irony also addressed very acute economic challenges.[17]

### On Being a Mother in Ukrainian Art

Born into an artistic family, Ilya Chichkan himself modeled and sewed clothes, but never left his artistic practice. His personal and artistic life always complimented one other and were inseparable. However, the same cannot be said about his first wife, the artist Tetiana Iliakhova, who simultaneously took care of their children and fulfilled commercial orders.[18] While her partner could afford to experiment with art forms and themes, she, for example, was engaged in the restoration of icons. Performing such technical work, she moved

---

[15] Taia Galagan (real name Tetiana Gershuni, b. 1968, Kyiv) is an artist and curator. She participated in exhibitions beginning in 1994. She graduated from private drawing and painting courses in 1987-1988 at A.G. Poluyanov Studio, Kyiv. She holds a BA in Art History and Theory from the Ukrainian Academy of Fine Arts in Kyiv and an MFA from the University of Saskatchewan, Saskatoon, Canada. See: Taia Galagan, Yuri Kaplun, and Kostiantyn Klymashenko. "Galagan pro Galagan" (Galagan about Galagan). *Mitec: Suchasniy mitetstvo ukrainy.* May 18, 2020. https://mitec.ua/galagan-o-galagan/.

[16] Natalia Radovinska (b. 1971, Kyiv) is an artist and was a member of the Paris Commune. She left the professional art world in 1993 for the fashion industry, where she works to this day. Viktoria Parkhomenko (b. 1971, Kyiv) is an artist, was also a member of the Paris Commune and left the professional art scene in 1996, switching to the restaurant business. She is now a culinary expert.

[17] See: Kateryna Iakovlenko, "The Establishment and Development of the Paris Commune Squat in Kyiv," in *The ParCommune: Place, Community, Phenomenon* (Kyiv: Publish Pro, 2019), 18-49.

[18] Tetiana Iliakhova (b. 1954, Kyiv) is an artist. A graduate of the T. H. Shevchenko Republican Comprehensive Art School, she was Ilya Chichkan's first wife. She lived and worked in the studios on Sofiivska Street.

away from the contemporary art field. In addition, Ilyakhova "found herself" in motherhood; she taught her children drawing and painting. Today David Chichkan and Sasha Chichkan continue the artistic line in the biography of their famous family. Over the years, however, Iliakhova continued her interest in painting and especially "batik," a special technique of painting on fabric, and created an impressive body of work that has yet to be shown to the public.

Iliakhova's biography is not an exception. For example, another female artist, Svitlana Selezneva, who at the time had recently received a degree in fine arts, found herself working first in art restoration, and then as a seamstress and clothing designer.[19] After maternity leave, she could not return to work as an art restorer and was forced to look for alternative livelihoods. Custom tailoring served as an alternative source of income. Selezneva mentions that the field became profitable because many people wanted to look good in the new context, which permitted individuals with more freedom to explore decorative self-styled appearances, but nobody could afford to buy expensive clothes in stores. Eventually, she was approached by television stars and writers. Later, as the state's economic development progressed, the need for individual sewing disappeared, and the artist began to look for other options again: jewelry appeared as a fascinating new avenue.[20]

Although economic factors forced the artist Selezneva to postpone her artistic career, she still debuted on the international stage in 2018. For the installation *Diploma Thesis* Dariia Kuzmych, Svitlana Selezneva's daughter and an artist in her own right, asked her mother to collaborate with her on a project.[21] The installation, which includes a quilt (multi-layered textile object), multiple drawings from 1982-1998, bead embroidery, and a visual archive in notebook

---

[19] Svitlana Selezneva is an artist and designer from Kyiv who works with different textile techniques: sewing, quilting and beaded embroidery; beaded jewelery is also an important theme in her work.

After graduating from art school in 1986, Selezneva worked in restoration at the National Museum of Art of Ukraine, the Kyiv Art Gallery, and as dressmaker throughout the 1990s.

[20] Svitlana Selezneva, Oral unpublished interview with the author, December 10, 2021.

[21] See: https://www.dariiakuzmych.com/Diploma-thesis. Dariia Kuzmych (1991) is an artist from Kyiv, also based in Berlin. She completed her BA in monumental painting at the Fine Arts Academy in Kyiv in 2015 and her MA at the Berlin University of Arts in 2020, in the art and media program taught by Professor Nina Fischer and field research based program by renown artist Ai Weiwei. Her practice encompasses both traditional media, such as painting, drawing, text, textile, and new media including video, animation and computer-programmed architectural interfaces. She often connects her pieces in spatial installations in which verbal and written language often plays an important role. A central theme in her multimedia practice are points of historical transition in society and their deeper impact(s) on the individual.

form, raised the question of artistic work, productivity, maternity and success. This biographical case study shows the story of an artist told through her daughter's artwork, whose career started before the collapse of the USSR, but was postponed because of the demands of family life.

**Figure 8.1.** Dariia Kuzmych in collaboration with Svitlana Selezneva. 2018. Diploma Thesis. Installation, quilt (multi-layered textile, 210 x 210 cm), multiple drawings from the years 1982-1998, bead embroidery, visual archive in a notebook. Installation view in the Künstlerhaus Bethanien. Courtesy of the artist.

Selezneva's biography raises the question about the notion of youth as a determining factor in both opportunities and limitations for women artists at different points in their lives.[22] Who counts as a young artist: does the notion refer merely to one's age, or does it also address one's work experience? Can an artist realize his or her creative potential and create a career long after graduating from university? What opportunities and programs are there for academic or institutional support for continuing artistic careers? Unlike

---

[22] Despite the urgency of the issue of categorizing "young artists," only recently has this topic entered into any wider critical discourse concerning art as a profession. In Ukraine in 2021 the critic Yulia Hnat initiated a critical platform of essays and events on this topic. See: Yulia Hnat, *Statistichnyi portret molodoi hudozhnitsi* (*Statistical portrait of young artists*), Cedos.org, BUT System Solutions Bureau, Info Sapiens, March 11, 2021. https://cedos.org.ua/researches/statystychnyj-portret-molodo_yi-hudozhny_czi/.

governmental or private institutions and corporations with clear rules of maternity leave, such support does not exist in the artistic field, which mainly relies on freelance work: having spent their active years on child-rearing, it is a fact that many women artists find it more challenging to re-integrate into the artistic field afterwards.

Moreover, galleries and museums concerned with showing artworks, especially in the case of pleasing donors and collectors, often tend to prioritize the younger generations of emerging artists. Is it possible to combine motherhood and artwork? If so, who is responsible for the childcare? For example, can an art institution, museum, or gallery take on the function of caring for and supporting young artists and parents, thus creating the necessary conditions for their creativity? These days, there are examples of institutions which offer additional funding for family scholarships or assistance with insurance or babysitting. However, even only slight improvements in closing the gender gap among the majority of art institutions in Ukraine and globally are still fairly uncommon.

The 1990s changed the career trajectory for another artist, Iryna Lastovkina, who chose to teach at the National Academy of Fine Arts and focus her career on art restoration.[23] In 1995, Lastovkina debuted at the feminist exhibition *Mouth Of The Medusa* with her sculpture "Madame Butterfly." Made of metal and mesh, the artwork resembled an exquisite dress. Recalling the primary concept behind the work, the author said that she wanted to do something feminine and robust: "I correlated this sophistication inherent in a woman with a metal frame that cannot be changed or broken."[24] However, she also claims that she aimed for an idea of femininity as something exquisite, which she has never been herself. In describing her work on the object, she focuses on the material component:

---

[23] Since 1997, Iryna Lastovkina has been teaching at the National Academy of Fine Arts and Architecture, collaborating with the Museum of the History of Ukraine, the Institute of Archeology of the National Academy of Sciences of Ukraine, the National Military History Museum, the Museum of the History of the Church of the Tithes and others. She also regularly participates in archaeological expeditions and works on the restoration of decorative and applied art objects and paintings. She is one of the few working in the field of contemporary art restoration in Ukraine.

[24] See: Kateryna Iakovlenko, "Irina Lastovkina: Kogda my uvideli ukrainskuyu zhivopis, u nas vsyo perevernulos s nog na golovu" (Irina Lastovkina: When We Saw Ukrainian Painting, Everything Turned Upside Down Inside Us), *KORYDOR*, December 14, 2018. http://www.korydor.in.ua/ua/woman-in-culture/irina-lastovkina-kogda-my-uvideli-ukrainskuju-zhivopis-u-nas-vse-perevernulos-s-nog-na-golovu.html.

Welding itself did not take much time. However, it was necessary to purchase the materials, which posed a problem. Today anyone can go to the store and choose everything they need. At that time, we had to look for all the necessary materials on the black market, negotiate, search, or buy from construction workers. I needed smooth fittings, so I dragged them myself from one construction site to the next before I could get to bending and welding. I bought the materials from construction workers, who took everything from their construction site. They also had to pay for materials. In my sculpture, by the way, a chain-link fence was used. It was almost impossible then to find the netting.[25]

Taia Galagan, one of the first artists in Ukraine to have started using ultraviolet light in her work, also reaffirms this idea of materiality: "In the 1990s, there was no special technical support from galleries, so you had to do everything yourself. I bought parts, developed diagrams, designed lamps, and installed them in the exhibition spaces myself."[26] Galagan revived her career as an artist after earning her MFA in Canada. Returning to Kyiv and her native artistic environment was a challenge because the art market had changed during her absence, and as a result, she had to work all the more just to reaffirm her presence as an artist.[27]

## Technology and Maternity

In her Manifesto, Kyiv-born artist Yana Bystrova, who emigrated to Paris in 1991, speaks about the need to change one's career path.[28] Tackling the question of identity, loss of home, and departure from one's cultural roots, she realized that she could not continue with her traditional painting practice. She did not have a personal studio in Paris and urgently needed to earn money just to survive. She describes this period as an experience of intense personal mutations:

---

[25] Iakovlenko, Ibid.

[26] Kostyantyn Doroshenko, "Taya Galagan: Hudozhnik kak proizvedenie" (Taya Galagan: Artist as a masterpiece), *ArtUkraine*, March 5, 2015. https://artukraine.com.ua/a/taya-galagan–khudozhnik-kak-proizvedenie/#.YW3GSy1t5QK.

[27] Galagan, Kaplun, and Klymashenko, "Galagan pro Galagan" (Galagan about Galagan), Ibid.

[28] Yana Bystrova was born in Kyiv, Ukraine, and is a third-generation artist. She studied at the School and Academy of Fine Arts of Ukraine in Kyiv, having received a traditional "official" education in Soviet Socialist Realism. She participated in the lively art scenes of Kyiv and Moscow after graduation and moved to Paris in 1991. She continued to develop her career by working with additional media in Paris, such as photography, digital art, silkscreen, and computer programming.

The radical change in my situation, the absence of a studio, and the impossibility of practicing painting in the way I was taught to and accustomed to doing, as well as the state-of-the-art scene of those years, made me explore other practices. In turn, I tried tiny formats, then silkscreen, photography, graphic design, and finally programming, at which point I stopped practicing traditional forms of art for a while. But then, somehow, this chosen interruption of art practice felt like a major loss of identity.

These mutations, or shape-shiftings, or searches for a place or status, the questioning of art practice, digital experiments, along with a period of programming and office work (!): these metamorphoses are best represented, I think, by a series of experimental self-portraits, done in a proprietary technique. This cycle took me more than ten years to complete and ended with a return to painting.

This time it was by choice.[29]

It is crucial to note that for many artists in the 1990s, computer technology-generated artwork became something of a lifeline, as it did not require the purchase of additional material resources for each new piece. Rather, they could be synthesized onscreen. Moreover, thanks to the open digital laboratory of the Soros Center for Contemporary Art, many artists have taken courses in art and technology and learned to experiment with video and digital art. Based on work in this laboratory and with the center's support, such artists as Natalia Golibroda, Olga Kashimbekova, Solomiya Savchuk, Margaryta Zinets, and others created significant moving image art. However, after this laboratory was shut down, most artists returned to their painting practice, leaving these experiments behind. For many of them, this turn in their professional activity was also connected to maternity and family life. In essence, experiments in some forms of physical (non-digital) media and new topics were also indicative of the artist's privileged position. Such freedom could be afforded only by those who had economic support.

Speaking about different stages in the trajectory of her work, the Odesa-born artist Natalia Golibroda who in the 1990s primarily focused on digital and video art, addressed motherhood and stated that this experience allowed her to look at her artworks differently. This experience coincided with her return to painting and her diminishing involvement with technology and computer art. In addition to the desire to work with physical materials and to return to visual

---

[29] See: Yana Bystrova, *Secondary Archive Project*, Ukraine section curated by Oksana Briukhovetska, Kateryna Iakovlenko, Iryna Polikarchuk, and Kateryna Rusetska (Warsaw, Poland: Katarzyna Kozyra Foundation. 2021). https://secondaryarchive.org/?s=troubina&id=435.

thinking, there was another reason for this choice: digital art was not in demand on the art market, unlike painting.[30]

The topic of motherhood and the iconography of the mother both occupy prominent positions in the Ukrainian context. One of the most famous Soviet symbols of Kyiv is a monument to the Motherland, which takes the form of a statue of a woman on a pedestal holding a militantly raised shield and sword, designed by the sculptor Vasyl Borodai (1917—2010). In total, the pedestal and statue, taken together, stand 102 meters tall. Among contemporary artworks, Vlada Ralko's *Kyiv Diary* graphic series, which she worked on for several years, should be mentioned in this context. The well-known icon "Mother of God's Protection," which Ralko conveys expressively, depicts a woman with an open womb or breastfeeding two infant sons; today, it embodies the traumatic present, the pain of loss, and the wounds of the Russian war in Ukraine. Describing Ralko's work, notably her *Kyiv Diary*, critic Taras Wozniak remarked that she is perhaps the only man in Ukrainian contemporary art to have boldly faced the issue of the war. Therefore, looking at the diverse artistic landscape of today's Ukraine, we have reasons to reiterate that Vlada Ralko is indeed "almost the lone male figure in the whole of contemporary Ukraine."[31] It is not that Ralko embodies masculine traits or tackles stereotypically masculine topics: she symbolizes courage and possesses resilience and patriotism that in Soviet culture were primarily represented by male society. However, it is worth paying attention to the problematization of courage and civic engagement in the art context. During Soviet times, there was a stereotype about a masterpiece in art: it needed to be "pure" and "honest." However, of course, such characteristics were primarily addressed not directly to art itself but to artists, and such high historical praise was given exclusively to men. Thus, the Soviet government controlled the patriotism of the artists and their loyalty to the system. [32] However, no matter what we mean by this word today, the legitimacy of such

---

[30] See: Natalia Golibroda-Boyko, *Secondary Archive Project*, Ukraine section curated by Oksana Briukhovetska, Kateryna Iakovlenko, Iryna Polikarchuk, and Kateryna Rusetska (Warsaw, Poland. *Katarzyna Kozyra Foundation*, 2021). https://secondaryarchive.org/?s=troubina&id=435.

[31] See: Wozniak, Taras. "Oche-Vydytsya Vlada Ralko." (Eyewitness Vlada Ralko). *Chasopys Ji.* Blog Post. http://www.ji-magazine.lviv.ua/2019/voznyak-oche-vydytsya-vlada-ralko.htm.

[32] This topic was developed for a public talk and article on masculinity; See: Kateryna Iakovlenko, "Art Between Manliness and Activism: The Role of Ukrainian Women Artists During Political Transformation," Lecture, *Unwritten Stories: Women Artists in Central and Eastern Europe Conference* (Arton Foundation Warsaw, Latvian Center for Contemporary Arts Riga, SCCA-Ljubljana, Center for Contemporary Arts Ljubljana, and the Office for Photography Zagreb. September 2–3, 2021).

claims, which support stereotypes and myths about the "honest" nature of art, can and should be contested.

Wozniak's phrase "lone male figure" is an allusion to Ivan Franko (1856-1916), who famously described his contemporary, the female writer and today national symbol, Lesia Ukrainka (1871-1913), as "the lone male figure in Ukrainian literature."[33] Such a reference is essential in the links between art and literature, but today such a phrase could also be perceived as undermining the struggle for women's rights and equality. Ralko refers to female images as powerful metaphors, containing humanistic ideas worthy of the universal meanings and elevation to the eternal truth that also take epic form in representing revolution and war. Although the artist denies feminist references and involvement in this movement, all her works manifest the core of any feminist struggle; they amplify the voices of the marginalized who may not be capable of independent expression.

Suzanna Danuta Walters pointed out that for feminists, redressing this absence and beginning to formulate alternative histories and theories of motherhood.[34] The artist and curator Oksana Briukhovetska has pursued a similar goal.[35] Commenting on her curatorial exhibition, entitled *Motherhood*, she said: "My curatorial position is also affected by the fact that I am an artist myself, and usually, as an artist, I take part in exhibitions that I organize. This abolishes the hierarchy in the positions of curators and artists for me. In reality, artists can be, and often are, curators." [36] Briukhovetska argues that her perception of her practice and work changed after she experienced firsthand how the double burden on women functioned, in which women are expected to take on all domestic chores and caring for children, while also working outside of the home. More precisely, motherhood reveals some previously hidden topics and allows society to rethink this experience and creativity in general.

---

[33] Wozniak, Ibid.

[34] Suzanna Danuta Walters, *Lives Together/Worlds Apart: Mothers and Daughters in Popular Culture* (Berkeley: University of California Press, 1992), 141.

[35] Oksana Briukhovetska is an artist, and curator. She is currently pursuing an MFA at the School of Art and Design of the University of Michigan. She is a member of the Center for Visual Culture and curator of many exhibitions, including: *Ukrainian Body* (2012); *Motherhood* (2015); *What do I have from a woman?* (2015); *TEXTUS: Embroidery, Textiles, Feminism* (2017); *Women's Texts* (2017). She co-edited a book of seminal interviews about art and feminism launched in the framework of the 2019 "Black Cloud" Kyiv Biennale. See: Oksana Briukhovetska and Lesia Kulchynska, Eds. *The Right to Truth: Conversations on Art and Feminism* (Kyiv: Visual Culture Research Center; Paris: European Alternatives, 2019).

[36] Oleksandra Pohrebnyak, Dmytro Chepurnoy, and Kateryna Iakovlenko, Eds. *Kuratorskyi Posibmyk* (*Curatorial Handbook*), (Kyiv: Izolyatsya, 2020), 107.

Another artist, Oksana Chepelyk, uses her experience of motherhood as a topic in her artistic practice. [37] Having received a degree in architecture in early 1990s in Kyiv and having studied feminist theory in Paris, she turned to contemporary art and started practicing filmmaking and performance. Throughout the 1990s, Chepelyk's work predominantly focused on gender and its visual representation. She addressed the commodification of women, the role of sexuality in politics and in popular consciousness, power and intercultural relations and the influence of history on the treatment of gender binaries. Describing the role of Chepelyk's experience on her art, the philosopher Tamara Zlobina emphasizes the close connection between the individual and the political. The artist's statements fit the feminist axiom that the "personal is political":

> By installing images of infants in public spaces, the artist raises the issue of responsibility for the survival of a community that the public hypocritically lays exclusively on the shoulders of mothers and fathers, all the while promulgating the tales of "the joys of motherhood." Meanwhile, the government institutions shirk their duty of ensuring a healthy environment, a favorable social climate, and adequate material security.[38]

For the artist Marina Skugareva, maternity was also an equally inspiring and politically radicalizing experience. [39] While staying at home, doing housework, and caring for her daughter, she created a series of drawings entitled *The Good Housekeepers* begun in 1997, wherein materiality appears on both the symbolic and the physical planes. She combined depictions of domestic scenes of cleaning, cooking, and resting with printouts from Internet chats featuring women in discussion about various pressing issues, seeking support from one

---

[37] Oksana Chepelyk is an established multimedia artist with a long repertoire of international exhibitions and residencies. She began her career as an architect, having studied Architecture at the Art Institute in Kyiv (1978-1984). In the early 2000s, after completing a program at the Bauhaus Kolleg (Dessau, Germany), Chepelyk's focus in her video and digital art shifted towards the social and aesthetic structures of urban life to explore the synthesis of architectural spaces, contemporary aesthetics and new media.

[38] Tamara Zlobina, "Zhinka siogodni: materynstvo ta emansypatsia u proektah Oksany Chepelyk" (Today's Woman: motherhood and emancipation in Oksana Chepelyk's projects), *Ukrainskyi Zhurnal* 5 (2011), 55. See also: Oksana Chepelyk, "Genesis Project as a Model of Gender Study Research." *UCLA CSW: Center for the Study of Women.* Newsletter, March 1, 2011: 26–34.

[39] Marina Skugareva (b. 1962, Kyiv) is a painter and a representative of the New Ukrainian Wave in contemporary art. She graduated from the Dzhemal Dagestan art school in 1981 and then studied at the Lviv State Institute of Decorative and Applied Arts Textiles Department from 1982–1988.

another. She later continued this series in the form of paintings on canvas and fabric sheets.

**Figure 8.2.** Oksana Chepelyk. 2000. Genesys. Installation view. Rio de Janeiro, Brasil. Courtesy of the artist.

### On Being a Daughter in Ukrainian Art

Despite the joy of learning a new social role, many women artists still face the pressure of social stereotypes about motherhood and the role of women in society and the family; accordingly, they feel the effects of long-standing inequality. Interestingly, I did not find a single example of art that would problematize the mother-daughter relationship in the 1990s from the position of a daughter. In turn, the artists whose childhood came in the 1990s, to a greater extent, reflected on the practice of their fathers. Vivid examples are the artists Ksenia Hnylytska and Anna Zvyagintseva. The latter did several projects dedicated to her father, particularly the artwork "Sculptures of my father." Therefore, in this paragraph, I will deviate a little from the context of the 1990s and turn to a more modern example of the mother-daughter relationship in Ukrainian art, which, in my opinion, more vividly and intensely reveals the topic more distinctly and vividly.

Suzanna Danuta Walters emphasizes that "many feminists have acknowledged the importance of rethinking the mother/daughter relationship."[40] Ukrainian

---

[40] Walters, *Lives Together/Worlds Apart: Mothers and Daughters in Popular Culture*, 142.

contemporary art bears many critical examples of this process. For instance, in 2018, the 44-year-old artist Alevtina Kakhidze created a video entitled *44*, in which she films herself saying the word "NO" in forty-four different ways. This was her response to reproductive violence and social expectations that reduce every woman's choices to an oppressive binary: to become or not to become a mother. This question elicits a different reaction in every woman, especially as it pertains to any questions about why she does not have children because of women's rights, physical conditions, health considerations, economic and social factors, or any other number of reasons. The social demand placed on women to care for children is so strong that it serves as a fundamental mechanism for labeling an individual not only as female but, she notes, as acceptable/unacceptable: "But even if a woman cannot have a child, society asks her to adopt."[41]

According to Kakhidze, the gender drama of the current era in Ukraine is such that a woman cannot raise a child independently, save for a few positive examples that only further prove the rule. Alevtina Kakhidze is a Ukrainian artist who has taken an active civic stance and has engaged the themes of war, peace, and security in her art since the beginning of the Russian war in Ukraine in 2014. A large body of her recent work is dedicated to her mother, who lived in the occupied territories of the Donetsk Oblast. The series began with her posts on social networks, where she created a separate account for her mother.

Kakhidze has been keeping an artistic diary for more than four years, describing and drawing the life "along that frontline" based on her mother's stories. Her drawings about her mother's life are done in a childlike aesthetic. Broken lines in pencil and felt-tip pen convey the difficult situation in the region. A naive visual language describes the role of the ordinary, everyday person in this war. In the winter of 2019, Alevtina Kakhidze's mother died on a routine trip to pick up her pension check, which required her to stand in a very long line to cross a checkpoint from the occupied territories into sovereign Ukraine. She died of heart failure. Kakhidze posted on her Facebook wall on 17 Jan. 2019:

> My mother, whom many knew as Strawberry Andreevna, died yesterday at a DPR [Donetsk People Republic — Ed.] checkpoint [ . . . ] Many pensioners go through this process, traveling from uncontrolled territory to collect their Ukrainian pension. She left her house at 4 in the morning, but never reached the territory controlled by Ukraine.

---

[41] Kateryna Iakovlenko, "Dolzhna i vse: Hudozhnytsya Alevtyna Kakhidze o reproductivnom nasilii" ("That should be all:" the artist Alevtyna Kakhidze on reproductive violence), *Bird in Flight* 3, December 3, 2018, https://birdinflight.com/ru/portret/20181203-alevtina-kahidze.html.

According to the DPR, her death by heart failure was recorded at 10:25 am. It turns out that in the 5 hours she stood in line, she did not even get to the checkpoint.

She added:

Strawberry Andreevna never demonized any side of this war.
She always said that we needed to stop using the words "yours" and "ours."[42]

Kakhidze's personal story raises deep issues of everyday life during a military conflict, such as ordinary people crossing the frontline, access to social benefits and healthcare, information policy, voting rights, etc. The story of an artist's mother, the biography of a woman as imagined by her daughter, who has become a character in an art project, grows in proportion as an allegory for both the broken connections, but also strengthened continuities between generations in the experience of war. Once again, artistic devices are employed to reveal the complex and inhuman relationship of war and civilians. Originally, Kakhidze created a Facebook page for these works; subsequently, they became a basis for a staged play, and fragments of these dialogues have also been incorporated into many later works by the artist.[43]

**Figure 8.3.** Alevtina Kakhidze. 2021. Alevtina Kakhidze's mother's house: a monument to all who did not participate in the war, but were present there. Muzychi, Kyiv region. Photography by Margo Didichenko. Courtesy of the artist.

[42] Alevtyna Kakhidze, "Strawberry Andreevna," Facebook post, January 24, 2020. https://www.facebook.com/truealevtina/.
[43] Kakhidze, Ibid.

Suzanna Danuta Walters argues that:

> Although feminist theory has opened a new and exciting range of study
> on mothers and daughters, much of it repeats these same old dichotomous
> stories. The relationship between mother and daughter is either valorized
> as a transcendent bond of almost sexual plenitude or pilloried as the
> "bond" that keeps women tied to self-destructive behaviors and patterns of
> submission. Once again, mothers are either victims or agents, pawns in
> the game of male domination or sneaky operators in their own psychic
> power plays.[44]

In contrast to Danuta's emphasis on depictions of mothers and daughters
through a fetishization of either/or the sacred versus profane, in the case of
Kakhidze's storytelling, her mother's voice is not supra-human but is also not
weakened as that of an imperiled war victim — she is shown as an empowered
individual, who has her own opinions and even disagrees with her daughter
about critical changes in society, including the Maidan Revolution in 2013-14.
This imperfect relationship and outward disagreement are familiar to many
daughters and mothers, even a ritual, but the ability to imbue this ritual with
humor, love, and care stands out in Kakhidze's representations of her mother.
At some point, the story of Strawberry Andreevna began to appear on different
virtual platforms: it appeared in public and political discussions. Both state and
public sympathy for the woman who continued to live on the other side of the
frontline appeared as a rare example where, elsewhere, broader criticism of the
war and violence tended to instruct people to shut out excess concern and
focus on one's problems. Strawberry Andreevna's story about her personal
experiences with the state and society became a way to declare a shared
democratic, liberal view.

The conflicted relationship between a mother and daughter has also been
represented by the artist Taia Galagan. Rethinking her life, she decided to change
her last and first name, reclaiming her mother's maiden name; she writes:

> I believe that, at birth, a person should receive a double surname: that
> of their father and mother; otherwise, the whole family line is deprived
> of continuation. So I decided to officially change my name. I took my
> mother's maiden name, Galagan and the name "Taia" is derived from
> my birth name, Tatiana. So now, I sign my works with a double last
> name.[45]

---

[44] Walters, *Lives Together/Worlds Apart: Mothers and Daughters in Popular Culture*, 161.

[45] Galagan, Kaplun, and Klymashenko, "Galagan pro Galagan" (Galagan about Galagan), Ibid.

This gesture undermines the patriarchal structure of society and suggests a different understanding of the function of motherhood and parenthood in Ukraine.

## Conclusion

In her book, the philosopher Renata Salecl talks about the problem of ignorance, noting how, over time, the knowledge economy has transformed into an ignorance economy: between truth, post-truth, lies, and lack of information, some representatives of society choose a path of non-knowledge that is more convenient for itself, building further communication and knowledge upon deception.[46] The lack of easily accessible information about Ukrainian art in the 1990s, or rather the lack of high-profile women artists, does not mean that women did not participate in creative and intellectual processes. Nevertheless, when dealing with art history, the authors of feminist theory constantly and rightly emphasize the inequality of conditions under which women and men coexisted.

Analyzing the work of women artists in Kyiv in the early 1990s, one is constantly confronted with the challenges they faced. A dire lack of economic and social support forced some to move on to other fields, abandoning art altogether or putting their artistic careers on hold. Meanwhile, this same period in the history of Ukrainian art was so rich in experiments because the male artists finally had the opportunity to carry out their ideas. They had the time, the support of their partners, and later the support of collectors. To a great extent, however, their women partners were artists in their own right who nevertheless took on domestic and family responsibilities. The artists whose careers didn't fully develop until later had previously tried their hand at many random styles, looking for found objects at flea markets or experimenting with shapes and textures. By contrast, due to the double burden of making art while raising children, women artists could not afford to make mistakes; they could not afford to create random, "non-serious" and "fun" works. Because of their lack of free time, their complicated living and professional conditions, housework, the pressure of other responsibilities, and socioeconomic challenges, they often abandoned art. That explains why their body of work is often much smaller than that of their male colleagues: women artists couldn't afford to make mistakes.

Considering the above, motherhood today should not be seen as a career hurdle or the framework that renders art practice inaccessible. Along with this,

---

[46] Renata Salecl. *A Passion for Ignorance*. Princeton, (New Jersey: Princeton University Press, 2020).

the current critical view of the art that emerged in the 1990s raises another issue: who is a young artist? What are the opportunities to support the artists who have put their creative work on hold to pursue motherhood? The example of Svetlana Selezneva and many others underlines an unstable art system, focusing exclusively on young authors with the energy, strength, and diligence to succeed. The experiences of Ukrainian women artists who navigated the 1990s and paved the way for later artists show an opposite change: most women artists and curators today have consciously taken claim of "the female" heritage in art and have changed their attitudes to art, modifying their choice of topics and creating a new discursive field that includes and pays tribute to the domestic routines associated with femininity, overturning what that word means, and taking aim at society's unequal expectations and judgments that place limitations and boundaries around parenthood, the experience of motherhood, or childlessness. This open discourse also invites not just male/female artistic representations but claims new ground for expressive will and aesthetics capable of showing a gender as a gradient, or self-identification, rather than a category.

I started work on this text before the start of the full-scale invasion by the Russian army into the territory of Ukraine. My text is primarily dedicated to the artistic context of the 1990s and gestures toward the context of recent times. As I edit this text today, and especially places where my thinking concerns the topic of motherhood, I cannot notice the profound impact that the war has had on gender issues. Some of my thoughts find their thematic reflection in the works of the artist Kateryna Lisovenko, a mother of two sons. The experiences of motherhood, raising children, and the family are some of the central ones in her work, and speak of the artist's perspective, and her view of everyday life and war.

Men who are Ukrainian citizens aged 18-60 are not permitted to leave the territory of Ukraine under Martial Law, which was instituted beginning in February by President Volodymyr Zelenskyy. Civilians of both genders are fighting in volunteer units, but a draft remains in place for men. Some male artists, curators, and students can cross over the border on exchanges, but only for a short period with the permission of the Ministry of Culture in Ukraine. Hundreds of international academic and artistic institutions have simplified the conditions for entry, and increased their interest in Ukrainian art. Many women, not only artists but of all professional and working classes, have left the territory of Ukraine among the now 6 million refugees — some forever, while others continue to return. Throughout the country, at least weekly across many regions, if not daily in the South and East of Ukraine nearest the frontline with occupied territories, our hospitals and maternity wards are all under fire. Children there and everywhere face trauma under the sounds of sirens, insecurity in many displaced living conditions, and loss of their parent(s) in extreme cases. An estimated 450 children have been killed and 890 wounded by rocket fire and other attacks since February 24, as of November 2022. Undoubtedly, the war crimes and crimes against humanity that are taking place in Ukraine amount to serious humanitarian challenges now and in future. The moment must be seized upon by women, including in the creative professions, to communicate a language capable of capturing the atrocities now, in the future, and also to re-envision that future. These women who find themselves inside of history, inside of these rapid changes, will rewrite the gender order along with more expansive perceptions, media discourses, power agendas, and new horizons for future research.

## Bibliography

Barshynova, Oksana, and Olena Martynyuk. "Ukrainian Art of the Independence Era: Transitions and Aspirations." In *From "the Ukraine" to Ukraine: A Contemporary History 1991—2021*. Edited by Matthew Rojansky, Georgiy Kasianov and Mykhailo Minakov. Berlin and New York: Ibidem and Columbia University Press, 2021.

Bystrova, Yana. *Secondary Archive Project*, Ukraine section curated by Oksana Briukhovetska, Kateryna Iakovlenko, Iryna Polikarchuk, and Kateryna Rusetska. Warsaw, Poland: Katarzyna Kozyra Foundation. 2021. https://secondaryarchive. org/?s=troubina&id=435.

Briukhovetska, Oksana and Lesia Kulchynska, Eds. *The Right to Truth: Conversations on Art and Feminism*. Kyiv: Visual Culture Research Center; Paris: European Alternatives, 2019.

Chepelyk, Oksana. "Genesis Project as a Model of Gender Study Research." *UCLA CSW: Center for the Study of Women*. Newsletter. March 1, 2011: 26–34. https://escholarship.org/content/qt3zx338p3/qt3zx338p3.pdf.

Doroshenko, Kostyantyn. "Taia Galagan: Hudozhnik kak proizvedenie" (Taya Galagan: Artist as a masterpiece). *ArtUkraine*. March 5, 2015. https://artukraine. com.ua/a/taya-galagan–khudozhnik-kak-proizvedenie/#.YW3GSy1t5QK.

Galagan, Taya, Yuri Kaplun, Kostiantyn Klymashenko. "Galagan pro Galagan" (Galagan about Galagan). *Mitec: Suchasniy mitetstvo ukrainy*. May 18, 2020. https://mitec.ua/galagan-o-galagan/.

Golibroda-Boyko, Natalia. *Secondary Archive Project*, Ukraine section curated by Oksana Briukhovetska, Kateryna Iakovlenko, Iryna Polikarchuk, and Kateryna Rusetska. Warsaw, Poland: Katarzyna Kozyra Foundation. 2021. https://secondaryarchive.org/?s=troubina&id=435.

Hnat, Yulia. *Statistichnyi portret molodoi hudozhnitsi* (*Statistical portrait of young artists*). *Cedos.org; BUT System Solutions Bureau; Info Sapiens*. March 11, 2021. https://cedos.org.ua/researches/statystychnyj-portret-molodo_yi-hudozhny_czi/.

Iakovlenko, Kateryna. "'Telo' Parizhskoy Kommuny: Chast pervaya" ("The Body" in the Art of the Paris Commune: Part One). *KORYDOR.UA*. March 7,

2017. http://www.korydor.in.ua/en/context/telo-parizhskoj-kommuny-part-one.html.

————. "Irina Lastovkina: Kogda my uvideli ukrainskuyu zhivopis, u nas vsyo perevernulos s nog na golovu" (Irina Lastovkina: When We Saw Ukrainian Painting, Everything Turned Upside Down Inside Us). *KORYDOR*. December 14, 2018. http://www.korydor.in.ua/ua/woman-in-culture/irina-lastovkina-kogda-my-uvideli-ukrainskuju-zhivopis-u-nas-vse-perevernulos-s-nog-na-golovu.html.

————. "Dolzhna i vse: Hudozhnytsya Alevtyna Kakhidze o reproductivnom nasilii" ("That should be all:" the artist Alevtyna Kakhidze on reproductive violence). *Bird in Flight* 3. December 3, 2018. https://birdinflight.com/ru/portret/20181203-alevtina-kahidze.html.

————. "The Establishment and Development of the Paris Commune Squat in Kyiv." In *The ParCommune: Place, Community, Phenomenon*. Kyiv: Publish Pro, 2019: 18-49.

————, Ed. *There Are Such Great Women Artists in Ukrainian Art*. Kyiv, Publish Pro, 2019.

————. "Art Between Manliness and Activism: The Role of Ukrainian Women Artists During Political Transformation." Lecture, *Unwritten Stories: Women Artists in Central and Eastern Europe Conference*. Arton Foundation Warsaw, Latvian Center for Contemporary Arts Riga, SCCA-Ljubljana, Center for Contemporary Arts Ljubljana, and the Office for Photography Zagreb. September 2–3, 2021.

Kakhidze, Alevtyna. "Strawberry Andreevna," Facebook post, January 24, 2020. https://www.facebook.com/truealevtina/.

Kochubinska, Tatiana. "The Late Soviet Kyiv Bohemians: On the Significance of the Paris Commune Squat." In *The ParCommune: Place, Community, Phenomenon*. Kyiv: Publish Pro, 2019: 12-17.

Lozhkina, Alisa. *The Permanent Revolution: Art of Ukraine from the 20th–early 21st century*. Kyiv: ARTHUSS, 2019.

Parker, Rozsika, and Griselda Pollock. *Old Mistresses: Women, Art and Ideology*. New York: Pantheon, 1982.

*PinchukArtCentre Research Platform*. Kyiv, Ukraine. Official website. https://new.pinchukartcentre.org/en/research.

Pohrebnyak, Oleksandra, Dmytro Chepurnoy, and Kateryna Iakovlenko, Eds. *Kuratorskyi Posibmyk (Curatorial Handbook)*. Kyiv: Izolyatsya, 2020.

Pollock, Griselda. "Women, Art and Ideology: Questions for Feminist Art Historians." *Women's Art Journal* 4, no. 1 (1983): 39-47.

Salecl, Renata. *A Passion for Ignorance*. Princeton, New Jersey: Princeton University Press, 2020.

*Secondary Archive Project*, Ukraine section curated by Oksana Briukhovetska, Kateryna Iakovlenko, Iryna Polikarchuk, and Kateryna Rusetska. Warsaw, Poland: Katarzyna Kozyra Foundation. February 23, 2022. https://secondary archive.org/?s=troubina&id=435.

Selezneva, Svitlana. Oral unpublished interview with the author. December 10, 2021.

Troubina, Valeria. *Secondary Archive Project*, Ukraine section curated by Oksana Briukhovetska, Kateryna Iakovlenko, Iryna Polikarchuk, and Kateryna Rusetska. Warsaw, Poland: Katarzyna Kozyra Foundation. February 23, 2022. https://secondaryarchive.org/?s=troubina&id=435.

Walters, Suzanna Danuta. *Lives Together/Worlds Apart: Mothers and Daughters in Popular Culture.* Berkeley: University of California Press, 1992.

Wozniak, Taras. "Oche-Vydytsya Vlada Ralko." (Eyewitness Vlada Ralko). *Chasopys Ji.* Blog Post. http://www.ji-magazine.lviv.ua/2019/voznyak-oche-vydytsya-vlada-ralko.htm.

Zhmurko, Tetiana. "A Few Words About Painting." In *The Parcommune: Place, Community, Phenomenon.* Kyiv: Publish Pro (2019): 68-75.

Zlobina, Tamara. "Zhinka siogodni: materynstvo ta emansypatsia u proektah Oksany Chepelyk." (Today's Woman: motherhood and emancipation in Oksana Chepelyk's projects). *Ukrainskyi Zhurnal* 5 (2011): 55–56.

# Chapter 9

# Beyond Three Colors:
# Exploring Soviet Memory of Race

Oksana Briukhovetska

### Abstract

This text is about my political discoveries about race after arriving in the United States for the first time in my life at the beginning of 2020. The Black Lives Matter protests which were taking place at the time pushed me to expand my artistic and research interests, which previously focused on feminism, to race and racism. This was not only a shift in my research subject, but also a considerable shift in my personality. As a Ukrainian artist, I started to look for my position in the discussion about race, which is not only American, but a global discussion. This text was written in 2021, before the war in Ukraine started. In the summer of 2022, it was finalized, taking the current Russian war in Ukraine into consideration.

In this text, I present fragments of my research and reflections that preceded and accompanied the making of two works of art during the first year of my MFA program at Stamps School of Art and Design at the University of Michigan in 2021-22. The first work, the remake of the Soviet poster of the 1960s, "For the Solidarity of Women of the World!" was a response to my investigations of the legacy of Soviet racism. The second one, "In Solidarity with Ukraine," I started in January 2022, before the full-scale Russian invasion on Ukraine, and finished during the first month of the war. It is no coincidence that the word "solidarity" appears in both titles, as I was trying to express the meanings of solidarity. I started the second work as a continuation of promoting the topic of race within the Ukrainian context, but at the end it was significantly contextualized by the war and the wave of solidarity with Ukraine that rose all over the world. I started with the attempt to understand the possible ways for Ukraine to be in solidarity with the anti-racist struggle, and later I, like many Ukrainians, found myself seeking solidarity with Ukraine and the Ukrainian people who are fighting to defend their homeland and democracy.

In the research that accompanied my work in the field of art, I try to go deeper into the history of Soviet racism to understand its influence on the perception of Eastern European countries of the Black Lives Matter protests in 2020. I try to understand manifestations of unconscious racism in Ukraine, a country that was for 70 years a part of the USSR and under the influence of Soviet ideology. Today, more than ever, the people of Ukraine, along with their military fight against Russian invaders, are liberating themselves from the toxic Russian imperialist domination and its ideologies. Racism, as a crucial component of the ideology of superiority, needs to be reflected upon and rejected in Ukrainian society. The struggle of the Ukrainian people can help foster solidarity in the struggle and liberation of other people, including people of color in the U.S. and all over the world. For Ukraine to be a democratic country that accepts diversity and freedom for all peoples means to demonstrate attitudes opposed to Putin's Russia, which is a brutal aggressor confident in its superiority.

**Keywords**: race, racism, anti-racism, blackness, whiteness, bias in art and language, post-Soviet

***

My interest in the topic of race first emerged when I arrived in the United States in 2020. This was the year not only of the global pandemic, but also of one of the largest anti-racist protest movements in the world, which began in the U.S. after the killing of a black man, George Floyd, by a white police officer, Derek Chauvin. That was just one more murder in the often-repeated murders throughout history and the present day, and the protests against brutality—a continuation of a long history of anti-racist protests. While I was in the U.S., I was able to attend and observe the Black Lives Matter (BLM) street demonstrations in the city of New Orleans, where I lived at the time, and to also follow the broader anti-racist agenda in the U.S. media. I also observed the media coverage of BLM in my own country. [1]

Many of the social media posts coming from Ukraine regarding the BLM protests expressed disdain for the protestors, which was also characteristic of the portrayal of the protests by many Eastern European and Russian media figures, bloggers, and politicians. The president of the Czech Republic, Milos Zeman, called the BLM slogan of "Black Lives Matter" a "racist" idea—proclaiming

---

[1] I express my gratitude to Serhiy Yekelchyk, Professor of History and Germanic & Slavic Studies of the University of Victoria, Canada; and Jennifer Metsker, Lecturer at Penny W. Stamps School of Art & Design, University of Michigan; and Jessica Zychowicz, Director of Fulbright Ukraine, all of whom made contributions to early drafts of this chapter; and to Martin Curran for reading the final version.

instead that "All Lives Matter."[2] I even encountered the same misunderstanding of the anti-racist struggle among some of my Ukrainian friends.

This led me to wonder how some Ukrainians, who can acknowledge and articulate the history of their own oppression throughout the centuries, especially in having to fight for independence from Russia, including in two revolutions (Orange Revolution of 2004 and the Maidan Revolution of Dignity in 2013-2014), and since 2014 have had to live under Russian military aggression, were not able to sympathize with black people in their struggle? As an artist and thinker, I came to the question whether our own trauma might help us in feeling more sympathy for the struggles of other people? Or are we doomed to grieve only about our own tragedies, easily "identifying with the oppressor" when it comes to the struggles of other oppressed groups?

To start this conversation in my country I need to understand why in Ukraine and in Eastern Europe in general, the denial of racism persists in specific ways that are shaped by the legacy of communism. I aim to reflect in my artistic work upon the various stereotypes that have been forged during the Soviet era and have ceased to disappear even after the fall of the USSR and Ukraine's gaining of national independence. The Black Lives Matter protests, in spite of uncovering once again the deep roots of American racism, were an example of an open and ongoing discussion about racism. Creating a similar discussion in Ukraine is an important challenge for the future.

### America as a Land of Opportunity and the Soviet Legacy of Stalinism

Ukraine is a diverse country in the post-Soviet context and former Eastern Bloc. Aside from the majority who are ethnically Ukrainian — many other minorities comprise its population. Alongside the new immigrants, there are dark-skinned peoples in Ukraine who are descendants of the waves of immigrant Africans who arrived in the Soviet Union in the 1960-70s, in large part due to campaigns to bring students and professionals to the republics in order to later spread communist influence in mainland Africa. Still today in Ukraine these individuals are perceived as "different," even though they were born and raised in Ukraine. There are also Roma people in Ukraine who face much discrimination based on race, though the perceptions and stereotypes of Roma have their own unique historio-social dynamic. Some Ukrainian citizens could be marked as

---

[2] *Kafkadesk.org Prague Office*, "Czech President Calls Black Lives Matter Slogan 'Racist,' Says 'All Lives Matter.'" News Blog Post. July 1, 2020. *Kafkadesk.org*. https://kafkadesk. org/2020/07/01/czech-president-calls-black-lives-matter-slogan-racist-says-all-lives-matter/

foreign or "others," for example, those who have darker skin. Some self-identify as ethnically Crimean or Armenian but have Ukrainian passports.

America, in the post-Soviet imagination, is a rich country, a "land of opportunity" and for the most part, Ukrainians would deny that there is any racism in Ukraine. Ukrainian popular culture often is organized in representations of America and the West that refer primarily to a white version of America. Common perceptions tend to hold that since Ukraine is a poor country, one can justifiably complain about their fate, but those who live in a rich country — like America, have no right to complain because they have an opportunity to build their lives. This is a common stereotype which stems from an envy of America's wealth, and from the mythic proportions of American freedom and democracy. Ukrainians, counting on America's protection in their conflict with Russia, overwhelmingly tend to focus on the discourse of official American power, which at the time of BLM, was represented by the Trump administration. It is remarkable that today the military support for Ukraine during the full-scale Russian invasion on its territory is provided by the administration of Joe Biden who was, arguably, elected largely because of the incredible electoral activism of black people at the time. So, this is a new perspective Ukrainians can utilize to understand the BLM protests today.

Ukrainians who come to the United States for education or work oftentimes face issues with integration due to their accent and cultural difference, but those who are less marked as "others" in the American context are quickly able to "pass" as white in the terms of how whiteness is understood in America. Passing is a goal that some strive for in immigrant communities, even if it means losing their attachment to their homeland and its culture. This is a tragic loss that one could argue is brought on by the host country, the new country that claims to invite immigrants, but demands from such newcomers that they assimilate to whiteness, rather than integration (and preservation of difference). For Ukrainians with white skin, once they or their children from the next generation master the language perfectly, without an accent, their integration into U.S. society is much easier than for people with darker skin. Due to their skin color, Ukrainians don't have much reason to think about race, as this is "not their problem."

The concept of being "white" discussed in this paper (including, of course, different gradations of whiteness) is related specifically to the American context. In Ukraine, many oftentimes do not readily identify with the categorical term "white," one might argue differences notwithstanding, that the dynamic shares similarities to individuals in Africa who do not derive binary categories by self-defining as "black."[3] In the American context, the division of people into groups based on skin color who ascribe to these groups a superior or inferior status was established during early American economies that profited from the forced labor of the enslaved peoples brought from Africa, the Caribbean, and Latin America. This division is still deeply ingrained in the American consciousness. The author Isabelle Wilkerson in her book *Caste* gives a historical account of the social hierarchies that later persisted in immigrants' assimilation into American society according to their skin color:

> To gain acceptance, each fresh infusion of immigrants had to enter into a silent, unspoken pact of separating and distancing themselves from the established lowest caste. Becoming white meant defining themselves as furthest from its opposite – black. They could establish their new status by observing how the lowest caste was regarded and imitating or one-upping the disdain and contempt, learning the epithets, joining in on violence against them to prove themselves worthy of admittance to the dominant caste. They might have arrived as neutral innocents but would have been forced to choose sides if they were to survive in their adopted land. Here they had to learn how to be white.[4]

Ukrainian national identity since 1991 primarily depended upon denying the legacy of the Soviet state, which represents a historically imperial and oppressive relationship toward Ukrainian culture. The politics of *decommunization* in Ukraine's public institutions and cultural field have passed through a few stages, beginning in the early 1990s, then again during and after the Maidan Revolution of 2013-14. But the strategies in the rejection of traces of the past are never a good guarantee that it will not return; indeed, in form, components of the laws that were passed unilaterally that aimed at erasure of the communist era were rather more of an endorsement of loosely interpreted or regulated acts of censorship that robbed people of any true opportunities for civic involvement in these decisions or critical reflection on their legal origins and basis.

Today we see how the demons of the Soviet past along with the demons of the Russian Empire feed Putin's ideological attacks on Ukraine. But the fact that Ukraine for seventy years was a part of the USSR means that Soviet perceptions and identifications remain, because they are not so easy to eradicate in

---

[3] In her book, *Caste,* Isabel Wilkerson mentions how a Nigerian-born playwright once said to her: "You know that there are no black people in Africa. They are Lgbo and Yoruba, Ewe, Akan, Ndebele. They are not black. They are just themselves. They are humans on the land. They don't become black until they go to America or come to the U.K." See: Isabel Wilkerson, *Caste: The Origins of Our Discontents* (New York: Random House, 2020), 54.

[4] Wilkerson, Ibid.

demolishing monuments and renaming the streets. One of these Soviet remains is a specific view on race and racism. We need to reflect on our lived memory and discuss it in interdisciplinary conversations, including art.

My personal memories of my early childhood that was spent in the Ukrainian Soviet Republic are significant to my identity personally and as an artist. I return to them often in attempting to understand many aspects of contemporary Ukrainian history. In this text, I refer to my personal memories, alongside references to a few literary sources — both of which have inspired me while making my art works. My parents were born under Stalinism, thus it still appears to me as recent history; it has had a destructive impact that is still notable through the generations and many aspects of it have survived the emancipative 1960s, or the "thaw" (Ukrainian: *vidlyga*) which my parents lived through in their early twenties. Similarly, racism in other parts of the world has remained durable over the centuries despite waves of social liberation. I continue to explore the hypothesis that post-Soviet racism, including contemporary racism in Ukraine, has retained some of the racialized politics of Stalinism.

The Soviet Union, on the one hand, promoted the ideals of diversity and solidarity between the different ethnicities of the Soviet state, insisting in official discourse that "all Soviet republics are brothers." On the other hand, the Soviet Union promoted Russian culture above all others, leading to a widespread understanding that if "all Soviets are brothers," Russians are the "older brothers" and the guardians of all. This preference for Russians and Russian culture above other ethnic groups can be seen in the policy of "Russification" and the ethnic makeup of high-ranking Soviet officials. This official preference for Russian culture filtered down to attitudes of common Soviet people, with Ukrainians being no exception. By the late Soviet era, the Ukrainian language, although being the language of publications and school education in Ukraine, was thoroughly discouraged in usage and perceived as second-rate, even within Ukraine. I remember at the Ukrainian secondary school I attended in Kyiv, how teachers and students used to switch to Russian in informal communication during breaks from the lectures in Ukrainian. The general attitude was that the Ukrainian language was more of an artifact, a "dead language" not suitable for daily communication. Russian was not only "the greatest and the most important" but also "the most alive." At the time of my childhood, most people in Kyiv, the capital of Ukraine, spoke Russian. Furthermore, it was often considered shameful to speak Ukrainian in Kyiv (which was spelled "Kiev" in English, according to the Russian transliteration). People from rural areas who were native Ukrainian speakers who relocated to larger cities like Kyiv often changed their spoken language to Russian in order to assimilate, but their specific accent and vernacular mixture of two languages often became the subject of ridicule by Russian-speaking inhabitants. Today, during wartime, many previously Russian-speaking Ukrainians have started to switch to Ukrainian, discovering their "native" language and reclaiming their identity. Today, the Ukrainian language has acquired political meaning like never before – it has become a strong symbol of identity along with the yellow-blue flag or the image of sunflowers.

In the USSR, racism was proclaimed not to exist; at the official levels the Soviet Union repeatedly declared itself to be "an internationalist country." Racism was an accusation made against the United States in Soviet propaganda, which was denigrated as a capitalist and imperialist society which was said to brutalize people of color in the United States and around the world. At the same time, there was a specific racial logic being deployed around how to perceive non-Russian nations in the USSR. According to the scholars Nikolay Zakharov and Ian Law, the hierarchy between Slavic nations with Russia at the top and others below was a foundation for "racial Russification, racial Sovietization, ethnic cleansing and post-communist racial and ethnic hostility."[5] The idea of a Soviet citizen who obligatorily participated in political life and demonstrated loyalty to the regime was well-established during Stalin's rule. Russification, a long-range strategy utilized in Tsardom, was renewed, and applied outwardly to define Soviet citizens not by ethnicity, but by ideological and political belonging. Russian language and culture were seen as something which united Soviet citizens, while the other ethnic identities and languages were seen as something to be celebrated and represented as an achievement of the progressive socialist state, but always in subjugation to the common unifying Russian culture. This complicated dialectic established a firm racial hierarchy wherein Russian culture and language was official, unifying and most important, while the cultures and languages of the other ethnicities were considered merely decorative and less important.

In the 1920s, during the early Soviet era, Ukraine underwent a flourishing of Ukrainian culture, which later came to be known as the "Executed Renaissance." This is because the renaissance of Ukrainian writers and artists was brutally crushed during Stalin's purges in the 1930s, when expressions of national identity were outlawed by the dictatorial regime as "bourgeois nationalism." Thus, the Ukrainian artists and authors who were not considered by the Politburo to be conforming to Soviet ideology (by virtue of their expressions of national identity) were suddenly doomed to extermination. Millions of Ukrainians, along with writers, poets, artists, and people of other professions, were arrested under the label "enemies of the people" and consequently killed, or forced to

---

[5] Nikolay Zakharov and Ian Law, *Post-Soviet Racisms: Mapping Global Racisms* (London: Palgrave Macmillan, 2017).

live the rest of their lives in the far reaches of Siberia's penal colonies — the infamous GULAG. Many of them, ironically and tragically, had believed themselves to be earnest communists who indeed did make a significant impact on the development of Ukrainian culture during their short lives. We can see a similar tragic trajectory in the life and death of Lovett Fort-Whiteman, an African American communist, described in *Time* magazine in 1925 as "the reddest of the blacks." *The New Yorker* recently published an article about Lovett Fort-Whiteman's life.[6] In the 1920s, many African Americans came to the Soviet Union to find freedom and to escape the brutal racism of American Jim Crow laws. Fort-Whiteman came to the Soviet Union in 1924 and chose to stay in the USSR in order to become a free and productive individual with full participation in society. He felt himself welcomed in the Soviet Union and considered communist ideology as a tool for liberation for blacks in America as well. But with the rise of Stalin's power, he vanished in Moscow in 1936 and his life ended dramatically in the GULAG.

The cruelty of Stalin's ethnic purges exhibited a thoroughly racist politics as they were carried out: along with the millions who perished or became "disappeared persons," different ethnic groups were deported en-masse from their homeland, such as the Crimean Tatars who were deported in 1944 from Crimea to Uzbekistan. Russian superiority and suspicions of any national or ethnic manifestations, apart from the official versions developed through the years, had a significant impact on the treatment of non-Russian nations within the USSR. Another example: the film *Koryo Saram: The Unreliable People* by David Chung and Matt Dibble, explores how, in 1937, a population of Koreans who inhabited the Russian Far East, and who were fleeing the war with Japan, were deported to Kazakhstan. The physical lives of Korean people were harshly destroyed by forced deportation, and later, their language and culture were brashly oppressed. After depriving a whole generation of children of the opportunity to learn their native language, the Soviet state in the frame of performing "multinational representations and friendship," published a newspaper in the Korean language for the Korean community in Kazakhstan, but by that time only a handful could read it.

The historian Serhiy Yekelchyk in his book about post-World War II Ukraine describes how the hatred and search for enemies was a cornerstone of Stalin's politics in his cultivation of Soviet citizens:

[6] Joshua Yaffa, "A Black Communist's Disappearance in Stalin's Russia." *The New Yorker*. October 18, 2021. https://www.newyorker.com/magazine/2021/10/25/a-black-communists-disappearance-in-stalins-russia-lovett-fort-whiteman-gulag.

Typical of revolutionary and revisionist states that possessed an exclusionary vision of the world, hatred of enemies emerged in Stalin's time as a core component of ideal Soviet identity, on par with love and gratitude to the Leader. Prewar denunciatory campaigns against "enemies of the people" gave way during the war to hatred of external enemies, the Nazis, and, in the words of official discourse, the "internal" Ukrainian nationalists, with whom they were linked. After the war, public hatred of the nationalists was muted since its prominence in the official discourse served as an acknowledgment of the strength of the nationalist insurgency in Ukraine's western oblasts, but these wartime enemies also provided a link to new, Cold War-era, enemies: the United States in particular and the West in general. [7]

Ukrainian nationalism was a subject of manipulation during Stalinism and is today one of the central premises of Russian propaganda used by the Russian state to justify its war on Ukraine. In this regard, Russian propaganda seems to be a logical continuation of the Stalinist logic with its search for an "enemy of the people" and hatred toward those who are different from the dominant Russian identity. In fact, the official rhetoric of the current Russian state goes even further than that of the Soviet Union in denying Ukrainian identity. Whereas the Soviet Union promoted Ukrainian culture as a sub-identity to a more important and superseding Soviet identity, Putin, the leader of the modern Russian nation state, has denied that Ukrainians are a separate people from Russians altogether and has even gone as far as to claim that creating a separate Ukrainian Soviet Socialist Republic was a mistake. Thus, capitalizing on the old idea that Ukrainian nationalism is subversive to a more important Soviet identity, the current war, then, is being promoted as a campaign to assimilate Ukrainians by subjugating them to their proper place as not only a sub-identity, but as being Russian for all intents and purposes.

From Stalinism onward, the Soviet Union actively projected its own racism and hatred of "others" onto its opponents, the United States. Racism, according to Soviet propaganda, was a feature of the "enemy," totally absent from the Soviet Union, which claimed to be a force of good in the world opposed to all evils — racism included. According to Soviet propaganda, all 15 nations that had been incorporated into the republics of the USSR had dissolved happily into a general proletarian "friendship of the peoples" (Druzhba narodov). Thus, current Russian propaganda similarly uses a lie about Russian and Ukrainian closeness, which denies any meaningful differences between groups' civic

---

[7] Serhy Yekelchyk, *Stalin's Citizens: Everyday Politics in the Wake of Total War* (New York: Oxford University Press, 2014), 11.

aims, and creates an untouchable silence under which the worst crimes against humanity are taking place in the current war in Ukraine.

### Soviet-American Mutual Influences and Soviet Internationalist Propaganda of the 1960s

In the beginning of the 1960s (and after Stalin's death), the Western European colonies throughout the African continent underwent a process of decolonization and became independent countries. The Soviet Union attempted to assert its political and economic influence. In the 1960s, many Africans came to Moscow, Leningrad, Kyiv, Minsk, and other Soviet cities in order to obtain an education, or to make public appearances during festivals and events. However, according to their reports, they often faced racism while encountering Soviet citizens. In the paper, "Death of an African Student in Moscow," Julie Hessler describes unusual anti-racist demonstration that took place at the Red Square in Moscow on December 18, 1963. It was unusual because after three decades of Stalin's dictatorship, Soviet citizens were totally discouraged from protesting against authorities. That day hundreds of African students came out onto the streets of Moscow to protest racism. The demonstration was provoked by the death of a Ghanaian medical student, Edmund Assare-Addo, which was interpreted by African students as a racially motivated hate crime.

Hessler also gives an observation of typical manifestations of racism in the USSR. Hate crimes and racial attacks often occurred when black students were found out to be dating white women or were seen dancing with them at a party, they heard racist slurs in everyday life. They also complained about racial profiling and were often being stopped by the police. At the same time, policemen also turned a blind eye to racist attacks committed by their fellow citizens. Typical responses from the Soviet authorities pivoted upon assurances that racial disrespect was "alien" to the Soviet people, and that cases of crime and assault were carried out by "bad apples"—isolated hooligan "elements." They overtly refused to recognize racism as a widespread issue, and subsequently accused the African protesters as playing "into the hands of the imperialists." A similar discourse of "bad apples" was further exploited in a similar manner by the Trump administration during the Black Lives Matter protests to reject racism as a structural problem of American society and to blame only separate individuals who committed racial crimes.

In fact, the history of confrontation between the USSR and U.S. during the Cold War was full of mutual influence as well as competition. James Baldwin exclaimed about the 1954 Supreme Court decision outlawing segregation in the schools in the U.S., that most of the black people he knew didn't believe that "this immense concession would ever have been made if it had not been for the competition of the Cold War, and the fact that Africa was clearly liberating herself . . . "[8] Soviet propaganda, thus, introduced a doctrine of morality that, by competition, played a role in pushing the U.S. to counter it by meeting the demands of the 1960s Black Liberation and Civil Rights movement. This is not to convey that racism did not exist in the Soviet Union. Furthermore, Soviet citizens were exposed to American racist propaganda, but in more sophisticated applications. Though they did not read James Baldwin in official Soviet literary circles, the American canon of "white" literature enjoyed pride of place.

Toni Morrison, in her brilliant literary-critical essay *Playing in the Dark: Whiteness and the Literary Imagination* analyzes and deconstructs the texts of classical white American writers such as Edgar Allan Poe, Mark Twain, and Ernest Hemingway, all of which were very well-known to Soviet readers. Mark Twain's Huckleberry Finn, together with Tom Sawyer, were two favorite heroes promoted through adventure literature in the standard education of Soviet children of multiple generations. Toni Morrison discusses the attitude of Huck Finn and Tom Sawyer toward a black man, Jim, and their objectification of him: " . . . it would not have been possible for two children to play so painfully with the life of a white man (regardless of his class, education, or fugitiveness) once he had been revealed to us as a moral adult."[9] So, for white children in America, a black man, who was so loving toward them, was an appropriative tool in the national moral instruction on race, which declared that he should not be considered fully human. At its most essential, these racial attitudes were indirectly adopted by Soviet people. Thus, the discourse on race in the Soviet Union and the U.S., were mutually interdependent.

For Morrison, literature produced by white writers about white characters in a society rooted in racism, cannot be deprived of racism itself. She shows how, in American literature, the racial "other," often rejected and ignored, is always present in the texts. This dynamic persists as an important structural element, even as it is actively muffled or silenced from being spoken about out loud, in constructing white identity. Morrison said that the idea of human freedom in American history and culture is fed and reinforced by the presence of a bounded slave population: "Nothing highlights freedom – if it did not in fact create it – like slavery."[10] White characters use black presence to display their "superior" human qualities, in contrast to "inferior" black qualities. Power is a source and guarantee of white freedom.

---

[8] James Baldwin, *The Fire Next Time* (New York: Modern Library, 1995), 25.

[9] Toni Morrison, *Playing in the Dark: Whiteness and the Literary Imagination* (New York: Vintage Books, 1993), 15.

[10] Morrison, Ibid.

Soviet and post-Soviet readers alike identify themselves in these texts with the "good" white characters, and the influence of this co-constructed "white imagination" between the U.S. and the USSR, rooted in the historical past of slavery, still has its appeal. The ambiguous aspects of "whiteness" allow for dangerous ideologies and unconscious social bias.

If one looks at the Soviet culture's perception of non-Russian ethnicities in the USSR, a huge number of examples of racialized politics of everyday life and even of people's folklore can be found. Famous anecdotes about the level of stupidity of non-Russians is a perfect example of the Soviet racialized ethnic hierarchy. For example, the word "black" has been used in Russian as a slur from before Soviet times referring to people, who in the American context would be perceived as white, such as Armenians, Georgians or Azeris. The N-word is still perceived as acceptable in informal conversations in post-Soviet countries when referring to black people.

Soviet propaganda which on the surface purported to deliver anti-racist messages, itself was full of racist undertones. It was created by the Soviet regime with its opponent, the United States, as its main addressee, and was largely irrelevant to Soviet peoples' daily life experiences. Zakharov and Low describe the main features of such Soviet propaganda:

> Attacks on racism and racist practices such as South African Apartheid and American racism became a staple of Soviet propaganda which is evident in the work of Soviet writers, poets and filmmakers, yet they also contained key elements of racist discourse. Simplistic, idealized, exotic images of Africa were portrayed by the Soviet media and bureaucracy. School textbooks, posters and television in the 1960s contained images of communist compassion and the saving of helpless black victims of capitalist injustice and the Soviet civilizing mission, together with clearer racist messages about the bestiality of black men and warnings about the "racial crime" of black/white marriage.[11]

Many propaganda posters of the era are dedicated to internationalism, friendship, and solidarity of people of different races. They often depict "people of three races" — European (meaning Soviet ethnic, Russians), Asian and African — with "white" Soviet persons frequently being placed in the foreground, implying their leading role in the liberation of other peoples.[12] Race is prescribed in a very paternalistic way: a so-called Soviet (Russian)

---

[11] Zakharov and Law, *Post-Soviet Racisms: Mapping Global Racisms*, 6.

[12] Interestingly, Chinese communist propaganda mirrored the Soviets' visual messaging, but rather placed Asian ethnicities at the forefront of all social hierarchies.

citizen, is to be the leader of liberation of all mankind. In addition to constructing a stereotypical image of races reduced to three types of people — white, yellow, and black, Soviet ideology, in a way, reflected the American one in its designation of the dominant position to the white man —phrased as a competition between white American and white Soviet masculinities in their leading positions in the world.

I have chosen here to focus on a particular propaganda poster of the 1960s, which was designed at the time to convey solidarity with women of the world, an idea relevant to my own self-identification as a feminist. In this poster, a white woman was placed in the foreground, a black woman in the back, and an Asian woman found her position in the middle. The placement here, oddly, I might venture, actually refers to America's racial-hierarchical construct, which Isabelle Wilkerson explains as the direct outcome of slavery: "Slavery built the man-made chasm between blacks and whites that forces the middle castes of Asians, Latinos, indigenous people, and new immigrants of African descent to navigate within what began a bipolar hierarchy."[13]

During the Black Lives Matter protests that I attended in New Orleans in 2020, the black leaders of the street marches, when forming a column, always called upon the black marchers to come to the front. I have remade the image on the poster by changing the protagonist's position with a different leader, a black woman, representative of a shifting balance of power more relevant to the context of Black Lives Matter.

As an artist, in my practice, which is now deeply shaped by both my experience living and growing up in Ukraine, I was interested in looking at the Soviet images that provide examples of stereotyping in the representation of race, while at the same time claiming to project messages of solidarity. Rejecting the position of a white person on the foreground of a poster about solidarity, I as an artist reject racist logic of superiority established by Soviet Russia along with white America. This work, which is named after the original poster's slogan "For the Solidarity of Women of the World!" takes the remake of the Soviet poster as a starting point. After completing it, I continued to search for ways in which I can artistically communicate more nuanced and diverse representations of race, with an eye to the Ukrainian context.

Speaking as a Ukrainian artist, I would like to consider memories of race and racism in the Soviet era when expressing my position toward race, while considering the political challenges of the current time. In today's globalized world, the conversation about race should be relevant to the local context and, at the same time, take into account the history and cultural memory of the

---

[13] Wilkerson, *Caste: The Origins of Our Discontents*, 56.

region. To deconstruct Soviet propaganda, which finds its continuation in Russian propaganda nowadays, means to distinguish its lie component, which means to acknowledge that racism existed but was denied in the USSR, and that's why it persists to exist and is still rejected in post-Soviet space.

**Figure 9.1.** Oksana Briukhovetska. Remake of the Soviet poster of the 1960s "For the Solidarity of Women of the World!" Textile collage. 110x176 cm (43x69 in). 2021. Shared with permission.

## Socialization, Language and Culture

Julie Hessler notes that "the Soviet Union's ideological self-confidence and its tendency to treat shortcomings as anomalies limited its institutions' capacity to react constructively to social problems. Racism [as a form of denial of social problems *O.B.*], in this respect, was no different from alcoholism, domestic violence, homelessness, or mental illness."[14] This comment might be applied to the contemporary situation in post-Soviet space as well. It reveals the residual Soviet perceptions of racism and approaches to it in state building and popular culture as something to be silenced, and therefore falsely claimed to be invisible. In addition, for many post-Soviet people, localized forms of racism are still associated with the mythology of a dying Soviet past, and due to a lack of public debate, these associations are rarely or not addressed at all, and their manifestation is not recognized.

The complexity of the Soviet experience, in particular, drove individuals who were forced to conform to a mass identity to learn to live with a dual nature. The "official version of reality" was proclaimed and any deviation from it could lead to death, but the reality in which people lived was naturally very different and conflicted. Not a single individual was permitted to speak openly about any sense of reality that differed from the official version. More recent processes of decommunization in Ukraine, on the surface, point to these earlier traumas and fears, claiming to heal them through erasure. But in fact, as mentioned earlier, erasure of the past is never possible, and the suppression of social memory, between individuals or *en-masse* offers no critical distance. In fact, suppression only traumatizes even more, making the past intractable for analysis, and thus much harder to understand.

Soviet citizens lived under a dictatorship that imposed all forms of propaganda that they knew better than to trust, and indeed resented, because they could easily distinguish much of the propaganda from their own lived reality in the Soviet Union. According to Serhy Yekelchyk, Soviet citizens demonstrated evidence of passive and silent resistance to the political and ideological rituals that people were obliged to perform, and to the discourse of power emanating from the state. It became a long-lasting Soviet tradition to not trust authorities. Thus, the propaganda of the United States as a racist country and black Americans as oppressed was also not taken seriously, and was resented as falsehood.

The role of the Soviet Union's Cold War propaganda in relation to the sympathizers with the Communist Party inside the U.S. who supported Black

---

[14] Julie Hessler, "Death of an African Student in Moscow." *Open Editions Journals* 47, no. 1-2 (2006). https://journals.openedition.org/monderusse/9591?lang=de

Liberation was used as evidence to implicate individuals and manipulate propaganda; this dynamic is still weaponized by opponents of anti-racism movements today. During the Black Lives Matter protests, President Trump pejoratively labeled protesters "leftists" and "communists," fueling and reviving fears of the Cold War. The decommunization laws that were formally introduced in Ukraine were arbitrarily applied and arguably also played upon a similar fear of communism. While Soviet propaganda remains undoubtedly a source of falsehood for post-Soviet Ukraine, the history of manipulation of American racism by Soviets seems to be an old Soviet myth. Those who remember the Soviet era today often take these accusations against America ironically, usually simplifying everything into familiar stereotypes. Thus, BLM appeared to many as a chimera. Some audiences reacted to BLM in social media by posting old Soviet cartoons that grotesquely depicted racist American capitalists abusing black people. The aim of such posts was to declare in response to BLM: "Soviet propaganda again?" (meaning "Lie again?"). And Trump's nonsense accusations of communism towards BLM sounded in unison with this Cold War legacy. This is one of the pieces of evidence of how propaganda, even after its "official" end marked by the fall of the USSR in 1991, continues to dramatically underscore ignorance around race in post-Soviet societies. People whose education is rooted in the Soviet era, when exposed to the news about BLM in 2020, understood it through the lens of their own memories of Soviet propaganda. A generalized lack of education on American history, and adoption of stereotypes in "white" American literature and culture caused consumers of media to identify with a narrowly manipulated "white" identity—preventing them from understanding BLM or critically listening to its agendas.

While observing Black Lives Matter protests firsthand, I started to examine my own socialization in Soviet, and then independent Ukraine. As an artist, I continue to explore the unconscious consequences of my Ukrainian art education, and how race is understood in Ukrainian society.

During my art education in Ukraine, I painted portraits and nudes from live models for about a decade. I observed human skin very closely and learned what colors of paint I needed to blend to depict "human body colors." But what is perhaps most relevant to this discussion here about racism, from the knowledge I gained from painting, is that I was trained to think as if human skin were something universal. In traditional art training in Ukraine, the human body meant a "white" body, even though we didn't use this word. There was no need to use it, it was taken for granted. I never asked myself: if I paint a dark-skinned body, or a body of any person-of-color, which shades of colors would I need? None of the teachers ever asked this question. Before we started to draw live models, we practiced for a few years on plaster casts of antique sculptures completely painted in white. None of our teachers mentioned to us that in ancient master classes, the sculptures were usually colored. At the time, I was under the impression that their whiteness was equated with their value, and this idea was passed on to us by our teachers. I realized that my art history classes during my studies in the Ukrainian Art Academy that were partly focused on national art history, were in essence based on white [male] Western art history, considering ideas and examples we were introduced to.

I often drew as a child and my daughter also drew as a child – children are generally fascinated with the activity of drawing and painting people. I once explained to my daughter what kind of paints need to be mixed to produce a "human body color." It is true that many commercially produced packages of paint palettes in Ukraine (and Europe and the U.S.) include a special color designated for skin (so often it is a kind of pink-beige); children and students are pleased with this addition. I suddenly remembered this after seeing an exhibition of local children's drawings in the hall of the Contemporary Art Center in New Orleans. There were self-portraits of children four or five years old painted in dark brown. These drawings brought to light all the aforementioned preconceptions of my childhood. I believe that certain biases that are learned at an early age can continue to subconsciously bias our thoughts and actions, in the same manner as early traumas.

Isabelle Wilkerson's remark about the polarity of "black" and "white" in the binaries that people have established through history, these oppositions, and divisions are important to consciously claim and recognize as both socially and politically made. Wilkerson writes:

> In the same way that black and white were applied to people who were literally neither, but rather gradations of brown and beige and ivory, the caste system sets people at poles from one another and attaches meanings to the extremes, and to the gradations in between, and then reinforces those meanings, replicates them in the roles each caste was and is assigned and permitted or required to perform.[15]

In fact, there are many "human body colors," as American artist Byron Kim conveys in his ongoing painting project *Synecdoche*, begun in 1991. This project includes 400 small panels depicting the skin tones of different people that he met during his life, including many friends and family members.

"Black," "white" and "yellow" are the constructions of diminished vocabulary, a violent categorical language that does not correspond to lived reality and actual human skin but refer to the symbolic meanings of the so-called races. But being symbolic, these categories also obtain a meaning of self-identification while fighting for liberation. While in the past of the history of colonization

---

[15] Wilkerson, *Caste: The Origins of Our Discontents*, 56.

being black was prescribed to be oppressed, black people in their long way of liberation feel proud of their blackness and celebrate it (mentioning just the *Black is Beautiful* movement in the 1960s in the U.S.).

We need to reflect on how language functions as a carrier of historical meaning. There are negative connotations of "black" color in the Ukrainian language, that are not on the surface related to race. The black color often is associated in opposition to white, and is manifested in such contrasts as white day versus black night, white wedding dress versus black mourning dress, etc. As in most Judeo-Christian traditions, in Ukraine, white/black often represent the opposition of good and evil, which serves very well as an unconscious and irrational foundation for racism, as well as European colonialism. Translating the word "blackness" into Ukrainian can carry these negative associations. But it is not possible to understand history, anti-racism and contemporary politics without adding to the dictionary such terms. Blackness in the American context carries the meaning of empowerment, identity, and historical and cultural legacy of African Americans. The simplest introduction to the understanding of modern America can't be done without this term. The only way to revive "blackness" as a positive cultural and social phenomenon within the Ukrainian language is to break these older oppositions by creating new contexts of understanding. We need to get rid of out-of-date connotations that keep us being ignorant and still influenced by racist propaganda.

Drawings by the American artist Diane Edison have challenged me to think more deeply about this "opposition." During my art education in Ukraine, while drawing we usually used white paper and black pencil to draw portraits and bodies of white people. This formula finds its counter-position in drawings by Diane Edison, who takes black paper and white pencil to make portraits of people-of-color (she draws white people as well, but it will just confirm what I am about to say). Using white pencil, she creates images enhancing light, as opposed to when drawing with black pencil in which we create images by enhancing shadows. Playing with stereotypes, this opposition recalls associations with opposites in black-and-white photography, underscoring that, generally, in language, the word "negative" is opposed to "positive." [16] But the drawings of Diane Edison do not look like negatives at all. They are positives in all possible meanings. To overcome bias and stereotypes that are embedded in language, we need to prove that difference in color is not something that exists on opposite

---

[16] A common definition of photography underlines this negative contrast: "In photography, a negative is an image, usually on a strip or sheet of transparent plastic film, in which the lightest areas of the photographed subject appear darkest, and the darkest areas appear lightest." See: Entry for "Photography." *Wikipedia.org*. https://en.wikipedia.org/wiki/Negative_(photography).

poles, with plus and minus signs; as humans, we all might be perceived positively, regardless of skin color. This gradation and diversity enrich our life and art as an ecosystem of perception.

The legacy of Soviet racism (within proclaimed internationalism) was internalized by a large part of the population, and ideas of building a new Ukrainian national identity after 1991 still could not completely get rid of old Soviet stereotypes about race, or overcome discrimination and racism in many aspects of Ukrainian life. The Soviet reflexes that Ukrainians seek to discard are covered over with newer experiments in national identity building that superficially appear to be radically different than in earlier eras. But in the case of racism, in fact, I would observe that little has changed.

Ukrainian identity is experiencing a new wave of empowerment today. With the Russian aggression we can see clearer what we still bear that is internalized from the oppressor. Ukrainian nationalism in today's historical circumstances has a meaning of liberation, but as always, it comes with challenges. To insist on our national identity and to compare it with others, I would rather look at the historical precedents of the nationalism of the oppressed, as for example the black nationalism of Malcolm X, rather than trying to echo the ideas of [white] superiority.

Ukraine's turbulent history and emergence out of the structures of the Soviet Union provides a rich opportunity to strive for individual expression, pluralism, and to acknowledge — and reject — categories of oppression, wherever they appear on the globe. We need to recognize the caste system in Wilkerson's terms as a "human impulse," such that it must be vigilantly averted.[17] This vigilance is especially important for people who are able to "pass" as "white" in its various constructions, and to stand for independence means to stand on the side of the oppressed, not under a false "white" category, but to build solidarity and to end the dangerous spread around the globe of the ideology of white supremacy. And because Black Lives Matter is not only an American, but a global movement, the goal to overcome racism is now global. I feel a special responsibility as an artist, and a Ukrainian, to call upon my fellow Ukrainians even at a time of great peril, of war, to play a conscious role in this battle. To fight one's own oppressor also means not to accept any system of oppression.

With these thoughts in mind, I set about creating another work, whose title *Ukraine in solidarity with / In solidarity with Ukraine* is a reflection upon the mirroring effects implicit in acts of solidarity. The source of my inspiration and reference was a quilt of American artist Faith Ringgold *Sunflower quilting bee*

---

[17] Wilkerson calls us to think not only about race, but also broadly about caste in any dimension of identity: "The human impulse to create hierarchies runs across societies and cultures . . . " See: Wilkerson, *Caste: The Origins of Our Discontents*, 58.

*at Arles.* In this image, Faith Ringgold depicted known African American women gathered for quilting in the sunflower landscape. The work of Faith Ringgold is an homage to solidarity and the power of community. When I first saw Faith Ringgold's image, it reminded me of the Ukrainian sunflower landscape. As war has been ongoing in Ukraine, the sunflower, early on, became a symbol of Ukrainian resistance. This symbolic association grew even stronger after a story that became known during the first days of the full-scale war in Ukraine, in which a Ukrainian woman confronted a heavily armed Russian soldier who invaded her city. She offered him sunflower seeds, saying: "Put these seeds in your pockets so at least sunflowers will grow when you die here." In response to this association, I created a symbolic Ukrainian sunflower landscape in textile collage. I have inserted a large rainbow in the center of the piece in reference to the monument in the hills of Kyiv, which until recently was named the People's Friendship Arch (Arka Druzhby Narodiv). Originally, the arc was designed during late Soviet era in order to commemorate the reunification of Ukraine with Russia. Today the Soviet myth about "brotherly Ukrainian and Russian nations" which always assumed Russian dominance, is used as justification for the cruel invasion by Russia, the killing of thousands of my fellow-citizens, and the ongoing destruction of my country with the aim of erasing Ukrainian identity and independence.[18]

The idea of my work is to present a rethinking of "the friendship of peoples." In my work, women of different skin tones gather in front of the arch. Their skin tones are reflected in the rainbow. They embody solidarity with Ukraine that people from all over the world express today.

In April 2022, the sculpture under the arch in Kyiv was dismantled and the monument was renamed The Arch of Freedom of the Ukrainian People. The freedom of Ukraine has a symbolic meaning for the world today. It symbolizes democracy and freedom for people all over the world. The Ukrainian fight for its independence today is the fight against the oppressor, against the cruel and bloody dominance of the imperialistic colonizer. I have sought to understand solidarity together with the struggle against oppression. Today, during an unprecedentedly difficult time for Ukraine, I keep believing that what I have learned about the anti-racist struggle in the U.S. is important for the

---

[18] After Ukraine became independent there were different changes in the meaning of the monument. In 2016, the Ukrainian government announced plans to dismantle the arch as part of the decommunization laws, but the plan was not carried out. For the Eurovision Song Contest 2017, the arch was temporarily painted as a rainbow and renamed the Arch of Diversity. It doubled as the symbol of the Kyiv Pride parade and was illuminated as a rainbow at night. In 2018, human rights activists put a temporary sticker on the arch in the form of a crack. This was a sign of support for political prisoners who are illegally detained in Russia and annexed Crimea.

understanding of Russian imperialism as well. Ukrainian identity has been threatened by Russian domination symbolically and culturally for centuries, and today — Russia in a literal sense is destroying the lives of the Ukrainian people. A terrible and disgusting face of imperial power that seeks to dominate and subjugate, the ideological propaganda that implements an idea of "other" who need to be controlled, transformed and in the case of disobedience — exterminated — all this is visible in the current Russian aggression against Ukraine.

Today while fighting and praying for victory and peace for Ukraine, I also dream about its future. I believe that Ukraine, which is fighting a global fight for democratic values, will continue to transform into a country that will keep developing these values in a peaceful future. Anti-racism is an important part of these values. My work holds meaning for me in expressing a peaceful Ukraine open to solidarity and diversity.

## Bibliography

Baldwin, James. *The Fire next Time.* New York: Modern Library, 1995.

Hessler, Julie. "Death of an African Student in Moscow." *Open Editions Journals* 47, no. 1-2 (2006). https://journals.openedition.org/monderusse/9591?lang=de

*Kafkadesk.org Prague Office*, "Czech President Calls Black Lives Matter Slogan 'Racist,' Says 'All Lives Matter.'" News Blog Post. July 1, 2020. *Kafkadesk.org*. https://kafkadesk. /2020/07/01/czech-president-calls-black-lives-matter-slogan-racist-says-all-lives-matter/.

Morrison, Toni. *Playing in the Dark: Whiteness and the Literary Imagination.* New York: Vintage Books, 1993.

*Wikipedia.org.* Entry for "Photography." https://en.wikipedia.org/wiki/Negative_ (photography).

Wilkerson, Isabel. *Caste: The Origins of Our Discontents.* New York: Random House, 2020.

Yaffa, Joshua. "A Black Communist's Disappearance in Stalin's Russia." *The New Yorker.* October 18, 2021. https://www.newyorker.com/magazine/2021/10/25/a-black-communists-disappearance-in-stalins-russia-lovett-fort-whiteman-gulag

Yekelchyk, Serhy. *Stalin's Citizens: Everyday Politics in the Wake of Total War.* New York: Oxford University Press, 2014.

Zakharov, Nikolay, and Ian Law. *Post-Soviet Racisms: Mapping Global Racisms.* London: Palgrave Macmillan, 2017.

# IV.
# On Social Transformation:
# Text, Body, Protest, Ballot

Chapter 10

# How Feminist is the Belarusian Revolution? Female Agency and Participation in the 2020 Post-Election Protests

Natallia Paulovich

### Abstract

Belarusian women stand at the forefront of post-election protests. It did not start as a feminist project, however, but rather as a reaction to mass-scale arrests of male participants during the first days of protests. At the same time, is it possible to characterize female involvement in women's chains of solidarity and then regular Saturday demonstrations as a "feminist project" when one takes into account the usage of traditional feminine images and feminine aesthetics during the protests? This essay will examine the agentic nature of female protests and the ways of expressing dignity in times when a basic sense of security is lacking. I will look at situational individual acts of agency and how these acts characterize female participants of the protests as a group that is aware of its resources and power. The text will be based on the analysis of media discourse and visual materials.

**Keywords**: Belarus, elections, protest, women, agency, subversion

***

## Introduction

The scale of protests in Belarus after the August 2020 presidential elections is unprecedented. The protests began as a reaction to the falsified election results. They picked up steam following state-sponsored acts of torture against the people who had been detained during the first post-election demonstrations. Forms of protest have changed over time; women's marches, for example, started on August 14, just four days after the falsified elections. At this point, Belarusian women formed so-called "Solidarity Chains" along the streets of

Minsk as a reaction to police brutality and acts of torture in prisons targeted at men. Mothers, wives, daughters, and sisters poured out into the streets, expressing their pain and anger in face of the unfolding events. This put Belarusian women at the forefront of the protests. Their participation later developed into more organized actions, such as a weekly Saturday Women's March. Such activity is unprecedented and has become grounds for the international mass media calling the current protests "the revolution with a female face."[1]

However, the active participation of women in pushing for political change could be observed even before the August protests began. Three women led the change. One was Svitlana Tsikhanouskaya (Sviatlana Tsikhanoŭskaia), the wife of a popular Belarusian blogger who was imprisoned before he could register his candidacy; another was Veranika Tsepkalo (Veranika Tsapkala), the wife of a potential candidate who left Belarus to avoid arrest. The third in the "triumvirate" was Maria Kolesnikova (Maryia Kalesnikava), campaign manager for Viktar Babaryka, a jailed banker who had also hoped to beat Alexander Lukashenko (Aliaksandr Lukashènka). Together, they formed a coalition to support Tsikhanouskaya's presidential campaign. This suggests that the active participation of women before and after the elections did not start as a feminist project but rather as a spontaneous reaction to mass-scale arrests of male political actors.[2]

One of the main tactics of female protesters after the elections was dressing in white and attempting to shield male protesters with flowers. The usage of traditional feminine imagery and feminine aesthetics also raises the question about the validity of the claim that the Belarusian protests are a feminist project. However, I argue that the current mobilization of Belarusian women

---

[1] Anna Shadrina, "Tsvety protesta: Kak zhenshchiny stali novoĭ politicheskoĭ siloĭ Belarusi," *Forbes.ru*. News Post. March 9, 2020. https://www.forbes.ru/forbes-woman/408215-cvety-protesta-kak-zhenshchiny-stali-novoy-politicheskoy-siloy-belarusi?fbclid=IwAR2m8fjxXw86_7atbsnb9rTrEKiOj4fyOOdzjtQK34qnbZRyZQb_Kcc6Z9c. Also see: Ivan Nechepurenko, "In Belarus, Women Led the Protests and Shattered Stereotypes," *The New York Times*. News Post. October 11, 2020. https://www.nytimes.com/2020/10/11/world/europe/in-belarus-women-led-the-protests-and-shattered-stereotypes.html; Yasmeen Serhan, "When Women Lead Protest Movements: The Demonstrations in Belarus Point to a Broader Trend." *The Atlantic*. News Post. September 12, 2020. https://www.theatlantic.com/international/archive/2020/09/belarus-protests-women/616288/.

[2] Sociologist Elena Gapova has made several key insights into the nature of women's agency before the elections in 2020. See: Elena Gapova, "Svetlana Tikhanovskaia: ot lichnogo k politocheskomu." *opendemocracy.net*. News Post. August 6, 2020. https://www.opendemocracy.net/ru/tikhanovskaya-ot-politcheskogo-lichnomy/

might be analyzed as an agentic act, where agency is not simply a synonym for resistance to relations based on domination, but the capacity for action enabled by specific relations based on subordination.[3] In this article, I will examine acts of agency and attempt to see what they reveal about the female participants of the protests who are aware of their resources and power. The analysis is based on media discourse, visual materials, and social-media discussions among the participants and external observers of the Belarusian post-election protests.

## Agency or Heteropatriarchal Values

Anthropologist Saba Mahmood, in her research on women's participation in the Islamic piety movement in Cairo in the 1970s, claimed that "liberal assumptions about what constitutes human nature and agency become integral to our humanist intellectual traditions."[4] These assumptions are based on the belief that human agency consists of acts that challenge social norms, but practices such as women's active support for the piety socio-religious movement in Egypt that maintain principles of female subordination, cannot be perceived as agentic.[5] Mahmood's main contribution was calling attention to "different modalities of agency involved in acting, transgressing, or inhabiting ethical norms and moral principles," even if they take place within a system of inequality.[6] In her opinion, this understanding of agency as a modality of action allows for the broadening of debates about gender in non-Western societies beyond the analysis of the patriarchy. Moreover, it enables a conversation about the richness of female active agents, especially in regard to their embodied experience.[7]

The application of Mahmood's approach to the Eastern European context was subsequently undertaken by Alexei Yurchak in his ethnographic study of late socialism, when individuals were able to exercise their agency despite the

---

[3] Saba Mahmood, *Politics of Piety: The Islamic Revival and the Feminist Subject* (Princeton, New Jersey: Princeton University Press Kindle Edition, 2012), 773.

[4] Mahmood, *Politics of Piety: The Islamic Revival and the Feminist Subject*, 534.

[5] Ibid., 530, 538.

[6] Ibid., 5485-5486.

[7] Ibid., 547, 552, 566. See also the interpretation of Mahmood's approach towards female involvement in feasting culture in Georgia: Natallia Paulovich, "A Breadwinner or a Housewife? Agency in the Everyday Image of the Georgian Woman," *Anthropology of the Contemporary Middle East and Central Eurasia* 3, no. 2 (2016): 24-44.

repressive environment in which they lived.[8] Later, in 2017, in their introductory article to *The Journal of Soviet and Post-Soviet Politics and Society,* editors Felix Ackermann, Mark Berman, and Olga Sasunkevich, applied Yurchak's ideas by attempting to search for agency in Belarusian society, which had previously been analyzed through the lens of victimhood.[9] They stated that the permanent focus on state actions represented by Lukashenko and his "one-man-show character" could lead to a research perspective that pays little heed to the actions of ordinary people. According to them, the best way to avoid this bias is to look at "the subject's inner world, weave into their analysis examples of first-person testimony and other forms of public self-expression."[10] The effect of this careful attention to people's lives may reveal a broad range of hidden subjectivities.

This perspective could be applied to the interpretation of women's participation in the recent protests in Belarus, where female voices and actions serve as testimonies of their agency functioning within structures of subordination. These structures often support hegemonic discourses, including the most prevalent one that enacts heteropatriarchal values. In the opinion of Belarusian feminist and protester Irina Solomatina, Head of Council for the Belarusian Organization of Working Women, these values in Belarusian society are too persuasive to ignore. She is skeptical about whether Belarusian female protesters can successfully subvert these discourses, and thus doubtful about calling the current events a "feminist project."[11]

Furthermore, Solomatina stresses that it is exactly the women of the Belarusian opposition that reinforce these heteropatriarchal values. She reminds us that this trend was started by Tsikhanouskaya herself during the presidential campaign, through emphasizing her maternal experience and love for her

---

[8] Alexei Yurchak, *Everything Was Forever, Until It Was No More: The Last Soviet Generation* (Princeton, New Jersey: Princeton University Press, 2005).

[9] Felix Ackermann, Mark Berman and Olga Sasunkevich, "In Search of Agency: Examining Belarusian Society from Below," *Journal of Soviet and Post-Soviet Politics and Society* 3, no. 1 (2017): 1–20. For more on victimhood and Belarusian society, see: Nelly Bekus, "Agency of Internal Transnationalism in Social Memory," *British Journal of Sociology* 70, no. 4 (2019).

[10] Ackermann, Berman, and Sasunkevich, Ibid., 4.

[11] Nina Potarskaia, "U protesta ne zhenskoe litso. Interv'iu s Irinoĭ Solomatinoĭ o belorusskikh protestakh," (Interview with Irina Solomatina). *Commons.com.* News Post. October 6, 2020. https://commons.com.ua/ru/u-protesta-ne-zhenskoe-lico-intervyu-s-irinoj-solomatinoj-o-belorusskih-protestah/?fbclid=IwAR1q1SWZt5cwDP_DPJuAgNJx3 p0KHJpcDTS7f7Kn1JA05LtchHgOwFzCA80.

husband.[12] In fact, she was criticized for using gender essentialist tropes when she declared that instead of running in the election, she would rather return home and cook for her family. Local feminists immediately accused her of promoting a family structure with a dominant father, a subordinate wife, and their children, thus (re)enacting heteropatriarchal values in which the woman devotes her life to the man.[13] Furthermore, the joint representatives of the opposition — Tsikhanouskaya, Tsepkalo, and Kolesnikova — became active in place of the intended male presidential candidates, were fighting for "their men." In the public discourse, they immediately started to be called the "the three graces" and "our girls." They became the targets of misogynistic reactions on social media. One comment read as follows, "The regime sucks so bad that even a housewife could become president."[14]

Such an interpretation is reinforced by visual images of women protesting in white clothes with flowers who sing lullabies, sometimes even barefoot, embracing the representatives of the special military forces and giving flowers to them. As a result, innocence, whiteness, and even childishness became the main symbols of the protests. Solomatina and her co-author, the researcher Vica Schmidt, do not see power in these images. In their opinion, such acts merely constitute self-sacrifice in the name of heteropatriarchal values and, as such, are a betrayal of the feminist agenda.[15]

However, in feminist literature, the issue of (re)enacting heteropatriarchal values by women who are active in socio-political life is closely connected to the organization of political space, citizenship, and agency, which tend to be "polarized along gender lines."[16] For instance, research done by Suvi Salmenniemi in civic organizations in Russia at the beginning of 2000 shows that in the post-Soviet context, civic activity is often associated with femininity,

---

[12] Luba Fein, "Women and Feminism in Belarus: The Truth behind the 'Flower Power" (Interview with Irina Solomatina). *FiLiA.org.uk*. News Post. September 21, 2020. https://filia.org.uk/news/2020/9/21/women-and-feminism-in-belarus-the-truth-behind-the-flower-power?fbclid=IwAR1Xl4Qgi69JlinIagEBKzPyByZi-X5ldnucT2oVxRNidayYci7Irv4Ixw

[13] Anne McClintock, Aamir Mufti, and Ella Shohat, Eds. *Dangerous Liaisons: Gender, Nation, and Postcolonial Perspectives* (Minneapolis: University of Minnesota Press, 1997).

[14] Fein, "Women and Feminism in Belarus: The Truth behind the 'Flower Power."

[15] *syg.ma.* "Beloruskiĭ 'chernyĭ iashchik': Proizvol vlasti kak (ne)sostoiavshiĭsia politicheskiĭ tranzit?" *@syg.ma.* News Post. October 3, 2020. https://syg.ma/@sygma/bielaruskii-chiernyi-iashchik-proizvol-vlasti-kak-nie-sostoiavshiisia-politichieskii-tranzit?fbclid=IwAR2m8fjxXw86_7atbsnb9rTrEKiOj4fyOOdzjtQK34qnbZRyZQb_Kcc6Z9c

[16] Suvi Salmenniemi, "Civic Activity - Feminine Activity? Gender, Civil Society and Citizenship in Post-Soviet Russia," *Sociology* 39, no. 4 (2005), 735.

"where women bear the social costs of transformation,"[17] but this does not mean that such activity is deprived of agency. Therefore, there is a need to carefully analyze women's practices and the ways in which they subvert dominant associations. Such research can help find the answer to how these practices could be redeployed for not only the interest of researchers, but also the personal benefit of the women who apply them.[18]

### Dominant Discourses and Their Subversion

For individuals, civic activity is a form of practicing citizenship and negotiating one's relationships to the state.[19] As was previously mentioned, this practice is constructed as gendered, and various discourses support this interconnection. The most prevalent form for women is the discourse of *female moral agency*, through which qualities such as self-sacrifice and altruism are perceived as essential in achieving the "common good," and "woman's wisdom" as supportive.[20]

The Belarusian case shows that self-sacrifice, along with a perceived moral high ground, appear as the main drivers for women's participation in the protests. Fatima Kamara, a mother of five, claimed that her main motivation for taking part in the peaceful marches was a deep disagreement with the Belarusian government.[21] In Fatima's interview given with *tut.by*, an independent media outlet, the prevalent narrative is the woman's responsibility to protect her children for whom the current regime poses a significant threat, failing to provide any certainty about their future. Moreover, in August–October 2020, the emphasis on the so-called "protection of children" accrued special meaning when the current government tried to manipulate protesters by threatening to take away the children of parents who take to the streets. In this context, Fatima stresses, "Some services may try to put pressure on me through the children. If something like this happens, I will fight."[22]

Generally speaking, the Autumn 2020 protests saw a similar perception of the protection of children as a mother's duty. First of all, this could be seen on

---

[17] Ibid., 735, 748.

[18] Mahmood, *Politics of Piety*, 544.

[19] Salmenniemi, "Civic Activity - Feminine Activity? Gender, Civil Society and Citizenship in Post-Soviet Russia," 737-738.

[20] Ibid., 739.

[21] Dar'ia Chul'tsova, "'Ne mogla est' i pit' ot stressa. Mat' piaterykh o zaderzhanii, shtrafe i reaktsii detei na eë vozvrashchenie." *lady.tut.by.* Blog post. October 7, 2020. https://lady.tut.by/news/mylife/703056.html.

[22] Chul'tsova, Ibid.

numerous posters which women took to the streets: "Don't be sorry — beat me! Be sorry for your son" (an allusion to Lukashenka's son); "Using children as blackmail is mean"; "I'm a mother and not a target for OMON [the riot police]"; "I'm against violence. I'm here for the kids"; "Mothers won't forgive the torture and deaths of children." This shows that women perceived their protests as entirely justified because it had been the result of their emotional reactions to, among other things, the beatings and acts of torture against people they know. And this is what gave them strength.[23]

Through a liberal-feminist lens, such appeals to motherhood can be interpreted as the (re)enactment of heteropatriarchal values, according to which a woman's role is to take care of her children. Following, then, all the commotion of the protests, these women will return to their houses and continue to play out their normative gender roles. In my opinion, such interpretations are limiting. Even if the female protests in Belarus function within a patriarchal framework, this does not mean that these frameworks cannot be subverted and renegotiated. For example, certain posters presenting reworked patriarchal stereotypes could be seen as subversive: "Sasha, I don't want you" [24]; "Now everybody understands everything. Even blond women showed up"; "[This is a] march of women dissatisfied with the dictatorship." It follows that for many Belarusian women, the subversion of patriarchal prescribed gender roles is the only way – at least symbolically – to assert their power and dignity. These slogans thus appear as individual acts of maintaining agency, and, as such, become safe instruments for the expression of women's emotions.

Another form of women's protest is their situational reaction to police brutality. It is common for women to fight back; they try to break through police barricades, or attempt to prevent the detention of protestors who are dragged away by the riot police. They might even unmask men in combat gear. Most often, they simply embrace the officers and hand out flowers to them. Whereas the situations when women demonstrate power and fearlessness towards people in uniform are seen as an appropriate form of resistance, cases such as hugging and giving out flowers are perceived as a humble acceptance of the patriarchal authorities' methods of oppression.

However, women who are involved in these acts often do not agree with interpretations in which they are seen as uncritical objects of manipulation.

---

[23] To trace argumentation on the importance of emotions for social actions, see: Chris Shilling, "The Two Traditions in the Sociology of Emotions." *The Sociological Review* 50, no. 2 (2002): 10–32.

[24] Sasha is a short form from the name Alexander (Belarusian: Aliaksandr). This is a reference to Alexander Lukashenka.

The history of Ol'ga, a woman who was handing flowers to men in uniform, attests to this. Ol'ga's act took place at the moment of her arrest. In her *tut.by* interview, Ol'ga stated that she was not ashamed of what she had done.[25] Being a psychologist, she explained that she tries to understand the motives of those who detained her. At the same time, she stated that she cannot accept their behavior, and the only instrument with which she could confront these armed men was her courage. This shows that even though these acts are just spontaneous reactions to situations in which many Belarusian women appear on the streets, it allows them to regain the agency that had been taken away from them. Moreover, just like her fellow female protesters, Ol'ga appeals to women's self-pride and self-esteem, traits that allow them to claim a moral high ground over the regime. In her opinion, this moral high ground is also given to her through motherhood, "I'm a Belarusian woman. I'm a mother. I went to the march because I couldn't do otherwise. I have nothing to be ashamed of. I am proud of it."[26]

In the Belarusian context, the discourse of female moral agency, which is actively used by female protesters and reproduces the culturally strong conviction about the power of female self-sacrifice, functions as a reasonable discursive strategy.[27] Belarusian women who take part in protests are convinced that their biological role – the ability to bear children and be a mother – positions them differently in society and enables them to protect a sphere that is reserved for them with all its implied resources. They are aware that this strategy is essential for the "common good," which goes beyond caring for their families and stretches to encompass society at large.

At the same time, caring for the common good as a legitimate area of activity for women can also be done by methods that subvert the normative status quo. One of the ways to practice this is to playfully engage with entrenched stereotypical gender roles using ironic slogans. In this way, women engage in a form of a negotiation that makes the stereotypes work to their benefit. Protest slogans on women's posters play with normative femininity and masculinity through the reversal of stereotypical gender roles. Within the slogans, it is the women who feel the moral right to talk about dissatisfaction with the current

---

[25] Dar'ia Chul'tsova, 'Ne mogla est' i pit' ot stressa. Mat' piaterykh o zaderzhanii, shtrafe i reaktsii detei na eë vozvrashchenie." *lady.tut.by*. Blog post. October 7, 2020. https://lady.tut.by/news/mylife/702230.html?utm_source=telegram&utm_campaign=s hare&utm_medium=social&utm_content=desktop

[26] Ibid.

[27] Salmenniemi, "Civic Activity—Feminine Activity? Gender, Civil Society and Citizenship in Post-Soviet Russia," 745.

political regime and Lukashėnka himself. Women compare Lukashėnka to the stereotypical, idle husband who fails to provide safety, welfare, and sexual satisfaction.

These strategies are fully accepted by Belarusian female protesters as they see themselves as the only social actors who possess the sufficient moral high ground for action. Post-Soviet researchers of gender tend to see the source of this female moral advantage in the heritage of the Soviet past of the East-European region, where for decades women have played a leading role in taking care of the whole of society when, as it was during and after the wartime period, many men were killed or injured.[28] It was the women who then took over the reconstruction of the country, simultaneously maintaining the household and family. Such "total motherhood" may be considered a sphere of sacrum, or taboo that is unbreakable both by men and authorities. Meanwhile, this is a sphere in which women can exercise their freedom and agency. Thus, certain cultural patterns and specific underpinnings made visible under ethnographic scrutiny can shed light onto specific behaviors and strategies, allowing us to understand the "game" of subverting and negotiating women's roles in the fight against the regime. On the whole, this can open up a better understanding of the role of women and their "soft power" in resistance movements.

Furthermore, this shows that women can find their own niches of agency which they practice within oppositional movements that might at first glance be perceived as a masculine activity. Still operating within available gendered patterns, women's agentic acts appear as, following Mahmood, one of many numerous modalities of agency in which the fact of being subjected to established gendered norms does not eliminate the possibility of transgressing them.[29] The only further question in this context concerns the effects of this transgression: is there potential for a collective female formation which will support a women's agenda as the next step in their civic activism?

## Bibliography

Ackermann, Felix, Mark Berman, and Olga Sasunkevich. "In Search of Agency: Examining Belarusian Society from Below." *Journal of Soviet and Post-Soviet Politics and Society* 3, no. 1 (2017): 1–20.

---

[28] Salmenniemi, Ibid. See also: Oleg Riabov, *Matushka-Rus.' Opyt gendernogo analiza poickov natsional'noi identichnosti Rossii v otechectvennoi i zapadnoi istoriografii* (Moscow: Moskow, 2001).

[29] Mahmood, Saba, *Politics of Piety.*

Bekus, Nelly. "Agency of Internal Transnationalism in Social Memory." *British Journal of Sociology* 70, no. 4 (2019): 1602–23.

Chul'tsova, Dar'ia. "'Mne nechego stydit'sia. Zhenshchina, darivshaia tsvety silovikam vo vremia zaderzhaniia, rasskazala o svoikh motivakh." *lady.tut.by.* Blog post. September 29, 2020. https://lady.tut.by/news/mylife/702230.html ?utm_source=telegram&utm_campaign=share&utm_medium=social&utm_ content=desktop.

_____. "'Ne mogla est' i pit' ot stressa. Mat' piaterykh o zaderzhanii, shtrafe i reaktsii detei na eë vozvrashchenie." *lady.tut.by.* Blog post. October 7, 2020. https://lady.tut.by/news/mylife/703056.html.

Fein, Luba. "Women and Feminism in Belarus: The Truth behind the 'Flower Power" (Interview with Irina Solomatina). *FiLiA.org.uk.* News Post. September 21, 2020. https://filia.org.uk/news/2020/9/21/women-and-feminism-in-belarus-the-truth-behind-the-flower-power?fbclid=IwAR1X14Qgi69JlinIagEBKzPyBy Zi-X51dnucT20V-xRNidayYci7Irv4Ixw.

Gapova, Elena. "Svetlana Tikhanovskaia: Ot lichnogo k politicheskomu." *Open Democracy.net.* News Post. August 6, 2020. https://www.opendemocracy.net/ ru/tikhanovskaya-ot-politcheskogo-lichnomy/.

Mahmood, Saba. *Politics of Piety: The Islamic Revival and the Feminist Subject.* Princeton, New Jersey: Princeton University Press Kindle Edition, 2012.

McClintock, Anne, Aamir Mufti, and Ella Shohat, Eds. *Dangerous Liaisons: Gender, Nation, and Postcolonial Perspectives.* Minneapolis: University of Minnesota Press, 1997.

Nechepurenko, Ivan. "In Belarus, Women Led the Protests and Shattered Stereotypes," *The New York Times.* News Post. October 11, 2020. https://www. nytimes.com/2020/10/11/world/europe/in-belarus-women-led-the-protests -and-shattered-stereotypes.html.

Paulovich, Natallia. "A Breadwinner or a Housewife? Agency in the Everyday Image of the Georgian Woman." *Anthropology of the Contemporary Middle East and Central Eurasia* 3, no. 2 (September 2016): 24–44.

Potarskaia, Nina. "U protesta ne zhenskoe litso. Interv'iu s Irinoĭ Solomatinoĭ o belorusskikh protestakh" (Interview with Irina Solomatina). *Commons.com.* News Post. October 6, 2020. https://commons.com.ua/ru/u-protesta-ne-zhenskoe-lico-intervyu-s-irinoj-solomatinoj-o-belorusskih-protestah/?fbcl id=IwAR1q1SWZt5cwDP_DPJuAgNJx3p0KHJpcDTS7f7Kn1JA05LtchHgOwFz CA80.

Riabov, Oleg. *Matushka-Rus.' Opyt gendernogo analiza poickov natsional'noi identichnosti Rossii v otechectvennoi i zapadnoi istoriografii.* Moscow: Moskow, 2001.

Salmenniemi, Suvi. "Civic Activity—Feminine Activity? Gender, Civil Society and Citizenship in Post-Soviet Russia," *Sociology* 39, no. 4 (October 2005): 735.

Serhan, Yasmeen. "When Women Lead Protest Movements: The Demonstrations in Belarus Point to a Broader Trend." *The Atlantic.* News Post. September 12, 2020. https://www.theatlantic.com/international/archive/2020/09/belarus-protests-women/616288/.

Shadrina, Anna. "Tsvety protesta: Kak zhenshchiny stali novoĭ politicheskoĭ siloĭ Belarusi." *Forbes.ru.* News Post. March 9, 2020. https://www. forbes.ru/

forbes-woman/408215-cvety-protesta-kak-zhenshchiny-stali-novoy-politicheskoy-siloy-belarusi?fbclid=IwAR2m8fjxXw86_7atbsnb9rTrEKiOj4fyOOdzjtQK34qn bZRyZQb_Kcc6Z9c.

Shilling, Chris. "The Two Traditions in the Sociology of Emotions." *The Sociological Review* 50, no. 2 (2002): 10–32.

*syg. ma.* "Beloruskiĭ 'chernyĭ iashchik': Proizvol vlasti kak (ne)sostoiavshiĭsia politicheskiĭ tranzit?" *@syg. ma.* News Post. October 3, 2020. https://syg.ma/ @sygma/bielaruskii-chiernyi-iashchik-proizvol-vlasti-kak-nie-sostoiavshiisia-politichieskii-tranzit?fbclid=IwAR2m8fjxXw86_7atbsnb9rTrEKiOj4fyOOdzjt QK34qnbZRyZQb_Kcc6Z9c.

Yurchak, Alexei. *Everything Was Forever, Until It Was No More: The Last Soviet Generation* Princeton, New Jersey: Princeton University Press, 2005.

# Chapter 11

# 2020 Women's Emancipation in Belarus: From Housewives to Symbols of Freedom

Veranika Laputska

### Abstract

The history and wider political context of the electoral commissions in Belarus provides a deeper understanding of the Saturday demonstrations led by women against the regime of Alexander Lukashenka. This overview is a briefing on how authoritarian structures reinforce patriarchy within the post-Soviet Belarusian electoral system, and how female leadership challenged these two core problems in 2020 and beyond. Outlining a range of sociopolitical issues, systemic inequalities, and consequent demands put forward by the women-led Belarusian opposition, this analysis shows how women's emancipation in Belarus remains inseparable from the core electoral struggle for democracy.

**Keywords**: Belarus, feminism, protests, authoritarianism, women in politics, female leadership, post-Soviet

***

## Introduction

When in November 2019, the winner of a beauty contest, 22-year-old Maryia Vasilevich, became a member of the Belarusian Parliament, a number of international media outlets immediately wrote about "Alexander Lukashenka's favorite" and her new accomplishment. At that moment Belarusian Parliament again fulfilled an informal quota of itself consisting of more than 30 percent women. Many of them have previously served as the Belarusian President's proxies at elections, employees of state bodies, or his favorite singers or sportswomen.

Female members of the parliament have never been especially active or vocal in decision-making processes. The only exceptions are Alena Anisim and Hanna Kanapatskaya who both became deputies during the parliamentary elections of 2016 and were the only representatives of the opposition to participate. However, with the end of these women's term in 2019 and no sign of re-election, the Belarusian legislative branch was again at risk of remaining without any pro-active female voices.

Women of the executive branch never played a formative role in Belarusian politics. The highest positions of women in the Belarusian state apparatus never reached higher than the Minister of Education, Health, or Labor issues below the head of the president's administration. Thus, no key strategic ministerial positions connected with military, defense or foreign relations have ever been held by women. An exception to this has appeared only in the case of a body directly ensuring the continuation of the presidential power, such as in the election commissions or the President's Administration wherein absolute loyalty is a prerequisite. The clearest example for this case is one of the longest-serving Belarusian officials, the Head of the Election Commission (CEC) Lidziya Yarmoshyna, who has been falsifying elections and referenda in Belarus since 1996.

### Women in the Belarusian Elections Administration

Since gaining its independence, Belarus has undergone numerous transformations in the sphere of state administration. The figure of Lidziya Yarmoshyna, aforementioned in her role as the Head of Belarusian Central Election Commission since 1996, represents one of the longest-serving officials in Belarus; she was dismissed in the lead-up to the 2022 Constitutional referendum.

Yarmoshyna has truly become one of the most recognizable and well-known Belarusian female politicians, also thanks to her numerous anti-feminist statements. The one which gained her especially notorious media attention was her message addressed to Belarusian women protesting the outcome of the 2010 Presidential election in front of the Parliament Building, which houses the Central Election Commission. When the protesters were brutally suppressed and one of the journalists during the press conference pointed out that many of those detained were women, Lidziya Yarmoshyna replied: "these 'women' should stay at home and make *borshch!* It is shameful for women to participate in such events!."[1] For this statement, Ms. Yarmoshyna received the Award "Sexist of the Year-2010" from the Pro-Feminism group.

Despite such statements from the Head of the Central Election Commission in Belarus, the elections machine itself relies primarily on the work of women. Belarusian journalists calculated that during the 2010 Presidential elections, election commissions of different levels consisted of 48,307 women and 22,508 men, i.e., 68.2% and 31.8% correspondingly. As Vadzim Bylina stated in his

---

[1] Borshch is a traditional and very common Slavic soup made from beetroot broth.

article about the composition of election commissions, this figure has grown since 1999, when election commissions of various levels were composed of 60-70% of women.[2]

When Belarusian media tried to explain the reasons for such disproportion, they realized that most election commissions are located in schools, as well as other state-run institutions, hence primarily members of election commissions are teachers. In September 2010, there was an attempt to disable the possibility to include teachers into election commissions as they depend fully on their bosses and "have no rights," but the attempt failed. The practice of including teachers into election commissions did occur in later years.

The teaching profession has remained of the most underpaid occupations since the end of the Soviet era, and as a result, has suffered from the classic problem of the feminization of poverty, in other words, overwhelmingly fewer men become teachers. This, in turn, reinforces pervasive patriarchal stereotypes throughout Belarus, which deem men the main bread-winners in families. Men are given high salaries and lower-paid jobs on the labor market are offered to women. The Belarusian National Report on Sustainable Development for the period 2020 through 2030 indeed proves that the salaries of Belarusian women on average are only 75 – 80% of men's salaries due to the fact that "women mainly work in the budget-supported sphere, where the salaries are relatively low (for instance, education, health care, culture, social services)[3] with an average gap of 23% between men's and women's salaries."[4] Lukashenka also admitted this fact in his statement in August 2016, calling for the creation of conditions which would enable increasing the status of the teaching profession.

Certain Belarusian journalists also believe that women "traditionally incline to conformism" and will not argue, which makes them ideal in the falsification of elections. Some Belarusian political activists have publicly reproached Belarusian teachers for the falsification of election processes. The leader of "The Young Front" movement Zmicier Dashkevich called them the "teachers of

---

[2] Bylina, Vadzim, "Sklad vybarchykh kamisiy: asnounyia tendetsii va umovakh autarytarnay sistemy Belarusi (miastsovyia vybary 1994 – 2014)." *International Congress of Belarusian Studies* (2015). http://icbs.palityka.org/wp-content/uploads/2014/papers/02-02_Bilina.pdf.

[3] UN Sustainable Development Report: Belarus. *Natsionalnyi doklad Respubliki Belarus ob osuschetvlenii povestki dnia v oblasti ustoychivogo razvitiya na period do 2030 goda.* (2017), 29; https://sustainabledevelopment.un.org/content/documents/16357Belarus.pdf.

[4] Schyotkina, Marianna, "V Belarusi sformirovalos novoye pokoleniye zhneschin." *BelTA* (March 3, 2016); http://www.belta.by/interview/view/v-belarusi-sformirovalos-novoe-pokolenie-zhenschin-4588/.

lies"[5] after he had encountered one of the teachers who admitted she was forced to go on a picket for the incumbent during the 2015 presidential election campaign. Belarusian female politicians also believe that women "are more easily manipulated"[6] as they stated in their 2018 interview to the Radio Free Europe/Radio Liberty.

In 2015 during the presidential campaign Lidziya Yarmoshyna acknowledged that the share of women in territorial election commissions reached up to 59% whereas precinct election commissions were made up of 70% women.[7] Remarkably, the Belarusian Union of Women (BUW) systematically plays an important role in the election process. It also becomes the employer of former female officials who were dismissed from their posts in government structures. Thus, both former Minister of information Liliya Ananich, and former Head of the Belarusian National Bank, Nadzieya Yermakova, are deputies for the chairperson of the BUW as of February 2018.

During the 2015 elections, 119 members of the BUW were nominated for election commissions of various levels, representing up to 6.9% of the organization in the commissions.[8] In addition to that, 26 out of 422 nominees for domestic observation were from the Belarusian Union of Women. In her statement at the time, the Chairwoman of the BUW and former Head of the National Bank of Belarus, Nadzieya Yermakova, openly declared that the BUW would support current president Alexander Lukashenka during the 2015 Presidential Election.

The position of the next leader of the BUW turned out to be also vocal in terms of political activities of its members. Current Chairwoman of the Belarusian Union of Women and the Deputy Chairperson of the Council of the Republic (also former Minister of Labor and Social Protection and former Head of Alexander Lukashenka Campaign Headquarters), Maryjanna Shchotkina, stated in her speech at the national forum "Family XXI" in December 2017 that she expected women to be very active in local elections campaign of 2018.

Throughout all elections in Belarus, the Union of Belarusian Women has traditionally remained very active. Thus, many members of the Union are usually included into elections commissions along with the other five largest

---

[5] Dashkevich, Zmitser, "Nastauniki khlusni." *Nasha Niva* (August 5, 2015); https://nn.by/?c=ar&i=154070.

[6] Sous, Hanna, "Chamu vybary u Belarusi falsifikujuts zhanchyny." *Svaboda*. (January, 15, 2018); https://www.svaboda.org/a/28976207.html.

[7] "Vybory-2015. Dolya zhenschin v territorialnykh izbirkomakh sostavlyaet 59%." *BelTA* (August 15, 2015); https://www.belta.by/society/view/vybory-2015.-dolja-zhenschin-v-territorialnyh-izbirkomah-sostavljaet-59-159146-2015/.

[8] Ibid. "Vybory-2015. Dolya zhenschin v territorialnykh izbirkomakh sostavlyaet 59%."

public associations that are funded by the Belarusian state, such as: *Belaya Rus*; Belarusian Republican Youth Union; Belarusian Public Association of Veterans; and the Federation of Trade Unions of Belarus amounting altogether to 90% of all members. Together with other state-funded public associations, these groups also carry out observations during the elections.

Belarusian women indeed have played an active role in the formation of election commissions during the 2018 local elections, amounting to 73.58% of all commission members. The Belarusian Union of Women became one of the leading public associations together with *Belaya Rus*, Belarusian Union of Youth, Belarusian Public Association of Veterans and the Belarusian Federation of Trade Unions, nominating many of their members for elections commissions. Overall, the number of representatives of these top organizations reached 37.59% in precinct election commissions.[9]

During the 2018 local elections the four pro-government public associations and one trade union (*Belaya Rus*, Belarusian Republican Youth Union, the Union of Belarusian Women, Belarusian Public Association of Veterans and the Federation of Trade Unions of Belarus) were largely represented in the TECs (Territorial Election Commissions) by 3,678 members, which was 97.3% of their nominees; by 1,871 representatives in the DECs (District Election Commissions), or 95.5% of the nominees; and by 97% in the PECs (Precinct Election Commissions). The proportion of women in the PECs amounted to 72.58% of the total number of their members. In the regional TECs there were only 41% female members.

Along with this evidence, statistics show that women in Belarus go to vote and participate in local elections far more actively than men. In their interview to Radio Free Europe/Radio Liberty, female politicians running in the 2018 local elections declared that they did not feel any difference in the attitude of potential voters due to their female gender. At the same time, other politically active women stated in their conversation with the same media outlet that Belarusian women do not demonstrate an active civic position and interest in the political processes and the only way women participate in elections is by being members of election commissions.

In order to counterbalance the problem of women's participation in manipulations during election processes, Belarusian female oppositional activists created a campaign "Women Against Falsification" before the 2015 Presidential Elections. They believed that Belarusian men often hide

---

[9] Hlod, Uladzimir, "Khto budzie lichyts' halasy na miastsovykh vybarakh: 5 halounykh prykmetau." *Svaboda* (January 5, 2018); https://www.svaboda.org/a/28956645.html.

themselves behind "weak" women because the responsibility for falsification is huge. For this reason such campaigns should become necessary in Belarus.

### Women in Belarusian State Bodies

The Belarusian National Report on Sustainable Development until 2030 mentions that 70.1% of all civil servants and 68% of judiciary sector employees are women.[10] Ms. Shchotkina in her March 2016 interview with the state news agency *BelTA* stated that Belarus tries to follow its National Plan on Gender Equality for 2011 – 2015. The head of the Belarusian Union of Women said that altogether the share of women is 55.4% in executive, legislative and judicial branches of power. Women also prevail in local executive bodies with 62.7% (excluding the village executive councils).[11]

In her December 2017 speech, Ms. Shchotkina cited the data from the Report stressing the fact that the number of women in the Council of Republic and the House of Representatives is constantly growing. Thus, during the 2016 Parliamentary Elections, 33.7% of women were elected for both Chambers of the National Assembly (Belarusian Parliament) whereas in 2012 this proportion was 29.7%. Moreover, before the 2018 local elections, 46.3% of local deputies were women and they also headed 30% of local executive bodies in Belarus.[12]

The rapid growth of the number of women in the Belarusian legislative body followed the requirement to maintain 30% of women declared by the Belarusian President in 2004. Similar quotas are promoted by the UN conventions and international best practices. To date, Belarus also holds the leading position with its 33% female deputies among the members of the Eurasian Economic Union and is at the 29th position in the world according to the Inter-Parliamentary Union. These figures improve Belarus' image on the gender equality map of the world. The active participation of such women in leadership, though, begs a question mark. They hardly ever initiate any laws, remain absent from mass-media, and hardly make any public statements. The exemption to this rule are two women who became deputies of the House of Representatives during the last parliamentary elections.

---

[10] Ibid. UN Sustainable Development Report: Belarus.

[11] Schyotkina, Marianna, "V Belarusi sformirovalos novoye pokoleniye zhneschin." *BelTA* (March 3, 2016); http://www.belta.by/interview/view/v-belarusi-sformirovalos-novoe-pokolenie-zhenschin-4688/.

[12] "Schyotkina ozhidayet aktivnogo uchastiya zhneschin v metsnykh vyborakh 2018." *BelTA* (December 5, 2017); http://www.belta.by/society/view/schetkina-ozhidaet-aktivnogo-uchastija-zhenschin-v-mestnyh-vyborah-2018-278998-2017/.

In 2016 two out of 38 elected women for the House of Representatives (Lower Chamber of the Belarusian Parliament) Alena Anisim and Hanna Kanapatskaya represented the Belarusian opposition. Both women tried to maintain an active policy and remained vocal during the wave of social protests throughout Belarus in winter-spring 2017. Interestingly, Hanna Kanapatskaya ran at the same precinct as the former candidate for the president Tatsiana Karatkevich, but managed to win the post. Some uncertainties remain regarding how reliable the results of the elections were in light of numerous violations noted by international observers. However, the new trend that, for the first time since constitutional reforms of all branches of power were enacted in 2004, resulted in the election of two opposition politicians was indeed welcomed by the international community. Many male politicians and experts, however, responded by marking the outcome as a token benefit for the Belarusian president stating that he "allowed" the women to be elected because he does not see women as his political opponents.

Despite these declarations on the presence of female leaders in public administration, the Belarusian government demonstrates a different dynamic. Currently, all Deputy Prime-Ministers in the Belarusian government are men, save two. The Presidium of the Council of Ministers includes only one woman—Natallia Kachanava—who is the Head of President Lukashenka's Administration. Remarkably, she became the first woman to hold this post, having previously been the first woman Vice-Premier. However, only one ministry out of 24 existing in the current government—the Ministry of Labor and Social Protection—is headed by a female official, Iryna Kastsevich. To sum up, men hold the majority of key positions in the Belarusian government despite the ritual declarations on developments in gender policy in Belarus.

Women who are part of state bodies often become headliners in oppositional media. The personal life or appearances of these female politicians often attract particular media attention, especially from the oppositional media outlets. In 2017, when the son of Lidziya Yarmoshyna died, many Internet media reports allowed their readers to openly comment on that occasion, leaving the negative messages unedited. The Congress of the public association *BelayaRus,* which took place on January 19, 2018, also attracted the attention of the Belarusian Internet. As many state officials are members of "Belaya Rus," the event brought officials from all over Belarus to Minsk. Belarusian oppositional newspaper "Naša Niva" devoted several articles with photos especially ridiculing female representatives of the Congress, discussing their hair styles and outfits. At the same time, mass-media did not dare to publish similar articles discussing the appearance of Belarusian male officials, as they, together with the majority of Belarusian society, assume them to be real representatives of power whom they should not confront.

## Aliaksandr Lukashenka and His Female Proxies

During the twenty-three years of his presidency, Alexander Lukashenka has created quite an oppressive workforce structure of female employees who participate not only in the official, but also unofficial activities of state politics. The Belarusian president married when he was elected for his post in 1994, but his wife never fully entered the scenes on which his public life has played out. Halina Lukashenka stayed in a small town where Mr. Lukashenka had lived before he became Deputy of the Belarusian Supreme Council (this was the name of the Belarusian Parliament before the constitutional reforms under Lukashenka). Lukashenka's mother-in-law stated in her interview in 2014 that her daughter Halina was happily married and loved the president.

In 2008 the Belarusian president revealed his illegitimate son Mikalai who since then has served as the president's companion in all official visits abroad and important events within the country and, in a way, has substituted in for the First Lady in this role. Mr. Lukashenka himself declared in 2009 that his son was "from God." Mikalai's mother was never publicly named, but many Belarusians believe it is the former president's personal doctor, Iryna Abelskaya, who now manages the most prestigious state medical center. Ms. Abelskaya's mother, Liudmila Pastayalka, for several years was the Minister of Health in Belarus after her appointment by Alexander Luksahenka. Ms. Abelskaya never publicly admits that Mikalai Lukashenka is her son, although she mentions him without pronouncing his name as her younger son in her interviews with Belarusian journalists.

In May 2014, Mr. Lukashenka gave an interview to the Russian independent television channel *Rain.* Russian socialite and journalist Kseniya Sobchak who ran for presidency in Russia in March 2018 was the interviewer. The interview threw the light on many personal details of Lukashenka's life. He admitted that he did not want to divorce his wife, despite the fact that they had not lived together for almost 30 years because he did not want to "traumatize the mother of his children." The mystery and speculations about the acting first lady never stopped, and both Belarusian and foreign journalists alike continue to catch the image of the women who appear during official international and national events with the Belarusian president.

Alexander Lukashenka tends to portray himself as a man popular among women and it seems he tries to preserve such an image. In the same interview to the television channel *Rain*, he confirmed he liked to be accompanied by young women, and not state officials during various public events. Alexander Lukashenka also admitted that one of his new companions was a young woman named Darya Shmanai who is officially employed in the President's Protocol Service. Reportedly she was noticed by Mr. Lukashenka after a beauty contest, in which she won and afterwards was recruited to the President's Protocol Service, where attractive young women resembling models are always available for assistance during international receptions and public celebrations.

Among his other companions to whom he paid visits or watched sports games were television journalists such as Palina Shuba, or pop stars including Alena Lanskaya, who presented Belarus in the Eurovision song contest, and Belarusian professional sportswomen such as Kseniya Sankovich. Some of these women even became Lukashenka's proxies during the presidential election of 2015, such as the Belarusian gymnast Liubou Charkashyna. Others succeeded further in their political careers, as happened in the case of Belarusian singer Iryna Darafeyeva, who became a Deputy in the House of Representatives, having previously been unofficially referred to as the president's favorite singer.

One of Lukashenka's earlier companions, Natallia Eysmant, made a successful career in television before becoming his Press Secretary. Her husband, Ivan Eysmant, was appointed on February 6, 2018, as the Head of the National State Television Radio Company, one of the most important positions in Belarusian media. This proved to provide both her own and her husband with key roles in the state political hierarchy. Interestingly, the husband of Lukashenka's previous Press Secretary, Natallia Piatkevich, was also appointed by the Belarusian president to the position of Chief Director of the main state channel "Belarus 24." Ms. Piatkevich herself rose in her career to become the Deputy Head of the President's Administration and his personal assistant.

The Belarusian public follows not only the personal life of the president but also pays much attention to his statements regarding women. On March 9, 2017, during a meeting with key government officials and while discussing the consequences of the infamous Decree 3 (unofficially known as "Decree on Social Parasitism"), which had provoked numerous protests all over the country, Mr. Lukashenka called officials to ensure the employment of their "wives, husbands, female and male lovers, family members and friends."[13] Such a statement provoked ironic comments by many Belarusians on social media who declared that they wanted to attain the position of a female lover so that they might obtain employment. These lines were later removed from the president's official website but left a negative impression within Belarusian society.

---

[13] "Lukashenko: trudoystroyte svoikh zhyon, muzhey, lyubovnits! Zastavit rabotat tekh, kto dolzhen I mozhet!" *Svoboda Slova* (March 10, 2017); https://www.youtube.com/watch?v=dDn-8invJww.

## Women's #Evalution

The year 2020 saw an evolution in the female leadership of the country, protest, and self-identification of voters in Belarus. Never before had so many Belarusian women run in the presidential race, organized campaigns, or participated in protests on a massive scale, nor demonstrated so much bravery and pride in simply being women.

Pictures of Belarusian women wearing white clothes and holding flowers spread globally, providing a strong impulse for the evolution of feminism and female protests. Photos of women's faces from Belarus were featured in the headlines of The New York Times, The Guardian, Deutsche Welle, The Atlantic, BBC, Al Jazeera and Euronews. Traditional and social media were flooded with high-spirited and bright female faces and voices. Belarusian women demand to be heard and recognized. They demand an end to violence and the protection of the Belarusian people from state violence.

When the first visual symbol of Belarusian women's demonstrations emerged, the painting entitled *Eva*, discussed below, very few expected that it would soon come to signify women's demands as an entirely new and lasting phenomenon within the wider Belarusian protests. Intertwined with the story of this particular painting is the way in which Belarusian authorities invented mechanisms to silence one of Lukashenka's major rivals, the long-term head of *Belgazprombank*, Viktar Babaryka, this was carried out through the usual repressive measures applied by the Belarusian regime to its dissenters. Mr. Babaryka was reknown throughout the country not only for his professional success, but also for his love and dedication to art. For years he had been collecting priceless Belarusian art pieces, which he was managing to return to Belarus from various countries. Many of the outstanding pieces were exhibited in various art galleries in Belarus; the *Belgazprombank* art collection kept growing thanks to its head patron who at the time enjoyed ironclad support from the regime. Several days before the registration of presidential candidates in the election, Viktar Babaryka and his son Eduard were arrested for alleged financial crimes committed by the *Belgazprombank* leadership and businesses related to their family. The bank art collection turned into yet another "victim" of the criminal investigation. All the pieces were arrested, including one of the most expensive artworks in contemporary Belarus: the painting *Eva*, by Chaim Soutine, an expressionist artist of Jewish origin born in Belarus.

The Belarusian Internet immediately exploded with collages depicting the painting's heroine, Eva. On such collages and memes, Eva was shown making rude gestures hinting at the resistance of the Belarusian people to the Belarusian authorities. Eva thus became the most popular image to be printed on a T-shirt, cup, or sticker. Later on, with the growth of the female protest movement in Belarus, Eva's image was transformed multiple times. In some renderings, Eva is dressed in white clothes and holding flowers, as in the Belarusian women's demonstrations. In other renderings, Eva is depicted behind bars, resembling countless peaceful protesters, including the mostly female protesters in the Saturday marches who were beaten and jailed en masse for their political activities. Thousands of people inside Belarus and abroad have reproduced and spread images of Eva, giving rise to a new visual phenomenon depicting a feminist, pro-woman semantic identification with a freer future for Belarus.

## Belarusian Presidency — Not for Women?

On the eve of the 2020 presidential campaign in Belarus, nothing signaled any significant change in the overall subjugated position of women's status or involvement into Belarusian politics. Nevertheless, when four women declared their intention to run in the presidential elections, Alexander Lukashenka did not seem to be concerned. Known for his many sexist statements and surrounded by men and women who demonstrate misogyny and male chauvinism daily, the Belarusian strongman continued to play his usual role of a self-sufficient leader who adorns himself with women as decorative accessories. As in earlier campaigns, Mr. Lukashenka never appeared in public with his wife while on the campaign trail; instead, young attractive women from the Presidential Protocol Services continued to accompany him in public. The Presidential Protocol Services became the most infamous state apparatus for recruiting young attractive women from beauty pageants to accompany the Belarusian leader and his close milieu for both formal and informal events.

The moment that Svetlana Tsikhanouskaya (Sviatlana Tsikhanouskaya) announced that she would run for president, taking the place of her husband the jailed popular vlogger and opposition figure, Siarhei Tsikhanousky (Siarhei Tsikhanouskiy), huge crowds started to gather in support of her candidacy in every region of Belarus. Lukashenka was taken by surprise. He went into immediate defense mode, applying his characteristically brutal tactics of targeting any dissent or political competition to his iron fist. These tactics had seemed by his logic to ensure a stable following, but he would be proven wrong. He began his crackdown on the nationwide rallies in support of Svetlana Tsikhanouskaya by first publicly condemning the viability of any female presidency. He declared that the Belarusian constitution: "is not written for a woman" because "it is too hard for a woman to bear the burden" of the presidential post.

Belarusian public opinion reacted immediately. Many Belarusian women, including celebrities, denounced Lukashenka's statement, which attracted wide media coverage. Most popular social media spread the video that later went viral featuring many women condemning such statements. Belarusian women felt deeply insulted and irritated by the statements of the Head of State and kept referring to them throughout the post-election protests.

## Women in the 2020 Presidential Race

Sviatlana Tsikhanouskaya became the only viable oppositional candidate, after two of Lukashenka's main rivals in the presidential election, Viktar Babaryka and Valery Tsepkalo (Valery Tsapkala), were denied registration. The Belarusian president was obviously not deterred by the appearance of a female contender, and most likely, her supposedly unthreatening semblance of unqualified credentials due to her gender was the reason Lukashenka still "allowed" her to run in the race. Mrs. Tsikhanouskaya appeared to be shy and unprepared for any political battle, but only on the surface.

However, almost immediately, she declared her unification with two more women to run the campaign – Maria Kolesnikova (Maria Kalesnikava), as the representative of Viktar Babaryka, and Veronica Tsepkalo (Veranika Tsapkala), wife of Valery Tsepkalo (Valery Tsapkala) and head of his election headquarters. The three women stated that it had taken them only fifteen minutes to find common ground and decide to merge their joint efforts during the presidential campaign.

When declaring their unification, Tsikhanouskaya, Kolesnikova, and Tsepkalo immediately and as they later stated, unintentionally, invented their own visual slogan: a heart, a fist and a victory sign in the form of a hand making a peace sign. These symbols went viral on the Internet and offline. Belarusians started to reproduce them during rallies, display them on their T-shirts, and distribute them on merchandise. The ways in which the three women communicated with the public and behaved were like a breath of fresh air in the stifling Belarusian political arena. They organized an excellent campaign in social media which had never been of interest to Mr. Lukashenka, who had earlier felt so confident in his iron power over public support.

The female trio embraced and projected values of female strength, but also empathy and justice. They underlined multiple times that they were almost forced into politics to protect their men, and that they did not intend to stay, nor did they see themselves as representing a feminist protest. This messaging was welcomed by various camps within Belarusian society. Those who claimed themselves anti-feminist enjoyed the constant referral of the women to the men who they were representing, and their rhetorical adherence to traditional values. The trio was, for this conservative faction of society, thus re-confirming of the idea that women cannot lead, but can only represent men in politics. Nonetheless, even despite this maneuvering to retain the conservative factions, the Belarusian feminist movement still celebrated the fact that women in Belarus were the ones finally leading the long-awaited political awakening and, in their opinion, this would inevitably inspire many Belarusian women to fight for an even more long-awaited emancipation in the struggle for women's rights.

Beyond the extremely visible trio of women whose success in rallying massive support remains undeniable, there was another female candidate, Hanna Kanapatskaya, who remained overshadowed. As a successful and outspoken lawyer and a former Member of Parliament, she had been re-elected to the Belarusian Parliament in 2016. Together with another woman, Alena Anisim, the two represented the only oppositional force within government at the time. Mrs. Kanapatskaya became well-known for her persistent struggle with the shortcomings of the Belarusian legislation; her followers deeply admired her unconventional stance, persistence, and adherence to democratic values. But a very different Mrs. Kanapatskaya decided to run in the presidential campaign in 2020. Some of her former colleagues stated that she must have been taken under control of the Belarusian special services, as her rhetoric had become so different. Although she was publicly condemning the Belarusian authorities and Alexander Lukashenka, her statements towards other presidential candidates were lacking her usual ethics and tact. Mrs. Kanapatskaya was openly labeling many of her competitors Kremlin puppets.

After the new oppositional female trio of leaders publicly united, Kanapatskaya launched a series of posts attacking Tsikhanouskaya on her public profile, questioning her political experience along with her professional and personal qualities. Later she labeled all three women — Tskihanouskaya, Kolesnikova, and Tsepkalo — "laughing girls," juxtaposing their experience and younger age to her more robust background working for the state in professional politics. Needless to say, the Belarusian public did not welcome such statements from Mrs. Kanapatskaya. Many believed that the former MP was either jealous of the trio's successes, or was harshly and openly discrediting them for more covert purposes in the service of the regime. Some brave supporters of the new oppositional leadership trio went so far as to react to these attacks by publicly criticizing Kanapatskaya, even openly condeming her, growing more bold in their statements as the mass protests ensued after the 2020 election results. But by that time the bright new and greatly admired female trio of oppositional leaders had already become the main target for destruction in Lukashenka's repressive crackdown.

## State Repressions Against Female Leaders

The female trio had successfully united hundreds of thousands of people in Belarus, and brought dozens of thousands into the streets in demonstrations for fair and transparent elections ahead of the 2020 vote. Belarusians cordially greeted these women wherever they went. They became the face of the oppositional movement in Belarus. The three women created a powerful message of the legitimate and trustworthy female leadership able to treat the people of Belarus with empathy and love; their platform remained authentic and emotional even amid the crackdowns, relying on images of bravery and strength. The trio initiated great inspiration for Belarusian women who for years had been deprived of their chance to be part of political decision-making. Yet by August, the three women faced a number of repressive measures and threats. Tsepkalo joined her husband in Russia one day ahead of the election due to the palpable threat of persecution inside Belarus. Tskihanouskaya was forced to leave the country for Lithuania on August 11 due to similar reasons: she left just after a conversation at the Central Election Commission, where she had been forced to make a humiliating video address to her electorate.

The Coordination Council Presidium was established on August 14, 2020, to ensure a fair transition of power; it included five women and three men. In addition to Sviatlana Tsikhanouskaya and Maria Kolesnikova from the initial election women's trio, three more remarkable women joined the Presidium: Sviatlana Alexievich, a Nobel Prize Winner of Literature and author of the reknown book, *The Unwomanly Face of War*; Volha Kavalkova, Belarusian Christian Democracy Co-Chair, who initially also ran as a presidential candidate herself but then joined Tsikhanouskaya's team; and Liliya Ulasava – an experienced and well-known lawyer and mediator. All became Members of the Coordination Council Presidium.

Soon after the formation of the Presidium, the Belarusian authorities acted swiftly to invent and apply mechanisms by which to act against the Presidium's women. At first they detained Volha Kavalkova. After several days of imprisonment, they then forcibly transported Ms. Kavalkova to the border with Poland and deported her from Belarus. Next, the Belarusian Committee of State Control arrested and detained Liliya Ulasava. Following this brutal act of repression, Maria Kolesnikova was abducted from the city center of Minsk and taken to the Belarusian-Ukrainian border the following day, where she was joined by her fellow oppositionists Anton Radniankou and Ivan Krautsou. Unlike the men accompanying her, Kolesnikova managed to tear up her passport and flee back into Belarusian territory. After this ordeal, she faced criminal charges, including "seizure of power" and was subsequently imprisoned. From that moment onward, Maria Kolesnikova's face became even more recognized amid the protests taking place across the nation as a key symbol of the new female-led Belarusian opposition.

Soon after, Presidium member and Nobel Prize winner and famous author Svetlana Alexievich, mentioned above, declared that unknown forces were trying to break into her Minsk apartment. European diplomats and journalists immediately arrived at Alexievich's personal home in order to protect her from "unknown people." Diplomats stayed with her and lent their protection for several days. The timing of this incident was likely connected to the fact that Alexievich had acted in defense of the Coordination Council Presidium of which she was a member; she had provided contrary evidence in the criminal case against Kolesnikova.

The outcome of the formation of the women-led Presidium and its targeting led to harsher repressions and crackdowns on women protesters who had earlier been much safer, in comparison with their male protesters. Those women who joined student protests and solidarity chains after the abduction of Maria Kolesnikova on September 7, 2020, were all brutally beaten and detained. The cruelty of the riot police had no limits, and the human rights infringements are only beginning to be known, including severe beatings of pregnant women. In one case, a woman lost her child after a round of beatings; the Belarusian state media cynically lied about her death on television, stating that she had performed an abortion.

Belarusian authorities continued to invent and apply severe means against protesters, often their targetings belied a gendered logic, for example, they would weaponize women demonstrators' parental rights. Many women claimed that school and police authorities threatened them with the possibility of taking their children into custody and stripping them of all future parental rights, should they continue to demonstrate against Lukashenka in the women's marches. In one case, a detained female activist had to pick up her son from an orphanage, even as other members of the family had pleaded with authorities to take temporary custody of him while his mother was serving time in a detention center.

### The White Protests: Flowers, Lipstick, and Tears

During the initial and most brutal days of the post-election crackdown, hundreds of people were detained. When released, most women claimed that they had faced less violence inside the detention centers and prisons than on the streets, even though while held in captivity by the state they had also been humiliated, beaten and, in some cases, raped. Several hundred women self-organized on Telegram to call for an end to the violence.

On August 12 and 13, 2020, Belarusian women across the country started to form "chains of solidarity." In white clothes and holding hands, they called upon the authorities to stop the violence and hear their voices. This new phase of the organized female-led opposition movement took Lukashenka's riot police by surprise. On August 14, when a massive demonstration took place in front of the House of Parliament in Minsk, military forces put down their shields in front of the female protesters. In response, the women started hugging and kissing the soldiers. The female protesters realized that their strongest weapon were themselves, remaining peaceful, but persistent and strong.

Members of the female trio kept thanking the Belarusian people in their struggle for freedom. They also admired the bravery of the Belarusian protesting women. In September 2020, Svetlana Tskihanouskaya, Volha Kavalkova, and Veronica Tsepkalo re-united in Warsaw for an official meeting. When speaking to journalists, they praised the courage of their colleagues and friends, especially their "feisty girlfriend" Maria Kolesnikova, who, despite the risk of persecution at home, opted for imprisonment instead of forced emigration. In her several statements from abroad exiled Svetlana Tsikanouskaya honored the courage of the women who stood up for freedom, and condemned the Belarusian state police for mercilessly beating women and children.

The name of the women's demonstrations, "white protests," evokes strong sentiments of patriotism because "*belo,*" which is the term for the color *white*, is also at the root of the word "*Belo-*rus," transliterated from Cyrillic into Latin letters as Belarus. The women's marches would take place across every region of the country, uniting the entire nation at least once a week, usually on Saturday. Women marched through Belarusian cities and towns, and also united abroad. They held hands in large chains of people symbolizing an invincible spirit, carried flowers and posters, recited poems, and sung folk songs such as the famous traditional Belarusian song *Kupalinka* about the sad destiny of a village girl. Many female Belarusians organized flash mobs and created videos for Belarusian and international audiences. With strong female leaders such as the women's initial trio, along with the women members of the Coordination Council Presidium, and Belarusian actresses, sportswomen and artists, the cumulative effect of these public denunciations of the Belarusian authorities, and Alexander Lukashenka, first of all, solidified thousands of Belarusian female voices into the leading force for the entire opposition movement.

Yet nothing so powerful emerges without challenges calibrated by the regime at each and every step. In a futile attempt to de-fang the movement by mimicking it, the Belarusian authorities organized a concert named "Women for Belarus," featuring Russian and Belarusian pop-stars. The performances all expressed support for Alexander Lukashenka and the singers were deliberately selected and staged to represent every region of the country. The regime was obviously attempting to juxtapose itself against the popular followings behind the women leading the opposition, who had managed to unite the entirety of

Belarus in dissent with Lukashenka and ongoing falsified elections. The concert was a poor and imitative attempt to neutralize the power of the women-led oppositional trio by entrenching into society a weak counter claim to the opposition by introducing a falsification: that many women support Lukashenka. After this propagandistic concert, the media disseminated staged photos showing Mr. Lukashenka being fawned over and kissed by members of the concert's mostly female audience.

### "Beloved [Belarus] cannot be given away," Lukashenka's Statements Against Women, Post-Detention Violence

One of the slogans of pro-Lukashenka loyalists involved a metaphor for matrimony to the state: "a beloved (Belarus) cannot be given away," which tries to equate "a woman" with a loyal state. Never before in recent history had women enjoyed so much attention from the Belarusian leadership. The Belarusian women's opposition movement responded in-kind to the slogan by comparing Mr. Lukashenka to an abuser who usually forces his partner to stay, despite their partner's will to leave — as in the case of the abused Belarusian people, who continued protesting against the authorities for months, even under severe duress including near-death beatings with batons.

At the time of writing this chapter, the women of Belarus have been heard, but unfortunately, not listened to. Although the repressive machine keeps inventing new ways of targeted attacks against specifically women, the Belarusian female leaders and protesters demonstrate their courage and determination to go on with their fight for freedom and justice. The emancipation of Belarusian women in their unified will to fight for an end to oppression and violence took no time at all to manifest, but has not reached its full potential. It remains a bright and unforgettable start to an ongoing battle. The Belarusian authorities will now never be able to go back; they can no longer ignore the new, fierce, and unstoppable driving force that is changing the course of history – the power of Belarusian women.

### Bibliography

Bylina, Vadzim. "Sklad vybarchykh kamisiy: asnounyia tendetsii va umovakh autarytarnay sistemy Belarusi (miastsovyia vybary 1994 – 2014)". *International Congress of Belarusian Studies,* 2015. http://icbs.palityka.org/wp-content/uploads/2014/papers/02-02_Bilina.pdf.

Dashkevich, Zmitser. "Nastauniki khlusni." *Nasha Niva.* August 5, 2015. https://nn.by/?c=ar&i=154070.

Hlod, Uladzimir. "Khto budzie lichyts' halasy na miastsovykh vybarakh: 5 halounykh prykmetau." *Svaboda.* January 5, 2018. https://www.svaboda.org/a/28956645.html.

"Lukashenko: trudoystroyte svoikh zhyon, muzhey, lyubovnits! Zastavit rabotat tekh, kto dolzhen I mozhet!" *Svoboda Slova*. March 10, 2017. https://www. youtube.com/watch?v=dDn-8invJww.

Schyotkina, Marianna. "V Belarusi sformirovalos novoye pokoleniye zhneschin". *BelTA*. March 3, 2016. http://www.belta.by/interview/view/v-belarusi-sformirovalos -novoe-pokolenie-zhenschin-4688/.

"Schyotkina ozhidayet aktivnogo uchastiya zhneschin v metsnykh vyborakh 2018". *BelTA*. December 5, 2017. http://www.belta.by/society/view/schetkina-ozhidaet-aktivnogo-uchastija-zhenschin-v-mestnyh-vyborah-2018-278998-2017/.

Sous, Hanna. "Chamu vybary u Belarusi falsifikujuts' zhanchyny." *Svaboda*. January, 15, 2018. https://www.svaboda.org/a/28976207.html.

UN Sustainable Development Report: Belarus. *Natsionalnyi doklad Respubliki Belarus ob osuschetvlenii povestki dnia v oblasti ustoychivogo razvitiya na period do 2030 goda*. 2017. https://sustainabledevelopment.un.org/content/documents/16357Belarus.pdf.

"Vybory-2015. Dolya zhenschin v territorialnykh izbirkomakh sostavlyaet 59%". August 15, 2015. *BelTA*. https://www.belta.by/society/view/vybory-2015.-dolja-zhenschin-v-territorialnyh-izbirkomah-sostavljaet-59-159146-2015/.

# Chapter 12

# "People Have Nothing to Oppose to State Violence Except their Fragile Bodies"[1]: Configurations of Feminism in Belarusian Protest Art

Antonina Stebur

## Abstract

This text is devoted to the analysis of feminist configurations within the protests in Belarus (2020–2021) and relevant political gestures by contemporary artists. On the one hand, the text analyzes the reasons why the feminist agenda is hardly heard amid the broader opposition. On the other hand, the author considers a possible feminist reconfiguration of protest through the prism of feminism not as a struggle for women's rights, but as an attempt to propose alternative social, ontological, and political structures – based on attempts to understand the fragility and concreteness of human existence. Is it possible to build collective infrastructure based upon the principles of care – as opposed to authoritarian, hierarchical, patriarchal forms of social organization?

**Keywords**: Belarus, feminism, contemporary art, art-activism, solidarity, care, horizontal system

\*\*\*

---

[1] A quote from the Belarusian artist and activist Marina Naprushkina, from an interview with Sergei Shabohin for his 2020 archival project *Social Marble: Dynamic Archive of the Rise of Civil Society in Belarus*, which was exhibited as part of the major exhibition of Belarusian art in Kyiv the following year; See: Aleksei Borisionok, Andrei Dureika, Marina Naprushkina, Sergey Shabohin, Antonina Stebur, Maxim Tyminko. *Every Day. Art. Solidarity. Resistance.* Visual Art Exhibition. Kyiv, Ukraine: Mystetskyi Arsenal. March 25–June 6, 2021. https://artarsenal.in.ua/en/vystavka/evere-day-art-solidarity-resistance/.

## Introduction

In August 2020, Rufina Bazlova, a Belarusian artist living in Prague, started working on her embroidery-based project, *The History of Belarusian Vyzhavanka,*[2] dedicated to the central events and images of the Belarusian protests against the illegitimate reelection of Alexander Lukashenko to the office of President. The artist defines this project as "comics" and "saga," emphasizing its multi-layered and complex nature, which is often perceived as elusive due to the seeming simplicity and even decorativeness of embroidery as a craft.[3] The Belarusian artist Rufina Bazlova describes her artworks, or "protest vyshavankas," in reference to ideas of resistance against a corrupt regime: "I can't put up with the fact that one can lie and hate one's own people so much."[4] *The History of Belarusian Vyzhavanka* can be approached in three main directions in research. These three interpretations, explicitly or implicitly present in the artwork, create friction and discussion around its reading. In a sense, Bazlova's project is open to interpretation and can be captured and reworked by both sides of the political spectrum, entering into either/both right and left discourse.

It is important to note that *The History of Belarusian Vyzhavanka* was shown as part of the 2021 exhibition *Every Day. Art. Solidarity. Resistance.* exhibition that took place in Kyiv, Ukraine, in the large and well-known museum, Mystetskyi Arsenal.[5] This was the largest exhibition globally to date focused on contemporary Belarusian art and was also groundbreaking in its presentation of activist and sociopolitical artistic practices. Describing the exhibition, the curator and art critic Olga Kopenkina defined it as "a continuous flow of video documentation, photography, prison drawings, handmade and printed posters, mixed media installations, paintings, sculptural objects, diagrams, and info-graphics documenting and articulating multitudes creating a new temporality,

---

[2] The title of the work contains a pun since in Russian there are two words that differ in spelling by only one letter, but have vastly different meanings: "vyshuvat" (вышивать) means "to embroider" while "vyzhyvat"(выживать) means "to survive."

[3] Sasha Razor, "Rufina Bazlova: The History of Belarusian Vyzhavanka," *Chrysalis Mag,* Blog Post. February 17, 2021. https://chrysalismag.by/project/rufina-bazlova-istoriya-belarusskoy-vyzhivanki.

[4] Maria Lasheva, " 'I can't put up with the fact that one can lie and hate one's own people so much' The Belarusian artist Rufina Bazlova talks about her ornament of 'protest vyshavankas' with riot police and paddy wagons." *MEDUZA.io.* August 18, 2020. https://meduza.io/feature/2020/08/18/ya-rosla-s-oschuscheniem-chto-lukashenko-navsegda.

[5] Borisionok, Dureika, Naprushkina, Shabohin, Stebur, and Tyminko, *Every Day. Art. Solidarity. Resistance, Ibid.*

in which 'every day' (the protest's slogan and the exhibition's token word) appeared as the eternal 'today.' "[6] During the curatorial discussions in the preparation of the exhibition, the discussion of the work of Rufina Bazlova was one of the most thought-provoking. On the one hand, her works are a kind of archive of the Belarusian protest, recognizable and understandable in any language. On the other hand, this work can be interpreted as nostalgia for traditional culture, the reconstruction of the right-wing political conservative discourse to emancipatory cyberfeminist reflections. This complexity was both a strength and a weakness of *The History of Belarusian Vyzhavanka*. Perhaps the multi-layered meanings of this work, its openness to multiple interpretations, can serve as the key metaphor for the feminist dimension of the Belarusian protests that began in 2020.

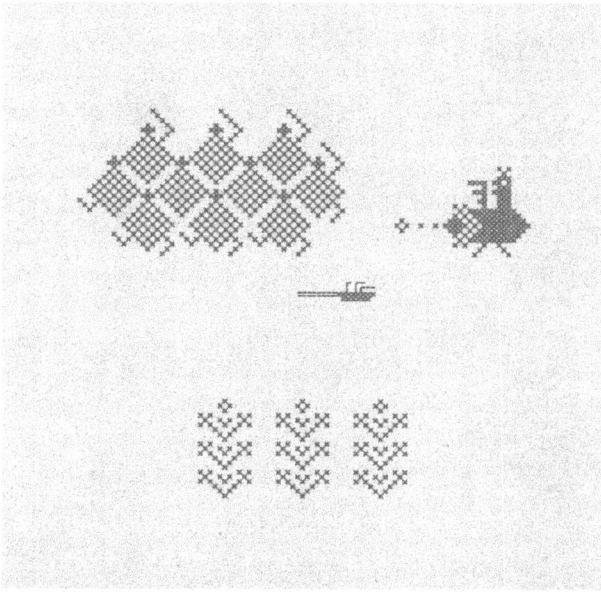

**Figure 12.1.** Rufina Bazlova, from the series "The History of Belarusian Vyzhyvanka" 2020-2021. Source: © provided by the artist. Reproduced with permission.

---

[6] Olga Kopenkina, "Exhibition Review: Every Day. Art. Solidarity. Resistance Mystetskiy Arsenal. Kyiv, Ukraine: May 3–June 6, 2021," *Afterimage* 48 (2021), 83.

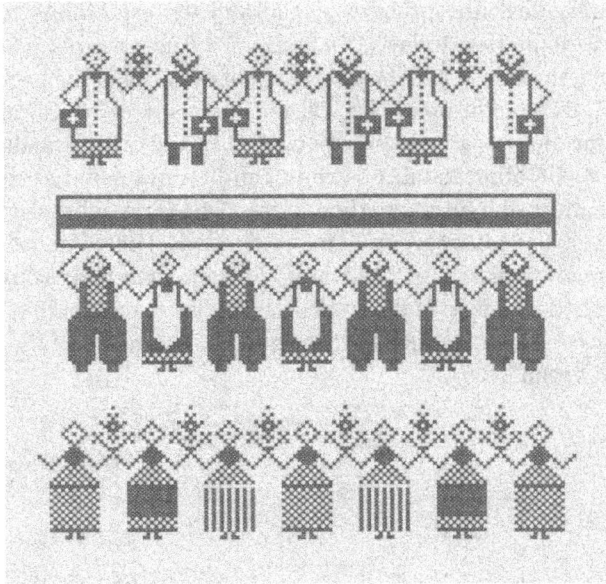

**Figure 12.2.** Rufina Bazlova, from the series "The History of Belarusian Vyzhyvanka" 2020-2021. Source: © provided by the artist. Reproduced with permission.

**Figure 12.3.** Rufina Bazlova, from the series "The History of Belarusian Vyzhyvanka" 2020-2021. Source: © provided by the artist. Reproduced with permission.

The first approach activates mass appeal by evoking traditional Belarusian folk culture. Vyshyvanka (Belarusian: Vyzhavanka) refers to cloth, usually linen, with cross- or half-stitched colorful embroidery. This form of folk art is popular across both Belarus and Ukraine and in both countries, vyshyvanka garments are worn during ceremonies, holidays, and at other moments of significance. In terms of Bazlova's installation, the use of vyshyvanka becomes a signifying language by which she outlines the symbolic boundaries of Belarus: its national aesthetics and political movements. This folk backdrop enables us to view her artworks as commentary about controversial subjects, but cast in a conservative dimension—where we would usually be least likely to find such commentary. The works are also an attempt by the artist to locate her own roots, distinct from the signs and symbols circulated by the official authorities who seek to obscure individuality for the sake of an enforced national identity, severed from organic experience and certainly cut off from critique of any kind. At the same time, the embroidered shirt turns out to be not only an internal, but also an externally recognizable system of signs, a kind of ideologeme exoticized in media. It is no coincidence that Rufina's works have appeared on the covers of numerous publications, such as *e-flux, Iskusstvo Kino (Film Art)* and others. The topicality of the scenes of protest within her embroidery might also be interpreted within the frame of mass-media as a continuation of the exoticization of Eastern Europe. In this latter interpretation, the idea of a resisting subaltern finds itself in this instance in the inclusion of flickering and transient "otherness" in the politics of identity that are projected into the asymmetrical global art and cultural industry.[7] As the theorist, curator, and artist Hito Steyerl has remarked on inequalities and Western dominance in the global art system: "Hierarchies of different cultural hybrids and genres also emerge within the framework of a global, western-dominated capitalism that is nourished by local differences."[8] To be included into the global cultural industry the "local differences" must be captured in a clear distinction which inscribes the artist and their work as "other." A "local difference" often takes form as a simple, recognizable symbol, often referring to national identity and traditional folklore.

The process of exoticization of Eastern Europe as "other" should be viewed not only aesthetically, but primarily as a dimension of political and economic exchange. As the critic Cristian Nae writes of identity politics and the role of

---

[7] Cristian Nae, *Retrospective Exhibitions and Identity Politics: The Capitalization of Criticality in Curatorial Accounts of Eastern European Art After 1989* ( Bratislava and Frankfurt am Main: Peter Lang, 2013). https://is.gd/VH8ntc.

[8] Hito Steyerl, "'Can the Subaltern speak German?' Postcolonial Critique," *Beyond Representation* (2016), 206.

capitalism in the production of East-West relations by curators after 1989: "Currently, exoticization is produced by the market, operating in accordance with the decontextualization logics, commodity fetishism, and cultural consumption."[9] In other words, Rufina Bazlova's embroidered shirts can be decoded as a simple and accessible representation of the position in Western lenses of Belarusian otherness, and specifically in its associations with the return to pre-Christian culture; while, at the same time, mirroring and playing on the surfaces of the local discourse of nostalgia, which drive formulations of the Belarusian national identity, supposedly only waiting to later be capitalized.

The second perspective is concerned with critical analysis from the point of feminist criticism, which addresses not only the struggle for women's rights but also the awareness of all forms of oppression, the disclosure and undermining of hierarchies in various forms.

Throughout the history of contemporary art, beginning in the 1970s, embroidery has not been positioned as a neutral medium, being used in feminist art to deconstruct the hierarchy of art history as an attempt at its re-assembly by the incorporation of such excluded or oppressed spheres as the applied arts. The classical art system had its own hierarchy, where painting and sculpture were placed at the top, followed by graphics and then — in descending order — photography. Embroidery, weaving, and textile art were generally excluded from the canon of "high art." Artists who consciously chose to work with such marginalized forms and techniques were in essence articulating not only their aesthetic, but primarily political position. It is not the nostalgia for her traditional roots that underlies Bazlova's art — on the contrary, she employs weaving and textiles as representative of the techniques that have, over time, been oppressed, excluded, and underprivileged within the hierarchies of art in its designation of women and women's work as subsidiary. This choice, on Rufina's part, serves her visual language by embedding it into a field of political tension.

In the case of vyshyvanka, artworks which include political commentary, but still appear within this media and its low-ranking historical place in the aesthetic hierarchy actually serve to challenge social oppression through illustration. By contrasting the visual idiom of textiles, traditionally produced by women, with images about women resisting oppression the pieces manifest an act of protest not only at the level of the choice of technique, but also in the medium's inclusion into the artistic system as folk brought into "high art." This is especially powerful because vyshyvanka is stereotyped as "female" in neo-

---

[9] Olia Sosnovskaya and Aleksei Borisionok, "Former West and New East," *Khydozhestvennyi Zhurnal* 101 (2017), 153.

conservative appropriations of it in framings of traditional femininity usually constructed from a voiceless, excluded, and invisible female laborer. As a rule, in traditional folk-art, embroidery was done by women who did not have access to education and were often illiterate. We do not know their names and stories because they could not sign their works. For them, vyshyvanka was the only visual language that they could access in a systematic way. In an interview for the Russian journal *Meduza*, the artist Rufina Bazlova mentions that, while studying the history of Belarusian ornament (the characteristic features of Belarusian traditional weavings and embroidery), she was impressed by a story about "a woman who could neither read nor write, but managed to express her feelings through embroidery — her only way of recording events."[10] The artist remarks that this episode played a crucial role in defining the message of her own works. Thus, taking into account the artist's claim to revive where other woman artists do not, or simply cannot, for lack of education, challenge the lesser evaluation of their textile forms within the art system, Bazlova's series *The History of Belarusian Vyzhavanka* can be interpreted from the point of feminist criticism as an appeal to exclusion zones and oppressed groups in order to attempt to find other ways of recording the history of the Belarusian protests, based upon the principles of egalitarianism and inclusiveness.

And finally, the third interpretation which can be applied to the analysis of Bazlova's works is their connection to modern technologies, rather than a return to traditions. In line with cyberfeminist theory, turning to needlework, embroidery or weaving, in particular, one takes aim at the actualization of the technical and political potential of traditionally female labor. In this regard, the theorist Sadie Plant argues that computer programming should be reconsidered as a traditionally female occupation. Since weaving is a complex technological process involving formulas that repeat, this is the same logic that underlies the logic of the first computers: "Weaving is the exemplary case of denigrated female craft which now turns out to be intimately connected to the history of computing and digital technologies."[11] Sadie Plant mentions Ada, who is known as one of the inventors of the mechanical computer, and can be considered the first programmer since she was the first to recognize that the machine had applications. When creating the computer, Ada relied on the structure of the loom: more specifically, on the experience of organizing and working with the Jacquard machine. The open system of such traditionally

---

[10] Lasheva, " 'I can't put up with the fact that one can lie and hate one's own people so much' The Belarusian artist Rufina Bazlova talks about her ornament of 'protest vyshavankas' with riot police and paddy wagons," Ibid.

[11] Sadie Plant, "On the Matrix: Cyberfeminist Simulations, cyberfemzine's," *Cyberfemzine.net*, Blog Post. 2021. https://cyberfemzine.net/plant_matrix/.

female crafts as weaving or embroidery is similar to the open stake in programming, which makes it possible to connect craftivism on the one hand, and the latest technologies on the other. Turning to embroidery can be seen as an innovative emancipatory strategy of "restitching" social relations, that is, of reinstalling a qualitatively different system of social and political relations.

It is interesting to note that Bazlova's cross-stitching is also a model of networks that mirror complex networks of protesters' solidarity, where neither hierarchical nor linear systems can be identified between the repeated female chromosomal connotation of X-shaped stitches (since it is difficult to rank them while embroidering according to their importance, access to power, etc.). Moreover, in order to form a pattern in cross-stitch embroidery, stitches have to coexist next to one another, which repeats the idea of nodes in the solidarity-based network model. *The History of Belarusian Vyzhavanka* might be considered as a project dedicated to an alternative social structure rooted in the principles of solidarity and cooperation, and opposed to the rigid patriarchal system of the authoritarian rule of Lukashenko's regime.

All three approaches, described here through close analysis of Rufina Bazlova's work, repeat the configurations of feminist action and intellectual problematization of women's exclusion that discursively have become the core of the aims of the wider Belarusian protests: decolonial critiques of the model of patriarchal nostalgia, which feeds on authoritarian nationalism; a process of inclusion of the excluded; and finally, the formation of alternative sociopolitical structures opposed to the patriarchal order.

## The (Im)Possibility of Feminism

The protests that began in Belarus in the summer of 2020 were marked by the active involvement of women — a phenomenon that was not limited to the female leaders of the three candidates' offices of Svetlana Tsikhanouskaya, Veronica Tsepkalo, and Maria Kolesnikova. A large number of protest actions were attended mostly by women: so-named "Women's Chains of Solidarity," as they became known among participants, flash mobs, women's marches, retirees' marches dominated by women, and the "walks" of women carrying red and white umbrellas. As many researchers note, [12] the reasons for such

---

[12] Vasil Navumau and Olga Matveieva, "The gender dimension of the 2020 Belarusian protest: Does female engagement contribute to the establishment of gender equality?" *New Perspectives* 29 (September 3, 2021), 20. Also see: Tatyana Nevedomskaya, "COVID-19 and the protests in Belarus: is Lukashenko regime worse than the pandemic?" *Deutsche Welle*, News Post. September 10, 2020. https://www.dw.com/ru/covid-19-i-protesty-v-belarusi-ne-tak-strashen-koronavirus-kak-rezhim-lukashenko/a-54869439

prominent female civic activism are rooted in Lukashenka's disregard of the pandemic, overt vote-rigging, and unmotivated violence (especially in the early days of the protests) on the part of law enforcement agencies against peaceful protesters. According to the Belarusian philosopher Olga Shparaga, it was women who shaped both the peaceful dimension of the protests and their distinctive features she defines as "wide solidarity, creativity, empathy."[13]

The female face of the protests also quickly became iconic in global media. On August 1, 2020, the cover of *The Guardian* circulated an image of a girl holding a rose in direct reference to the protests in Belarus.[14] The caption read: "Flower Power: The Women Driving Belarus' Movement for Change." On October 11, 2020, *The New York Times* published an article entitled, "In Belarus, Women Led the Protests and Shattered Stereotypes."[15] Despite the headlines about broken stereotypes and feminist revolution, researchers and analysts, unfortunately, continue to point out that women are unlikely to become the main beneficiaries after the fall of Lukashenko, since the female face of the protests does not automatically mean it is a feminist one. Despite the fact that very different women holding very different beliefs and views participated in the protests, the vast majority of them did not problematize their concerns at marches and in discussions on social networks. As the researcher Victoria Schmidt and the activist Irina Solomatina note: "The question about opportunities means that women have to develop their own goals and agendas, openly declare them, and be recognized as independent subjects of the political transition towards the much-desired democracy in today's Belarus; this remains unanswered."[16]

Among the reasons why feminist ideas, despite women's active participation in the protests, are not articulated as political demands, one should mention the patriarchal structure not only of power, but also of society, on the one hand,

---

[13] Olga Shparaga, "Women have made this protest peaceful," *Radio Svaboda*, News Post. February 3, 2021. https://www.youtube.com/watch?v=%20PtcvxW9bVWw.

[14] Will Dean, Ed., "Revolt in Belarus and the rise of Kamala Harris: the 21 August Guardian Weekly," *The Guardian Weekly*. News Post. August 21, 2020. https://www.theguardian.com/us-news/2020/aug/19/revolt-in-belarus-and-the-rise-of-kamala-harris-the-21-august-guardian-weekly?utm_referrer=.

[15] Ivan Nechepurenko, "In Belarus, Women Led the Protests and Shattered Stereotypes," *The New York Times*, News Post, October 11, 2020. https://www.nytimes.com/2020/10/11/world/europe/in-belarus-women-led-the-protests-and-shattered-stereotypes.html.

[16] Victoria Schmidt and Irina Solomatina, "Belarusian 'black box': arbitrariness of the authorities as an (un)political transit?" *Syg.ma*, News Post, September 03, 2020. https://syg.ma/@sygma/bielaruskii-chiernyi-iashchik-proizvol-vlasti-kak-nie-sostoiavshiisia-politichieskii-tranzit.

and associations with Western hegemony and coloniality of the idea of feminism both in Belarus and other post-Soviet countries, on the other. In her 2015 work of art entitled "Of our women," the Belarusian artist Olia Sosnovskaya analyzes the subordinate position of women in Belarus, which manifests itself through sometimes subtle social exchanges or official rituals. In her performance, Sosnovskaya captures male officials presenting women with flowers at award ceremonies and official meetings. She poses an important question: "How does one love another who is subordinate?"[17] This paternalistic gesture of handing over a bouquet reproduces a woman's position as "a tool of reproduction" and an aesthetic object that requires protection. The rhetorical question about subordination challenges viewers to consider how in any asymmetrical relation a woman turns out to be an apolitical figure, devoid of her own political initiative.

It is interesting to mention that at least two of the three female leaders of the Belarusian opposition demonstrators' United Headquarters – Svetlana Tsikhanouskaya and Veronica Tsepkalo – got their start in politics by standing up for their husbands. In public they often emphasized how, before their husbands went to jail and they decided to run in their places, they were both apolitical women; they constantly assured audiences that they do not hold any political ambitions or aims for future leadership of their own, but merely were "fighting in favor of their men who, for one reason or another, cannot participate in the political race."[18] This is disappointing because it de-fangs any present or future rhetoric on women's rights as worth fusing into the movement at the level of the broader opposition, but on the other hand, the women leaders' conscious distance from feminism and/or any agenda particular to women was also a pragmatic move to gain more followers.

The patriarchal nature of the authoritarian government at the official level in Belarus is painfully obvious in the jailing of Tsikhanouskaya's and Tepkalo's husbands, who, like many "disappeared" journalists or other dissenters with the regime, were stripped of their civil rights for challenging the presidency's continuation — cementation — into the next election cycle. However, one should keep in mind, that while holding power for twenty-seven years, Lukashenko has forged patriarchal systems of relations in society at every level from the top, to the middle-administrative institutions, all the way down to the unofficial relations between average citizens. This fact serves to partly explain

---

[17] Olia Sosnovskaya, "Of our women," Two channel video installation, Artist's Website, 2015. http://oliasosnovskaya.com/of-our-women/.

[18] Schmidt and Solomatina, "Belarusian 'black box': arbitrariness of the authorities as an (un)political transit?," Ibid.

how Tskihanouskaya, Tsepkalo, and Kolesnikova approached the stakes of their task: they created a modicum of immunity for themselves, even if only superficially, by making gestures to the apolitical nature of women's participation in protests. Yet, in taking this pragmatic approach, they also made a key compromise at the expense of women's rights. Tragically they lost an opportunity precisely where violence toward women was put on display in brutal crackdowns on protestors by the police. The clear illustration of the link between political repressions and domestic violence was brought forward in a major way, but there existed no language with which to capture it, neither in pre-existing social discourse, nor in the mouths of the three women leaders who failed to mention it, even when provoked by women protestors themselves — rather, they instead chose enfranchisement as their husbands' proxies. This amounted to a wider loss in the failure to adequately address the violence.

The level of violence and repression levied against the protesters is truly shocking: over 1% of the total adult population of the entire nation was detained during the demonstrations; of those jailed, over 1,000 prisoners were recognized as human rights defenders by watchdogs in the international community; thousands upon thousands of cases of police violence were recorded, along with instances of torture against those demonstrators who were arrested and held in captivity. The presence of mass violence in brutal crackdowns on protestors should be understood not only as unethical and corrupt policing, but as part of a wider systematic mechanism of control that permeates Belarusian society in all of its spheres, legitimizing and normalizing acts of violence in all relations between authorities and subordinates in a strict hierarchy. Further to this point, in parallel to statistics on political prisoners of the state and official sentences, there is also widespread evidence of domestic violence within the private sphere that is rarely, if at all, mentioned in the context of the women's demonstrations against Lukashenko, including in international media. Every third woman in Belarus is, or has been, subjected to violence at home; more than 70% of all domestic conflicts are complaints about violence against women and children.[19]

More efforts need to be made in order to understand the mechanisms behind the violence at the hands of the state in the Belarusian demonstrations, which was led by women, as NOT distinct from, but symptomatic of domestic violence. Domestic violence is a manifestation of Belarusian authoritarianism in its cyclical repetition not only through the state, but through families. The connection between political and domestic violence is the central subject of

---

[19] *Ministry of Labor and Social Protection of the Republic of Belarus,* "Stop the violence!" Official Belarusian State Public Campaign, 2020, Official Ministry Website. https:// www. mintrud.gov.by/ru/profilaktika_dom_nasiliya.

the works of such artists as: Antonina Slobodchikova; Marina Naprushkina in #дамаудобнаявбыту (convenient woman in everyday life); and Zhanna Gladko. In her installation "FORCE. FARCE. FALSE" (2020), shown at the 2021 exhibition "Every Day. Art. Solidarity. Resistance" in Kyiv, Ukraine, the artist Zhanna Gladko explores the mechanisms of power and force, comparing the political stage to interpersonal relations in the private sphere. The installation contains video documentation of rallies and the dispersal of protesters on one of Minsk's main avenues, filmed from the window of the artist's house, drawing up associations with Zhanna's personal history in her relationship to the authoritarian figure of her father. The famous slogan "The Personal Is Political" applies as the main message of this work of art in its most literal meaning. In such a context, not only the state authorities but also Belarusian society itself is seen as patriarchal and abusive, depriving a woman of her active political subjectivity mentally and physically, inserting barriers and obstacles for women to unify across the divides of domestic life, entering together into solidarity in public. The silence around domestic violence reinforces these divides; whereas articulating it, in visual or other forms, urges women to band together and seize their own power.

Along with the above silence around domestic violence, the second challenge women face in Belarus, despite their leading role in the protests against Lukashenka's dictatorship, partly stems from the colonial history of the term feminism itself. Feminism in its initial entrance into academic discourse in post-Soviet contexts in the 1990s was perceived as alien, and still often is, for several reasons. Firstly, it is seen as a single, mono-theory and political program with residuals of Soviet-era propaganda on equality, yet of a Western invasive version — an import into Belarus. In this instance, feminism is seen paradoxically as simultaneously Soviet and, above all, a mark of Soviet failure. It is rarely noted that in the early Soviet period of women's struggle for their rights they were largely ignored as "The Woman Question" did not ultimately aim at unification of genders or solidarity; rather, in practice, it was a way of ensuring separation between men and women in Soviet leadership and everyday life, with many documentations of social inequality as a result. Analyzing the history of the field of gender studies in the post-Soviet context, Elena Gapova notes that discourse and institutional engagement with the concept of gender studies arose as a part of an epistemological "Westernization," which developed through systems of academic knowledge and NGOs in close connection with Western foundations. She points out how this route of introducing feminism, perhaps unintentionally, contributed to its negative perception as well as actual inequalities it could only describe, not impact, as its foundations contained socioeconomic divisions replicated through unequal access to education by women of the working classes. This dynamic was further reflected in the separation of academia, and therefore also feminism, from studies on actual social problems (outside of pre-determined studies governed by the state), which Gapova describes as follows: "In general, feminist rhetoric was not supported by those women who had suffered most as a result of post-communist differentiation."[20] In contemporary Belarus, this observation rings true in the fact that, out of the three leaders of the demonstrations, only Maria Kolesnikova has ever openly declared herself to be a feminist. This fact emphasizes just how pervasive the allergy to feminism has become, and how deeply skeptical the majority of the population is to using this word, including its female half. Nonetheless, the Women's Solidarity Chains against Lukashenka's authoritarianism are indeed one of the most, if not the most, overt and bravest mass acts of feminism across the globe that we have yet witnessed in the twenty-first century.

The history of contemporary Belarusian art appears to indicate that the aforementioned gap is closing between perceptions of feminism as theory or methodology only, versus organized political acts that arise from within the Belarusian nation which have a widespread impact on women's rights. It is interesting to mention that the first projects concerning gender to have a major impact in the field of art did not arise from within the artistic field, but thanks to the academic initiative of the Center for Gender Studies at the European Humanities University. In 2002, the project *Women of Belarus: Creators of Culture* about Belarusian female artists emerged.[21] Since 2005 the group *Gender Route* has been installing exhibitions with the participation of Belarusian artists whose works are rethought in the feminist context.[22] Analyzing the art field of the 2000s, Tanja Setsko notes, "In recent years, gender anxiety and feminist imagery have clearly been present in the practices of Belarusian artists, but an articulate intelligible political statement can be found mainly as a part of the curatorial framework."[23] It was only in 2011-2012 when *Art Aktivist* magazine published a special issue *Feminism in Art* inviting as its editor

---

[20] Elena Gapova, "The class question of post-Soviet feminism, or on the distraction of the oppressed from the revolutionary struggle," *Gender Studies* 15 (2007), 160.

[21] *Women of Belarus: Creators of Culture* is an academic research project from 2002 that was dedicated to twelve women artists including contemporary artists. The project was initiated by the Center for Gender Studies at the European Humanities University, which is a key hub in the region for networks of research on gender in Belarus, and beyond. See: EHU Gender Studies Official Website https://en.ehu.lt/research/centers-laboratories-and-institutes/center-for-gender-studies/.

[22] *Gender Route* was started in 2005 as an interdisciplinary, subversive, feminist visual project. There were several festivals, exhibitions, research publications, and experimental public events. Official website: www.gender-route.org.

[23] Tanja Setsko, "Gender and sexual identity of Belarusian art," *Gender Studies* 22 (2017), 201.

Tamara Zlobina, a feminist activist from Ukraine and Romania, that an expert not from the Belarusian art field, but from abroad entered this symbolically laden context.[24] When considered together, the ideas of feminism, coloniality, and the patriarchial structure of Belarusian society, it is worth underlining how being a feminist is equated with taking an active political position, thus in the situation of the forcing of an apolitical status onto women in patriarchal societies, any position they take is already always rendered problematic. The essence of the issue, then, is not specific to Belarus, or to feminism, but to silencing mechanisms, conformity out of fear, and even self-censorship.

## Fragile Infrastructures

Returning to the work of Rufina Bazlova's *The History of Belarusian Vyzhavanka* and the third interpretation offered here, which approaches the use of embroidery not only as a technique, but a new technology which in the words of Sadie Plath shapes "the past, but also the future, which can change the patriarchal present."[25] Taking Plath's concept of history as a departure, we can revive past technologies for empowering women to devise a new configuration of feminism out of the Belarusian protests. This new configuration should be rooted in a definition of feminism that goes beyond prior notions of a women's movement, but primarily as an "appeal to history, including and using it as a way of being different from the traditional patriarchal call for violence."[26] In other words, it may be more apt, and certainly more useful for coalition-building, to think of feminism as an alternative way of organizing social, political, and everyday relations. This reorientation must be flexible enough to identify, but not identify with, durable authoritarian social reflexes; it should be that which opposes itself to the patriarchal model, which is always already based on unequal relations between dichotomies: subject/object, truth/lies, good/evil, man/woman, in which the secondary (feminine) category is defined as subordinate and devoid of political activity, while the primary (masculine) is stable and active.[27] In this new approach to the Belarusian context, not only do women achieve the opportunity to view from a feminist vantage point, but also

---

[24] *Art Aktivist* is an online platform for contemporary Belarusian art; it was founded on June 27, 2011, in Minsk, Belarus and was closed in 2014. Official website: artaktivist.org.

[25] Sadie Plath, "The future looms: weaving women and cybernetics," *syg.ma*, Blog Post, April 04, 2018. https://syg.ma/@lika-kareva/sedi-plant-tkatskiie-stanki-budushchiegho-tkachiestvo-zhienshchin-i-kibiernietika-1?utm_referrer=https:%2F%2Fsyg.ma

[26] Alexandra Pirich and Raluka Voynea, "Ginetsen's Manifesto. Notes on the margins of a new geological era," *Khydozhestvennyi Zhurnal* 113 (2020), 146.

[27] This idea developed in close discussion with the Belarusian artist and writer Aliaxey Talstou and the Russian feminist and philosopher Alla Mitrofanova.

to bring about such a vantage point in the first place, one which will not arrive on its own. The civic language by which to resist authoritarianism and dictatorships has proven itself to be closely intertwined with the language of women's movements. The Belarusian case mirrors mass women's protests since 2020 which align with women-led opposition marches in Poland, Iran, and the U.S. Belarus belongs in the global context, especially as 2020 also marked the pandemic around the world, which manifested in political crises and mass protests that have spawned ever-growing interest in alternative theories of the public sphere, the formation of other models of civic participation, and the drive toward the social and computer-aided technological re-organization of institutions. The twenty-first century resembles Chantal Mouffe's political field, in which feminism now means the struggle "against those forms of subordination that exist now in various types of social relationships, and not only those that are directly related to gender."[28]

The Belarusian protests of 2020-2021 have made possible a number of ways for understanding its participants along with the evolving relations between authoritarians in the region, and across the globe. Describing the actors of rallies, one can hardly define them as subjects; their existence can rather be seen as formed in antagonism with the very idea of the subject. The subject, as it has been discussed throughout this text in reference to a protesting woman, is the agent of power, who, according to Luce Irigaray, is seen as a fantasy of autogenesis and formed in inherently masculine categories. But apart from this, a subject is also formed through negation in a system of exclusions, that is, "through the creation of a domain of deauthorized subjects, presubjects, figures of abjection, populations erased from view."[29] It is precisely such systems of exclusion that the political struggle in Belarus against authoritarianism aims to dismantle. Returning again to Rufina Bazlova, who works with embroidery as a language excluded from the formal art system as the folk practice of the traditionally oppressed (woman) — the act of inclusion, in form and in content, captures the Belarusian events of 2020-2021. In the context of these mass demonstrations, which appear in Bazlova's cross-stitch in figures of police with batons in rows versus rows of people some without gender holding posters, flowers, and Molotov cocktails—it is the vast majority of the country's citizens that have become the excluded. Thus, "You do not represent us!" remains one of the most important slogans of the movement – it can be

---

[28] Chantal Mouffe, "Feminism, citizenship and radical democratic politics." In *Introduction to Gender Studies Reader, Part II* (Kharkiv: KhTSGI, St. Petersburg: Aleteya, 2001), 233.

[29] Judith Butler, "Contingent foundations: feminism and the question of 'postmodernism,'" *Introduction to Gender Studies Reader, Part II* (Kharkiv: KhTSGI, St. Petersburg: Aleteya, 2001), 248.

perceived not only in its direct reference to electoral fraud, but also as a global crisis of representative democracy, or a symptom of the fact that the majority of the country's population continues to be radically oppressed.

As have already mentioned earlier, one of the reasons for the timing of the protests exploding in 2020 was the COVID-19 pandemic, which, in converging with the elections, brought to the fore the awareness of fragility, corporeality, and transience of human existence. One of the key artistic statements about the pandemic in this context is artist Ulyana Nevzorova's political performance, which focuses on fragility not as a female quality, a breakdown, or a malfunction that needs to be fixed, but as a fundamental aspect of human existence. On October 22, 2020, Nevzorova took the subway and in one of the metro cars she unfolded a poster that said, "This Poster Might Become the Reason of My Detention." Despite being a solo performance by nature, one cannot notice any heroization in it, that is, Nevzorova does not seek to aestheticize her bodily presence — neither does she dramatize or hypertrophy the body. On the contrary, she presents her body to us in its rawest sociopolitical construction, a private self without a public one, a fragile existence. And this is where an important political shift emerges; just like in the performative poetic act "If the Past Doesn't End" (2020), where Aliaksey Talstou presents his body — his fragility, vulnerability, concern, worry, and uncertainty — by addressing the monuments and buildings of the late Soviet period. Nevzorova's fragility is the same as the spontaneous crowd populating the metro car around her; this fragility remains a distinctive feature of the Belarusian protests must be understood politically because Lukashenko still governs. Fragility is the antagonism of the patriarchal system of relations based on power and hierarchy, unequal access to privileges, and a system of inclusion/exclusion.

In the field of contemporary art today more broadly, and certainly in Belarus, the methods artists employ in their projects more often entails that they not only take the side of the oppressed, but become acutely aware of their own oppression as well. The artist may adopt the role of a mediator, exploring connections between themselves and others to trace precarity, describe common alternative social infrastructures, or offer a set of tools for new realizations. Oftentimes questions circulate around what is "utopia"? And how are the horizons of "political imagination," shaped, for example, as in the project called *The Museum of the Future* by eeefff group. The artists Dzina Zhuk and Nikolai Spesivtsev were living in one of the most underprivileged neighborhoods where they organized their project event. The event took place along with other activities organized by the residents of the area — concerts and various gatherings. The artists invited their neighbors to dwell on what a future museum to protest might look like. The goal of the protest was to initiate reflection on new alternative infrastructures, the artists write: "within the routine communication system toward building a temporary new reality that would provoke the rise of new forms of institutionality."[30] It is important that eeefff group itself was a part of the community of the locals. At the same time, they did not act as the creators of this museum, but rather as mediators of the situation, providing space for voices and interaction of a wide variety of people. Their process can be interpreted as a practice of caring for one's neighbors, which suggests thinking about joint care infrastructures. Such care practices are the basis of future infrastructures which aim at maintaining a freer human existence under a closed regime and in an unstable social environment, not through the acts of charity, services, or benefits distribution, but as a spontaneous practice of joint involvement, that is "caring is understood as a collective and structural practice not only for others but alongside them."[31]

**Figure 12.4.** Documentation of action The Museum of the Future by eeefff group, 2020. The faces in the photograph were sketched for security reasons since participation in the action could lead to detention. Cat-faces refer to the well-known protest phrase, "Belarusians are kitties." Photography by eeefff group. Source: © provided by the art group. Reproduced with permission.

---

[30] eeefff group, Interview with the author, December 9, 2020.

[31] iLiana Fokianaki, "The Bureau of Care: Introductory notes on the Care-less and Careful," *Khydozhestvennyi Zhurnal* 116 (2021), 127.

In the Belarusian protests, the recognition of fragility as a political category has become an important step on the way to building solidarities within society that have and will continue to lead to the creation of a number of care infrastructures and solidarity networks technologically facilitated through opposition networks across IT platforms: *Voice*; *Zubr*, *Honest People*; the call center Probono.by; various apps such as *Krama*; online communities and foundations aimed at helping victims such as *BySol*, etc. [32] These new infrastructures have been formed on completely different grounds than the protests themselves, being more logistically goal-oriented, horizontal, decentralized, distributed, leaderless, and flickering. But they are nonetheless reorganizing society in more self-sustaining and communicative ways that produce and ensure greater well-being and introduce the potential for serious discussions about violence, silence, and oppression, even while Lukashenko's regime (and its growing relations with Putin) still poses threats these advances.

Despite the fact that this text was written before Russia's large-scale invasion of Ukraine on February 24, 2022, as well as Belarus's complicity in this war through the provision of its territory to the Russian army, the tension in political and protest activity, described through a feminist focus, continues to persist. On the one hand, thanks to the formation of alternative horizontal protest infrastructures associated with the politicization of care, the citizens of Belarus continue to actively resist the country's involvement in the war. Belarusians resist even as the legal terms of punishment for political participation have drastically increased, for example, the death penalty has been introduced for attempted terrorism, which is interpreted very vaguely and applied broadly.

Many of these opposition technological infrastructures are made possible by thousands of contacts, social links, and networks that were forged in Belarus in 2020-2022 and now have quickly been adapted to help Ukraine. For example, since the beginning of the escalation of Russia's war on Ukraine in February 2022, the call center Probono.by, in cooperation with the Ukrainian initiatives Public Liberties Centre and EUROMAIDAN-SOS, created Probono.help. This serves as "a contact center for affected people in the war zone in Ukraine, as well as those who have moved outside of Ukraine."[33] Parallel to existing infrastructures, new ones have emerged, such as @Hajun_BY, which is

---

[32] See: The *Voice*, Official Website: https://belarus2020.org/home ; *Zubr: Civil Control of the Judiciary*, Official Website: https://zubr.cc ; *Honest People*, Official Website: https://honest-people.by/en ; *Krama*, Official Website: https://kramaapp.com/en ; Probono.by call-center, Official Website: www.probono.by.

[33] Probono.help Call Center, Official Website: www.probono.help.

organized in a horizontal and decentralized way, opposing authoritarian hierarchies.[34] It has been monitoring and tracking the activity of the armed forces on the territory of Belarus in order to warn residents of Ukraine about possible bombings. As is the case with other protest and antiwar infrastructures, ordinary residents of the country participate in @Hajun_BY. They trace the movement of military equipment and the launches of missiles and aircraft. In May 2022, over 12,000 people sent 40,000 messages. Such digital infrastructures are today important for civic engagement.

Within the cultural sector there is an important digital platform that serves a wider infrastructure for making protest statements: The International Coalition of Cultural Workers Against the War in Ukraine.[35] This is an open platform for artistic statements to be seen and heard all over the globe, and a network of solidarity that provides critical perspectives on the colonial context and the hierarchical worldviews that have led to this war. It includes international artists from Ukraine, Belarus, Turkey, India, Mexico, South Africa, Azerbaijan, Georgia, Germany, Great Britain, Croatia, Poland and other countries and territories that have themselves been war zones, or involved in war and political repression. Participants discuss issues of inequality, criticism of patriarchy and colonialism, as well as the consequences of resource economies.

On the other hand, despite all of this protest activity, the gender issue has not yet been explicitly discussed at the level of the wider political program of resistance in opposition circles in Belarus; not all women who actively participate in protests and the anti-war movement comprehend their rights. Feminist optics are still marginalized, relegated to secondary importance "for later after the war," or written off completely as unimportant. The conference of "New Belarus" which was held in Vilnius in early August 2022 and brought together representatives from almost all opposition forces in the country, is a clear confirmation of the lack of emphasis in the above-gendered terms. Of the twenty-one speakers at the conference, only five were women. The strength of every individual who participated in the Belarusian demonstrations is undeniable and the outcome is that they continue to build infrastructures for resisting authoritarianism that are resilient and lasting because they are open, horizontal, and decentralized. Structurally these infrastructures might be described as feminist or direct democracy; however, at the level of substantive articulation, feminist voices are inaudible. Women participating in the protests

---

[34] Hajun is a woodland spirit in Belarusian mythology.

[35] The International Coalition of Cultural Workers Against the War in Ukraine, Official Website, www.antiwar coalition.art.ua.

do not associate themselves with feminism; leaders do not put forward any demands in the global struggle for women's rights.

## Bibliography

*Art Aktivist*. 2011 (closed in 2014). Official Website. artaktivist.org.

Borisionok, Aleksei, Andrei Dureika, Marina Naprushkina, Sergey Shabohin, Antonina Stebur, and Maxim Tyminko, Curators. *Every Day. Art. Solidarity. Resistance.* Visual Art Exhibition. Kyiv, Ukraine: Mystetskyi Arsenal. March 25–June 6, 2021. https://artarsenal.in.ua/en/vystavka/evere-day-art-solidarity-resistance/.

Butler, Judith. "Contingent foundations: feminism and the question of 'postmodernism.'" In *Introduction to Gender Studies Reader, Part II.* Kharkiv: KhTSGI; St. Petersburg: Aleteya, 2001, 235-257.

Dean, Will, Ed. "Revolt in Belarus and the rise of Kamala Harris: the 21 August Guardian Weekly." *The Guardian Weekly.* August 21, 2020. https://www.theguardian.com/us-news/2020/aug/19/revolt-in-belarus-and-the-rise-of-kamala-harris-the-21-august-guardian-weekly?utm_referrer=. eeefff group. Interview with the author, December 9, 2020.

Fokianaki, iLiana. "The Bureau of Care: Introductory notes on the Care-less and Care-ful." *Khydozhestvennyi Zhurnal* 116 (2021).

Gapova, Elena. "The class question of post-Soviet feminism, or on the distraction of the oppressed from the revolutionary struggle." *Gender Studies* 15 (2007): 144-164.

*Gender Route*. 2005. Official Website. www.gender-route.org.

*Honest People*. Official Website. https://honest-people.by/en. The International Coalition of Cultural Workers Against the War in Ukraine. Official Website. www.antiwar coalition.art.ua.

Kopenkina, Olga. "Exhibition Review: Every Day. Art. Solidarity. Resistance. Mystetskiy Arsenal. Kyiv, Ukraine: May 3–June 6, 2021." *Afterimage* 48 (2021): 83-93.

*Krama*. Official Website. https://kramaapp.com/en.

Lasheva, Maria. " 'I can't put up with the fact that one can lie and hate one's own people so much' The Belarusian artist Rufina Bazlova talks about her ornament of 'protest vyshavankas' with riot police and paddy wagons." *MEDUZA.io.* August 18, 2020. https://meduza.io/feature/2020/08/18/ya-rosla-s-oschuscheniem-chto-lukashenko-navsegda.

*Ministry of Labor and Social Protection of the Republic of Belarus.* "Stop the violence!" Official Belarusian State Public Campaign, 2020, Official Ministry Website. https://www.mintrud.gov.by/ru/profilaktika_dom_nasiliya.

Mouffe, Chantal. "Feminism, citizenship and radical democratic politics." In *Introduction to Gender Studies Reader, Part II.* Kharkiv: KhTSGI; St. Petersburg: Aleteya, 2001, 214-234.

Nae, Cristian. *Retrospective Exhibitions and Identity Politics: The Capitalization of Criticality in Curatorial Accounts of Eastern European Art After 1989.* Bratislava and Frankfurt am Main: Peter Lang, 2013. https://is.gd/VH8ntc.

Navumau, Vasil, and Olga Matveieva. "The gender dimension of the 2020 Belarusian protest: Does female engagement contribute to the establishment of gender equality?" *New Perspectives* 29 (September 3, 2021): 20-45.

Nechepurenko, Ivan. "In Belarus, Women Led the Protests and Shattered Stereotypes." *The New York Times*. News Post. October 11, 2020. https://www.nytimes.com/2020/10/11/world/europe/in-belarus-women-led-the-protests-and-shattered-stereotypes.html.

Nevedomskaya, Tatyana. "COVID-19 and the protests in Belarus: is the Lukashenko regime worse than the pandemic?" *Deutsche Welle*. News Post. September, 10 2020. https://www.dw.com/ru/covid-19-i-protesty-v-belarusi-ne-tak-strashen-koronavirus-kak-rezhim-lukashenko/a-54869439.

Pirich, Alexandra, and Raluka Voynea. "Ginetsen's Manifesto: Notes on the margins of a new geological era." *Khydozhestvennyi Zhurnal* 113 (2020), 146–155.

Plant, Sadie. "On the Matrix: Cyberfeminist Simulations, cyberfemzine's." *Cyberfemzine.net*. Blog Post. 2021. https://cyberfemzine.net/plant_matrix/.

Plath, Sadie. "The future looms: weaving women and cybernetics." *syg.ma*, Blog Post. April 04, 2018. https://syg.ma/@lika-kareva/sedi-plant-tkatskiie-stanki-budushchiegho-tkachiestvo-zhienshchin-i-kibiernietika-1?utm_referrer=https:%2F%2Fsyg.ma

*Probono.by*. Official Website: www.probono.by.

*Probono.help*. Official Website: www.probono.help.

Razor, Sasha. "Rufina Bazlova: The History of Belarusian Vyzhavanka." *Chrysalis Mag*. Blog Post. February 17, 2021. https://chrysalismag.by/project/rufina-bazlova-istoriya-belarusskoy-vyzhivanki

Schmidt, Victoria, and Irina Solomina. "Belarusian 'black box:' arbitrariness of the authorities as an (un)political transit?" *Syg.ma*. News Post. September 03, 2020. https://syg.ma/@sygma/bielaruskii-chiernyi-iashchik-proizvol-vlasti-kak-nie-sostoiavshiisia-politichieskii-tranzit.

Setsko, Tanja. "Gender and sexual identity in Belarusian art." *Gender Studies* 22 (2017): 190-204.

Shparaga, Olga. "Women have made this protest peaceful." *Radio Svaboda*. News Post. February 3, 2021. https://www.youtube.com/watch?v=%20Ptcvx W9bVWw.

Sosnovskaya, Olia. "Of our women." Two channel video installation. Artist's Website, 2015. http://oliasosnovskaya.com/of-our-women/.

Sosnovskaya, Olia, and Aleksei Borisionok. "Former West and New East." *Khydozhestvennyi Zhurnal*, no. 101 (2017): 148-155.

Steyerl, Hito. "'Can the Subaltern speak German?' Postcolonial Critique." *Beyond Representation* (2016): 204-207.

*The Voice*. Official Website. https://belarus2020.org/home.

*Women of Belarus: Creators of Culture*. 2002. Center for Gender Studies at the European Humanities University. Official Website. https://en.ehu.lt/research/centers-laboratories-and-institutes/center-for-gender-studies/.

*Zubr: Civil Control of the Judiciary*. Official Website: https://zubr.cc.

# Chapter 13

# "You are not alone!" Poland's New Feminism and New Feminist Art

Agnieszka Graff

### Abstract

In one effect of the so-called Black Protests (2016-2018), a new collective entity has emerged in the Polish public sphere, in the collective imagination, and in the realm of art: angry women. The new feminism has broken a number of silences in Polish culture: around abortion, gendered violence, women's sexuality. It is audaciously anti-clerical, but not anti-religious – many participants are Catholics who are outraged by the political activity of the Catholic Church. This text examines the historical dynamic which led to the emergence of this mass-scale rebellion: the rise of populist nationalism, and the resulting breakdown of the long-lasting "compromise" between liberal elites and the Church. Next, it looks at the manifestations of the newly formed feminist consciousness in the realm of art. Among the works examined are Agata Zbylut's "Caviar Patriot" and Liliana Zeic's "Self-Portrait with a Rented Man," performances of The Witches' Choir, the radical artivism of The Black Rags Collective, and "memes" by Marta Frej. The new wave of feminist art is examined as a symptom of a deep political and cultural divide, one of the fronts of Poland's ongoing culture war.

**Keywords**: feminism, radicalism, Poland, art, Catholic Church, nationalism, political affect

*\*\**

In July 2018, shocking messages appeared on the buildings of the Metropolitan Curia in Warsaw: "Murderers!"; "THIS IS MY BLOOD AND THIS IS MY BODY – HANDS OFF! MITOCHONDRIAL EVE." And on the pavement: "NO MORE HELL FOR WOMEN." Under pressure from the Church, Poland's Parliament (Sejm) had recently admitted for deliberation the "stop abortion" project, a law pushed by the religious fundamentalists, which included an almost complete ban on abortions (including cases of severe fetal defects). The messages had been written hurriedly, in red and black spray paint. Their very appearance on a Church building breached a powerful cultural taboo, and the content of one of them constituted outright blasphemy: the words of Christ were paraphrased and attributed to humanity's hypothetical common ancestral woman, making her a defender of the women tormented by the Polish Church. The history of the Roman Catholic Church, recognized in Poland as the source and guardian of national tradition, was audaciously juxtaposed with the much older and more universal history. After all, the hypothetical Eve lived about 200,000 years ago.

The anonymous feminists' attack on church buildings was deemed more than just an act of vandalism – it was considered sacrilege. A few people spoke out in approval, suggesting this act constituted an appropriate response on the part of the women to the political involvement of the Church, to the war it was declaring on women by pushing through a complete ban on abortion. The feminist graffiti can be read as retaliation: an invasion of Church territory in response to the invasion of the women's bodies that the Church was enabling. My own response was mixed. At first, this event shocked and amazed me: a border had been crossed that would have been intransgressible just a year or two before. Soon, however, I experienced a strange sense of relief, not unlike the feeling that accompanies a coming storm after a muggy, stifling day. Yes, I thought, it had been hanging in the air, it was inevitable. But what was "it"? Let us call it a rupture, the angry breaching of a contract. In recent years, a new collective entity has emerged in the Polish public sphere, in the collective imagination, and in the realm of art: that of furious women. This new collective subject is angry, shameless, audacious, and loud. Importantly, for some time now, it has ceased to be perceived as marginal or weird. It may arouse indignation, but it is no longer being dismissed. A feminist rebellion is taking place at the very heart of Polish culture, where up until now, there had been silence – in the place where religion, national identity and corporeality meet. Until now, few had even peered into this space; now, all of a sudden, there was an uproar. It cannot be drowned out or silenced. Something has changed irreversibly. In order to understand the meaning of this change, and to accurately decipher its manifestations in art, we need to re-examine a chapter of Polish history.

For two decades following the political changes of 1989, the subject of gender equality was neglected in the public sphere and referred to as a mere distraction from real politics. People joked that the whole idea of gender equality was an abstraction that interested only a small number of feminists in Poland, while "normal women" were occupied with "real life." If disputes over women's rights were reported in the media, it was because the European Union was exerting pressure in this area – demanding legal regulations on discrimination in the workplace, for example. There was a consensus concerning the EU – this was a serious matter. First, we aspired to it, then we tried to adapt to it. After all, it was said, we were "returning" to Europe, a momentous historical process. And Europe had this strange obsession with equality, so we had to surrender – or rather, pretend to surrender. For there was a complication: the Catholic Church had clear views on this matter that happened to be contrary to those of the EU. It was under the pressure of the Church that an anti- abortion law was introduced in 1993; though one of the most restrictive in Europe, it was euphemistically labelled a "compromise." This compromise was not to be publicly discussed, and feminists who tried to do so were denounced as insane. Why? In the period leading up to the accession referendum in 2003, there was a clear message that the Church should not be angered, because without its support, Poland would not enter the E.U. Following the accession, the Church was still not to be angered because – so it was believed – without its blessing, liberal democracy in Poland would come to an end. Thus, the whole topic of gender – not only the reproductive rights of women, but also domestic violence, political representation, and LGBTQ+ rights – was silenced for many years pursuant to an unwritten contract. The law of the land remained in place: one cannot upset the Church because everything falls apart without it.

Today, we know that the calculation was erroneous. No one dared upset the Church, yet everything has fallen apart. We are witnessing the death of the young Polish democracy and the destruction of all the achievements of the Third Polish Republic. This is happening with the full approval of the Church; meanwhile, feminists have taken on a key role in defending democracy. This unexpected shift in roles has had profound consequences for the collective consciousness of Polish women, including those who do not identify as feminists.

During the bizarre "compromise" between nationalist Catholicism and European liberalism, the voice of female rebellion remained marginal, but it was nonetheless present in literature, art, scholarship, and occasionally also in the public sphere. It was the voice of opposition to the universally accepted "normality," a voice from the shadows. At times, feminism became a major talking point: a 1995 novel by Izabela Filipiak, *Absolute Amnesia* (*Absolutna amnezja*) caused quite a stir, the visual art of Katarzyna Kozyra and Anna Baumgart aroused interest, and Dorota Nieznalska's 2001 installation "Passion" ("Pasja"), caused a scandal and led to a court case that was widely spoken about in Poland.[1] The key figure is the cultural historian Maria Janion, who

---

[1] See: Izabela Filipiak, *Absolutna amnezja* (Absolute Amnesia), (Poznań: Obserwator, 1995); Dorota Nieznalska, "Pasja" (Passion), Artist website, 2001. https://nieznalska.com/; Katarzyna Kozyra, Artist website, http://katarzynakozyra.pl/en/; Krzysztof Jurecki, Ed.,"Anna Baumgart: biography," *Culture.pl*, 2004, https://culture.pl/en/artist/anna-baumgart.

introduced feminism into the discourse of Polish intelligentsia.[2] Janion also provided patronage for an important exhibition, *The Polish Woman: Medium, Shadow, Image* (Polka. Medium, cień, wyobrażenie) at the Center for Contemporary Art in Warsaw in 2005 – a powerful art show which brought contemporary feminist art into the history of Polish culture. Another extremely important work is the book-length poem by Bożena Keff entitled *On Mother and Fatherland* (*Utwór o matce i ojczyźnie*) published in 2009, in which the question of gender is interwoven with Polish-Jewish history and the grotesqueness of national martyrdom myths is ruthlessly exposed.[3]

From time to time, there had been flashes of energy around feminism in the public sphere. The so-called "Manifas" – annual feminist demonstrations taking place on International Women's Day across Poland from 2000 onwards – garnered media attention and radicalized younger women with provocative slogans and street performances. The Women's Party and the Congress of Polish Women were established (in 2007 and 2009, respectively) and brought talk of women's rights into the mainstream. Literary critic and activist Katarzyna Bratkowska caused an uproar in 2013 when she declared that she was pregnant and intended to get an abortion on Christmas Eve. Yet, there was no mass women's movement. Each of these political, media and artistic events – and many others which I have omitted here – was an isolated case in the collective perception. It was not clear for whom Polish feminism was speaking, and there were many indications that it spoke only for itself. There was no female "people," no demos, no collective body to which these statements and events could refer. But there was the unwritten agreement on the special role of the Church in Poland, and on women's silence – that unfortunate "compromise" which concerned not only abortion, but everything related to sex and sexuality that also has a political dimension. This agreement meant that the female "people" could not be construed as a fully-fledged subject of collective life. Women's claims to full rights simply did not fit into the official narrative of "Poland's return to Europe." Feminism remained a cultural niche – creative, vibrant, fascinating to watch, but marginal and having little impact on the course of history.

Somewhere around 2013, the "compromise" was terminated. The contract was broken by the Church, which openly cut itself off from liberal democracy,

---

[2] Maria Janion, *Kobiety i duch inności* (*Women and the Spirit of Dissidence*), (Warszawa: Sic!, 1996).

[3] Of the works mentioned here, it is the only one to have been translated into English. See: Bożena Keff, *On Mother and Fatherland*, translated by Benjamin Paloff and Alissa Valles (Cheshire, MA: MadHat Press 2017).

and entered into an alliance with the populist, anti-European right. Left-wing commentators had been observing the Church's anti-liberal drift for years, but for the liberal mainstream, this only became clear during the conservative campaign against so-called "gender ideology." Initiated by the Church, it grew into a hate campaign pursued by the populist right. This campaign attacked not only feminists, LGBTQ+ communities and sex educators, but also the entire liberal West, which is overtly demonized in anti-gender discourse as a "civilization of death." Poland plays a special role in this story: it is supposed to be the mainstay of Christian values, the last frontier for "family values." The anti-gender campaign has fomented social fears and antagonisms, strengthening not only homophobia and sexism, but also aggressive nationalism, which became a collective obsession during the refugee crises along the Belarusian border in 2015 and 2021. Attacks on gender equality activists are still combined with the demonization of refugees, spreading the message that gender equality weakens Poland, turning women into feminists and men into pathetic wimps, and that Poland needs to defend itself against the double-edged threat: the invasion of dark-skinned barbarians from the South, enabled by the plague of decadence from the West.[4]

This is, more or less, the right-wing vision of the world and Poland, which, in the autumn of 2015, led to the victory of the Law and Justice party (PiS) and allowed them to demolish the independent judiciary with impunity by 2018. Whereas in the 1990s and the first decade of the twenty-first century, the liberal elites were convinced that without subservience to the Church there would be no such thing as a European Poland, in 2018 (if not earlier) the same elites were willing to accept a different and more accurate version of recent history. In this narrative, it was the many years of subservience to the Church that led to the defeat of democracy, and may be about to lead us out of the E.U. The Church betrayed Polish democracy—this idea, which had previously resounded only on the margins of public debate, finally reached the awareness of the circle, which had long considered the alliance of the state with the altar as indispensable.[5]

---

[4] For an in-depth analysis of the anti-gender campaigns as a transnational phenomenon, see: Agnieszka Graff and Elżbieta Korolczuk, *Anti-Gender Politics in the Populist Moment* (London: Routledge, 2021). Chapter three of this book is focused on developments in Poland.

[5] An interesting example of this kind of analysis – angry and bitter – is Paweł Wroński, "Dokąd zmierza Kościół, który zdradził III RP" (Where the Church is headed, now that it has betrayed Poland), *Gazeta Świąteczna*, News Article, June 2, 2018. Wroński writes: "The vast majority of the hierarchical Polish Church has backed the political forces that aim to destroy the state, despite having co-founded this state in 1989 and despite supporting its key choices during the times of John Paul II. Why? Perhaps because the Church has

Consequently, the topic of gender unexpectedly found itself at the heart of the struggle for Polish democracy, with feminists widely recognized as key political players. On 25 July 2018, the front page of *Gazeta Wyborcza* — the liberal-left daily originally run by former dissident Adam Michnik — featured a photograph of female activists from the Women's Strike protesting outside the Senate against the law destroying the independence of the judiciary. The heroine of the protests against the attack on the independence of the courts was Klementyna Suchanow, a writer and feminist organizer associated with the Women's Strike. The image can be seen as emblematic of the configuration in the Polish political and cultural imaginary. Radical women — previously dismissed as mere trouble-makers — were now looked to with hope, as defenders of democracy. The fight for women's rights was now the same as the fight for democracy. After two decades of silencing, disrespect and ridicule, we have a female "people," a social movement capable of extremely efficient mobilization, well-connected, colorful and diverse.

Thus, the violent offensive of the right-wing in alliance with the Church had caused a new political subject to appear in Polish culture: that of furious women. This "people" has no leader, although several important and respected frontwomen have emerged. It also has no cohesive ideology or world vision. It is anti-clerical, but not anti-religious – many of its participants are Catholics who are outraged by the political attitude of the Church hierarchy. When I say we are dealing with a feminist "people," I am thinking of something more than a collective body ready to go out onto the streets. It is a community of the imagination, a revolution of images, texts, and songs. New phenomena have appeared in culture — not only individual works or trends in art, but also a certain language of expression, new forms of reception. The "black protests" that took place in 2016-2018 established a new female community of the imagination, expanding the space of what can be thought and said in Poland, including in the field of art.

What, then, is the nature of the newly emergent female subject that speaks to the female "people"? It is no longer the ironic artist, the theory-savvy researcher, or the solitary author of dissertations on gender equality, but a witch, a Cassandra, an avenger speaking on behalf of "ordinary women" who have run out of patience. The angry art of angry women draws on earlier achievements of Polish feminists but departs from them in an essential way. It is more radical, more embroiled in context, bolder, but also more egalitarian — it is pointedly directed towards a mass audience. It is remarkable how often it

---

received everything it has asked for from the Third Polish Republic." https://wyborcza. pl/magazyn/7,124059,23480424,dokad-zmierza-kosciol-ktory-zdradzil-iii-rp.html.

borrows from, appropriates, and transforms national symbolism.[6] However, it also aspires to universality — it talks about the global (not just the Polish) alliance of nationalism with religious fundamentalism, about the refugee crisis, and about ecology. These female artists draw strength from the long tradition of female anger, consciously referring to witches, revolutionaries, and avengers. To the forces of nature. To humanity. And yes, to Mitochondrial Eve.

The close relationship between the culture of female protest and the new women's art scene was brought to my attention by the exhibition *Polish Women, Patriots, Rebels (Polki, patriotki, rebeliantki)*, which I saw in Poznań's Arsenał Gallery in the fall of 2017.[7] As pointed out by the curator, Izabela Kowalczyk, the included works are immersed in the Polish political and cultural imaginary, but they do not succumb to its logic. They consistently apply a strategy of "appropriations": with angry irony, they adopt national symbolism for the female cause. They not only reveal the exclusion of women from the collective body known as "the nation," but also mock the grotesque flexing of manly muscles that occupies the center of the national imagination. An excellent example of this strategy is Agata Zbylut's "Caviar Patriot" (Kawiorowa patriotka) also known as "Suknia" (Gown) — the piece features a ball gown made of football fan scarves, which is a symbol of the nationalist aggravation of recent years.[8] To a large extent, this artwork's power results from the care with which it was made. With its extravagant elegance, the gown is clearly mocking football fan culture by suggesting that the rough masculinity and combativeness of the scarves is entangled in consumer culture, fashion, and gadgetry.

Another example of feminist appropriation of patriotic motifs and nationalist consumer culture is a work by Liliana Zeic (Piskorska) entitled "Self-Portrait with a Rented Man, AKA: I'm a Polish Man So I Have Polish Duties" (Autoportret z pożyczonym mężczyzną, aka: Jestem Polakiem więc mam obowiązki

---

[6] For a detailed analysis, see: Agnieszka Graff, "Claiming the Shipyard, the Cowboy Hat, and the Anchor for Women: Polish Feminism's Dialogue and Struggle with National Symbolism," *East European Politics and Societies* 33, no. 2 (2019), 472-496.

[7] The exhibition was curated by the feminist art historian Izabella Kowalczyk, and came with an edited volume containing insightful articles edited by her; See: Izabella Kowalczyk, Ed. *Polki, Patriotki, Rebeliantki . . . Sztuka feministyczna dzisiaj* (Polish Women, Patriots, Rebels... Feminist Art Today), (Poznań: Arsenał, 2017). Also see: Izabella Kowalczyk, Curator, Polki, Patriotki, Rebeliantki . . . *Sztuka feministyczna dzisiaj,* Visual Art Exhibition. Poznań: Arsenał Gallery, September 8–October 8, 2017. https://arsenal.art.pl/en/exhibition/polish-women-patriots-rebels/.

[8] Zbylut's work can be viewed at the artist's website: https://www.agatazbylut.com/Article/kawiorowa-patriotka.

polskie).[9] The artist, who openly identifies as a lesbian and is known for her lesbian art projects, captures an image of herself in a bed made up with commercially available "patriotic" bed sheets and a man with a shaved head sporting patriotic tattoos. The combination of the grandiose symbols with the idleness of the pose between the sheets, and the idea that a nationalist can be "rented," provide a comic effect. But the picture also contains an element of terror. The ironic gaze of the artist seems to ask: will this camouflage guarantee survival in today's Poland? Who is this man, where can he be rented, and what is the price for which he provides lesbians with protection? The photograph is part of the 2016 series "Methods of Camouflage in Contemporary Poland" (Sposoby kamuflażu we współczesnej Polsce), whose intention, according to the artist herself, is to question the monopoly of the extreme right on patriotic symbols. Interestingly, the work succumbed to the logic of cultural appropriation when it became a popular online meme: many commentators failed to see its critical edge and assumed it was an advertisement for the bedding used in the picture. It is hard to say whether this response demonstrates the success of the work or constitutes its defeat. It can be argued that the "camouflage" worked all too well, confirming the diagnosis that in today's Poland, the only widely understood language is the language of nationalism.

Works such as Zbylut's "Gown" and Zeic's "Self-Portrait" function in feminist circulation as signs of resistance against male nationalist hegemony. They are equally audacious as, for example, the ironically patriotic banners appearing during women's protests inscribed with "Cursed wombs" (Macice wyklęte), "Fighting Polish Woman" (Polka Walcząca) and—echoing the national anthem — "The Polish woman is not yet lost" (Jeszcze Polka nie zginęła).

How is this female "people" represented in the theatre? In recent years I have witnessed several important performances referring to the current struggle for women's rights. One of them is Oliver Frljić's *The Curse* (*Klątwa*), another is Jolanta Janiczak's *Wives of the State, Whores of the Revolution, or Maybe Learned Ladies* (*Żony Stanu, dziwki rewolucji, a może i uczone białogłowy*). The intensity of the political engagement of these performances is unprecedented in Polish theater. In both cases, the audience is called on to participate in the artists struggle against patriarchy, to make their experiences and views public. At some point during *Wives of The State*, the auditorium is transformed into a

---

[9] For a profile of the artist Liliana Piskorska, see: Agnieszka Sural, "Liliana Piskorska 17.12.1988." Translated by Patryk Grabowski, *Culture.pl*, Blog Post, October 2017, Updated by HSz April 2020. The artwork under discussion can be found on the artist Liliana Piskorska's official website: http://lilianapiskorska.com/en/praca/methods-of-camouflage-in-contemporary-poland/.

street demonstration, and the audience, equipped with banners, walk out of the theatre. In one of the scenes of *The Curse*, an actress — her exposed stomach bearing the message "1,000 zlotys" — enters into a dialogue with the audience. She asks the women present to declare if they have had an abortion, then claims that many women have not owned up and accuses them of hypocrisy. In the end, she shows an ultrasound and says that she's planning to have an abortion in the Netherlands.

This kind of audience participation is effective, but it remains theatrical. To my knowledge, it is only the musical performance of The Witches' Choir (Chór Czarownic) that has caused audience members to emerge from their role as viewers and to feel part of a political and simultaneously creative community. The musical performance of the Choir owes its emotional strength to a bold combination of music, theater and poetry, but also, I think, to the participation of people with no professional experience, enthusiasts. The majority of the Choir's members have never studied singing. In their day-to-day lives they work in various places. Inclusion in this project is for them the adventure of a lifetime.

The axis of the entire undertaking, and the main source of the fury and pathos it projects, is the way in which the condition of women in contemporary Poland is combined with a dark chapter of women's history. The Choir was formed in 2016, on the initiative of activist and artist Ewa Łowżył, as part of a social campaign to restore the memory of women killed in Poland for alleged "witchcraft" (and especially to commemorate the burning of the first Polish "witch" in 1511 in Chwaliszewo near Poznań). The lyrics are written by Malina Prześluga-Delimata and the songs are composed by Zbyszek Łowżył, Patryk Lichota and Malwina Paszek. As the creators state in the description of their show: "We don't see this project as an opportunity to beat our breast for the blindness and atrocities of five hundred years ago. It is an attempt to confront history and folk superstitions with the present times in which atrocities, although manifested in a subtler way, are still committed. It is also an occasion to stop and take a look at one another—our culture, diversity, our everyday eccentricities and obsessions."[10]

The hateful comments that appear under video clips of the Choir's performances include accusations of paganism, demonism and sectarianism. One reviewer accurately described the Choir's performance as "a bizarre, dark oratorio."[11]

---

[10] See: Chór Czarowic (Witches' Choir), "Pieśni Czarownic," Performance, Teatr Polski w Poznaniu, May 5, 2017. http://teatr-polski.pl/spektakle/czarownica/.

[11] Juliusz Tyszka, "Czarownice dają czadu" (The Witches Rock), *Teatralny.pl*, News Post, June 14, 2017. https://teatralny.pl/recenzje/czarownice-daja-czadu,2012.html

Indeed, the Choir strives to establish a female sacrum in a Catholic country whose culture persistently excludes women from the sacred sphere. A dozen or so women stand before us; their figures emerge from the darkness. They are of various ages and have very different bodies – from the conventionally beautiful to the explicitly non-normative. The outfits – or rather, the lack of outfit – is key. The Choir's members are demonstratively "undressed," wearing only skin-colored cotton petticoats. They stand in a tight formation, strong emotions showing on their faces: anger, determination, despair. After a piercing instrumental introduction, we hear around a dozen songs that seem to be sung in a trance. Each of the witches' songs is a powerful feminist poem, but it is not only the lyrics that are striking – it is also the extraordinary intensity of the performance, which resonates with the psychedelic music.

Each performance of the Choir is a spectacular, angry curse directed towards the patriarchy – a refusal to participate in the conventional game of femininity, the denunciation of duty. Witches from the past materialize as modern Polish women and speak – or rather, shout – in a unified, inspired voice. It is a voice that is incompatible with the endless demands on women, incompatible with accusations, with patriarchal obligation, with disregard, and with the anguish of everyday life:

I'm on fire, and still/
I'm on fire, and still/
There's dinner to cook/
Children to raise/
Nails to bite/
Elbow-deep in laundry/
Make yourself a deity/
Potatoes and cabbage/
Non-fat yoghurt/
A pill for the headache/
The butter's finished/
Be nice, be nice . . . be nice, be nice.[12]

The witches' songs are not all complaints about women's fate. There is also a dark fantasy about rebellion, escape, and sometimes revenge. The show's opening song, "Chwaliszewo" is an eruption of swearing and blasphemy sung from beyond the grave. The song "Pack of Women" (Wataha kobiet) projects a strange, oneiric vision in which we participate from within, adopting the perspective of a group of hounded, wronged females at the threshold of

---

[12] Chór Czarowic (Witches' Choir), "Już płonę" (I'm on Fire), Performance, *Chór Czarowic YouTube Channel*, October 9, 2017. https://www.youtube.com/watch?v=7yaG7cvypTg.

awakening. They have been fleeing persecution for too long now and are about to start pursuing their torturer: "We dream of escape . . . The pack of women who know how to defend themselves... Is still escaping but will one day chase you off."[13]

Ewa Łowżył has commented in an interview on the therapeutic dimension of the Choir's activities: "The ability to sing and hear such simple, distinct songs often becomes an act of collective therapy – both for the group and for the listeners. As we know, once something that is named and spoken out loud, it loses its negative charge: suddenly, it turns out that we all have similar fears and experiences."[14] The healing power of singing is undeniable, but I would argue that – due to the context – the political dimension is stronger than the therapeutic one. During the Choir's performances, audience members spontaneously stand up and join in the singing, shouting and dancing. This is accompanied by extremely intense emotions: a sense of community, as well as both dread and hope. Women embrace each other, hold hands, weep.

How does this relate to the new wave women's movement? Arguably, the relationship is one of symbiosis. The Choir was formed a few months before the Polish Women's Strike; subsequently, one of their songs "Your Power" (Twoja Władza) became the movement's anthem. In 2017 they performed during the Women's Congress in Poznań and received a standing ovation.[15] However, their work cannot be reduced to public service activity. The Choir is an autonomous artistic project likely to endure and evolve independently of the Black Protests. In the meantime, it is working in harmony with women's mobilizations, expressing and at the same time strengthening female rebellion. It is co-creating the new collective consciousness, the suddenly expanded imagination and emotionality. The witches from Poznań conclude each performance with a rhythmic, poignant protest song, which was also sung during the protests:

Your power
Your faith
My fault

---

[13] Chór Czarowic (Witches' Choir)."Wataha kobiet" (Pack of Women). Performance. *Chór Czarowic YouTube Channel*. September 21, 2017. https://www.youtube.com/watch?v=e6WrqyH BAAs.

[14] For an interview with Ewa Łowżył, see: Aleksandra Skowrońska, "Rzeczywistość nas dogania" (Reality is catching up with us), *Dziennik Teatralny*. 7 July 7, 2017. http://www.dziennikteatralny.pl/spektakle/piesni-czarownic.html.

[15] For the group's performance at the 9th Women's Congress, See: Chór Czarowic (Witches' Choir), "Chór Czarowic at the 9th Women's Congress," Poznań, *Chór Czarowic YouTube Channel*, September 2017. https://www.youtube.com/watch?v=xJyzTlSsuxU.

My punishment
My world is in your hands
You've had me over a barrel for a million years!
Look me straight in the eyes
I am your mother, sister
I am your daughter, wife
I stand with my head held high
A million of us are standing now, none of us are afraid
I stand, I shout, I stand, I shout . . .[16]

A very different, more direct symbiosis with the culture of the black protests comes into play in the case of the artivist collective Czarne Szmaty (Black Rags, CzSz), who, in their own words, "work within what is broadly defined as performative art – performance, street art and happenings."[17] Their best-known action, entitled "Greetings from Lesbos" (*Pozdrowienia z Lesbos*) took place on June 9, 2018 during the Equality Parade in Warsaw (i.e., the annual LGBTQ+ march). Three young women set up an improvised beach in the middle of the Charles de Gaulle Roundabout, one of the busiest intersections in the capital. Crucially, since 2002, this spot has housed the installation "Greetings from Aleje Jerozolimskie" (Pozdrowienia z Alej Jerozolimskich), the famous Warsaw palm tree created by feminist artist Joanna Rajkowska. With Rajkowska's permission, CzSz transformed her project by placing a green sign displaying the word "Lesbos" under the palm tree. The sign resembled the official large road signs used to mark towns across Poland. They set up deckchairs and spent several hours there dressed in bathing suits and reading lesbian poetry. The reactions were wide-ranging: some passers-by gave them a friendly wave, others thought they were out of their minds, cars honked, police officers stayed in sight, but did not intervene. Pictures from the performance made by the collective's photographer Pat Mic were circulated online and sent to the media, causing amusement, indignation and numerous discussions. Some commentators objected to the fact that refugees had been omitted from the performance. One of the artists, Karolina Maciejaszek, offered the following response:

---

[16] Chór Czarowic (Witches' Choir). "Twoja władza" (Your Power). Performance. *Chór Czarowic YouTube Channel.* October 2, 2017. https://www.youtube.com/watch?v=UCYH 3O_e9DI.

[17] The group's activities are presented on their Facebook page, Czarne Szmaty (Black Rags). https://www.facebook.com/czarneszmaty/. For an extended study of their work, with photographs from key performances, see: Katarzyna Niedurny, "Czarny Album," *Dialog* 9 (September 2021), 778. https://www.dialog-pismo.pl/w-numerach/czarny-album.

We all have our Lesbos. For me, this action has a surreal character. The sign is like one from a Polish village, and we've put it on a roundabout in Warsaw. We were thinking about Lesbos itself in two dimensions. The first association is a cultural one: the connotation with the island of Sappho, which has always been associated with female homosexuality, but also with the space of sisterhood and female culture. The second association relates to the present. Nowadays, Lesbos evokes the tragedy of refugees. Here we had some doubts. I wouldn't equate lesbians in Poland with refugees on Lesbos. That would be a misappropriation.[18]

Black Rags had appeared in public space long before *Lesbos* made them famous. The group was created on October 3, 2016 in Warsaw; its members are Marta Jalowska, Karolina Maciejaszek, Monika Sadkowska, and Magda Staroszczyk. Their first action was reckless and theatrical. It took place during the Women's Strike known as Black Monday: the group blocked street traffic in Warsaw, standing across multiple streets with a several-meter-long black banner displaying huge letters in white that read "BORDER OF CONTEMPT" (GRANICA POGARDY). Asked about their motivation, they explained: "We felt the need to finally say: enough. Enough of treating women like dirt, we're setting the border right here."[19] This happening drew my attention because it was so bold and poetic. The Rags used a trope that is rarely adopted in art: a metaphor gone literal, or visual pun, which can give a ludicrous effect, but in this case, happened to be an extremely strong means of conveying political meaning. The silent act of holding the "rag" was an expression of resistance, but also of powerlessness and despair in the face of violence. There is an element of absurdity and bitter irony in this literalism. Where is the border of contempt towards women? Here, at this crossroads, on this street. Who determines it? We, the women holding the black rag, the group known as The Black Rags. The group's name, it is worth noting, is a feminist appropriation of one of the vilest, most misogynist, contemptuous terms used against women in Poland. "Szmata" as a term of abuse is the equivalent of "whore" or "slut." Of course, it was impossible to hold the "border" for long — impatient drivers began to beep their horns, the police intervened, and they had to withdraw, moving the border to another busy spot. And so the "border of contempt" roamed the city

---

[18] Sistrum, "Czarne Szmaty. Razem znaczymy więcej niż każda osobno" (Black Rags: Together we mean more than each one of us separately), *Akulturalgbtq.pl*, Interview, July 2018. http://akulturalgbtq.pl/wpcontent/uploads/2018/07/aaakulturalnik_sistrum_CzarneSzmaty.pdf.

[19] Karolina Domagalska, "Nie jesteś sama" (You are not alone), *Wysokie Obcasy*, October 28, 2017. https://www.wysokieobcasy.pl/wysokie-obcasy/7,163229,22573549,czarne-szmaty.html

center, other participants of the Strike joining the Rags spontaneously, thus becoming co-creators of the risky event.

The repertoire of Black Rags includes the equally powerful message "WE (STILL) HAVE THE RIGHT" ((JESZCZE) MAMY PRAWO), which appeared in 2017 during protests against the breaking of the Constitution and dismantling of the independent judiciary by the Kaczyński regime. Another banner – "END(LESS) HATE" ((BEZ)KRES NIENAWIŚCI) – was displayed during the Black Friday demonstration in Warsaw on March 23, 2018. At a certain point, two members of the collective attacked the "LESS" with a bottle of red paint, so "ENDLESS" became "END." The group celebrated the first anniversary of the Women's Strike by decorating several mermaid monuments in Warsaw with sashes bearing the words "YOU ARE NOT ALONE" (NIE JESTEŚ SAMA). The appeal of this action lies in the ambiguity of the message. In the context of the ongoing struggle over the right to abortion in Poland, the characteristic black banners can be read as words of encouragement for oppressed women from the courageous activists. It is a manifestation of female resistance — pathos, the struggle, and a sisterly community of indomitable women. Yet, the humorous dimension of this event is also clear: here are Warsaw's mermaids — historically isolated and immobilized on their pedestals — greeting each other from different parts of the city.

The Rags' messages popping up around the city unexpectedly could easily be seen simply as huge banners created with great care. But they are something more, just as The Witches' Choir is more than a musical group to accompany the Black Protests. It is a form of performative art, simultaneously radical and surreal, inspired by the work of the American group Public Movement and consciously referring to the situationists, as well as to the traditions of the Academy of Movement and Orange Alternative, Polish performance groups from the time of state socialism.

Lastly, a few words about one of the most popular manifestations of female creativity in recent years: the memes of Marta Frej. This phenomenon straddles the border between art, pop culture, politics and a woman-run business. Frej's home environment is the internet; her memes are computer-processed photos (she works in Photoshop, using the brush tool) circulated on social media and available for sale as posters and gadgets. The key element in these images is the text added by the artist: it is the dialogue or commentary that gives each meme its provocative or subversive meaning. Her work keeps apace with political developments, providing witty – sometimes lyrical, sometimes malicious — commentary on various contemporary phenomena and events. Many women identify with these images, wear them on T-shirts, bags and pins. At the height of the Black Protests, in 2018, Frej's Facebook page had 160,000 fans, and each of her memes would get several hundred shares.[20] Users appreciate the political message of her work, especially her way of making fun of the Church's power in Poland. One of her most popular memes features a group of bishops with the tagline: "We know all there is to know about women." In another image, two girls are walking down the school corridor; one says: "My tummy really hurts," and the other replies: "I'll take you to the chapel, that's where the school nurse's office used to be." There are also memes commenting on the ills of Polish capitalism. In one, a group of people are seated in a circle; a woman says: "I'm Magda and I've got a mortgage in Swiss francs." Some of Frej's work is self-consciously personal; she uses her own image, talking frankly about her family life, her fantasies, dreams, insecurities, as well as her mistakes and indecent thoughts. On behalf of the female "people," she comments on gender norms and various manifestations of patriarchal culture, including the unequal division of housework, domestic violence, as well as hypocrisy and prudishness that prevail in the sphere of sexuality. The images she creates do not have the status "art" as it is typically understood in Poland, i.e., they are not original works exhibited in galleries and museums, addressed to the elites and sold at exorbitant prices. They are pretty in a feminine way, even stylish, and they are put into mass circulation in the form of gadgets: mugs, calendars, T-shirts, bags, phone cases, and so on.[21] Unlike the Black Rags projects or The Witches' Choir performances described above, Frej's memes are neither angry nor dark. But despite their lightness, they can be surprisingly radical. The political messaging of her work is both provocative, sincere, rebellious and humorous.

Frej has created a mural commemorating the Women's Strike of October 3, 2016, the famous "Black Monday." It was painted on the wall of a building on Targowa Street in Warsaw's Praga district and depicted a crowd of women with umbrellas, with protest signs falling on them instead of rain. It included a tagline, one of the protest's slogans: "I won't give birth to a child (if I'm) dead." Marta Frej gave the following commentary on this piece: "The mural is not only to commemorate the day when Polish women came out in solidarity to fight for their rights and protest against the Polish state's discriminatory policy, but also to remind us that the struggle has only just begun . . . Polish women have immense power, but they also have an immense job to do."[22]

---

[20] The artist Marta Frej's Facebook page: https://www.facebook.com/martafrejmemy/; as of Decemeber 2021, the page has 231, 770 followers.

[21] The artist Marta Frej's work can be purchased in her online store: https://martafrejsklep.pl.

[22] Marta Kowalska, "Mural Marty Frej na Targowej – #czarnyprotest ma swój 'pomnik'"

The works described here are not works of art whose creators are experimenting with or referring to feminism. They are radical feminist statements whose creators chose an artistic form of expression because they happen to be artists. Feminist engagement is simply a part of their lives. All the artists discussed here are active participants in protests in defense of democracy; Frej is an icon of contemporary Polish feminism – a regular at demonstrations and the Women's Congress, an organizer of numerous cultural projects, meetings and debates in her hometown of Częstochowa (and more recently Gdańsk). The key feature of this creative work – arguably, one that distinguishes it from the feminist art of the transition era – is its accessibility and egalitarianism. This is not elite art that assumes significant cultural capital on the part of viewers, as did the critical art of the previous twenty years. Feminist art of the 1990s and 2000s tended to be ironic, allusive, self-referential. It often signaled its own marginal status, its separateness from mainstream culture. From a marginal vantage point, it explored women's problematic relationship to the new democracy.[23] The works and projects discussed here are positioned differently vis-à-vis the public sphere. They are confrontational without being marginal; they are inclusive without being either crude or primitive. In fact, some works are formally sophisticated; their creators are professional artists who are familiar with art history and theory of culture. There is, however, nothing cryptic about this art, no assumption of marginality. Even when they draw on codes of modern art such as performance or situationism, one is not required to know this to be a fully-engaged recipient, or even participant in their performances. This wave of feminist art rejects hermeticism and self-irony and embraces pathos, anger and humor instead – just as contemporary street feminism, the feminism of the Black Protests and the Women's Strike, rejects the elitism of academic feminism.[24]

---

(Marta Frej's Mural on Targowa Street – The Black Protest has its monument). *Elle.pl.* November 3, 2016. https://www.elle.pl/artykul/mural-marty-frej-na-targowej-czarnyprotest -ma-swoj-pomnik.

[23] For insightful explorations of Polish feminist art of the 1990s and early 2000s and its complex relationship to national culture and democratization, see: Elżbieta Matynia, "Feminist Art and Democratic Culture: Debates on the New Poland," *PAJ: A Journal of Performance and Art* 27, no. 1 (2005): 1-20. Elżbieta Matynia, "Poland Provoked: How Women Artists En-Gender Democracy," *Current History* 105, no. 798 (2006): 132-138.

[24] For an extended version of this argument, see: Agnieszka Graff, "Angry Women: Poland's Black Protests as 'Populist Feminism,'" in *Right Wing Populism and Gender: European Perspectives and Beyond,* edited by Gabriele Dietze and Julia Roth (Bielefeld: Transcript Verlag, 2020), 231-250.

Perhaps the key to this new poetics lies in grasping the rejection of irony in favor of pathos and sincerity — a phenomenon widespread in post-postmodern literature and art, in which affect plays a vital role. The message is at times ambiguous and multidimensional, but there is no distancing from lived experience. This is politically engaged art that encourages recipients not only to actively receive, but also to express themselves radically. The goal is to create an affective community, to infect the audience with shared emotion, building an affective solidarity, to use Clare Hemmings's term.[25]

The theme of darkness appears in the new feminist art on a strikingly regular basis. It is not just the use of black as demonstrated by Black Rags, and the Witches' Choir emerging from the darkness – but also the numerous references to dark motifs: witches, madness, night, even death. This thematic can be explained, in part, by the fact that we are living in dark times; these works are a response to the situation, an expression of dark emotions. However, a thread of dark female power is also to be noted. Rejecting the saccharine feminine aesthetics of post-feminism, where women's strength is supposed to lie in dynamism, optimism and entrepreneurship, many of these works are inspired instead by the trend of feminism in which darkness is the source of female power. This trend certainly includes Agnieszka Holland's film *Spoor* (*Pokot*, 2017). Based on the novel by Olga Tokarczuk, the movie tells the disturbing story of an eccentric old woman – half madwoman, half witch – who sets out on a mission to defend animals from hunters. The protagonist gathers a group of hyper-sensitive people around her, outcasts from the small-minded and often violent world of small-town Poland, and together they declare war on this world. In a key scene, the local church is set on fire – allegedly by birds, but de facto by the protagonist. The film caused quite a stir; it was accused of promoting "ecoterrorism" and "paganism" – and if you read the plot literally, this interpretation makes sense. Holland's work, however, should be read as a metaphor expressing a particular collective emotion. Like the song "Pack of Women," *Spoor* is a revenge fantasy. In today's Poland, Christianity has the face of cruel old men who, as Frej's meme suggests, claim to "know all there is to know about women." No wonder female rebellion is assuming wild and desperate forms, consciously referring to pagan rituals.

By quoting the blasphemous inscription on the wall of the Warsaw Curia at the beginning of this article, I deliberately took a risk, exposing myself to disdain and censure. Acts of vandalism and sacrilege are supposed to be off-limits to art, as is violence and cruelty. Such things are in excess of symbolic

---

[25] Clare Hemmings, "Affective Solidarity: Feminist Reflexivity and Political Transformation," *Feminist Theory* 13, no. 2 (August 2012): 147–161.

struggle. Or are they? The same can be said about the radical art described here that does not aim to please. Instead, they demand to be taken seriously. Their creators – perhaps with the exception of Frej – do not try to ingratiate themselves with their recipients. They shock with violence, pathos, and desperation. Just as the inscriptions on the walls of the Curia and the Women's Strikes which constitute its proper context. The new wave of feminist art gives voice to pain, fury, intensity, and determination that has never before been seen in Polish culture, at least not in connection with women.

This angry art is a symptom of a deep political and cultural divide, one of the fronts of the culture war into which Poland has plunged. This war – involving the rise of radical nationalism and described by sociologists in terms of "symbolic thickening" – has what may be termed a spiritual dimension.[26] It is experienced by many as a struggle between good and evil. Against the rise of fascism, against the dissolution of democratic dreams, there is an equally radical rebellion. Witches, madwomen, and rebels are emerging from the darkness in defense of the good – democracy, freedom, and pluralism. On the other side, they see evil – nationalism, misogyny, ossified tradition, unspeakable cruelty. It is hard to foresee what women's art will look like if the authoritarian right-wing government and the rise of fascism turns out to be just a brief episode in our history. But one thing is certain: traces will remain in collective consciousness from the time of darkness and defiance, the eruption of female fury.

NOTE: This article was originally published in French in the collected volume *Hourras et désarrois. Scènes d'une guerre culturelle en Pologne,* edited by Agnieszka Żuk (Paris: Noir sur Blanc, 2019). It was translated to English by Kate Webster and published in the online journal *Switch on Paper* on 20 August 2020. I extend my thanks to the editors of both publications, and to the translator, for their kind permission to include the text here. The present version has been edited and updated by the author.

## Bibliography

Chór Czarowic (Witches' Choir). "Już płonę" (I'm on Fire). Performance. *Chór Czarowic YouTube Channel.* October 9, 2017. https://www.youtube.com/watch?v=7yaG7cvypTg.
_____. "Twoja władza" (Your Power). Performance. *Chór Czarowic YouTube Channel.* October 2, 2017. https://www.youtube.com/watch?v=UCYH3O_e9DI.

---

[26] Marta Kotwas and Jan Kubik, "Symbolic Thickening of Public Culture and the Rise of Right-Wing Populism in Poland," *East European Politics and Societies*, 33, no. 2 (2019): 435-471.

_____. "Chór Czarowic at the 9th Women's Congress." Poznań. *Chór Czarowic YouTube Channel.* September 2017. https://www.youtube.com/watch?v=xJyz TlSsuxU.

_____. "Pieśni Czarownic." Performance. Teatr Polski w Poznaniu. May 5, 2017. http://teatr-polski.pl/spektakle/czarownica/.

_____. "Wataha kobiet" (Pack of Women). Performance. *Chór Czarowic YouTube Channel.* September 21, 2017. https://www.youtube.com/watch?v=e6WrqyHBAAs.

Czarne Szmaty (Black Rags). Facebook Page. https://www.facebook.com/czarneszmaty/.

Domagalska, Karolina. "Nie jesteś sama" (You are not alone). *Wysokie Obcasy.* October 28, 2017. https://www.wysokieobcasy.pl/wysokie-obcasy/7,163229, 22573549,czarne-szmaty.html.

Filipiak, Izabela. *Absoluta amnezja* (Absolute Amnesia). Poznań: Obserwator, 1995.

Frej, Marta. Facebook Page. https://www.facebook.com/martafrejmemy/.

_____. Online store. https://martafrejsklep.pl.

Graff, Agnieszka. "Angry Women: Poland's Black Protests as 'Populist Feminism.'" In *Right Wing Populism and Gender. European Perspectives and Beyond.* Edited by Gabriele Dietze and Julia Roth. Bielefeld: Transcript Verlag, 2020: 231-250. https://doi.org/10.14361/9783839449806-013.

_____. "Claiming the Shipyard, the Cowboy Hat, and the Anchor for Women: Polish Feminism's Dialogue and Struggle with National Symbolism." *East European Politics and Societies* 33, no. 2 (2019): 472-496. https://doi.org/10. 1177/0888325419835914.

Graff, Agnieszka and Elżbieta Korolczuk. *Anti-Gender Politics in the Populist Moment.* London: Routledge, 2021.

Hemmings, Clare. "Affective Solidarity: Feminist Reflexivity and Political Transformation." *Feminist Theory* 13, no. 2 (2012): 147–161. https://doi.org/ 10.1177/1464700112442643.

Janion, Maria. *Kobiety i duch inności* (*Women and the Spirit of Dissidence*). Warszawa: Sic!, 1996.

Jurecki, Krzysztof, Ed., "Anna Baumgart: biography," *Culture.pl,* 2004.

Keff, Bożena. *On Mother and Fatherland.* Translated by Benjamin Paloff and Alissa Valles. Cheshire, MA: MadHat Press 2017.

Kotwas, Marta and Jan Kubik. "Symbolic Thickening of Public Culture and the Rise of Right-Wing Populism in Poland." *East European Politics and Societies* 33, no. 2 (2019): 435–471. https://doi.org/10.1177/0888325419826691.

Kowalczyk, Izabella, Ed. *Polki, Patriotki, Rebeliantki . . . Sztuka feministyczna dzisiaj* (Polish Women, Patriots, Rebels... Feminist Art Today). Poznań: Arsenał, 2017.

_____, Curator. Polki, Patriotki, Rebeliantki . . . *Sztuka feministyczna dzisiaj.* Visual Art Exhibition. Poznań: Arsenał Gallery, September 8–October 8, 2017. https://arsenal.art.pl/en/exhibition/polish-women-patriots-rebels/.

Kowalska, Marta. "Mural Marty Frej na Targowej – #czarnyprotest ma swój 'pomnik'" (Marta Frej's Mural on Targowa Street – The Black Protest has its monument). *Elle.pl.* November 3, 2016. https://www.elle.pl/artykul/mural-marty-frej-na-targowej-czarnyprotest-ma-swoj-pomnik.

Kozyra, Katarzyna. Artist website. http://katarzynakozyra.pl/en/. https://culture.pl/en/artist/anna-baumgart.

Matynia, Elżbieta. "Feminist Art and Democratic Culture: Debates on the New Poland." *PAJ: A Journal of Performance and Art* 27, no. 1 (2005): 1-20. https://doi.org/10.1162/1520281052864024.

_____. "Poland Provoked: How Women Artists En-Gender Democracy." *Current History* 105, no. 798 (2006): 132-138. https://doi.org/10.1525/curh.2006.105.689.132.

Niedurny, Katarzyna. "Czarny Album" (The Black Album). *Dialog,* September 2021, 9 (778). https://www.dialog-pismo.pl/w-numerach/czarny-album.

Nieznalska, Dorota. "Pasja" (Passion). Artist website. 2001. https://nieznalska.com/.

Piskorska, Liliana. Artist's Website. http://lilianapiskorska.com/en/praca/methods-of-camouflage-in-contemporary-poland/.

Sistrum. "Czarne Szmaty. Razem znaczymy więcej niż każda osobno" (Black Rags: Together we mean more than each one of us separately). *Akulturalgbtq.pl.* Interview. July 2018. http://akulturalgbtq.pl/wpcontent/uploads/2018/07/aaakulturalnik_sistrum_ CzarneSzmaty.pdf.

Skowrońska, Aleksandra. "Rzeczywistość nas dogania" (Reality is catching up with us). Interview with Ewa Łowżył. *Dziennik Teatralny.* 7 July 7, 2017. http://www.dziennikteatralny.pl/spektakle/piesni-czarownic.html.

Sural, Agnieszka. "Liliana Piskorska 17.12.1988." Translated by Patryk Grabowski. *Culture.pl.* Blog Post. October 2017. Updated by HSz April 2020.

Tyszka, Juliusz. "Czarownice dają czadu" (The Witches Rock). *Teatralny.pl,* News Post. June 14, 2017. https://teatralny.pl/recenzje/czarownice-daja-czadu,2012.html

Wroński, Paweł. "Dokąd zmierza Kościół, który zdradził III RP" (Where the Church is headed, now that it has betrayed Poland). *Gazeta Świąteczna.* News Article. June 2, 2018. https://wyborcza.pl/magazyn/7,124059,23480424,dokad-zmierza-kosciol-ktory-zdradzil-iii-rp.html.

Zbylut, Agata. Artist's Website. https://www.agatazbylut.com/Article/kawiorowa-patriotka.

# Index